OECD Territorial Reviews: Peru 2016

OECD
BETTER POLICIES FOR BETTER LIVES

This work is published under the responsibility of the Secretary-General of the OECD. The opinions expressed and arguments employed herein do not necessarily reflect the official views of OECD member countries.

This document and any map included herein are without prejudice to the status of or sovereignty over any territory, to the delimitation of international frontiers and boundaries and to the name of any territory, city or area.

Please cite this publication as:
OECD (2016), *OECD Territorial Reviews: Peru 2016*, OECD Publishing, Paris.
http://dx.doi.org/10.1787/9789264262904-en

ISBN 978-92-64-26284-3 (print)
ISBN 978-92-64-26290-4 (PDF)

Series: OECD Territorial Reviews
ISSN 1990-0767 (print)
ISSN 1990-0759 (online)

Revised version, October 2016
Details of revisions available at: *http://www.oecd.org/about/publishing/Corrigendum-TerritorialReviewsPeru2016.pdf*

The statistical data for Israel are supplied by and under the responsibility of the relevant Israeli authorities. The use of such data by the OECD is without prejudice to the status of the Golan Heights, East Jerusalem and Israeli settlements in the West Bank under the terms of international law.

Latvia was not an OECD member at the time of preparation of this publication. Accordingly, Latvia is not included in the area totals.

Photo credits: Cover Illustration © Jeffrey Fisher.

Corrigenda to OECD publications may be found on line at: *www.oecd.org/about/publishing/corrigenda.htm*.

Foreword

Policies for economic growth, jobs, human capital and environmental sustainability have greater impact when they recognise the different economic and social realities where people live and work. National governments are thus challenged to rethink how to harness the potential of different types of cities and regions to prepare for the future. Policies for regions and cities can generate opportunities for skills development, investment and innovation, and directly contribute to improving quality of life. Such policies actively complement traditional macro and structural approaches in enhancing national performance.

Regional policies are particularly important for Peru, which has the fifth-largest land mass when compared with OECD countries. Peru has a diverse economic geography with unrealised potential in its cities and rural areas. Coastal regions tend to have better socio-economic conditions than uplands and rainforest regions in the interior of the country. These different areas are not well connected and have vastly different levels of service provision and infrastructure. In terms of population, Lima is the fifth-largest urban area in Latin America and dominates the economy and population of the country. Given its size relative to other cities, there is scope for additional agglomeration benefits by addressing problems associated with informal settlements and pressures on the transport network. Better adapting national policies to the circumstances and needs of these different regions is a key challenge for Peru.

This regional dimension will need to be taken into account as Peru continues to develop its economy. Peru decided to undertake this review to ensure this territorial dimension is reflected in future policies to lift the productivity and competitiveness of the country. This includes ensuring that subnational governments have the capacity and tools to deliver on this agenda.

This *Territorial Review of Peru* sets out how regional policies in Peru can be improved. This includes ensuring the preconditions (such as mechanisms to ensure a more equitable distribution of transfers to the regional level) are in place for decentralisation to work. Lifting the productivity of the country has a lot to do with how Peru's cities can work better. This review includes recommendations for how Peru can develop a comprehensive approach to urban policies, including enhancing linkages with rural areas. It also identifies how regions can play a stronger role in the government's efforts to diversify the economy away from natural resources by increasing the scope for regions to identify and mobilise areas of comparative advantage. The implementation of these recommendations will help ensure all of Peru's regions maximise their contribution to national well-being and prosperity.

This review was carried out by the OECD Regional Development Policy Committee (RDPC) as part of the OECD Country Programme for Peru, which is built around given key areas: economic growth; public governance, anti-corruption and transparency; human capital and productivity; and the environment. The RDPC provides a unique forum for international exchange and debate on regional economies, policies and governance. The RDPC has developed a number of activities, including a series of national Territorial Reviews. These studies follow a standard methodology and a common conceptual framework, allowing countries to share their experiences and disseminate information on good practices. The RDPC has also endorsed the Principles for Effective Public Investment across Levels of Government, and adherence to this instrument will enable Peru to address some of the governance challenges outlined in this report.

Acknowledgements

This review was prepared by the Directorate of Public Governance and Territorial Development (GOV) of the OECD, in collaboration with the Peruvian government. The OECD would like to thank the Peruvian authorities at the national and subnational levels for their co-operation and support during the review process, and in particular, the National Centre for Strategic Planning (CEPLAN) for its technical and financial support.

We acknowledge the hospitality and insights from the government, civil society and business representatives in the regions of San Martín, Arequipa, Piura and Lima. The OECD Secretariat expresses its special gratitude to Victor Vargas Machuca, Elizabeth Vargas and the team from CEPLAN for their valuable involvement in the process of this review, particularly to Natalia Cabrera, Karen Guerrero and Jose Talavera. The review also benefited from comments and participation by representatives from other ministries including the Presidency of the Council of Ministers, the Ministry of Economy and Finance, the Ministry of Production, and the Ministry of Agriculture, the Ministry of Environment, and the Ministry of Housing.

The Secretariat would like to acknowledge the valuable co-operation of the peer reviewers that were involved in this report:

- Lillian Salerno, Department of Agriculture, United States
- Elena Martin Cordova, Minister of Finance and Public Administration, Spain
- Elizabeth Arciniegas Muñoz, National Planning Department, Colombia
- Manuel Fernando Castro, National Planning Department, Colombia
- Alessandro Alasia, Statistics Canada, Canada
- Carman Schlotfeldt, Ministry of Interior and Public Safety, Chile.

The review was directed by Joaquim Oliveira Martins (Head, Regional Development Policy Division) and José Enrique Garcilazo (Head of Rural Policy Unit). The review was co-ordinated and drafted by Chris McDonald and Raffaele Trapasso with the support of Guillaume Lecaros de Cossio of the OECD Secretariat and benefited from comments and input by Isabelle Chatry, Karen Maguire, Aimee Aguilar, Paqui Santonja, Jorge Carbonell, Sebastian Nieto Parra, Jose-Luis Alvarez-Galvan and Elodie de Oliveira. External contributors were: Alessandro Alasia, Elena Martin Cordova and Marco Magrassi. Thanks are also due to Kate Lancaster and Andrea Uhrhammer for their editorial assistance. Jeanette Duboys, Ulrike Chaplar and Pilar Philip prepared the review for publication.

Table of contents

Tables

Figures

Acronyms and abbreviations

UUBN	Unsatisfied Basic Need
CCT	Conditional monetary transfer programme
CEPLAN	National Strategic Planning Centre
CITES	Network of centres for technological innovation
CNC	National Competition Council
CONCYTEC	National Council for Science, Technology and Innovation
FAE	Savings and Stabilisation Fund (Colombia)
FDI	Foreign direct investment
FONCOR	Regional Equalisation Fund
FUA	Functional urban area
GDP	Gross domestic product
GPFG	Government Pension Fund – Global (Norway)
GPT	General purpose technology
GVA	Gross value added
GVC	Global value chain
INAP	National Institute of Public Administration (Spain) *Instituto Nacional de Administración Pública*
INEI	National Institute of Statistics and Informatics *Instituto Nacional de Estadística e Informática*
IRS	Increasing returns to scale
LAC	Latin America and the Caribbean
MEF	Ministry of Economy and Finance
MIDIS	Ministry of Development and Social Inclusion
MINAGRI	Ministry of Agriculture and Irrigation
NGO	Non-governmental organisation
NRP	New Rural Paradigm
NUDP	National Urban Development Plan
OpI	Works for Taxes" *Obras por Impuestos*

PCM	Presidency of the Council of Ministers
PDRC	Concerted regional development plan
PEDN	National Strategic Development Plan
PEN	Peruvian soles (currency)
PESEM	Sector-specific strategic plan
PISA	Programme for International Student Assessment
PNDP	National Production Diversification Plan
PRODUCE	Ministry of Production
R&D	Research and development
RDA	Regional development agency
RDPC	Regional Development Policy Committee
SAT	Tax administration agency
SENACE	National Environmental Certification Service
SINACYT	National System of Sciences, Technology and Innovation
SINAPLAN	National Strategic Planning System
SLO	Social license to operate
SNIP	National System of Public Investment
STI	Science, technology and innovation
TL2	Territorial Level 2
TL3	Territorial Level 3
USD	United States dollar

Executive summary

The economic performance of Peru in recent times has been impressive. Since 2000, gross domestic product (GDP) growth has averaged 5% per annum compared to the Latin American average of 3.2% per annum and the OECD average of 2% per annum. A commitment to fiscal discipline and open markets has enabled the country to take advantage of favourable external conditions. Growth has been supported by increased exports of agricultural and mining products, and foreign investment has flowed into the country. The people of Peru have benefited from this growth. Household incomes have risen and poverty rates have declined significantly. However, GDP per capita is USD 11 438, which is about 30% below Mexico, close to 40% below Turkey and significantly below the OECD average of USD 37 270.

A transition is now under way as commodity prices fall, and the key challenge for Peru is how to improve productivity and maintain this growth trajectory. Mining, finance and telecommunications have relatively high productivity, whilst lower levels of productivity are evident in agriculture and other service sectors, where most of the labour force is employed: over one-quarter of the labour force works in agriculture whereas the OECD average is 5.6%. Peru needs to take a more strategic approach to investing in the key enabling factors of productivity growth that remain significantly below OECD standards (skills, innovation, infrastructure and the business environment). To enhance the effectiveness of these investment policies, Peru will also need to take a more comprehensive approach to managing the growth and development of its cities and rural areas.

Peru's regions are diverse, and each region has different sources of and potential for growth. Realising this regional growth potential will require integrated policies that are tailored to the unique circumstances of each place and that can simultaneously improve skills, innovation, infrastructure and the business environment. Better prioritisation of public investment and the integration of these priorities within fiscal frameworks at a regional level should be a key reform priority. Within this context the OECD has identified four main challenges.

1. Since 2002, Peru has made strong advances in terms of political decentralisation, with the election of regional governments and the transfer of significant responsibilities to the subnational level. However, this has not been accompanied by changes to tax and transfer arrangements, or a coherent strategy to increase skills and capabilities at the subnational level. This situation, coupled with overlapping responsibilities and competencies between levels of government and limited levels of horizontal and vertical co-ordination, has prevented the country from achieving the objectives of decentralisation. The regional level is the weakest link in Peru's system of government, and will need to be strengthened to address the economic challenges the country now faces.

2. Peru's sectoral and innovation policies focus on diversifying the economy and increasing the complexity of the country's export basket, and are primarily designed and executed at a national level. The rise of global value chains, the

increasing importance of networks and technological platforms for innovation, and dynamic nature of business start-ups all point toward the need for a more "bottom-up" innovation strategy. This should not only focus on increasing exports, but also on generating additional value from imports. The strategic planning and co-ordinating role of subnational governments needs to be strengthened, along with better-targeted incentives and more effective partnerships with the national level, to help realise this place-based approach.

3. There is a lack of a strategic approach to urban and rural policies. The institutional framework for urban and rural development policies is fragmented and lacks effective mechanisms to co-ordinate and align planning and resource allocation. Strategic spatial plans are not connected to resource allocation decisions in a co-ordinated way, nor is their implementation consistently monitored and evaluated. Rural programmes are mainly orientated toward alleviating poverty, and are not adequately connected to economic development opportunities. There is significant variation in how urban and rural development policies are implemented at a subnational level, and a lack of alignment between different levels of government. The current arrangements for decentralisation favour national or municipal decision making, largely bypassing regions; this contributes to a lack of collaboration between provincial and district municipalities.

4. Peru is a territorially diverse country and the delivery of better policies will need to be supported by good spatial statistics. Currently, there is a lack of consistency and quality in the system of statistics at a subnational level. As a result, there is diversity of standards, concepts, definitions and, in several cases, inconsistent statistics. Consolidating and streamlining territorial statistics and information systems will be crucial for improving the quality of policy-making processes and the delivery of sectoral policies. This includes harmonising rural definitions, and developing statistical definitions that better capture functional urban areas.

This review identifies 11 key recommendations that have been designed to address these challenges and achieve the following strategic objectives:

- making decentralisation work by strengthening subnational governments and encouraging a partnership-based approach to public investment
- implementing a better approach to regional policies, including by strengthening regional institutional capacity
- developing a comprehensive approach to urban policies
- implementing a pro-growth rural development agenda
- improving statistical definitions and the system of territorial statistics.

Assessment and recommendations

Peru's recent growth performance has been strong but challenges remain.

Peru's recent socio-economic performance has been impressive with strong growth and progress in reducing poverty. Since 2000, gross domestic product (GDP) has averaged 5% annually, much higher than in previous decades. This rate of growth is impressive compared to the OECD average of 2%. Peru's export performance has benefited from rising commodity prices and increased production of key mineral resources. Poverty rates have more than halved since 2001, to a level of around 23% in 2014, and extreme poverty rates have also fallen, from close to 25% to around 5% in the same period.

The Peruvian economy is going through a transition from the commodities boom. The mining sector is dominated by large multinationals, which are globally integrated, and employs less than 1.5% of the labour force. As a result, the benefits to other sectors of the economy in terms of intermediate inputs, and increased household incomes and consumption, are not as significant as its share of GDP and exports would suggest. The decline in commodity prices presents downside risks for Peru. Although its sound macroeconomic policies and open economy will stand it in good stead, the country does face some challenges.

Improving productivity across the economy is a key challenge. Despite recent improvements in productivity, Peru's international competitiveness is impacted by historically slow productivity growth. Peru's total factor productivity has grown at an annual rate of less than 2% over the last two decades, which has not been enough to close the gap with OECD economies. Peru's level of labour productivity (USD 14 043) is more than three times lower than the OECD average (USD 48 449), and more than half of the level for Turkey (USD 29 342). There is a large informal sector, at close to 70% of the total employment, which shows particularly low levels of productivity. This includes 25.8% of the labour force employment in agriculture compared to the OECD average of 5.6%. When considering Peru's comparatively younger population, there is significant potential for future economic growth. High levels of informality, low levels of skills and innovation, poorly designed and organised cities, and under-developed infrastructure are holding Peru back.

Addressing this productivity challenge will require a strategic and integrated approach to investing in key enabling factors (skills, innovation, the business environment and infrastructure). The first is challenges associated with human capital and informality. The quality of human capital is not adequate, it is insufficiently developed and not effectively used by firms, and widespread informality in the labour market reduces incentives for firms and individuals to invest in it. The second is the low innovation performance of businesses, universities and other actors within the innovation system. This reduces the scope for diversification and the capacity to participate in higher value activities within global value chains (GVCs). The fourth is poor infrastructure performance, which also reduces competitiveness within GVCs, and the productivity of the non-tradable sector. Peru faces a challenge to design structural policies that can deliver sustained improvements to key enabling factors (skills, innovation, the business environment and infrastructure) in an integrated way.

Peru is territorially diverse and these growth dynamics and challenges are playing out differently across the country.

Compared to OECD countries, Peru would rank as one of the largest countries and is very territorially diverse. It is the 19th largest country in the world, and only 4 OECD countries (Canada, the United States, Australia and Mexico) have a larger land mass. Population density is low at only 24 people per square kilometre, which is similar to relatively low density countries such as Chile and Sweden. The physical geography of the country is shaped by a thin coastal region, the Andes and the Amazon forest in the interior. Coastal regions tend to have better socio-economic conditions than uplands and rainforest regions in the interior of the country. These different areas are not well connected and have vastly different levels of service provision and infrastructure. When assessing regional growth trends in detail, it is apparent that the economic geography of the country is also marked by heterogeneity and difference, which emphasises the importance of taking a place-based approach to policies designed to promote inclusive growth.

A key feature of Peru's economic geography is the over-dominance of the capital Lima, compared with OECD countries. Lima dominates the urban system of Peru with a population of approximately 8.5 million, which represents 30% of the national population and close to half of the national economy. In terms of population, this makes Lima the fifth-largest urban area in Latin America and one of the top 30 metropolitan areas of the world. Arequipa is the second-largest metropolitan area in Peru, and is less than one-tenth of Lima in population size. Lima is the location of the vast majority of Peru's high-value services, manufacturing, and transport and logistics, which reflects its role as an international gateway for the country. Although Lima is performing well compared to other regions, it is not performing that well considering the size of the population and the industry mix. Addressing problems such as over-crowding on the transport network in Lima would have a significant productivity pay-off. There are also significant inter-regional disparities between Lima and the rest of the country, and between coastal areas and the interior, which reflects the weaknesses of other regions, and most likely the underperformance of second-tier cities.

Rural areas make an important contribution to the national economy but are not performing to their potential. Three-quarters of Peru's exports is composed of mining, hydrocarbons and agriculture, and this share of total exports has not shifted significantly in the last 40 years. Although rural areas are rich in resources, the people living there are generally poorer. Nearly half of the individuals in poverty were estimated to live in rural areas, indicating that individuals in rural areas were nearly twice as likely to be poor than individuals living in urban areas. Moreover, about 47% of the poor were living in the region of the Sierra, which also has a higher proportion of indigenous people. Some of the most important development challenges for Peru are located in rural areas, and better connections with urban settlements will help address them. The linkages between rural and urban areas are weak due to factors such as ineffective strategic spatial planning, poor quality infrastructure and a lack of incentives to facilitate the co-ordination of investment and service delivery at a functional scale.

There is a need to support territorial policies with better evidence.

National policies are based on different ways of defining regions and using evidence about social, economic and environmental conditions, which reduces the effectiveness and efficiency of public policies. Peru's regions are diverse, and each region has different sources of and potential for growth. There are significant differences in socio-economic conditions between coastal, highland and jungle areas and these places are not well connected. However, Peru's regional taxonomy for statistical purposes does not capture this diversity and is a very basic (binary) one, which defines rural in terms of non-urban status. This definition does not include factors such as population density or proximity to urban centres. National ministries and agencies also have different definitions of urban and rural areas for policy purposes, and there is a lack of common platforms to integrate data and its use in policy development. The multiplicity of actors involved in the production of regional statistics results in diversity of standards, concepts, definitions and in several cases in discrepant statistics. Consolidating territorial statistics and information systems will be instrumental in improving the quality of policy development processes and integrating and adapting the delivery of sectoral policies.

Defining functional urban areas will be a key part of delivering more effective urban policies and improving urban-rural linkages. These territorial definitions are based on political boundaries and administrative units. The usage of these boundaries does bring disadvantages, such as an arbitrary definition of a territory that often does not correspond to patterns of life, job markets or business flows. For example, the administrative boundaries of a city often do not capture the economic flows and interactions which constitute its functional area. The mismatch between functional and administrative boundaries can result in difficulties in co-ordinating policies from different administrative units and lead to sub-optimal outcomes. Currently there are no statistical or administrative geographies that correspond to the concept of functional region or labour market area. The analysis of functional urban areas in Peru would support the development of better policies for urban and rural areas.

Adopting the OECD regional typology to Peru will help facilitate international comparability. To help improve the system of territorial statistics and improve international comparability the OECD regional typology is applied to the case of Peru. For the purpose of comparability with the OECD territorial grid, the following classifications are recommended:

- Territorial level 2 (TL2) can be properly represented by 25 departments (*departamentos*); these include 24 departments, as such, plus the Constitutional Province of Callao (Provincia Constitucional del Callao), to which the state recognised a special status, reflected also in most of the statistical reporting.
- Territorial level 3 (TL3) can be properly represented by 195 provinces (not included the Constitutional Province of Callao).
- Below TL3, the building block of the regional typology is the community level, which in this report is identified with the term of district and district municipality. Throughout this report, the terms local governments and municipal governments

will be used to identify both provincial municipality and district municipality (if not otherwise indicated).

Recommendations to improve statistical definitions and the system of territorial statistics

1. Develop harmonised statistical definitions of urban and rural areas by:

- undertaking a stocktaking of existing regional definitions across national ministries and develop harmonised statistical definitions for urban and rural areas
- advancing rural definitions to take into account the physical geography of the country (coastal, highlands and rainforest), areas of strong interaction with urban centres, population density/size and accessibility/remoteness
- advancing urban definitions with journey to work and travel time data which enable the creation of an agreed definition of functional urban areas within the system of national statistics
- developing indicators aligned with the OECD regional typology to allow for international comparability.

2. Expand the system of territorial statistics by:

- developing a framework and set of indicators for measuring multi-dimensional well-being at a regional level that aligns with the OECD Better Life Index
- incorporating the measurement of GDP at the scale of regions and functional urban areas into Peru's national accounts
- developing an agreed set of environmental and land-use indicators at the regional level, which would include the National Institute of Statistics and Informatics (Instituto Nacional de Estadística e Informática, INEI) linking existing datasets into a single data portal to improve access.

Peru will need to strengthen its approach regional policy to unlock the growth potential of its regions.

Across the OECD it is increasingly recognised that place-based policies are complementary to structural policies and improving aggregate growth potential. There are strong differences in the economic performance between regions and these differences tend to persist over time due to regional factors. These factors can be influenced by integrated and tailored investments in "enabling factors" such as skills, infrastructure and innovation that are designed to unlock regional growth potential. Tailoring these policy interventions at a place-based level is important because of the mutually reinforcing impacts of complementarities between policies (e.g. infrastructure investment alone has little impact on growth unless it is co-ordinated with investments in human capital and innovation). Enabling this place-based approach is dependent upon local and regional governance arrangements that can tailor and adapt policies to local needs and circumstances.

Peru still has some way to go in shifting toward this place-based approach as sectoral and innovation policies are still primarily designed in a top-down way. Over the past two decades Peru has demonstrated a commitment to sound macroeconomic policies which has enabled the growth and diversification of exports. Peru's industry and innovation policies, which are primarily designed and executed at a national level, have focused on further diversifying the economy and increasing the complexity of the country's export basket. Capabilities have been built within national ministries to design and deliver these policies, and constituencies have been built with key private and public sector stakeholders around these core ideas. However, these policies are still primarily designed around industry sectors at a national level (with some exceptions, such as the Policy Strategy for Territorial Innovation).

Peru already has a planning and institutional architecture that can provide the foundation for implementing a place-based approach. Over the last decade the Peruvian government has invested in improving its strategic planning capabilities. In 2008, the SINAPLAN (National Strategic Planning System) and its National Strategic Planning Centre (CEPLAN) as its governing and guiding body were created. The National Strategic Development Plan (PEDN in Spanish) establishes a policy framework to guide development policies which incorporates economic, social and environmental considerations. CEPLAN has also established a hierarchy which links national development planning to sectoral and territorial plans. Concerted regional development plans (PDRC) provide a framework for guiding development policies at a regional level. They are prepared by the regional governments, using an eight-year planning horizon.

However, there is insufficient vertical and horizontal co-ordination to implement this approach, particularly concerning the fiscal framework. Mechanisms to ensure whole-of-government participation are lacking in the policy and investment cycle at a subnational level. These planning frameworks are also not clearly linked to, or conditional upon, the allocation of resources (e.g. fiscal transfers). CEPLAN does have a monitoring and evaluating role in regards to these subnational planning frameworks. However, it is in an advisory capacity and focuses upon in the degree of alignment between national, sectoral and strategic spatial planning frameworks, and the articulation between objectives, indicators and targets within each plan. There do not appear to be clear incentives to develop better quality plans or to ensure co-ordination across the planning cycle. In addition, there is significant variation in capabilities between regional governments, and a lack of consistency and depth in measures to build these capabilities.

Recommendations to implement a better approach to regional policies including by strengthening regional institutional capacity

3. Consider the establishment of more effective and strategic institutional support capacity to facilitate a partnership-based approach to regional development between departments and the national government. Two strategic options to achieve this outcome are: 1) deconcentrated agencies of the Presidency of the Council of Ministers (PCM) and Ministry of Economy and Finance (MEF) that can work in partnership at a macro-regional level; and 2) regional development agencies (RDA) that are constituted as a partnership between departments and the national government:

- developing the skills and technical capacity of regional governments (departments) in areas such as policy development and evaluation, strategic planning, procurement, and project/programme delivery
- providing support to departments and municipal governments to better integrate strategic plans with fiscal frameworks and investment strategies
- communicating strategic priorities of the departments to the national government, identifying opportunities for strategic alignment between departments, and ensuring these priorities inform the national budget and planning cycle

Recommendations to implement a better approach to regional policies including by strengthening regional institutional capacity *(continued)*

- ensuring that national policies and priorities are considered and reflected in departmental planning
- co-ordinating investments and programme delivery at a regional and inter-regional scale
- evaluating and monitoring departmental and municipal level planning to ensure plans are effective and aligned with the national system of strategic planning.

4. Improve the quality and effectiveness of concerted regional development plans (PDRC) by:

- ensuring that within the next two years that all departments have an endorsed PDRC
- Supporting the Regional Government in gathering input and advice from national ministries during the formulation of the Concerted Regional Development Plan (coordinated by the deconcentrated agency or RDA model).
- mandating a formal review of the implementation of PDRCs every three years, synchronised with other regions, and which is publicly available (co-ordinated by the deconcentrated agency or RDA model)
- mandating publicly available annual reporting on progress in implementing the PDRC by the regional governor (which also includes a summary of the activities and achievements of the regional co-ordination councils)
- strengthening the economic analysis within these plans, for example, incorporating further analysis of the industry and business structure within regions at the scale of functional economic areas (including at a macro-regional scale), including how regional businesses are integrated with GVCs, and the identification of key bottlenecks and growth opportunities at these scales
- creating opportunities for policy makers at a departmental level to learn from each other and good practices nationally and internationally (e.g. through targeted training, and a bi-annual conference on regional planning and investment).

5. Better integrate regional planning with the fiscal framework by:

- Introducing competitive-based funding programmes that are designed to encourage innovation, infrastructure and skills initiatives at a regional level. Ensure that the criteria for prioritising funding includes demonstrating alignment with PDRCs, the integration of investment between national ministries and co-contributions from regions, different municipalities, business and other actors.
- Tasking the Ministry of Economy and Finance (MEF, through the RDA or deconcentrated agency) to work in partnership with departments to identify and prioritise medium-term (three to five years) capital investment programmes in the regional PDRCs to deliver on strategic priorities in the territory (derived from the national and subnational plans and programmes). Through the RDA, the MEF should also contribute to the development of these investment programmes.
- Including the annual report on progress in implementing the PDRC in the department's budget and plans, demonstrating alignment with budget instruments.

A framework for urban policy has been established, however, it needs to provide stronger policy direction with clear mechanisms for implementation.

To diversify the economy and lift productivity Lima and secondary cities will need to be better connected and more inclusive. With Lima playing such a dominant role in the economy, the productivity and well-being of the city is a national policy issue. Considering its size relative to other regions in Peru, there is scope to generate additional agglomeration benefits and lift the productivity of Lima. More can also be done to foster a system of cities by increasing connectivity and improving integration with rural areas. To realise these benefits it is increasingly recognised across the OECD that national governments should play a more proactive role in urban policy. Effective urban policy requires clear differentiation and alignment between the roles of different levels of government, and mechanisms to co-ordinate "city shaping" land-use, infrastructure and environmental policies. As urban policy tends to involve trade-offs between different policy options, citizen engagement is also important to the design and implementation of policies at a metropolitan and local scale.

Leadership from the centre of government is required to deliver effective urban policies. The National Urban Development Plan (NUDP) (2006-15) was developed by the Ministry of Housing, Construction and Sanitation, and provides a platform to better co-ordinate policies to support better urban development outcomes. However, the NUDP has not accomplished its goal of serving as guide and catalyst for the development of Peruvian cities. Peru's urban policy is primarily focused on social policy issues and needs to complement this with a focus on the economic performance of cities. Linkages with implementation also need to be strengthened. This includes strengthening the system of land-use regulation and integrating strategic spatial planning with public investment. Leadership from the PCM and MEF is required to achieve these outcomes.

Urban policies need to be better integrated with fiscal frameworks. Mechanisms to link urban policies with resource allocation at a national level are lacking, which means that the NUDP has not unlocked the investment required to support urban development objectives. Importantly, this is also about ensuring that investments are delivered at the right time, in the right location and in the right sequence (e.g. the co-ordinated delivery of economic and social infrastructure to support the development of new urban areas). This is not occurring consistently because urban policy objectives are not considered systematically by line ministries or the MEF in terms how decisions are made on programmes and investments.

Urban policies are not co-ordinated or aligned at a subnational level. There is a well-developed urban planning framework at a provincial and district level; however, it has not been implemented consistently across the country. These inconsistencies in implementation reinforce the point that there are not effective mechanisms in place to co-ordinate and align the various actors involved in urban policy. It also indicates differences in capacity between different provinces and district municipalities, and a lack of effective monitoring and evaluation of performance at regional and national levels. Even larger districts and provinces, which are likely to be better resourced, have low rates of implementation for key planning instruments. The regional level is largely absent from urban policy, which reduces the scope for co-ordination and alignment between districts and municipalities and the national level.

Recommendations to develop a comprehensive approach to urban policies

6. The Peruvian government should develop a comprehensive approach to urban policy which builds upon the lessons of the National Urban Development Plan (NUDP) 2006-2015, and encompasses the following elements:

- clear policy objectives and indicators, which are outcomes-based, and monitored and evaluated
- leadership of the PCM and MEF to ensure co-ordination in urban policies across national ministries (in particular Housing, Construction and Sanitation; Transport and Communications; Environment; and Production)
- incentives and technical assistance for provincial and district municipalities to implement planning instruments and systems for land management (land-use zoning, development approvals and cadastre)
- enforcement of laws to protect public land and property rights, which is currently lacking
- the incorporation of strategic spatial planning into the fiscal framework (for example funding proposals for infrastructure should be required to demonstrate alignment with strategic spatial plans)
- incentives to encourage the matching and co-ordination of policies at the scale of functional urban areas
- an articulation of how cities can contribute to national strategies to lift productivity and promote economic diversification, and an identification of the economic roles and functions of cities within Peru's urban system.

7. In parallel to this work, the government should also work with key stakeholders to identify options for improving the governance of land use and infrastructure for functional urban areas. This includes ensuring each city has an endorsed strategic spatial plan and urban plans, and that there is a co-ordinated process for linking this with investment decisions about infrastructure at a subnational and national level. The government should prioritise reforms for the metropolitan region of Lima, which will then provide lessons for improving planning and governance arrangements in intermediate cities.

Linking programmes to address poverty with initiatives to promote economic development under a common rural policy framework would help rural areas maximise their assets and address development challenges.

The OECD's New Rural Policy can provide a framework for better enabling Peru's rural areas to maximise their assets and address development challenges. Peru's strong national economic performance that has characterised the past two decades depends on capitalising on rural assets, including oil, minerals and agricultural products. Rural areas also face development challenges with higher levels of poverty, less skills and lower quality infrastructure. OECD countries are increasingly implementing integrated approaches to address these kinds of challenges, maximise assets and opportunities, and support rural areas to unlock new growth opportunities. In this context, innovative governance structures have been created in many OECD countries to strengthen co-ordination across sectors and across levels of government; and innovative policy instruments aimed at identifying and exploiting the varied development potential of rural areas. The OECD has labelled this as the "New Rural Policy 3.0", which includes a focus on integrated investments, urban-rural partnerships and building capacity at the local level.

The current approach to rural policy is largely sectoral and focuses on poverty alleviation. Addressing poverty has been a policy focus of successive national governments in Peru. The Ministry of Development and Social Inclusion, and the Ministry of Agriculture and irrigation play major roles in rural development policy. There are also a number of other national ministries – such as Transport and Communications, and Health – which have developed rural-specific policies. A large number of different social programmes have evolved which provide transfers to poorer households, and invest in public services and basic infrastructure. There are comparatively less resources dedicated to economic development programmes. Subsidies to agriculture were removed in the 1980s, and support focuses on extension services and the development and diffusion of irrigation technologies. Since the 1990s there has also been significant investment in the road network, which has benefited rural producers and helped to reduce rural poverty.

There is a disconnect between these programmes to alleviate poverty and policies to promote rural economic development. Peru's social programmes are largely detached from the country's competitive agenda, focusing instead on the creation of employment and income-generating opportunities. The Ministry of Economy and Finance and the Ministry of Production do not, for example, actively participate in efforts to address poverty and promote local economic development in rural areas. The same disconnect is evident at the subnational level, and in non-governmental organisations (NGOs) and citizens' organisations the engagement of the business community is minimal. For instance, *Juntos* (and the large pool of information the programme collects about households and communities) could operate in co-ordination with a pro-growth programme, or better a policy, that empowers people and helps to create in the right conditions that would allow them to leave the conditional cash transfer system.

To realise this outcome, governance arrangements for rural policy will need to be improved. Mirroring the situation in cities, rural regions would benefit from the creation of stronger regional governments that can co-ordinate investment and the delivery of public services. These include rural-urban partnerships that help adjacent communities interact and that facilitate the delivery of services and public goods at the right territorial scale. In fact, the lack of an intermediate government level that co-ordinates different streams of national policies is a key challenge in Peru that particularly affects the capacity of the public sector to promote the sustainable development of the country. An effective co-ordination body will also be needed at the national level, coupled with a clear vision and political leadership. For this reason, and given the importance of rural development in the country, the PCM and the MEF should play a more proactive role in the national rural development agenda to facilitate a genuinely whole-of-government approach.

Recommendations to implement a pro-growth rural development agenda

8. The development of a pro-growth rural agenda can be achieved in the following ways:

- ensuring that the vision, objectives and priorities for rural development have a strong focus on productivity and diversification and are included in relevant policies across government (the centre of government – the Presidency of the Council of Ministers and the Ministry of Economy and Finance – should work in partnership to ensure buy-in and commitment from different national ministries to this policy agenda)
- prioritising the development of initiatives which are designed to enhance productivity and diversification opportunities for rural communities (e.g. mining, agriculture, fisheries and tourism)
- adapting existing social programmes such as *Juntos* and better linking clients with opportunities for skills development, employment and entrepreneurship (this will provide a platform to make further inroads into poverty reduction and reduce reliance on transfers over time)
- strengthening the role of regions in the planning and co-ordination of rural development initiatives by ensuring concerted regional development plans include a strong focus on rural economic development.

Reforms that strengthen subnational governments and encourage a partnership-based approach to regional development policies are required.

Making decentralisation work is central to improving social, economic and environmental outcomes at a regional level. Peru's regions face diverse challenges and opportunities, and public policies need to be tailored to effectively address them. Improving co-ordination between levels of government and improving subnational capacities will enable this place-based approach. Since 2002, Peru has undergone a decentralisation process driven both by democratic and economic and regional development objectives. The process sought to bring democracy closer to the people, enhance accountability while at the same time improve the provision of public goods and reduce regional disparities. Peru has made strong advances in terms of political decentralisation, with the election of regional governments and the transfer of significant responsibilities to the subnational level.

Roles and responsibilities are not clear and subnational governments lack the skills and capabilities to carry them out effectively. The current decentralisation process, which was initiated in 2002, based the division of responsibilities between levels of government on the principle of subsidiarity. However, in practice there is an overlap of roles and responsibilities across governments. In addition, these responsibilities were transferred simultaneously to all regions independently of an assessment of their capacities to carry them out. The national government has not devolved responsibilities related to resource allocation, and subnational governments (particularly regions) do not have an adequate tax base. As a result there is a systemic problem in relation to lack of accountability for outcomes at a subnational level. The national government seeks to overcome this issue by directly delivering services at a regional and local levels, and placing tight controls of expenditure decisions on subnational governments.

Co-ordination rather than fragmentation is the problem facing the public administration in Peru. Peru displays levels of regional and municipal size above the OECD average (both in terms of area and population). However, over 60 new municipalities have been created over the past 6 years, which is a potential risk and requires closer consideration. Without effective co-ordination mechanisms various risks can emerge between levels of government, such as gaps between responsibilities and fiscal capacity, the lack of capacities to deliver services, and policies that are designed without consideration of synergies and overlaps between sectoral areas. Mechanisms that address these risks such as mutually agreed contracts and agreements, the monitoring of nationally agreed standards and regulations for service delivery, and co-ordinating committees and partnerships are lacking or not effectively operationalised in the Peruvian context.

The transfer system is unequal and subnational governments do not have the fiscal space to effectively tailor and adapt policies and resources to regional and local circumstances. The vast majority of taxes (87%) are collected by the national government and resources that are allocated to the subnational level are tightly controlled. For example, subnational governments are heavily dependent upon central government transfers, particularly on "ordinary resources", which constituted 78% of regional revenues and 22% of municipal revenues in 2014. Most of these resources are transferred from the central government for particular projects and programmes, and the capacity for regional governments to modify them is limited. Subnational governments in those cases are confined to a role of executing national policy directions and resource allocation decisions. In this sense they act more as deconcentrated agencies of the central government than as subnational governments in a decentralised system. An increase in revenue from natural resources (the *canon*) in recent years has increased imbalances in expenditures between local municipalities and regions. *Canon* transfers are strongly concentrated with six regions receiving 77.7% of the overall transfer between 2002 and 2014. Three-quarters of this revenue is allocated to the municipal level with the remaining 25% allocated to the regional level. In this period, the level of transfers from the *canon* increased significantly, from 164 million PEN to 7.1 billion PEN. Together with the lack of effective co-ordination mechanisms, the transfer system contributes to the problem of fragmentation of public investment at a subnational level.

Recommendations to make decentralisation work by strengthening subnational governments and encouraging a partnership-based approach to public investment

9. Develop more effective partnerships between levels of government to deliver better policy outcomes by:

- strengthening the role of the Inter-governmental Coordination Council including by refocusing its role on policy co-ordination between the national and regional governments, and streamlining its agenda on a small number of mutually agreed policy issues
- strengthening governance arrangements that facilitate policy and investment co-ordination between levels of government at the scale of functional urban areas, and macro-regional scale

Recommendations to make decentralisation work by strengthening subnational governments and encouraging a partnership-based approach to public investment *(continued)*

- developing a coherent strategy to build the skills and capabilities of subnational governments, which is linked to an accreditation system for increasing responsibilities (including applying the national Law on Civil Service Reform to the local and regional levels)
- putting in place an asymmetric approach to decentralisation, particularly for metropolitan areas, which would allow for the flexibility to better match responsibilities with resources and capabilities
- clarifying the criteria for the creation/amalgamation of new municipalities (including consideration of factors such as fiscal sustainability, efficiency and effectiveness of services, service catchments), and establishing a more transparent and consultative process which includes a public statement providing the evidence and rationale for these decisions
- creating a task force with a mix of technical skills and capabilities (strategic planning, public finance, procurement, project management and evaluation), which can be applied in a flexible way to address critical gaps in skills and capabilities at a subnational level.

10. Develop a coherent package of actions to enable better public investment outcomes at a subnational level by:

- strengthening support for subnational governments to apply results-based budgeting, which is integrated with local and regional concerted development plans
- incorporating multi-year (three-to five-year) capital investment and service delivery plans into the fiscal framework at a regional level and making national transfers conditional upon them (the PCM/MEF should also ensure co-ordinated input from across national ministries to these plans)
- developing a system of public reporting of service delivery performance at a subnational level, which is transparent, user friendly and enables comparisons between jurisdictions.

11. Designing and implementing an integrated reform to subnational finances which includes the following features:

- increasing the proportion of investment funds (such as the *canon*) which are allocated to the regional level, and reducing the proportion allocated to the provincial and district levels in order to increase the overall effectiveness of public investment at a subnational level by generating increased economies of scale and the scope for policy complementarities
- creating a stability fund managed by an independent board appointed by the Government, would help balance the cyclical nature of the royalties system (the *canon* in Spanish)
- strengthening equalisation mechanisms to help compensate for inequalities between regions that are exacerbated by the *canon*
- improving tax administration at a subnational level by pooling administrative capacity at a regional level, enabling regions to collect taxes on behalf of municipalities
- providing subnational governments with the mandate and capacity to mobilise their own revenues (e.g. property tax at a municipal level), which would help stabilise public finances while providing clearer accountability for outcomes.

Chapter 1.

Regional development trends and statistics

This chapter provides a diagnosis of the main subnational trends in Peru. The analysis focuses on the performance of Peru's regions in respect to each other and OECD countries. The first part of the chapter focuses on the key macroeconomic challenges and opportunities facing Peru. The second part goes beyond these national averages to describe the main characteristics of the country at a subnational level. The third part evaluates the performance of Peru's regions, and assesses growth enablers and bottlenecks at a regional level.

The statistical data for Israel are supplied by and under the responsibility of the relevant Israeli authorities. The use of such data by the OECD is without prejudice to the status of the Golan Heights, East Jerusalem and Israeli settlements in the West Bank under the terms of international law.

Key findings and recommendations

Key findings

- Peru is experiencing a transition away from a growth dynamic driven by increasing commodity prices. The country benefited from the global commodity boom, and sound macroeconomic policies have delivered high rates of growth with low inflation. In turn, this has enabled significant reductions in levels of poverty.
- The decline in commodity prices presents downside risks for Peru. Levels of productivity are low due to the legacy of political and economic instability, and the majority of the economy is stuck on a low productivity and value-adding pathway. Low innovation levels reduce the scope for diversification and the capacity to participate in higher value-adding activities within global value chains.
- This transition generates a number of interrelated structural challenges that will need to be addressed. These challenges include a low level of skills in the workforce and high rates of informality, and comparatively poor infrastructure and innovation performance. Peru is territorially diverse and these growth dynamics are playing out differently across the country.
- Cities will be the key to lifting the productivity performance of the services sector. The metropolitan region of Lima-Callao is the leading economic region of the country, and a centre for high-value professional services. Although these trends are positive, they also indicate weaknesses in other regions of the country, and most likely the underperformance of second-tier cities.
- Many of Peru's rural areas are rich in assets but the people living there are generally poorer. Mining and agriculture account for 74% of Peru's exports but 50% of rural people live below the poverty line. Getting the framework conditions right in rural areas – including investment in social and transport infrastructure, and fostering the development and effective use of the skills needed (such as entrepreneurship) – will be a key to realising the growth potential of the national economy.
- Improving the system of regional statistics would enable a better understanding of these issues at a subnational level. Peru's regional taxonomy is a very basic (binary) one, which defines rural in terms of non-urban status. National ministries and agencies have different definitions of urban and rural areas, and there is a lack of common platforms to integrate data and its use in policy development. The multiplicity of actors involved in the production of regional statistics results in a diversity of standards, concepts, definitions and in several cases in discrepant statistics.

Recommendations

1. Develop harmonised statistical definitions of urban and rural areas by:
   - undertaking a stocktaking of existing regional definitions across national ministries and developing harmonised statistical definitions for urban and rural areas
   - advancing rural definitions to take into account the physical geography of the country (coastal, highlands and rainforest), areas of strong interaction with urban centres, population density/size and accessibility/remoteness
   - advancing urban definitions with journey to work and travel time data which enable the creation of an agreed definition of functional urban areas within the system of national statistics

Key findings and recommendations (*continued*)

- developing indicators aligned with the OECD regional typology to allow for international comparability.

2. Expand the system of territorial statistics by:
   - developing a framework and set of indicators for measuring multi-dimensional well-being at a regional level that aligns with the OECD Better Life Index
   - incorporating the measurement of gross domestic product (GDP) at the scale of regions and functional urban areas into Peru's national accounts
   - developing an agreed set of environmental and land-use indicators at the regional level, which would include the National Institute of Statistics and Informatics (Instituto Nacional de Estadística e Informática, INEI) linking existing datasets into a single data portal to improve access to data.

Peru's macroeconomic performance

This section summarises the main macroeconomic trends and challenges of the Peruvian economy. This macroeconomic analysis provides the general framework for the regional analysis which follows. Macroeconomic reforms which began in the 1990s have resulted in a stable monetary and fiscal framework, and a commitment to economic openness.

Peru's recent growth performance has been impressive. In the past ten years, gross domestic product (GDP) per capita growth was, on average, close to 5% annually, much higher than in previous decades. Peru's export performance has benefited from rising commodity prices and increased production of key mineral resources. Poverty rates have more than halved since 2001, to a level of around 24% in 2013, and extreme poverty rates have also fallen, from close to 25% to around 5% in the same period.

There is now a transition underway as commodity prices fall, and the key challenge for Peru is to improve productivity and maintain this growth trajectory. The country's stronger performance and rising terms of trade limited the scope to develop new export markets and value-adding opportunities. Despite recent improvements in productivity, many parts of the economy are impacted by Peru's historically slow productivity growth. There is a large informal sector, at close to 70% of the total employment, which shows particularly low levels of productivity (OECD, 2015e). This includes 25.8% of the labour force employment in agriculture compared to the OECD average of 5.6%.

There is now a strong imperative for structural reforms that can lift productivity and generate new value-adding opportunities. A regional approach will be the key to giving coherence to the implementation of these structural reforms. Peru's regions are diverse and each of these regions has different sources and potential for growth. Realising this regional growth potential will require integrated policies that are tailored to the unique circumstances of these places and can simultaneously improve skills, innovation, infrastructure and the business environment.

After a long period of underperformance Peru's recent macroeconomic performance has been strong

Peru's performance in terms of per capita income growth over the past 50 years has largely been modest with recent improvement over the past two decades (OECD, 2015e). Over the past 50 years the annual average growth rate of GDP per capita in Peru has been 1.6%. This is below the OECD average of 2.2%, and well below the performance of upper middle-income (3.7%), and middle-income (3.2%) countries. Peru's GDP per capita in 2014 was USD 6 541 and it is defined as an upper middle-income economy (World Bank, 2015e). This is significantly below the OECD average of USD 38 388 and similar to Colombia (USD 7 904). It is 37.8% below the GDP per capita of Turkey (USD 10 515) and 36.7% below the GDP per capita of Mexico (USD 10 326).

Figure 1.1. **GDP per capita, select countries and the OECD average, 2014**

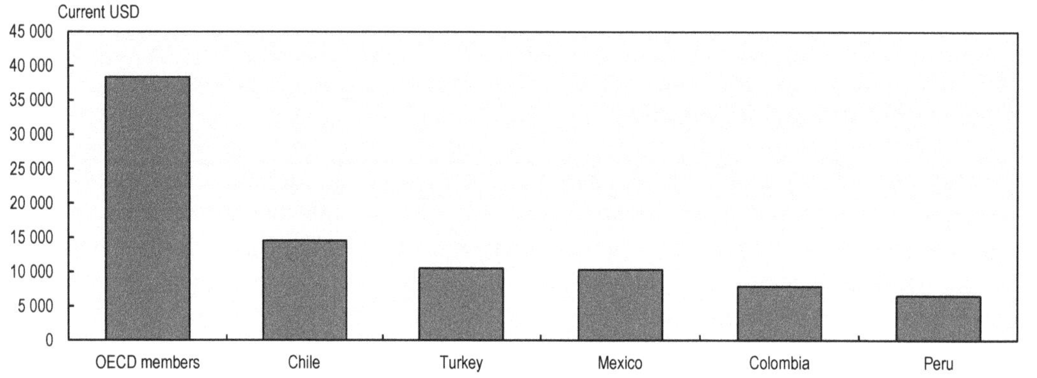

Source: World Bank (2015c), "GDP per capita (current USD)", http://data.worldbank.org/indicator/NY.GDP.PCAP.CD.

Since 2000 Peru's GDP growth has averaged 5% per annum compared to the OECD average of 2% per annum. The growth trajectory of the economy has followed the growth of the Chinese economy, which in part reflects for mineral resources. There was a period of strong growth from 2002 to 2008, a sharp slowdown associated with the crisis, followed by a rebound in growth from 2010. The rate of growth in the economy declined sharply again in 2013-14 from 6% to 2%. In the period 2002-14, inflation was steady and averaged 2.8%.

Despite this recent slowdown Peru has performed better than other benchmark countries such as Brazil. The implementation of structural reforms such as trade openness and sound macroeconomic management has played a key role in this strong performance (Diaz in Perales and Morón, 2010). Peru has been able to attract investment to exploit its mineral resources as global commodity prices began to increase from the early 2000s.

Productivity performance has been poor

Increases in per capita income and living standards in Peru since the early 2000s have been associated with rising commodity prices. However, sustainable and inclusive growth in Peru over the long term will depend upon increasing productivity (OECD, 2015e). Productivity growth will enable Peru to move up the value chain from activities driven by low-skilled labour toward higher value activities. It will also enable Peru to maintain international competitiveness and adjust to changes in external market conditions.

Figure 1.2. **Annual GDP growth, Peru compared to the OECD average and select countries**

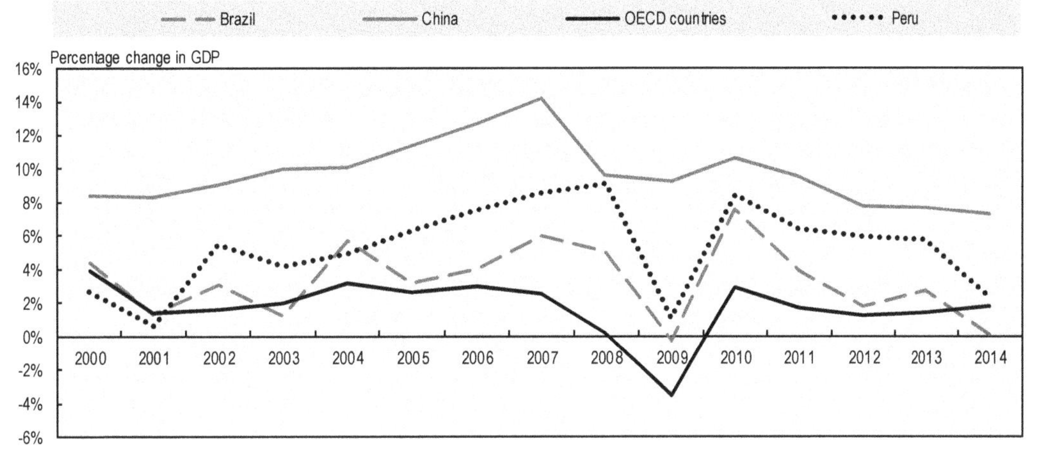

Sources: World Bank (2015c), "GDP per capita (current USD)", http://data.worldbank.org/indicator/NY.GDP.PCAP.CDW; World Bank (2015b), "GDP at market prices (constant 2010 US$)", http://data.worldbank.org/indicator/NY.GDP.MKTP.KD/countries?display=graph.

Low productivity has been an important contributing factor to the historically poor performance of the Peruvian economy. Peru's level of labour productivity (USD 14 043) is more than three times lower than the OECD average (USD 48 449), and more than half of the level for Turkey (USD 29 342).

Figure 1.3. **Labour productivity: Peru compared to select averages and countries, 2014**

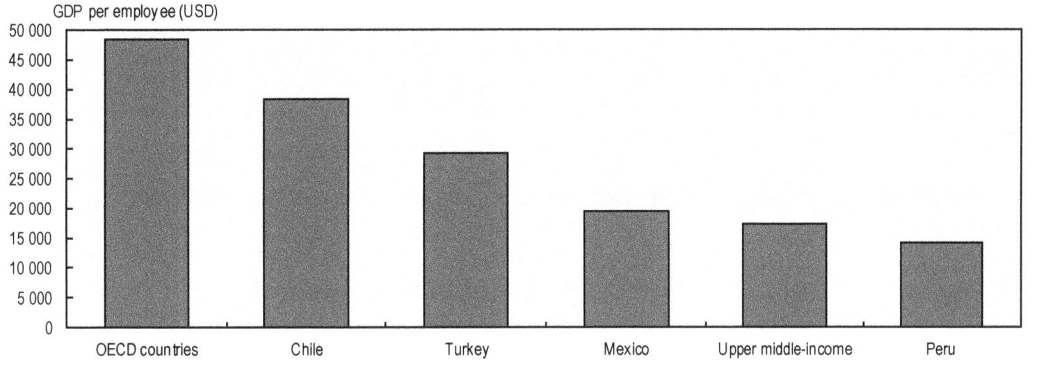

Source: World Bank (2015d), "GDP per person employed (constant 2011 PPP $)", http://data.worldbank.org/indicator/SL.GDP.PCAP.EM.KD.

Low levels of productivity are apparent across much of the economy (OECD, 2015e). Mining, finance and telecommunications have relatively high productivity whilst lower levels of productivity are evident in agriculture and other service sectors where most of the labour force is employed. Over a quarter of the labour force is employed in agriculture, compared to the OECD average of 5.6%. These are also sectors affected by high levels of informality. Although this is a challenge, it also represents a significant opportunity to lift productivity and transition workers to higher value market segments and activities.

Box 1.1. Productivity trends and policy recommendations for OECD economies

Labour productivity growth is considered a key indicator to assess competitiveness and an essential driver of change in living standards. Living conditions are raised by continued gains in labour productivity, along with an increase in labour utilisation. In fact, only economies that manage to simultaneously sustain employment and productivity growth will increase their gross domestic product (GDP) per capita and maintain it in the long run.

Productivity gains have been decelerating over recent decades in most advanced economies. This productivity slowdown, which reflects a mixture of structural and cyclical factors, is fuelling concerns of persistent low global growth and has ignited a spirited debate on the future of productivity. One view posits that the low-hanging fruit of the recent technological explosion have already been picked, whilst the contrary position holds that the IT revolution is continuing apace, fuelling disruptive new business models and enabling a new wave of productivity growth across the economy.

The period 1950-95 saw some degree of convergence in labour productivity performance between the United States, where the level of productivity was the highest, and other advanced economies. Those economies whose productivity levels started the furthest behind the United States saw relatively faster productivity growth. While for some economies this phenomenon partly reflected the rebuilding of war-ravaged capital stocks, it was also likely the result of technology and knowledge spillovers from the global productivity frontier which facilitated the adoption of more advanced technologies and better practices (Aghion and Howitt, 2006).

Yet the catch-up effect was short lived. From the mid-1990s, many countries, particularly in Europe, were not able to keep pace with the acceleration of productivity growth associated with rapid diffusion in ICT in the United States and the gap in productivity levels between the United States and other advanced economies started to widen again. Moreover, from 2004, the benefits from the ICT revolution began to wane in the United States. Overall labour productivity slowed in a number of OECD countries before the crisis.

Since the crisis, the further slowdown in labour productivity growth in the OECD was driven by a – possibly partly temporary – decline in the contribution of capital per worker. Indeed, the weakness in capital deepening is stark and the recovery in investment is sluggish compared with previous cycles (OECD, 2015e). For 40% of OECD countries in 2014, the estimated capital per worker contribution to trend productivity growth was less than 0.25% per annum, while this was true for only two countries in 2000 and 2007. The post-crisis weakness in tangible investment reflects a number of structural but also cyclical factors. It notably reflects soft aggregate demand, in line with a typical accelerator-type model. Impaired financial systems and elevated levels of uncertainty likely also play a role. Therefore, more balanced global demand and less uncertainty could be expected to propel investment to a higher level equilibrium, particularly if accompanied by market reforms.

Research from the OECD (2015d) points toward several policies that are important in sustaining productivity growth, which include:

- improvements in public funding and the organisation of basic research
- innovation policies, including R&D fiscal incentives, collaboration between firms and universities, and intellectual property rights protection (which do not favour particular market players)
- lifting barriers to trade and easing services regulation to facilitate participation in global value chains
- well-functioning product, labour and risk capital markets as well as policies that do not trap resources in inefficient firms
- reforms to policies to increase labour mobility and address skills mismatches (e.g. funding for lifelong learning).

Sources: OECD (2015d), *The Future of Productivity*, http://dx.doi.org/10.1787/9789264248533-en; OECD (2016b), "The productivity-equality nexus: A concept paper", 7th New Approaches to Economic Challenges (NAEC) Group Meeting.

Productivity growth is determined by human capital, physical capital, natural resources and innovation. Poor productivity performance in Peru is due to differences in the quality of human capital and how efficiently factors are combined in processes of production. Total factor productivity is used to identify how efficiently resources are used by identifying the portion of production not explained by increasing the amount of inputs (capital and labour) used in production. Peru's total factor productivity has grown at an annual rate of less than 2% over the past two decades, and growth has been lower than benchmark countries such as Brazil, Chile and Turkey (OECD, 2015e).

Figure 1.4. **Total factor productivity in Peru and selected benchmark countries (base 100 = 1961)**

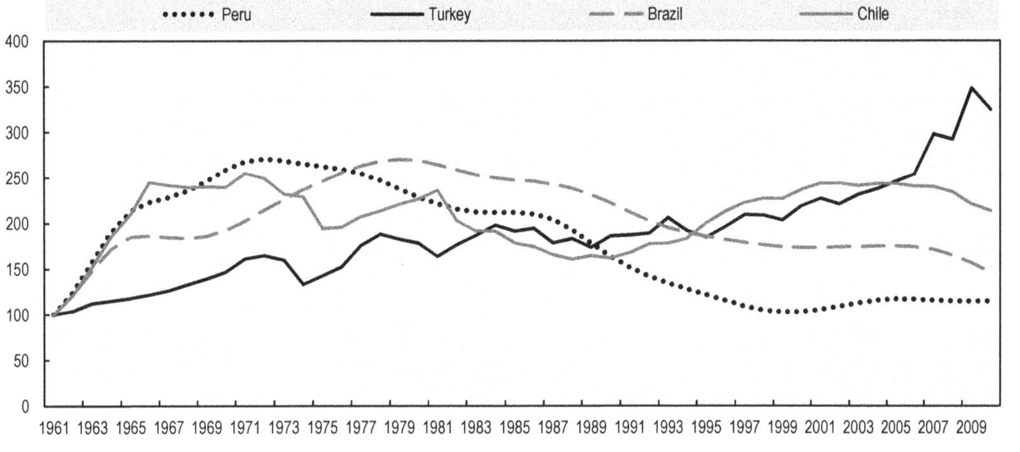

Source: OECD (2015e), *Multi-dimensional Review of Peru: Volume 1. Initial Assessment*, http://dx.doi.org/10.1787/9789264243279-en.

There has been progress in addressing poverty but inequalities are still high

Peru's recent economic performance has enabled significant reductions in poverty, with more than 20% of the population lifted out of poverty since 2000 (World Bank, 2015e). This progress is typical of many developing countries which have improved per capita incomes. However, poverty still remains a challenge with levels above 25% and extreme poverty above 5% (OECD, 2015e). As Peru's economy continues to develop, relative rather than absolute differences in income and well-being will become a more important policy issue.

In sum, Peru is experiencing a transition from a growth dynamic driven by increasing commodity prices. The country benefited from the global commodity boom, and sound macroeconomic policies have delivered high rates of growth with low inflation. In turn, this has enabled significant reductions in levels of poverty. Peruvians have experienced rising incomes and job opportunities, are living longer and participating more in education. However, levels of productivity are low due to the legacy of political and economic instability, and the majority of the economy is stuck on a low productivity and value-adding pathway. Peru is lagging in terms of the quality of employment and education, and this growth is also generating environmental costs. The following section will further explore the main drivers and bottlenecks for growth in Peru.

Figure 1.5. **Poverty and extreme poverty in Peru**

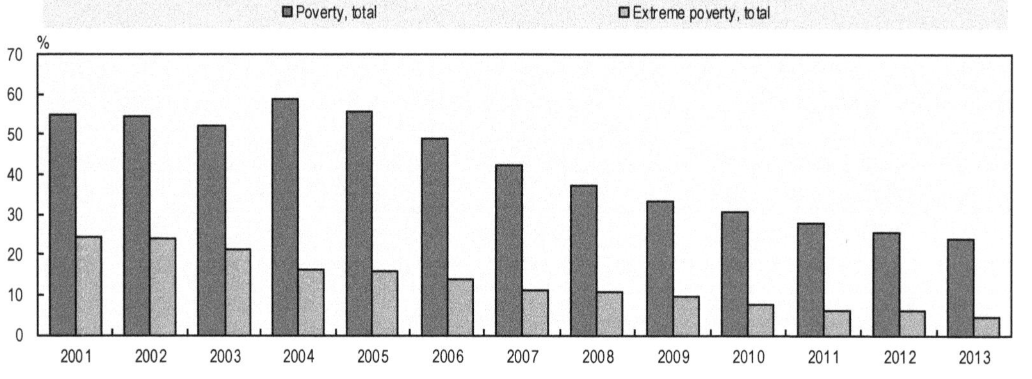

Note: 2013 data are estimates. According to INEI, total poverty includes individuals who belong to a household where either income or consumption per capita is less than the cost of a minimum basket of minimum and essential goods and services; extreme poverty includes those where this is below the value of a minimum basket of food.

Source: OECD (2015e), *Multi-dimensional Review of Peru: Volume 1. Initial Assessment*, http://dx.doi.org/10.1787/9789264243279-en.

Box 1.2. **Inclusive Growth**

The OECD's Inclusive Growth (IG) initiative was launched in 2012 in the midst of the crisis, in a context of high joblessness and growing inequalities. Inclusive Growth is about identifying policies that can deliver improvements in the population's living standards with a more even distribution of the benefits of increased prosperity among social groups. In a context of widening worldwide inequalities – in the distribution of income and social outcomes that matter for people's well-being – policy makers in advanced and emerging market economies, alongside their counterparts in developing countries, are examining the potential of inclusive growth policies to kick-start growth by turning equity into a driver of economic performance.

Absolute poverty has fallen worldwide, but relative poverty has risen in many OECD countries and many emerging-market economies. Rising income inequality is often accompanied by greater polarisation in educational and health outcomes, perpetuating a vicious circle of exclusion and inequality. Moreover, growing unequally bears a cost on future economic growth, particularly where inequality of opportunity locks in privilege and exclusion, undermining intergenerational social mobility. Inequalities and the problems to which they give rise have a spatial dimension both within cities, and between rural and urban areas.

There are a number of policy levers that can help achieve more inclusive growth: more progressive tax systems and targeted social protection; competition reforms along with support for groups affected by restructuring; liberalising labour markets along with policies to enable workers to upgrade skills and groups to enter the labour force; and education reforms such as increasing pre-school enrolments and improving low performing schools.

For inclusive growth to work well, appropriate institutions are needed, and citizens must feel that they can trust them. New technologies can play an important role in strengthening inclusiveness in policy making and implementation, by enabling new forms of collaborative and participatory governance. Inclusive policy making and service delivery requires an effective decentralisation of policies which allows for better targeted place-based approaches.

Source: OECD (2015c), *All on Board: Making Inclusive Growth Happen*, http://dx.doi.org/10.1787/9789264218512-en.

Box 1.3. Measuring well-being for Peru

Economic prosperity is only one among several pillars that supports an individual's well-being and quality of life. The OECD has developed a framework for measuring well-being in OECD countries which encompasses two broad pillars (OECD, 2011b). The first pillar, material conditions, comprises the dimensions of consumption possibilities, work, housing conditions and infrastructure. The second pillar, quality of life, comprises health status, education and skills, social connections, empowerment and participation, vulnerability, and life evaluations, feelings and meanings.

This framework has also been adapted to measure well-being in non-OECD countries, taking into account the literature on measuring development outcomes, and the socio-economic and institutional conditions in these countries (OECD, 2015e). This framework has been applied to Peru and a number of key strengths and weaknesses have been identified. These assessments are based on international benchmarks for these different dimensions, and in particular outcomes expected for Peru at the country's level of development.

The assessment of Peru against this well-being framework presents mixed outcomes for the country (OECD, 2015e). In terms of the economic dimension, Peru compares well in relation to income and labour force participation. However, it is weaker in terms of the quality of employment due to informality and vulnerability in the labour market. Peru ranks strongly in some social dimensions, in particular life expectancy, personal security, life satisfaction and educational attainment. But in terms of the quality of education, the country ranks poorly in relation to scores for reading, maths and science. In terms of the environment, Peru underperforms in relation to air and water quality, and reasonably well in relation to deforestation and emissions.

Figure 1.6. **Peru compared to OECD average: Select well-being indicators**

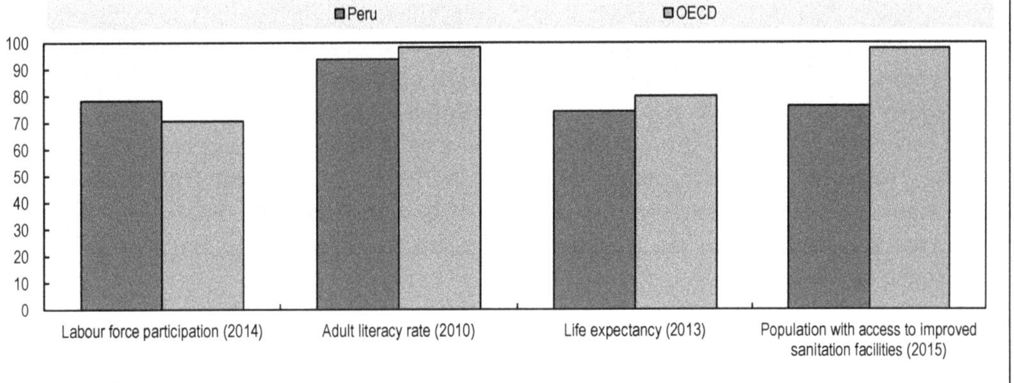

Source: World Bank (2015e), "Peru", http://data.worldbank.org/country/peru.

There are also significant inequalities across socio-economic groups in relation to some of these well-being outcomes, in particular for indigenous communities (OECD, 2015e). However, there currently is not a clear framework or set of indicators for measuring multi-dimensional well-being at a regional level. This is an area for future policy and statistical development for Peru.

Growth drivers and bottlenecks at a national level

Export commodities have been important to growth and there are downside risks

Exports have historically been an important driver of growth for Peru. As global commodity prices increased from the early 2000s, exports as a proportion of GDP nearly doubled, from 17% in 2000 to 30% in 2007. The financial crisis resulted in a levelling of exports before a sustained decrease from 2011. These export peaks pushed Peru slightly above the OECD average but below that of Chile, which is another commodity exporter.

Figure 1.7. **Exports as a proportion of GDP: Peru compared to the OECD average and select countries**

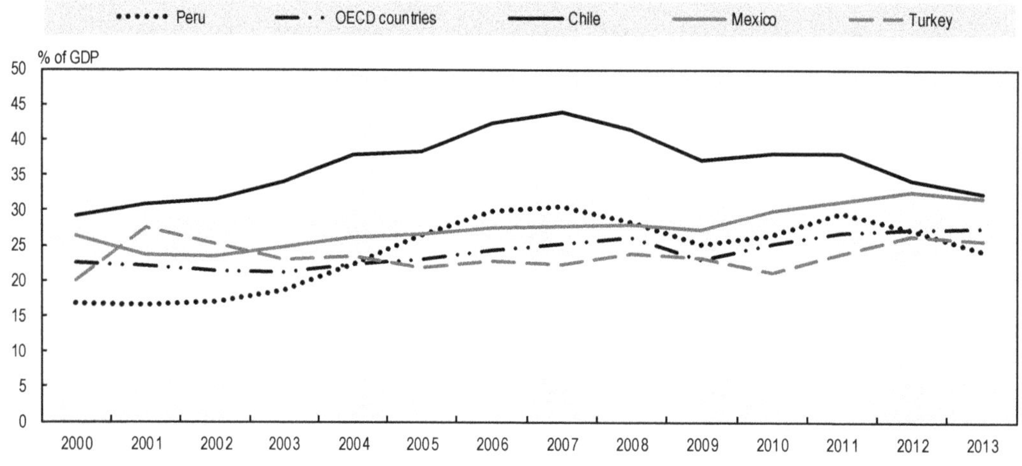

Source: World Bank (2015a), "Exports of goods and services (% of GDP)", http://data.worldbank.org/indicator/NE.EXP.GNFS.ZS.

Extractive industries have been a key component of this export growth and now account for 12% of GDP and only 1.3% of employment. Mining contributed 52% of total export revenues for Peru in 2014. This proportion of export revenues is lower than other commodity-based economies (Australia, Colombia and Norway) but higher than the OECD average (18.5%). Peru has large reserves of different mineral resources and is a leading producer of silver, copper, gold, zinc and tin. Copper and gold accounted for more than 76% of its mineral exports in 2014. This will continue to be a key comparative advantage for Peru due to the quality of its resource endowments and low production costs (OECD, 2015e).

This increase in exports is similar to many other commodity-based economies over the past decade. Increases in Chinese demand led to higher metal prices from the early 2000s. In turn, this translated into substantial investment and increases in supply. The combination of increasing export revenues and investment to increase production capacity has led to an appreciation of the exchange rate. Peru achieved trade surpluses between 2002 and 2012. As metal prices have dropped, Peru has experienced declining terms of trade, and trade deficits since 2013. These movements have affected the growth performance of the national economy, and present risks to future growth performance. Growth in the Peruvian economy has historically been related to movements in the terms of trade and the prices of metal products (Hausmann, 2008).

Figure 1.8. **Terms of trade (2000-14): Peru compared to the OECD and Latin America and Caribbean averages (base 100 = 2000)**

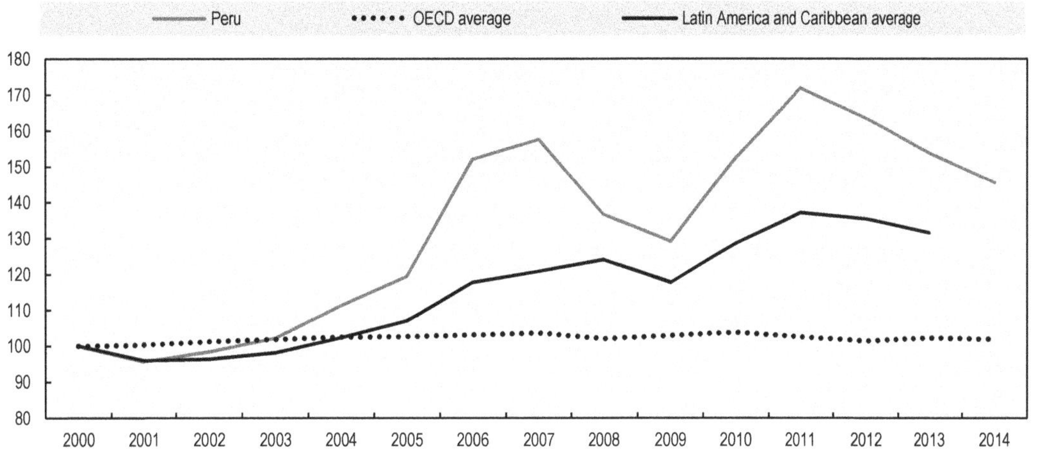

Sources: OECD (2015e) *Multi-dimensional Review of Peru: Volume 1. Initial Assessment,* based on *OECD Terms of Trade Indicators* (database), https://data.oecd.org/trade/terms-of-trade.htm; BCRP (2015), *Annual Series database*, https://estadisticas.bcrp.gob.pe/estadisticas/series/anuales; and OECD calculations based on export data from WITS/UN Comtrade.

Box 1.4. **The relationship between tradeables and non-tradeables**

Resource booms can have various impacts on the broader economy by inducing an appreciation of the exchange rate. A higher nominal exchange rate reduces the competitiveness of other tradeable sectors particularly agriculture, mining and tourism. Increasing prices for commodities attracts labour and capital from these tradeable sectors to the mining industry. Increasing income also generates spending effects within the domestic economy which primarily benefits the non-tradeable services sector. However, this also increases prices in the services sector and the domestic economy, and leads to an appreciation of the real exchange rate.

These effects are commonly known as "Dutch Disease", which is characterised by structural decline in tradeable sectors outside of resource extraction. Growth can be sustained in a resource-based economy in a number of ways: taxing resource rents and using this for debt relief and lowering general taxation; implementing regulatory reforms to reduce barriers to business start-ups and growth; and innovation and export facilitation policies to encourage diversification of the tradeable sector (Ahrend, 2006).

There is a lack of strong evidence that this is an issue at an aggregate level in Peru. Peru's real exchange rate increased from the early 2000s until the crisis in 2008, and declined to below 2009 levels since then (see Chapter 2). Extractive industries as a proportion of GDP rose quickly between 2000 and 2005, and have declined since then. Agriculture experienced a decline over this period, which may indicate reduced competitiveness. The largest growth has been in the services sector, including construction. This may be due to the investment cycle in the mining sector during this period. Manufacturing has experienced a decline since 2008, which is probably shaped by the crisis.

Box 1.4. **The relationship between tradeables and non-tradeables** (*continued*)

Figure 1.9. **Compositional shift in GDP by sector**

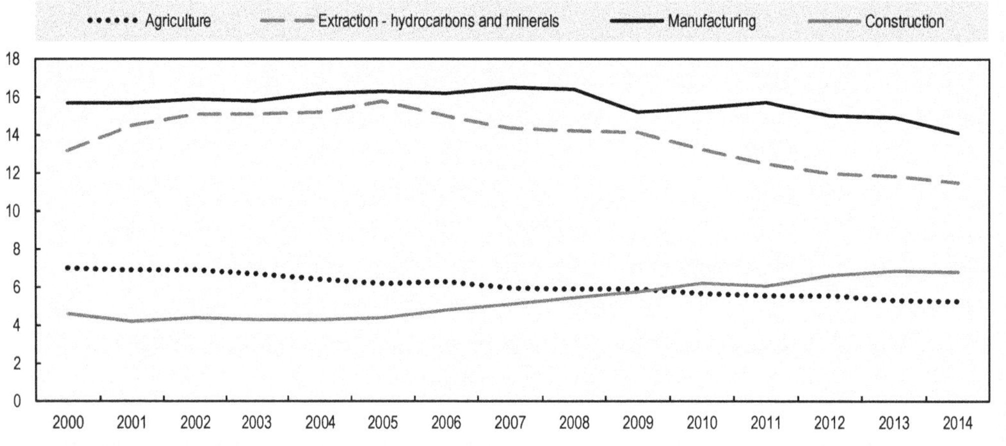

Source: INEI (2016), "Economía", www.inei.gob.pe/estadisticas/indice-tematico/economia.

There is some evidence that some of the impacts of extractive industries are also localised through indirect effects associated with increased public expenditure on infrastructure (Natural Resource Governance Institute, 2015). As local municipalities increase expenditure on public works this may have the effect of drawing labour away from the local agricultural industry. These localised impacts warrant further investigation.

Source: INEI (2016), "Economía", www.inei.gob.pe/estadisticas/indice-tematico/economia.

The rate of informality is high

Labour force participation is high in Peru at 73.3% in 2013, compared to the OECD average of 65.7%. The employment rate in Peru has increased by 8.2% since 2004.[1] An important feature of the labour market is the prevalence of informal (not officially registered) activities. Although the existing estimates of the size of the informal sector vary considerably, there is no doubt that the informal sector is an important contributor to the national economy (INEI, 2014a). The relevance of the informal sector is particularly large when measured in terms of employment. There appears to be some agreement on the fact that three out of four jobs are not captured by formal employment statistics. However, estimates of value added generated by the informal economy vary largely (from a low of about 20% to as much as 70% of total GDP). INEI puts the contribution of the informal economy to the national GDP at about 20%, suggesting that although relevant in terms of employment, the labour productivity of the informal sector is extremely low.[2]

Human capital and innovation are key bottlenecks

Improvements to education and skills are critical to the performance of firms within global value chains (GVCs) (see Chapter 2), and inclusive growth. Human capital indicators are relatively poor in Peru and the country lags behind the OECD in terms of quality of education:

- Participation rates in school education are similar to other Latin American countries (OECD, 2015e). However, scores for Peru on the Programme for International Student Assessment (PISA) are generally amongst the lowest for participating countries. In the 2012 survey Peru ranked last in terms of scores for mathematics, reading and science (OECD, 2013a). An average 15-year-old student in Peru is behind the average Latin American student by the equivalent of eight months of secondary schooling, and around three years behind the average OECD student (OECD, 2015e). Due to this gap in quality it can be argued that a year of schooling in the OECD is not equivalent to a year of schooling in Peru. This quality gap is apparent when average years of schooling are adjusted by quality based on the 2012 PISA scores (OECD, 2015e).
- Overall, Peruvians have become more educated over time. The share of the population with no schooling has fallen, from 17% in 1980 to close to 5% in 2010. The largest increase was in the proportion of the population who completed secondary education, which increased from 14% to 37% in the same period. The proportion of the population with a tertiary degree increased from 7% to 12% (OECD, 2015e).
- In terms of workforce skills there are a number of issues related to skills gaps and whether the higher education and vocational training systems are matched to demand in the labour market. In Peru, about 28% of firms report that they cannot find workers with the right skills, which is lower than the average for Latin America and the Caribbean countries (LAC) (36%) but higher than the OECD average of 17% (OECD, 2015e). Participation in the vocational education system is low due to quality issues, and this is likely to be impacting on the capacity to develop technical skills within the workforce (OECD, 2015e).

Figure 1.10. **Informal employment in benchmark countries and among socio-demographic groups in Peru**

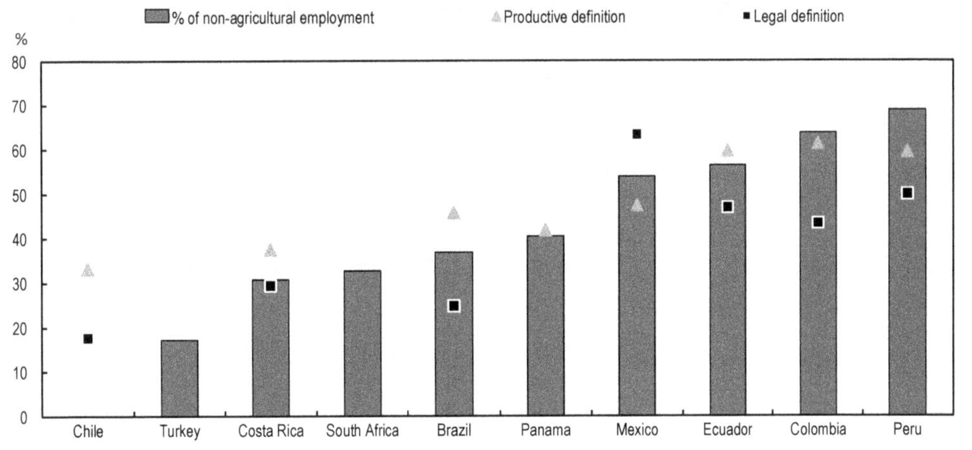

Notes: The non-agricultural employment rate is based on 2013 data for Brazil, Colombia, Costa Rica, Mexico, Panama, Peru and Turkey; 2010 data for Ecuador and South Africa. No data available for Chile for that indicator. Productive and legal definitions are based on 2011-12 data.

Sources: OECD (2015e) *Multi-dimensional Review of Peru: Volume 1. Initial Assessment* http://dx.doi.org/10.1787/9789264243279-en , based on CELDAS and World Bank (2014c), *Socio-Economic Database for Latin America and the Caribbean* (SELDAC) (database), http://sedlac.econo.unlp.edu.ar/eng/index.php for legal and productive definitions and ILO (2014), *Key Indicators of the Labour Market* for non-agricultural definition. http://dx.doi.org/10.1787/888933265385.

Figure 1.11. **Average years of schooling (ages 15-19), unadjusted and adjusted for academic achievement using PISA scores**

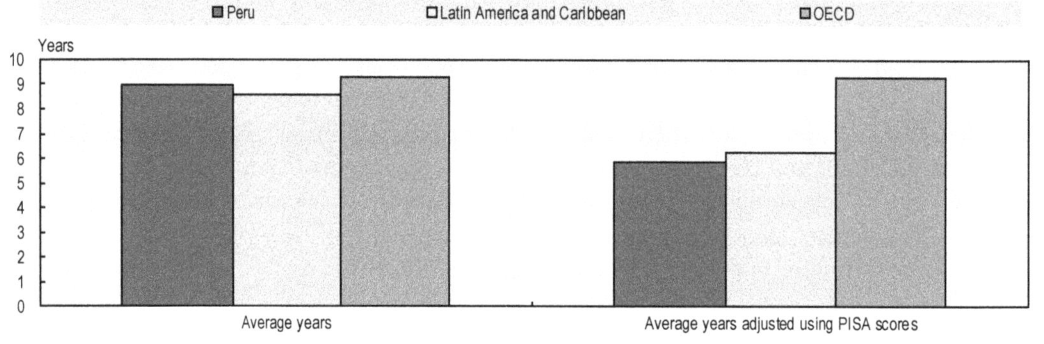

Note: Latin America and Caribbean here comprises Argentina, Brazil, Chile, Colombia, Costa Rica, Mexico, Peru and Uruguay, which are the countries in the region that participated in the PISA test in 2012.

Sources: OECD (2015e), based on OECD calculations based on *OECD/PISA 2012 database* and UNESCO/UIS (2015), *UNESCO Institute for Statistics Database*, www.uis.unesco.org/Pages/default.aspx.

Figure 1.12. **Educational attainment for total population over 15 years old, Peru**

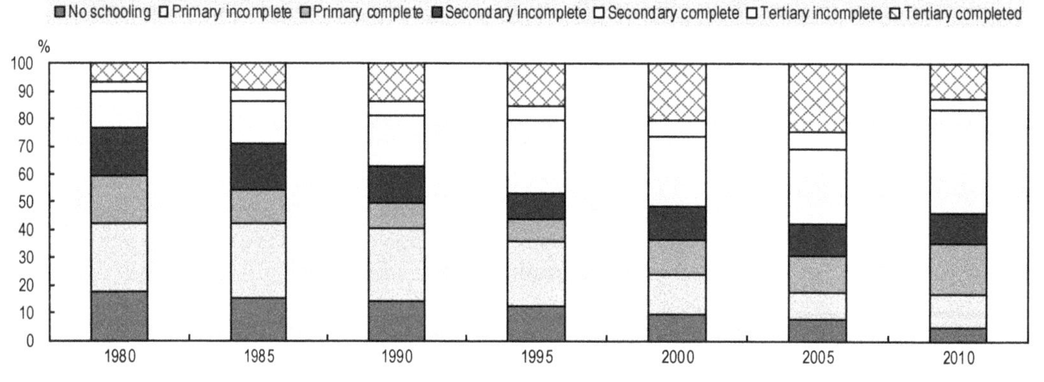

Source: OECD (2015e), based on OECD calculations based on Barro and Lee (2010), dataset, http://dx.doi.org/10.1787/888933265234.

Technological innovation and development will be central to enabling a shift to higher value activities by encouraging product diversification and increasing productivity. Peru performs poorly in relation to key input and output measures of innovation in comparison to OECD and other benchmark countries. Expenditure on research and development (R&D) remains low and patent applications are below all benchmark countries and LAC averages (Figures 1.13 and 1.14).

There are a number of factors contributing to this poor performance. There is a lack of domestic science and technology infrastructure that can generate new research linked to areas of comparative advantage for the country (OECD, 2011b). Businesses also face a number of barriers, including aversion to risk and long-term investment, weak competitive pressures and underdeveloped value chains, and weak interactions between firms and higher education and research institutes (OECD, 2011b). Low workforce skills are also a binding constraint and impact on the capacity of firms to absorb new technologies.

Figure 1.13. **Business expenditure on research and development, 2002 and 2013 (or latest available year)**

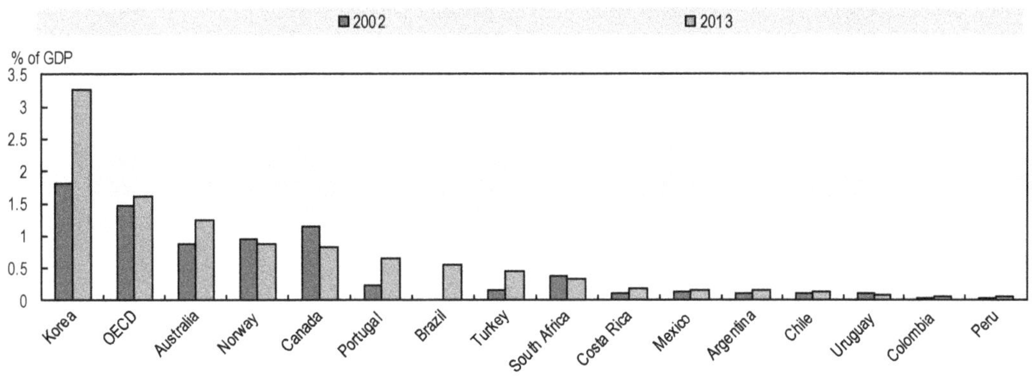

Notes: Latin American economies (excluding Argentina, Brazil, Chile and Mexico): 2012. Argentina and Chile: 2013. Australia and Mexico: 2011. Brazil: 2010.

Sources: OECD (2015e), *Main Science and Technology Indicators Database*, www.oecd.org/sti/msti; and OECD calculations based on RICYT (2015), Red de Indicadores de Ciencia y Tecnología – Iberoamericana e Interamericana website, www.ricyt.org/homeenglish.

Figure 1.14. **Patent applications per million people, comparing Peru and select benchmark countries and averages**

Number of Patent Co-operation Treaty patents, 2010-11 average

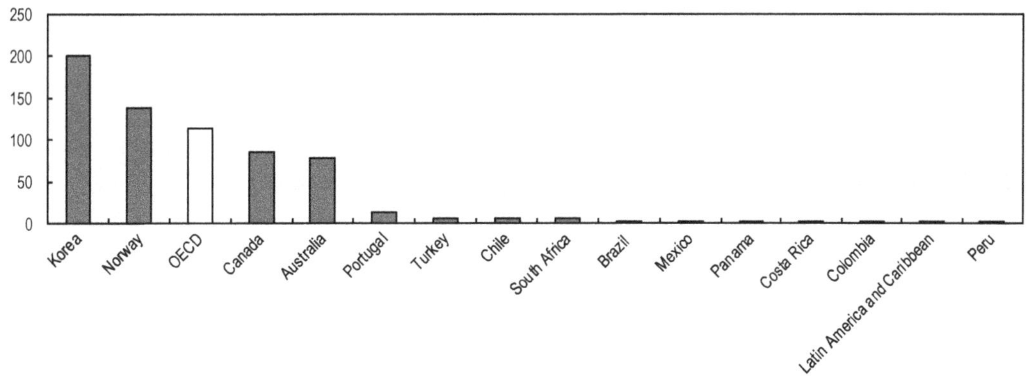

Notes: Data based upon 2010-11 averages. No values available for Ecuador from given source thus excluded from Latin American and Caribbean and benchmark countries.

Source: OECD (2015e), based on *OECD Patent Database* (database); www.oecd.org/sti/inno/oecdpatentdatabases.htm.

Infrastructure performance will need to improve

As a country with a large land mass and trade-exposed economy, the quality and efficiency of infrastructure is central to Peru's economic competitiveness. Improvements to water, energy, telecommunications and transport infrastructure are also important to addressing challenges associated with inequality and poverty in Peru (OECD, 2015e; Webb, 2013).

Quality and quantity of infrastructure has also been identified as one of the main binding constraints to both diversification and productivity in Peru (Haussmann, 2008; Webb, 2013). The investment requirement to cover the gap in infrastructure of the country has been estimated to be USD 68.8 billion over the next five years, or 8.4% of the country's projected GDP over that same period (AFIN, 2015). The largest infrastructure gaps are in the energy (37.5% and transport (23.8%) (OECD 2015e).

Peru has a similar ranking to other LAC countries for international standards in the perceived quality of infrastructure, despite some significant improvements (WEF, 2014). However, it still lags behind other benchmark countries and the OECD.

Figure 1.15. **Perceived quality of overall infrastructure, 2014**

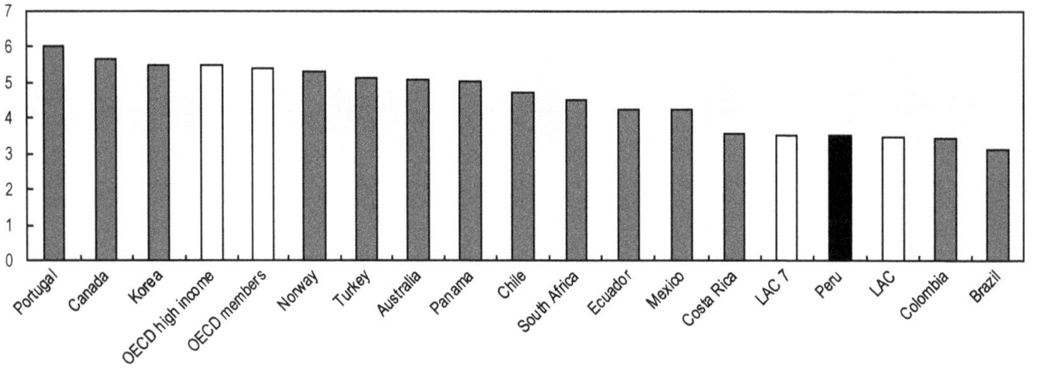

Note: This indicator uses a scale from 1 to 7 where a higher score means a better quality of infrastructure. Latest available data for Ecuador are for 2013. LAC: Latin America and Caribbean.

Source: OECD (2015), based on WEF (2014), *The Global Competitiveness Report 2014-2015*, www3.weforum.org/docs/WEF_GlobalCompetitivenessReport_2014-15.pdf.

Peru ranks particularly low in terms of the quality of different types of infrastructure that facilitate connectivity (roads, railroads, telephone and electricity). This poor quality of connecting infrastructure would be a constraint for Peruvian firms effectively participating in GVCs.

Figure 1.16. **Quality of public service infrastructure, 2014**

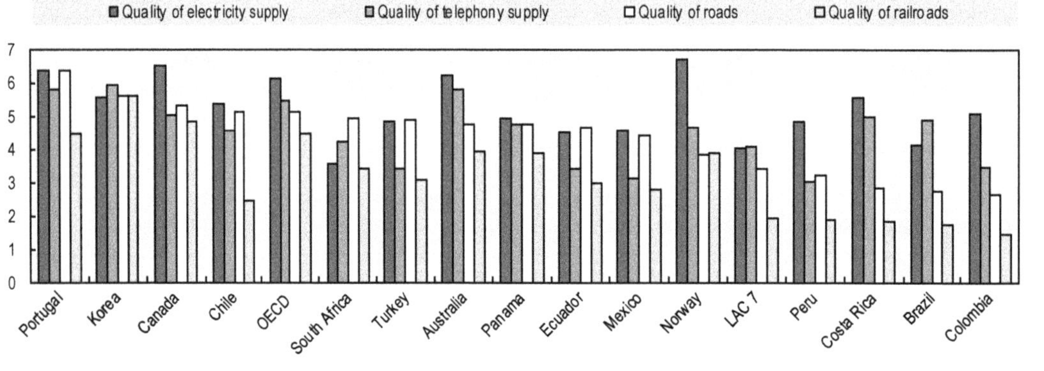

Notes: The indicator for quality of telephony supply corresponds to the weight on the electricity and telephony infrastructure component corresponding to mobile telephone subscriptions and fixed telephone lines. This indicator uses a scale from 1 to 7 where a higher score means a better quality of infrastructure. LAC: Latin America and Caribbean.

Source: OECD (2015), based on WEF (2014), *The Global Competitiveness Report 2014-2015*, www3.weforum.org/docs/WEF_GlobalCompetitivenessReport_2014-15.pdf.

Improving logistics services is particularly important for GVC participation by reducing transport-related costs (OECD, WTO and World Bank, 2014). This is important for a number of reasons including: the long-term cost competitiveness of agriculture and mining, creating opportunities for economic diversification, and supporting the role of secondary cities. The World Bank's Logistics Performance Index (LPI) provides a way of measuring logistics performance across seven components (Figure 1.17) (OECD, 2015e). Figure 1.17 indicates the gap in performance between Peru and the best-performing country within each domain, in addition to comparisons with the OECD and other LAC countries.

Figure 1.17. **Logistics performance gap to the best-performing OECD country and other Latin American countries, 2014**

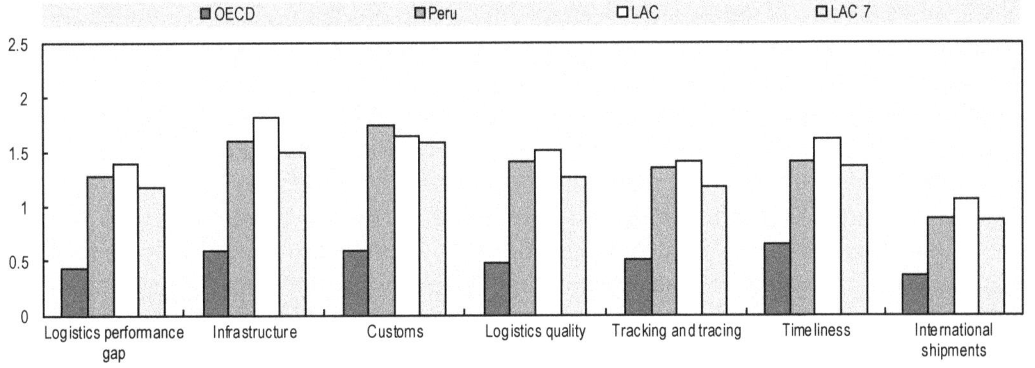

Note: The Logistics Performance Index (LPI) has a scale of 1 to 5, where 5 represents the best logistics performance. The gap refers to the difference for each logistics component with the best-performing OECD country, which is Germany for the overall LPI, infrastructure and tracking and tracing; Norway for customs and logistics quality; and Luxembourg for international shipments and timeliness. LAC 7 refers to the seven largest economies in Latin America and the Caribbean as measured by GDP: Argentina, Brazil, Chile, Colombia, Mexico, Peru and Venezuela.

Source: OECD (2015), based on data from World Bank (2014b), Logistics Performance Index 2014, http://lpi.worldbank.org.

In sum, the Peruvian economy is going through a transition from the commodities boom. The mining sector is dominated by large multinationals, which are globally integrated, and employment in mining is low. As a result, the benefits to other sectors of the economy in terms of intermediate inputs, and increased household incomes and consumption, are not as significant as its share of GDP and exports would suggest. The decline in commodity prices presents downside risks for Peru. Although its sound macroeconomic policies and open economy will stand it in good stead, there are a number of interrelated structural challenges that will need to be addressed.

The first is challenges associated with human capital and informality. The quality of human capital is not adequate, it is insufficiently developed and not effectively used by firms, and widespread informality in the labour market reduces incentives for firms and individuals to invest in it. The second is the low innovation performance of businesses, universities and other actors within the innovation system. This reduces the scope for diversification and the capacity to participate in higher value activities within global value chains. The fourth is poor infrastructure performance, which also reduces competitiveness within GVCs, and the productivity of the non-tradeable sector. Peru faces a challenge to design structural policies that can deliver sustained improvements to human capital, innovation and infrastructure in an integrated way.

Peru is territorially diverse and these growth dynamics are playing out differently across the country. Regions matter in terms of how the Peruvian government can give coherence to sectoral policies and achieve national policy objectives. This first requires an understanding of the growth dynamics and drivers of different regions. The following section will develop a framework for assessing the economic performance of Peru at a subnational level.

Regions, cities and rural areas: Moving beyond averages

When observing the geography of Peru a number of key features are apparent. The physical geography of the country is shaped by a thin coastal region, the Andes and the Amazon forest in the interior. Accessibility to international markets via sea ports is constrained by the Andes, and the major international airport is located close to Lima. Lima dominates the urban structure and population of the country with 8.5 million inhabitants (approximately 30% of the national population). Accessibility to Lima is an important factor in shaping economic performance. Accessibility to the Andes and rainforest regions is further made difficult by the extreme topography and weather conditions (such as landslides, amongst others). Coastal regions tend to have better socio-economic conditions than uplands and rainforest regions in the interior of the country. The economies of these areas are more diversified, with manufacturing, commerce and services activities. Rural economies are resource dependent and specialise in different mineral and agricultural commodities. Within these broader patterns each region has its own particular socio-economic and ecological features. When assessing regional growth trends in detail, it is apparent that the economic geography of the country is also marked by heterogeneity, which emphasises the importance of taking a place-based approach to policies.

Peru has a young and growing population, which is increasingly concentrating in cities

Peru has a population of 31 million people, which would make it the 13th largest country within the OECD. Peru is the 19th largest country in the world with a total surface area of 1.29 million km^2 (World Bank, 2015e). Only four OECD countries (Canada, the United States, Australia and Mexico) have a larger land mass. Population density is low at only 24 people per square kilometre, which is similar to relatively low-density OECD countries such as Chile and Sweden.

Peru also has a relatively young population when compared to many OECD countries and has the potential to reap a "demographic dividend" in terms of increased growth that comes from increasing numbers of people in the workforce. Peru's population growth rate is currently 1.32%, compared to the OECD average of 0.65%. Peru also has a higher proportion of people aged 0-14 of the total population than OECD member countries, although this gap is closing over time.

Taking full advantage of this demographic dividend is an enormous opportunity for Peru. This will require improvements in a number of key strategic areas such as lifting the quality of education, reducing informality and improving how cities function. In the longer term Peru will also need to consider how to financially support and provide adequate services for an ageing population, particularly in rural areas.

Figure 1.18. **Proportion of the population aged 0-14, Peru and OECD average**

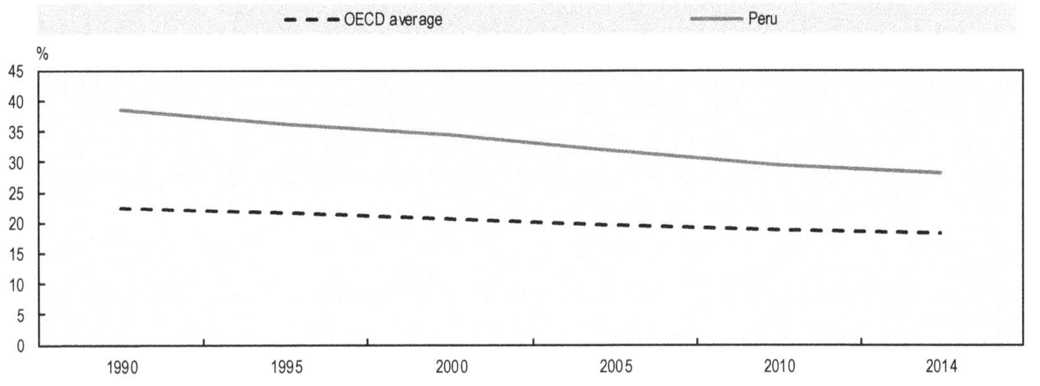

Source: World Bank (2016). "Population ages 0-14 (% of total)", http://data.worldbank.org/indicator/SP.POP.0014.TO.ZS.

In each of the 1961 to 2007 intercensal periods, although all departments reported long-term demographic gains, 12 departments generally recorded higher population growth than Peru: Lima, Amazonas, Arequipa, Huánuco, Ica, Lambayeque, Madre de Dios, Moquegua, San Martín, Tacna, Tumbes and Ucayali. Lima (including Callao) has maintained a population growth rate above the national average, but the pace of growth has decreased over time, from 70% during the intercensal period 1961-72, to 27% during the period 1993-2007 (nearly on par with the national overage of 25%).

Population changes over the most recent intercensal period, 1993 to 2007, indicate that most the population growth of each department is paralleled by a process of rapid urbanisation. Figure 1.19 shows the population growth of urban and rural areas between 1993 and 2007 (using INEI's definition of urban and rural), sorted by total population growth over the same period. It is clear from the figure that with the exception of Tacna and Tumbes, most of the population growth of each department is taking place in urban areas; moreover, 10 out of 25 departments reported a decline in the rural population.

Figure 1.19. **Population growth by urban and rural areas (INEI regional type), 1993-2007**

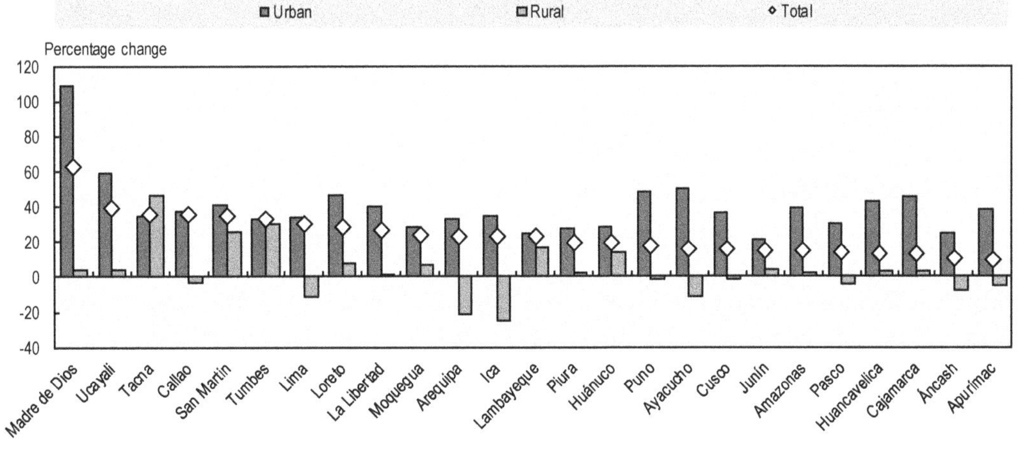

Notes: 1993 and 2007 are the last two census years. Changes computed in this figure might also reflect some reclassification of areas (particularly rural areas being reclassified as urban due to rapid development between the two census periods).

Sources: INEI data, http://www.inei.gob.pe.

Population estimates over the period 2007-15 confirm this pattern, showing a group of departments with a population growth rate higher than the national average. Over this time period, the population estimates suggest that Lima and Callao have maintained high population growth (12.6% and 13.0% respectively). A number of other provinces have also recorded higher than average population growth: Madre de Dios, Tumbes, San Martín, Ucayali, Tacna, La Libertad and Loreto. These trends provide support to the recent research on migratory flows across departments, which show that small to medium-sized cities are absorbing more population growth.

In contrast, a group of 12 departments reported lower population growth (less than 8% over the period 2007-15). Most of them are departments that are also lagging on a number of socio-economic dimensions as it will be discussed in the following sections, which suggest that comparative demographic dynamics remain an important indicator of well-being of a region. These departments are Puno, Lambayeque, Huánuco, Piura, Huancavelica, Pasco, Junín, Cusco, Áncash, Apurímac, Amazonas, and Cajamarca (with the lowest population growth at 3.6%).

Figure 1.20. **Population size (2015) and population growth (2007-15) by department**

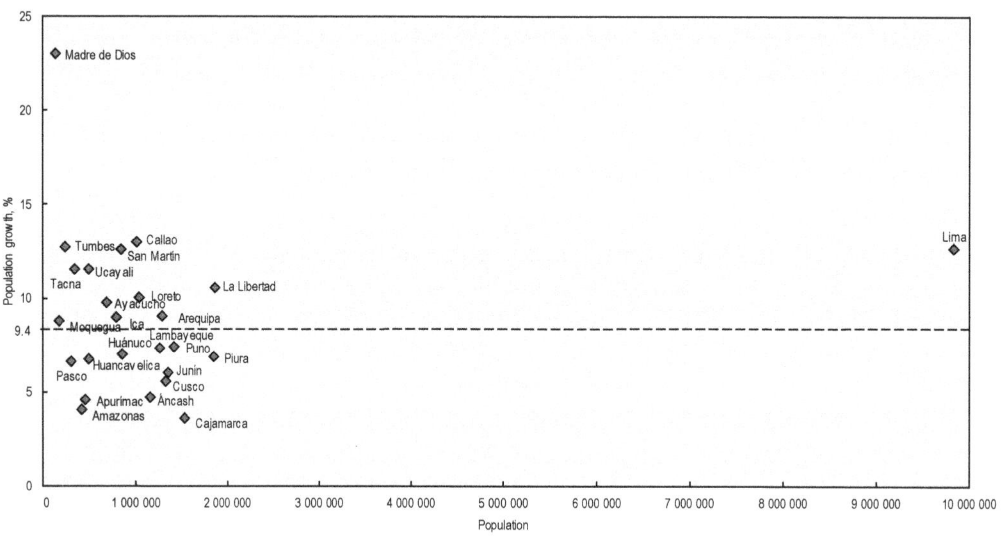

Note: The horizontal line represent the population growth of Peru (9.4%) over the period 2007-15.

Source: INEI data, http://www.inei.gob.pe.

Administrative areas

Peru has two levels of government at a subnational level: a regional level (department), with a subdivision at the municipal level between provinces and districts. Provinces include a number of districts and generally play a co-ordinating role amongst them. There are 24 departments (*departamentos*), and the Constitutional Province of Callao (Provincia Constitucional del Callao), which is given the status of a department. There are 195 provinces (not including the Constitutional Province of Callao), and 1 867 district municipalities. For a summary of these administrative and statistical definitions see Annex 1.A1.

Figure 1.21. **Peru's regions**

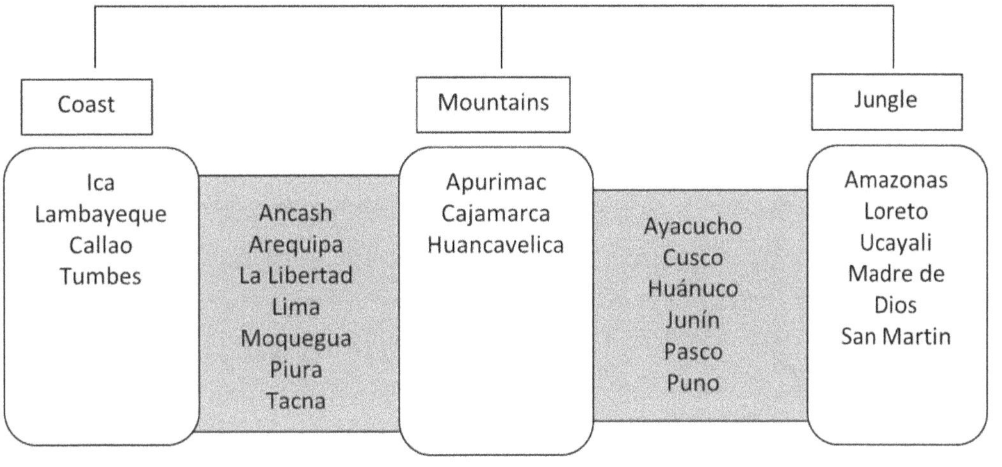

Note: Coast, mountains, and jungle indicate the different physical environments which exist across Peru's national territory. These areas do not have any formal status and reflect the main geographical features of the regions. Some regions have a combination of these physical environments, which is shown in the figure. La Libertad and Ica, both occupy a share of the three regions, but given that in both cases the majority of the territory is in two of these areas, they have been located in the box that best represents this reality.

Source: INEI (n.d.), http://www.inei.gob.pe.

The average geographic size of Peru's regions is relatively high compared to OECD regions and comparable to that of Chile and Mexico. The average population size is low, which is not surprising given the overall surface area of the country and low population densities.

Figure 1.22. **Average demographic and geographic size of OECD regional governments**

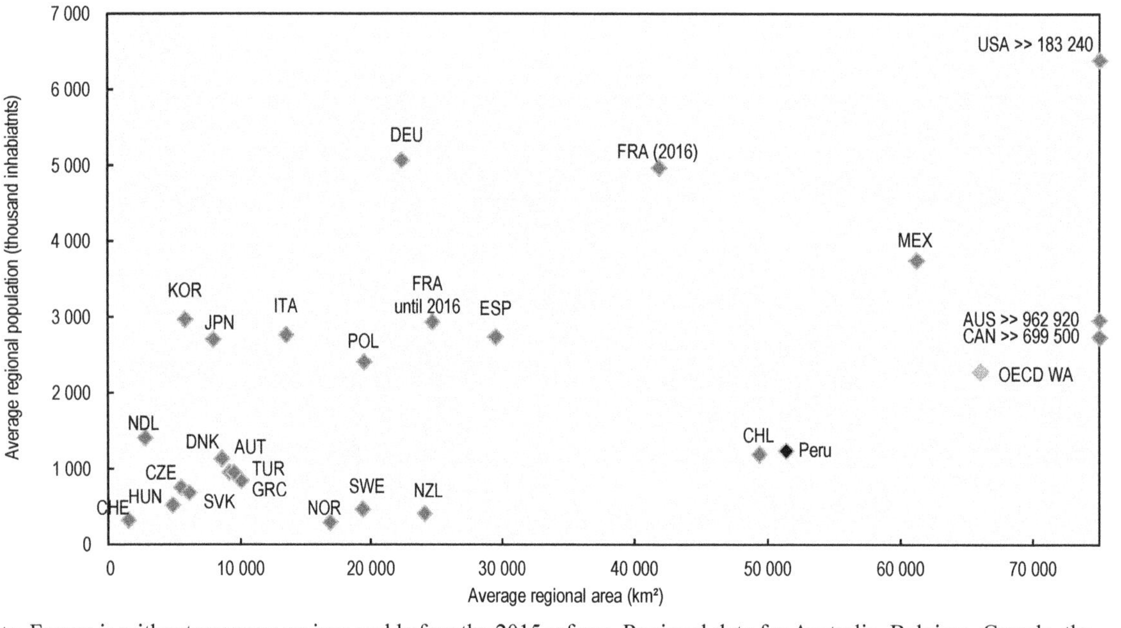

Note: France is without overseas regions and before the 2015 reform. Regional data for Australia, Belgium, Canada, the United Kingdom and the United States are not represented on this graph.

Source: OECD Regional database.

At the local level, the vast majority of municipal districts are located in rural areas and have low population density. Of 1 835 districts for which population density data are available, 1 625 (or nearly 90%) have a population density below 150 inhabitants/km². Many of the largest and mostly sparsely populated municipalities are located in the rainforest areas.

Figure 1.23. **Population density by district, 2015**

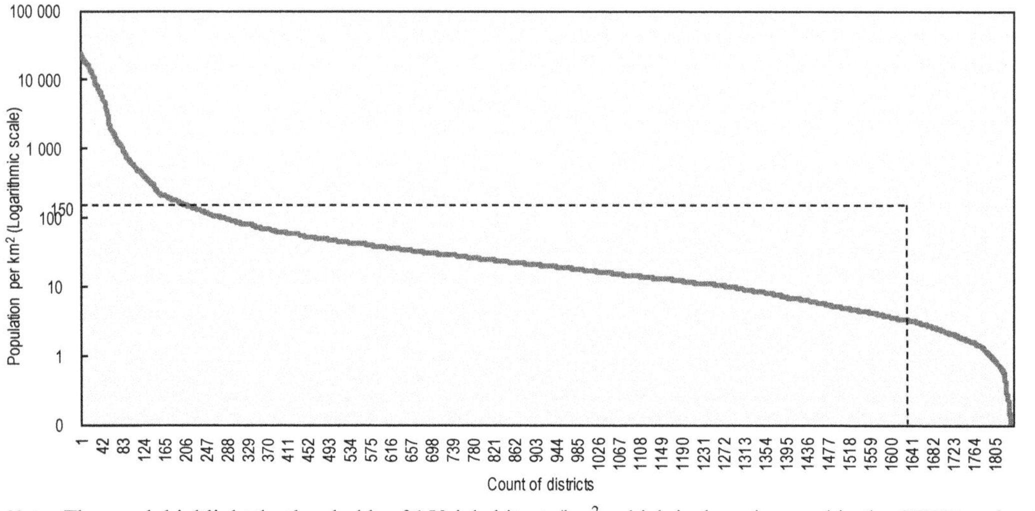

Note: The graph highlight the thresholds of 150 inhabitants/km^2, which is the value used in the OECD regional typology to define rural areas.

Source: INEI (n.d.), http://www.inei.gob.pe.

Peru's system of territorial statistics requires improvement

The system of territorial statistics has grown rapidly since the early 2000s, along with the impetus on regional decentralisation. Indeed, the statistical system itself remains relatively complex and decentralised across national entities, with a prominent technical role of INEI, and a multitude of statistical offices embedded in various ministries. INEI co-ordinates 27 regional statistical offices, which are also part of regional statistical committees. Various ministries have an active role in collecting, processing and disseminating national and regional statistics, and part of this work is also done with the technical assistance of INEI. Within this decentralised statistical landscape, a new set of public and private users of data are emerging. This is demonstrated by the rapid appearance of online open data portals.

Overall, this system is capable of generating a large amount of territorial statistics and geo-referenced data; however, due to the very nature of this system, coherence, interpretability and accessibility of information remains a concern. The multiplicity of actors involved in the production of regional statistics results in a diversity of standards, concepts, definitions and in several cases in discrepant statistics. Further measures are required to enhance the integration of database infrastructure, statistical process, analytical capacity and effective use of territorial indicators in the policy process.

The official definition of urban and rural areas for Peru is a simple binary one. For the purpose of the census, the urban areas (*área urbana*) are defined as those that have at least 100 contiguous dwellings (resulting in an average of 500 inhabitants), in addition all population centres that are district capitals are classified as an urban area even if they do not meet dwelling count. A rural area (*área rural*) is defined as an area that does not have 100 contiguous dwellings (and is not a district capital), or has more than 100 dwellings which do not constitute a contiguous agglomeration and are geographically disperse.

Various government departments have also established *ad hoc* definitions for policy development and programme delivery. In particular, there are five national ministries that share responsibilities for rural and urban policies: the Ministry of Housing, Construction and Sanitation; the Ministry of Development and Social Inclusion; the Ministry of Agriculture and Irrigation; the Ministry of the Environment; and the Presidency of the Council of Ministers (CEPLAN). Each uses a different definition, which results in overlapping and potentially conflicting perspectives on respective areas of competence and policy delivery. Over time, these definitional differences might require a process of harmonisation in order to ensure coherence and efficiency in the delivery of rural and urban policies.

Applying the OECD typology

Territorial policies will become more important to the development of Peru, and need to be supported by good spatial statistics. Harmonising territorial statistics and better co-ordinating information systems will be instrumental in improving the quality of policy development processes and the delivery of sectoral policies. Harmonising territorial statistics can also improve co-ordination in policy development, investment decision making and service delivery across level of governments, which is required to improve regional development outcomes.

To help improve the system of territorial statistics and improve international comparability, this section applies the OECD regional typology to the case of Peru. For the purpose of comparability with the OECD territorial grid, the following classifications are recommended:

- Territorial Level 2 (TL2) can be properly represented by 25 departments (*departamentos*); these include 24 departments, as such, plus the Constitutional Province of Callao, to which the state recognised a special status, reflected also in most of the statistical reporting.
- Territorial Level 3 (TL3) can be properly represented by 195 provinces (not including the Constitutional Province of Callao).
- Below TL3, the building block of the regional typology is the community level, which in this report is identified with the term of district municipality. Throughout this report the terms "local governments" and "municipal governments" will be used to identify both provincial municipality and district municipality (if not otherwise indicated).

Table 1.1. **Subnational territorial units of Peru (below Territorial Level 1 – National)**

Territorial unit	Count	Proposed OECD classification
Department	25	TL2
Province	195	TL3
District	1 867	x
Population centre	65 535	x

Notes: x: not applicable. The counts of districts and population centres had changed over time. The count of district reported here refers to the 2015 geographic frame. The count of population centres refers to the 2007 census geographic frame. The Constitutional Province of Callao (Provincia Constitucional del Callao) is counted as a department because of its unique and constitutionally recognised administrative status.

Box 1.5. **OECD regional typology**

The OECD regional classification is based on two main territorial levels. Territorial Level 2 (TL2) consists of macro-regions within each OECD country. Territorial Level 3 (TL3) consists of micro regions. Each OECD member country has identified the statistical or administrative geography that provides the best fit for this territorial classification.

The OECD taxonomy defines TL3 regions as predominantly urban (hereafter referred to as urban), intermediate and predominantly rural (hereafter referred to as rural). This taxonomy, established in 1991, is designed for facilitating international comparability of data. With this aim, it applies the same criterion and selects comparable units among OECD member countries. The OECD scheme distinguishes between two levels of geography within countries: a local community level and a regional level. Local communities are defined as basic administrative units or small statistical areas (districts in Peru). They are classified as either rural or urban using a population density threshold. In a second step, TL3 regions, which correspond to larger administrative units or functional areas, are defined as predominantly urban, intermediate or rural with a criterion measuring the share of population living in rural communities.

The first step in the OECD territorial typology is that of classifying "local units" (administrative entities at a geographical level lower than TL3) as rural if their population density is below 150 inhabitants per km^2. In a second step, the local units are aggregated into TL3 regions and classified as "predominantly urban", "intermediate" and "predominantly rural" using the percentage of population living in rural local units. A third step takes into account possible reclassification of predominantly rural and intermediate units based on the population size of their main agglomeration.

When applied to the Peruvian data, the OECD classification yields the results outlined in Table 1.2. There are 12 provinces (TL3) that are classified as predominantly urban (PU) regions, which include approximately 14.4 million people or nearly half of the Peruvian population. In addition, 19 provinces are classified as intermediate regions (IR). These regions encompass 3.9 million inhabitants or approximately 12% of the total population. The remaining 165 provinces are classified as predominantly rural (PR) regions. Predominantly rural regions include about 12.8 million people (about 40% of the total population). It should be noted that nearly 1.5 million of people living in predominantly rural areas are in fact living in an urban community (district).

Figure 1.24 provides further insights on the distribution of the Peruvian population by department and the OECD regional typology. Not all regional types are present in all departments. The following departments are entirely or largely constituted by predominantly rural provinces: Amazonas, Áncash, Apurímac, Huancavelica, Tacna and Ucayali. There is another group of departments largely constituted by predominantly urban or intermediate provinces: Arequipa, Callao, Lambayeque, Lima, Tumbes and La Libertad.

It is important to note that further work is required to address issues associated with the small size of some municipalities within urban areas and the lack of a "metropolitan area" concept within the statistical system of Peru. For example, Tacna has urbanised districts that are clustered together but none of these individual districts has a population large enough to be classified as "intermediate". This emphasises the importance of functional urban areas for the territorial statistical system and policy development in Peru.

Table 1.2. **Predominantly urban and intermediate regions (TL3), OECD definition, 2015**

Geocode (Ubigeo)	Province (capital city)	Urban population (district)	Rural population (district)	Total population	Rural share
			Units		
Predominantly urban					
1501	Lima (Lima)	8 828 000	67 000	8 894 000	0.7%
701	Prov. Const. del Callao (Callao)	995 000	0	995 000	0.0%
1301	Trujillo (Trujillo)	896 000	61 000	957 000	6.4%
401	Arequipa (Arequipa)	866 000	104 000	969 000	10.7%
1401	Chiclayo (Chiclayo)	747 000	111 000	857 000	12.9%
1201	Huancayo (Huancayo)	450 000	53 000	503 000	10.5%
801	Cusco (Cusco)	448 000	2 000	450 000	0.5%
2111	San Roman (Juliaca)	278 000	15 000	294 000	5.2%
1506	Huaral (Huaral)	162 000	28 000	191 000	14.8%
2209	San Martín (Tarapoto)	159 000	28 000	187 000	15.0%
1803	Ilo (Ilo)	67 000	4 000	71 000	5.4%
2403	Zarumilla (Zarumilla)	46 000	8 000	53 000	14.3%
Sub-total		13 942 000	481 000	14 421 000	3.3%
Intermediate					
2001	Piura (Piura)	482 000	283 000	765 000	37.0%
601	Cajamarca (Cajamarca)	289 000	99 000	388 000	25.5%
501	Huamanga (Ayacucho)	238 000	73 000	311 000	23.5%
2006	Sullana (Sullana)	222 000	96 000	318 000	30.2%
1001	Huánuco (Huánuco)	198 000	119 000	317 000	37.5%
1102	Chincha (Chincha Alta)	170 000	48 000	218 000	22.1%
2101	Puno (Puno)	146 000	103 000	248 000	41.4%
201	Huaraz (Huaraz)	138 000	29 000	167 000	17.4%
2401	Tumbes (Tumbes)	136 000	29 000	164 000	17.6%
608	Jaen (Jaen)	100 000	99 000	199 000	49.5%
1105	Pisco (Pisco)	93 000	42 000	136 000	31.2%
1502	Barranca (Barranca)	82 000	64 000	146 000	43.9%
607	Hualgayoc (Bambamarca)	82 000	21 000	102 000	20.1%
1307	Pacasmayo (San Pedro de Lloc)	71 000	33 000	104 000	31.3%
301	Abancay (Abancay)	66 000	40 000	106 000	37.9%
1304	Chepen (Chepen)	49 000	38 000	87 000	44.2%
2113	Yunguyo (Yunguyo)	38 000	10 000	47 000	20.2%
1209	Chupaca (Chupaca)	34 000	19 000	53 000	36.1%
101	Chachapoyas (Chachapoyas)	29 000	26 000	55 000	48.0%
Sub-total		2 663 000	1 271 000	3 931 000	32.3%
Predominantly rural					
Sub-total	165 provinces	1 475 000	11 348 000	12 823 000	88.5%

Notes: Population counts refer to 2015 population estimates. Counts might differ slightly from official statistics due to assumptions and different counts used for territorial units that do not have fully specified geographic boundaries. Data are rounded to the closest 1 000; as a result totals might not be the exact sum of their components. In this table, the Constitutional Province of Callao is included among the provinces; as a result, the total number of provinces in this table is 196.

Source: INEI data, http://www.inei.gob.pe.

Population growth estimates by type of region confirm that overall, predominantly urban regions grew the most, but several predominantly rural regions (by OECD standards) also maintained a high rate of population growth. Table 1.3 uses district level population estimates over the period 2007-15 to generate insight on population growth by type of OECD region. Overall, predominantly urban regions grew 12.3%, intermediate regions 9% and predominantly rural regions 6.4%. However, some of the most dynamic departments, which remain predominantly rural in OECD comparative terms, reported higher than average population growth. Population growth for these regions is likely to have occurred primarily in small towns or departmental capitals.

Figure 1.24. **Population distribution of departments by OECD regional typology, 2015**

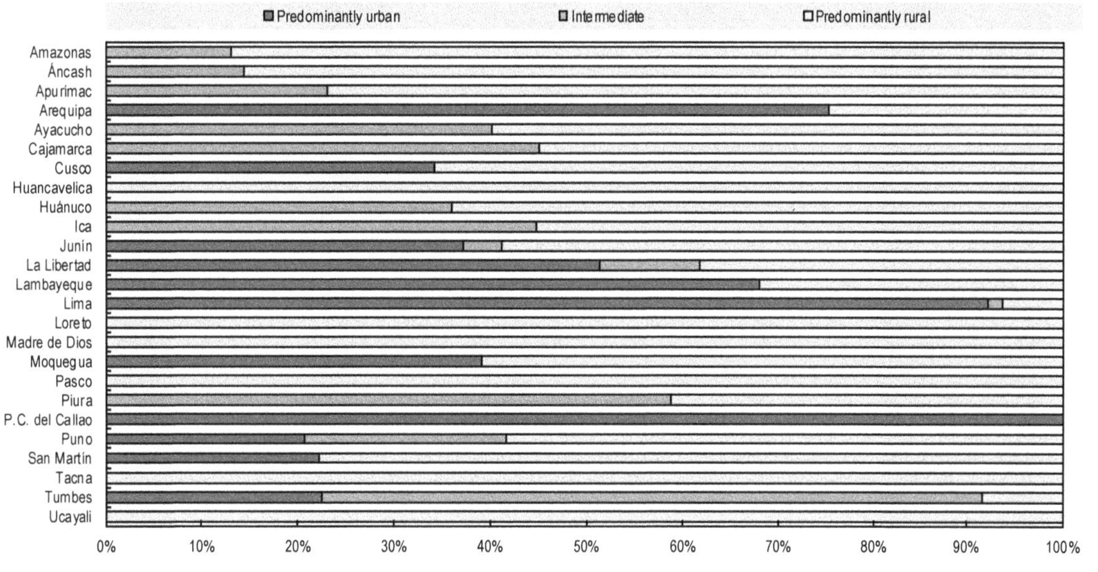

Source: OECD analysis based on data from INEI.

These territorial definitions are based on political boundaries and administrative units. The usage of these boundaries does bring disadvantages, such as an arbitrary definition of a territory that often does not correspond to patterns of life, job markets and business flows. For example, the administrative boundaries of a city often do not capture the economic flows and interactions which constitute its functional area. The mismatch between functional and administrative boundaries can result in difficulties in co-ordinating policies from different administrative units and lead to sub-optimal outcomes. As a response to this challenge the OECD has developed a new approach for classifying regions based on functional urban areas.

Currently there are no statistical or administrative geographies that correspond to the concept of functional region or labour market area. With the possible exception of the metropolitan area of Lima (see INEI, 2014d), the concept of functional region is not generally used in statistics reporting or policy development. The analysis of functional urban areas in Peru would support the development of better policies for urban and rural areas.

It is also important to note that Peru collects and disseminates statistics at a municipal level. This is important in providing the building blocks of a revised urban/rural definition, and providing more disaggregated analysis to inform policy design and delivery. However, due to constraints this chapter provides analysis mainly at a regional (or TL2) level.

Table 1.3. **Estimated population growth by department and OECD regional type, 2007-15**

In percent

Department	Predominantly urban	Intermediate	Predominantly rural	Total
Amazonas	...	2.9	4.2	4.1
Áncash	...	9.8	3.9	4.7
Apurímac	...	1.8	5.5	4.6
Arequipa	9.5	...	7.6	9.0
Ayacucho	...	17.2	5.3	9.8
Cajamarca	...	10.2	-1.2	3.6
Callao	13.0	...	...	13.0
Cusco	15.4	...	1.1	5.5
Huancavelica	...	...	6.8	6.8
Huánuco	...	8.7	6.1	7.0
Ica	...	8.8	9.1	9.0
Junín	3.8	-1.8	8.1	6.1
La Libertad	13.4	7.7	7.6	10.5
Lambayeque	7.3	...	7.5	7.3
Lima	13.1	5.4	8.4	12.6
Loreto	...	...	10.0	10.0
Madre de Dios	...	...	23.0	23.0
Moquegua	8.0	...	9.4	8.8
Pasco	...	...	6.6	6.6
Piura	...	10.5	2.1	6.9
Puno	17.9	2.7	5.8	7.4
San Martín	13.6	...	12.3	12.6
Tacna	...	...	11.5	11.5
Tumbes	23.9	9.7	11.6	12.8
Ucayali	...	...	11.5	11.5
Peru	12.3	9.0	6.4	9.4

Note: ..: not available.

Source: OECD analysis based on data from INEI.

Concentration in settlement patterns and economic activity

Lima dominates the urban system of Peru. The second-largest metropolitan area, as well as the second-largest region, is less than one-tenth of Lima in population size. According to the 2007 population census, metropolitan Lima had a population of approximately 8.5 million, with more than 7.6 million people residing in the Lima province and nearly 1 million in Callao, a constitutional province that is part of the same metropolitan area. This represents approximately 30% of the population of Peru, making it the largest metropolitan area of Peru, the fifth-largest urban area in Latin America and one of the top 30 metropolitan areas of the world.[3]

Following the metropolitan area of Lima, the other three largest cities (Trujillo, Arequipa and Chiclayo) are in the order of approximately 700 000-900 000 inhabitants. There are six cities which have a population size in the range of 330 000-700 000 (Piura, Maynas, Huancayo, Cusco, Santa and Coronel Portillo). The remaining cities (*centro poblando*) all have less than 320 000 inhabitants.

Box 1.6. Methodology for defining functional urban areas

The OECD-EU identifies functional urban areas (FUAs) beyond city boundaries to reflect the economic geography of where people live and work. Functional urban areas as relatively self-contained economic units, characterised by high levels of labour linkages and other economic interactions. Cities are widely accepted as important generators of wealth, employment and productivity gains. Moreover, large agglomerations are key players of transnational flows and work as essential spatial nodes of the global economy. Thus, often metropolitan areas are essential interconnected units in the global economy.

Defining urban areas as functional economic units can better guide the way national and city governments plan infrastructure, transportation, industrial and commercial developments, housing and schools, and space for culture and recreation. Improved planning will make these urban areas more competitive to support job creation, and more attractive for their residents.

The methodology identifies urban areas as functional economic units, characterised by densely inhabited "urban cores" and "hinterlands" whose labour market is highly integrated with the "cores". This methodology is a clear example of how geographic/morphologic information from geographic sources and census data can be used together to get a better understanding of how urbanisation develops. Information on the distribution of the population at a fine level of spatial disaggregation – 1 km² – are used to identify more precisely the centres or "cores" of the urban space, defined as contiguous aggregations ("urban clusters") of highly densely inhabited areas (grid cells). The hinterlands of these internationally comparable urban cores are defined using information on commuting flows from the surrounding regions.

Such a definition is applied to 30 OECD countries and identifies 1 179 FUAs with at least 50 000 inhabitants. Functional urban areas have been identified beyond their administrative boundaries in 30 OECD countries. They are characterised by densely populated urban cores and hinterlands with high levels of commuting towards the urban cores. The share of national population in FUAs ranges from 87% in Korea to less than 40% in Slovenia and the Slovak Republic.

Figure 1.25. **Percent of national population living in functional urban areas, 2012**

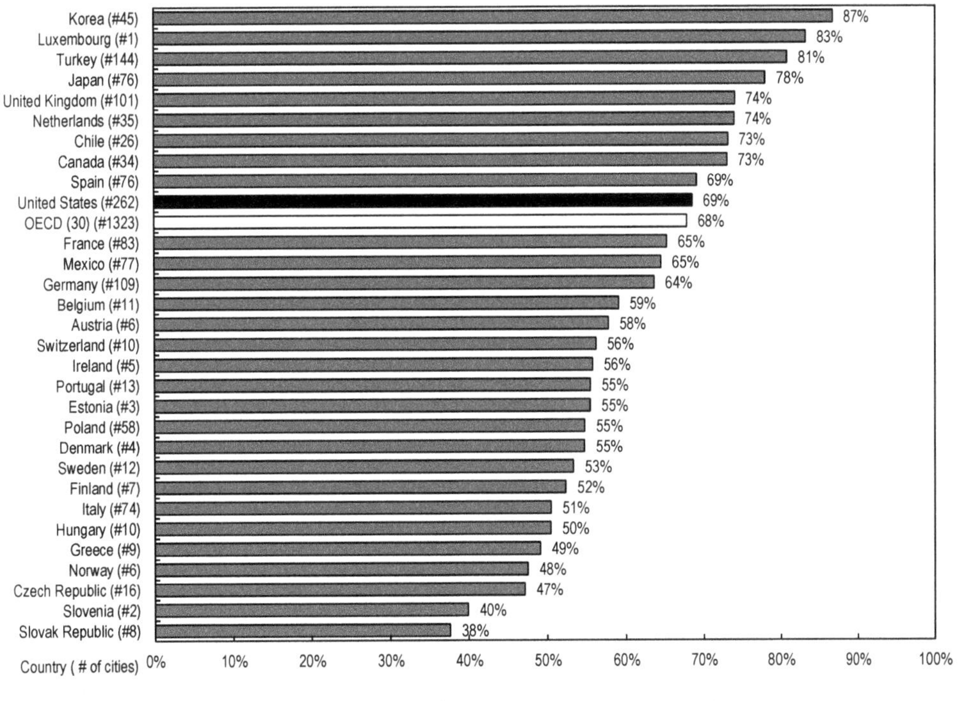

Source: OECD (2013a), *OECD Regions at a Glance 2013*, http://dx.doi.org/10.1787/reg_glance-2013-en.

Box 1.6. Methodology for defining functional urban areas (*continued*)

Among the 1 179 OECD functional urban areas, 77 have more than 1.5 million people, 198 between 500 000 and 1.5 million people, both groups concentrate almost 75% of the total urban population. Additionally, 406 were identified with a population of between 200 000 and 500 000 people, and 498 are small functional urban areas with a population below 200 000 and above 50 000 people (see below).

Figure 1.26. **Number of functional urban areas and population share by size, 2012**

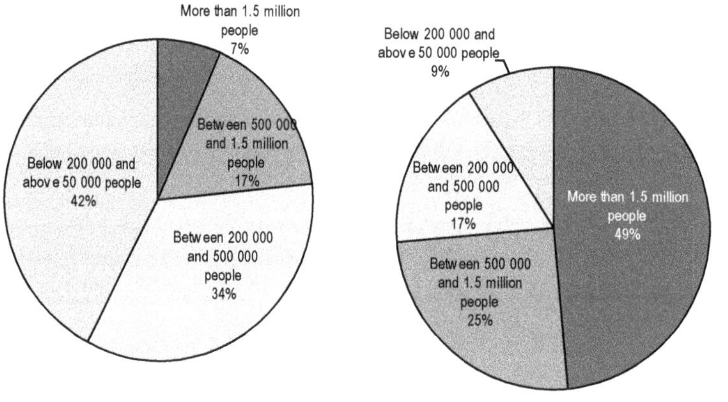

Source: OECD (2013b), *OECD Metropolitan Database*, http://dx.doi.org/10.1787/region-data-en.

Source: OECD (2014a), *OECD Regional Outlook 2014: Regions and Cities, Where Policies and People Meet*, http://dx.doi.org/10.1787/9789264201415-en.

Peru has a high level of concentration in population, according to the Geographic Concentration Index across its 25 TL2 regions. Only four OECD member countries record higher levels of concentration (Chile, Israel, Sweden and Canada), and only two enhanced engagement countries (Brazil and the People's Republic of China) also recorded higher levels of concentration. This high level of concentration is driven by the large concentration of population and economic activity in its capital region Lima. For a description of how the Geographic Concentration Index is constructed see Annex 1.A2.

Over the last 25 years, concentration in population has been increasing in Peru as a result of the gradual migration of population to Lima.

When compared to OECD member and non-member countries, the increase has been above the average, but not amongst the highest. It is interesting to note that other highly concentrated countries (Chile and Colombia) have reduced concentration in population over this time period.

How are Peru's regions performing?

There is diversity in regional performance with some evidence of convergence

Peruvian GDP has grown, in real terms, at an average annual rate of 6% between 2007 and 2013.[4] Over the same time period, however, there was large variation in regional economic performance. Regional economic growth, as measured by annual gross value added (GVA), varied largely by department and year.

Figure 1.27. **Geographic Concentration Index in population in select TL2 regions, 2014**

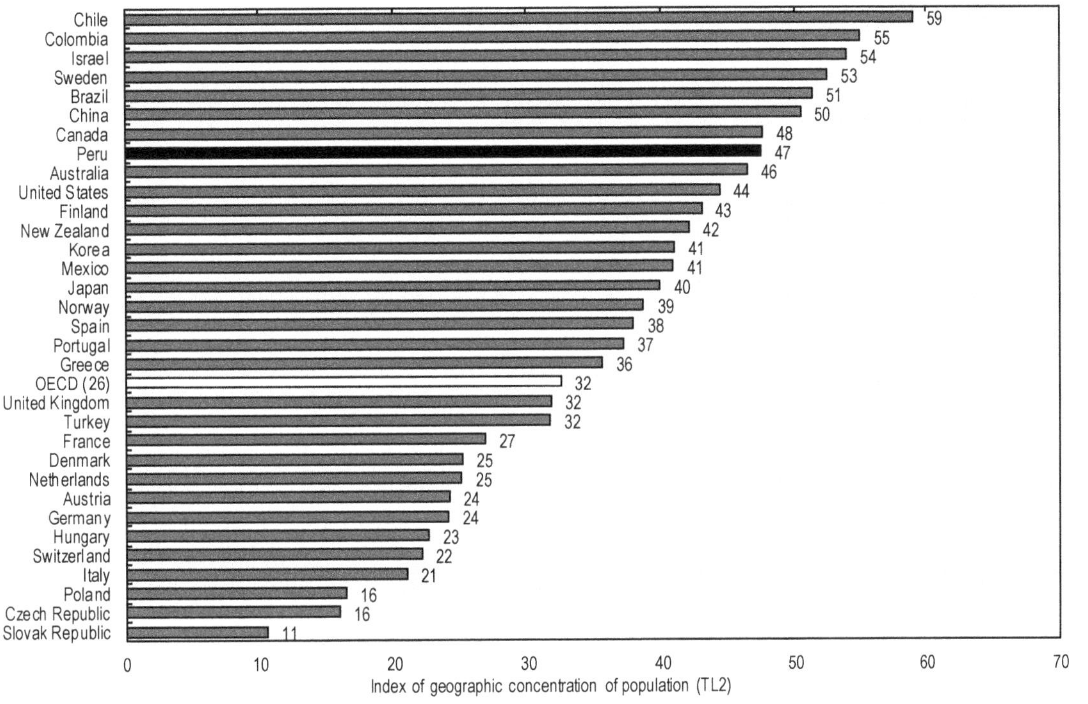

Source: OECD Regional Database.

Figure 1.28. **Geographic Concentration Index in population in TL2 regions, Peru**

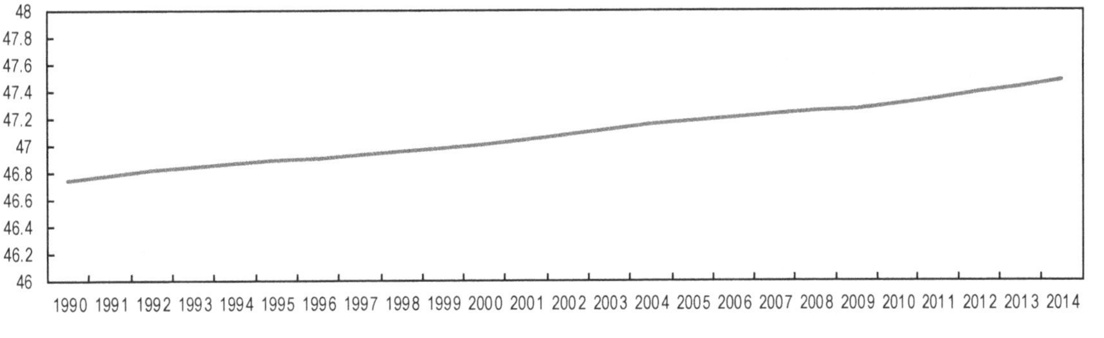

Source: OECD Regional Database.

Figure 1.29. **Change in Geographic Concentration Index in population in select TL2 regions, 1990-2014**

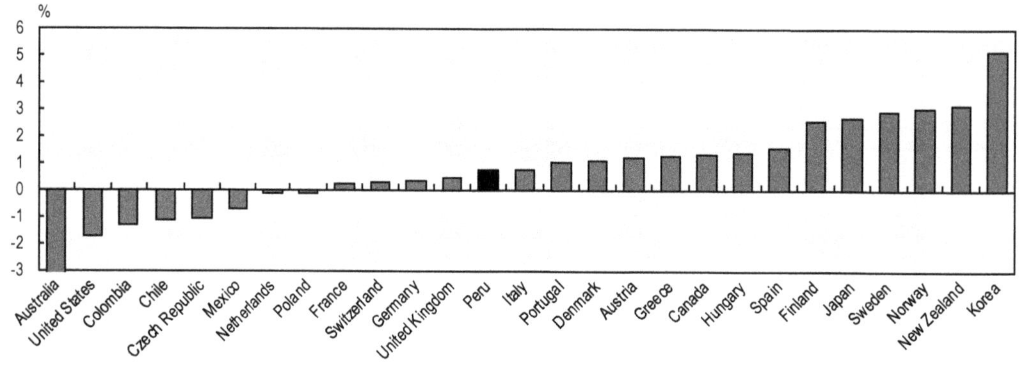

Source: OECD Regional Database.

The strongest growth performers were Cusco, Ayacucho and Ica, which all experienced average growth above 8% per annum for this period. There was a cluster of regions that experienced average annual growth rates above the national average in the range of 6-8% (Tumbles, Amazonas, Lambayeque, Lima, San Martín and Huánuco). Another group of regions grew very close to the national of average of 5% (Puno, Piura and Cajamarca). The remaining regions were at or below the national growth average for this period.

Figure 1.30. **Average annual growth rate, gross value added, by region, 2007-13**

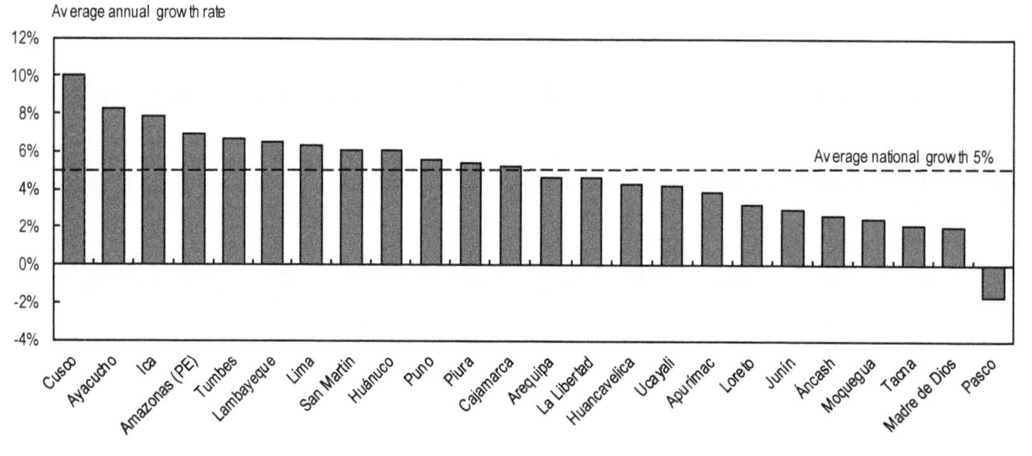

Source: INEI (n.d.), http://www.inei.gob.pe.

This average performance masks significant variations within years. In each year, the percentage point difference in GVA growth between the top and bottom performing department was 20% or more, with the largest differential of nearly 33% recorded in 2011/12 between Madre de Dios (-20.5%) and Apurímac (12.4%). This growth volatility is likely to be associated with the impacts that variations in commodity prices and capital investment in mining projects have in smaller rural economies.

There is some evidence of regional convergence between 2007 and 2013. Moquegua remains an outlier in terms of level of GVA per employee, and recorded a decline of about 8% in this period. Pasco and Madre de Dios also reported a decline in GVA per worker, although their GVA remain in the upper range. Cusco reported a major increase in GVA per employee (over 50%) and shifted toward the upper range of GVA per worker.

Growth has not been inclusive for some high-performing regions. Cajamarca, Amazonas and Ayacucho had high initial levels of poverty and also experienced large increases in GVA per worker between 2007 and 2013. Reductions in poverty during this period were relatively modest (Figure 1.31). In contrast, departments such as Ucayali, Puno, Piura and San Martín (which had a comparable level of GVA per worker) had smaller increases in GVA but substantially larger declines of poverty and improvements in other quality of life indicators.

Contribution of different regions to the national economy

National growth depends upon the contribution of all regions. Among OECD regions, a few large ones contribute disproportionately to aggregate growth whilst many smaller ones contribute only marginally on an individual basis. This pattern is apparent in the Peruvian context. The metropolitan area of Lima contributes to one-third of the country's population and produces almost half of the Peru's industry GVA. The next most economically important region, Arequipa, accounts for 5.4% of Peru's industry GVA. Nevertheless, a majority of Peru's economy is outside of Lima, and there are many regions which account for a small share of the national economy.

Figure 1.31. **Gross value added per employee: Level and growth by department, 2007-13**

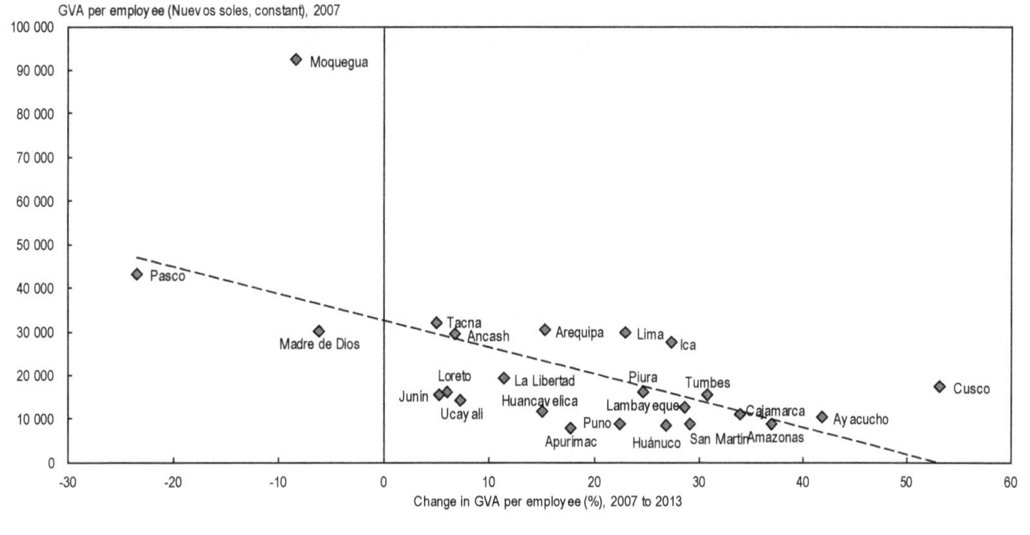

Notes: GVA per employee (vertical axis) is computed as an average for the year 2012 and 2013; the change in GVA per employee (horizontal axis) is computed as growth between the 2007-08 average and the 2012-13 average. Two-year averages are used to smooth the effect of an unusually high or low value for one single year. Callao is included in the department of Lima.

Source: OECD analysis based on data from INEI.

Figure 1.32. **Regional share of industry gross value added, 2013**

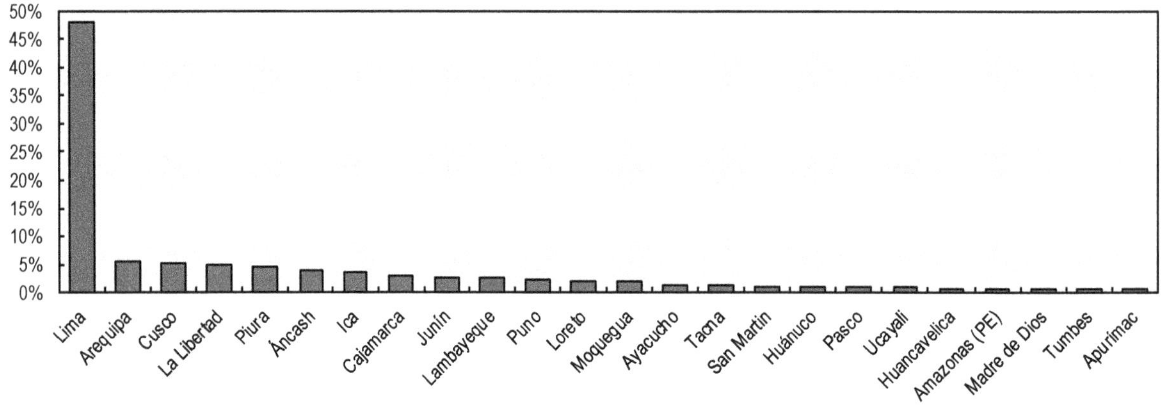

Source: OECD analysis based on data from INEI.

There is some alignment between the share of industry GVA and the contribution to growth (2007-13), particularly in terms of the importance of Lima. For some regions, their ranking in terms of contribution to growth is lower than their share of the national economy (Arequipa, Áncash, Moquegua, Tacna and Pasco) whilst some have been higher (Huánuco, Ucayali and Amazonas). There may be a number of reasons for this, including convergence (see Figure 1.33), population size and density, and framework conditions, which will be explored later in the chapter. Industry mix also influences regional performance, and this will be explored further in Chapter 2.

Figure 1.33. **Contribution to growth of industry gross value added, 2007-13**

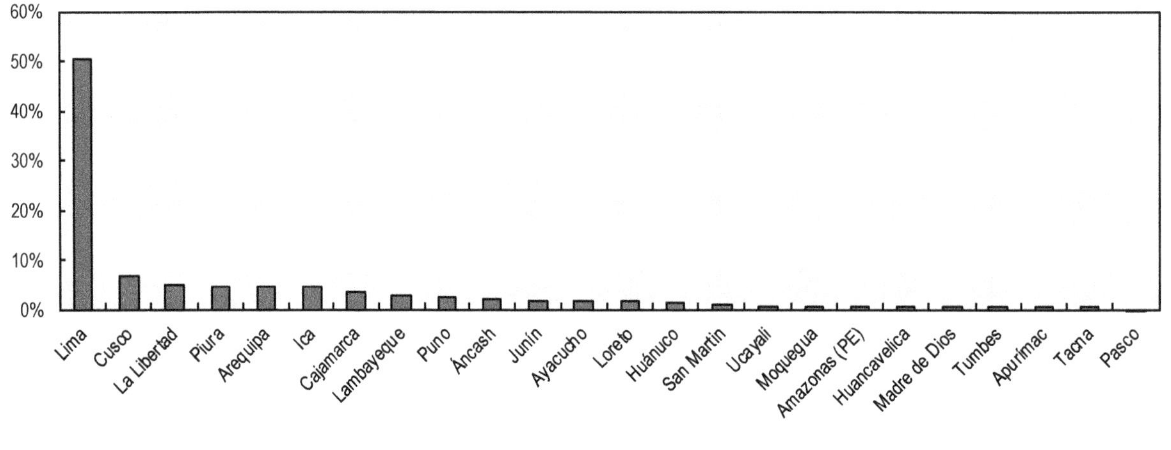

Source: OECD analysis based on data from INEI.

Poverty and inequality is spatially concentrated within rural areas

Substantial progress has been made over the past two decades in reducing poverty in Peru. However, the rate of reduction in poverty has slowed in recent years and is now around 20%. There are strong urban-rural disparities present in the distribution of poverty, and the most recent statistics show that poverty has increasingly become a rural issue. Using the INEI definition of rural, in 2013 only 25% of the population was living in rural areas, while 75% was living in urban areas (INEI, 2014f). However, nearly half of the individuals in poverty were estimated to live in rural areas, indicating that individuals in rural areas were nearly twice as likely to be poor than individuals living in urban areas. Moreover, about 47% of the poor were living in the region of the Sierra, which also has a higher proportion of indigenous people (INEI, 2014f).

A disaggregation of poverty incidence by department and OECD regional typology shows that predominantly rural regions generally have a higher incidence of poverty. Table 1.6 shows the incidence of poverty in each area relative to the national level in 2013 (the most recent year for which poverty estimates at the municipal level were generated). In this table, values greater than 1 indicate a higher regional incidence compared to the national incidence of poverty. With the exception of Ica, Lima and Tumbes, predominantly rural regions are those with the highest concentration of poverty.

Box 1.7. Contributions of regions to aggregate growth in the OECD

Recent OECD studies examining contributions to aggregate growth find a general pattern among regions. Around one-third of aggregate growth is driven by very few regions. The remaining two-thirds, while not dominated by any single region, stems from the combined contribution.

Among OECD TL2 and TL3 regions, while the distribution in gross domestic product (GDP) and GDP per capita growth rates follows an approximately normal distribution, the regional contributions to aggregate growth follow a power law, with a coefficient around 1.2 (in absolute terms). This implies that Few-Large (FL) regions contribute disproportionately to aggregate growth whereas Many-Small (MS) individual regions contribute only marginally. Nevertheless, because the number of these smaller regions is very large and the decay of their contribution to growth is slow (generating a fat tail distribution), their cumulated contribution is around two-thirds of aggregate growth. For the period 1995-2007, only 2.4% of OECD TL3 regions contributed to 27% of OECD GDP growth, but the remaining 97.6% corresponds to 73% of growth. The distribution of growth rates by size follows a non-monotonic pattern, with the largest concentration of above average regional growth rates being concentrated for middle-sized regions. Overall, the great heterogeneity suggests that the possibilities for growth seem to exist in all types of regions.

Figure 1.34. **Contributions of TL2 regions to OECD growth, 1995-2007**

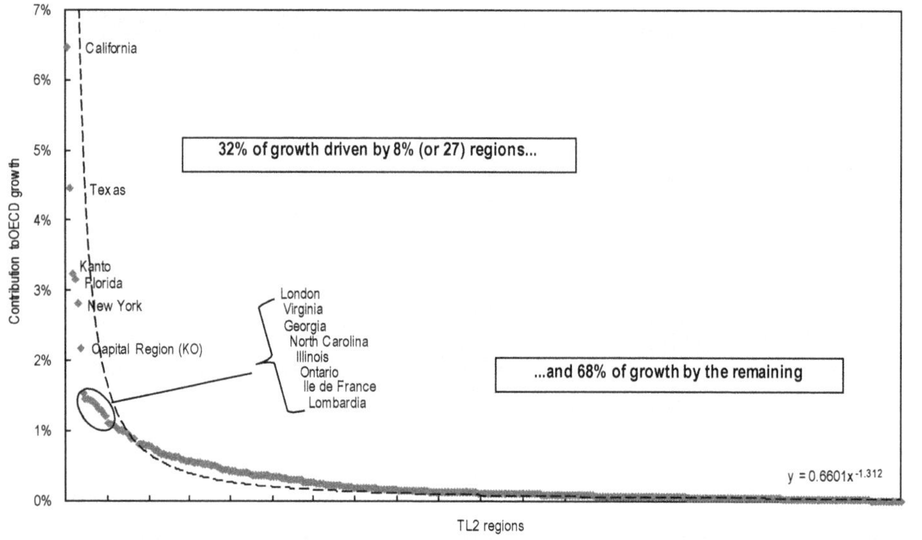

Functional urban areas (FUAs) also tend to follow this pattern. The 268 largest FUAs contributed on average to over half of the total OECD growth over the period 2000-08. The distribution of growth contribution also follows the shape close to a power-law distribution. The FL FUAs include Seoul Incheon (Korea), which appears in the first position, followed by New York (United States), London (United Kingdom), Los Angeles (United States), Tokyo (Japan) and Paris (France). Just the top 20 OECD FUAs contributed to 25% of the aggregate OECD growth during the period 2000-08. The remaining 92% of the OECD FUAs contributed to almost 75% of the aggregate growth, even if their individual contributions were below 0.5% of the GDP OECD growth (Figure 1.34).

Source: OECD (2011b), *OECD Regional Outlook 2011: Building Resilient Regions for Stronger Economies*, http://dx.doi.org/10.1787/9789264120983-en; OECD (2013a), *OECD Regions at a Glance 2013*, http://dx.doi.org/10.1787/reg_glance-2013-en.

Box 1.8. Territorial definitions and poverty: The case of Chile

The official definition delimiting urban and rural areas in Chile is constructed by the National Statistical Institute (INE). It classifies localities as either urban or rural. Urban localities are considered to be those inhabited by over 2 000 people, or by between 1 001 and 2 000 people when 50% or more of the economically active population is engaged in secondary or tertiary activities. As a special case, tourism and recreation centres which have at least 250 clustered dwellings but fail to meet the required population standard may also be classified as urban. According to the official definition, 87% of the Chilean population lives in urban areas.

There are a number of noticeable characteristics that emerge from this definition:

- the entire territory is classified dichotomously as either urban or rural
- the definition focuses primarily on urban characteristics defining the rural as the residual after urban is defined
- the definition does not differentiate among different types of rural areas in Chile
- it does not recognise mixed areas where there are strong urban and rural interactions.

The main shortcomings of this definition lie in its inability to capture basic elements of a modern rural economy, including: recognising areas of urban and rural interactions, differentiating among different types of rural areas, recognising and defining multiple types of rural towns and settlements, and finally, capturing rural areas attracting inhabitants with adequate human capital and skills – those rural areas which are emerging close to cities through improvements in accessibility and ICT connections that attract high-skilled dwellers wanting access to green spaces close to urban centres.

Poverty in Chile, based on figures employing the official definition of urban and rural areas, has been reported to be higher in rural areas (15%) than in urban ones (10.8%). These figures, however, are driven by the definition itself, which has a low population threshold and restrictive economic definition. Nevertheless re-estimating rural poverty rates based on a revised definition of urban and rural areas drawing on the OECD typology provides a very different picture. Poverty rates in urban areas (14%) are higher than nationally (13.3%) and in rural areas (9.3%).

Table 1.4. Poverty rates among rural and urban municipalities based on revised definition 1, 2013

	Rural	Urban	National
Official definition (INE)	15%	10.80%	14.40%
Revised definition (alternative 1)	9.30%	14.40%	13.30%
Change	-5.70%	3.60%	-1.10%

Note: The poverty baseline for rural areas (USD 48 613) is applied to rural households and the poverty baseline for urban areas (USD 72 098) is applied to urban households.

Source: Familia de la CASEN 2011 computations estimated by the Chilean Ministry of Economy.

Poverty appears to be a concern in mixed regions (urban and rural) displaying the highest poverty rates according to the second revised definition. Estimating poverty rates according to the second alternative definition which distinguishes between urban, mixed and rural regions (i.e. a simplified version of it) reveals a much higher poverty rate in mixed regions (16%) than in rural (9.2%) and in urban regions (13.9%). This estimate applies the urban poverty threshold (USD 72.098) to urban areas and the rural poverty line (USD 48.613) to rural and mixed areas.

Box 1.8. **Territorial definitions and poverty: The case of Chile** (*continued*)

Table 1.5. **Poverty rates among rural and urban municipalities based on revised definition 2, 2013**

	Rural	Mixed	Urban	National
Official definition (INE)	15%	..	10.80%	14.40
Revised definition (alternative 2)	9.20%	16%	13.90%	13.62%

Note: The poverty baseline for rural areas (USD 48 613) is applied to rural households and households living in mixed areas. The poverty baseline for urban areas (USD 72 098) is applied to urban households.

Source: Familia de la CASEN 2011 computations estimated by the Chilean Ministry of Economy.

Source: OECD (2014b), *OECD Rural Policy Reviews: Chile 2014*, http://dx.doi.org/10.1787/9789264222892-en.

Table 1.6. **Estimated concentration of poverty by department and OECD region typology, 2013**

Department	Predominantly urban	Intermediate	Predominantly rural	Total
Amazonas	...	1.2	2.0	1.9
Áncash	...	0.6	1.1	1.0
Apurímac	...	1.2	2.0	1.8
Arequipa	0.3	...	1.0	0.5
Ayacucho	...	1.4	2.4	2.0
Cajamarca	...	1.6	2.6	2.1
Callao	0.7	...	...	0.7
Cusco	0.2	...	1.3	0.9
Huancavelica	...	...	1.8	1.8
Huánuco	...	1.3	1.9	1.7
Ica	...	0.3	0.2	0.3
Junín	0.5	1.0	1.1	0.9
La Libertad	0.7	1.2	2.0	1.2
Lambayeque	0.7	...	1.3	0.9
Lima	0.6	0.5	0.6	0.6
Loreto	...	...	1.4	1.4
Madre de Dios	...	...	0.1	0.1
Moquegua	0.3	...	0.6	0.4
Pasco	...	...	1.8	1.8
Piura	...	1.2	1.8	1.4
Puno	0.7	1.1	1.9	1.5
San Martín	0.9	...	1.3	1.2
Tacna	...	...	0.6	0.6
Tumbes	0.6	0.5	0.5	0.5
Ucayali	...	...	0.5	0.5
Total	0.6	1.1	1.5	1.0

Notes: The concentration of individual in poverty (as measured by INEI) is computed as the percentage of individuals in poverty at the regional level divided by the percentage of individuals in poverty at the national level. Hence, values lower than 1 indicate that the percentage in poverty in the region is lower than the national share; values greater than one indicate that the regional percentage is higher than the national percentage.

Sources: OECD analysis based on data from INEI.

In spite of a substantial reduction of poverty at the national level, some of the departments with the highest incidence of poverty have recorded relatively modest improvements. A group of five departments maintains a relatively high incidence of poverty in the most recent years (2012-14 average), while recording relatively modest decline in poverty incidence over the past decade. These are Cajamarca, Amazonas, Ayacucho, Apurímac and Pasco.

Figure 1.35. **Poverty incidence and change by department, 2004-14**

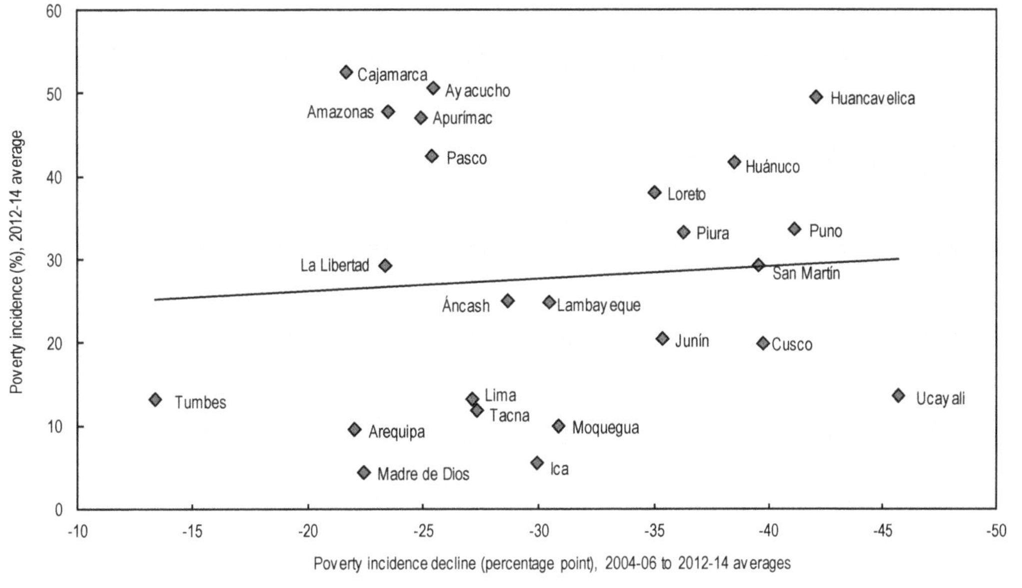

Notes: Poverty incidence (vertical axis) is computed as the average for 2012-14. The decline of poverty incidence (horizontal axis) is the percentage point difference between the 2004-06 average and the 2012-14 average. Three-year averages are used to smooth the effect of an unusually high or low value for one single year. Callao is included in the department of Lima.

Source: OECD analysis based on INEI data.

Analysis of poverty also needs to take account of other dimensions of inequality beyond income and consumption possibilities. These other dimensions of well-being include housing, health and education, safety, and the natural environment, which are captured by the OECD Better Life Index. Peru has developed a composite indicator to measure the number of unsatisfied basic needs (UBNss) of the population. Basic needs are defined as the quality of the housing, access to improved water and sanitation, enrolment in education amongst the children of the household, and level of per capita disposable income.

Despite improvements in reducing levels of poverty at a regional level, some areas still lag behind in terms of UBNs. Departments such as Loreto or Ucayali show levels above 50% of the households with at least one UBNss. In contrast, there are nine regions with less than 15% of their inhabitants with UBN. A more detailed look at UBNs per region shows that access to water and sewage are the most prevalent unsatisfied needs.

In sum, regions are central to the development challenges and opportunities facing Peru. Regional economic outcomes have been diverse, which largely reflects the shifts in population toward cities, the relative weight of extractive industries within the regional economy, and levels of poverty, particularly in rural areas. Inclusive growth may be a challenge for Peru in the medium term. It appears that progress in reducing poverty has diminished as it becomes more spatially concentrated within an overall trend of convergence between regions. A revised territorial definition for Peru will allow policy makers to have a clearer view of these growth dynamics and where they are occurring across the country. The following section will examine the growth factors and bottlenecks at a regional level.

Figure 1.36. **Share of population in monetary poverty and share of population with at least one unsatisfied basic need, 2014**

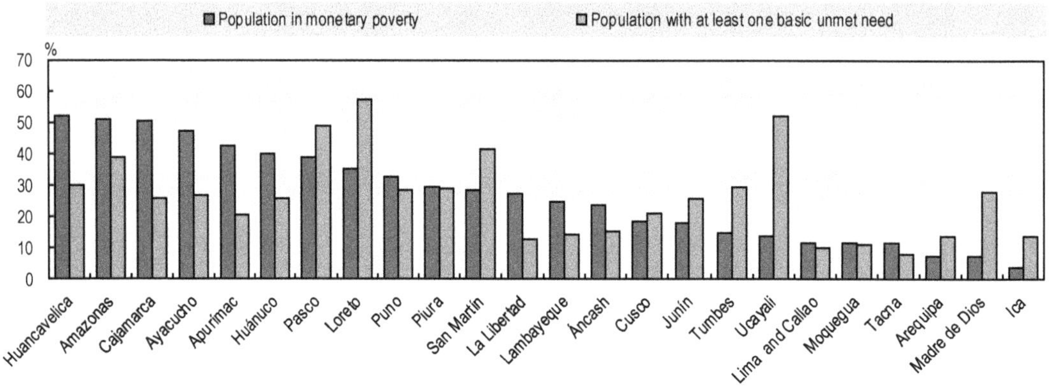

Note: Basic needs are defined as the quality of the housing, access to improved water and sanitation, enrolment in education amongst the children of the household, and level of per capita disposable income.

Source: OECD elaboration based on INEI data.

Growth factors and bottlenecks at a regional level

Recent OECD analysis identifies several key drivers of growth that are common to all OECD regions. These drivers, also called "framework conditions", are largely endogenous to the region and include agglomeration effects, sectoral specialisation, human capital, accessibility and infrastructure, innovation and institutional factors. Regions vary in their mix of assets and competitive advantages. Nonetheless, the OECD studies find evidence that sustainable growth rates only occur when regions mobilise their endogenous assets instead of depending upon transfers and subsidies.

The fluctuations in economic growth associated with resource-based economies are evident at a regional level. A larger share of GVA in mining (and to some extent in fisheries) is associated with increased GVA growth fluctuations over the period 2007-13. In contrast, a larger share of GVA in agriculture and service sectors tends to have a stabilising effect on the growth trajectory of a department. This pattern highlights the risk associated with some resource-dependent communities, particularly those reliant on extractive industries.

The mining industry is concentrated in few departments where it represents a large share of the regional economy. In 2013, four departments (Áncash, Arequipa, Cajamarca and Cusco) produced slightly over 50% of the national GVA in mining. Although mining was important for regional growth outcomes, it is not a necessary condition for high regional growth performance.

Box 1.9. Endogenous drivers of regional growth

OECD analysis examining the determinants of growth at the regional level identifies a number of critical drivers, including infrastructure, human capital, innovation and agglomeration (OECD, 2009). Perhaps the most important findings are, first, that the key factors are largely endogenous, i.e. they are things policy can address (as opposed to natural endowments or physical geography); and, second that these endogenous factors complement each other, suggesting the need for an integrated approach.

- Improvements in infrastructure at the regional level do not automatically lead to higher growth. Such investments need to be combined with improvements in education and innovation. This suggests that it could be useful to co-ordinate policies for building human capital, enhancing innovation and providing physical infrastructure. The effects of infrastructure investment appear to last around three to five years.
- Human capital – both the presence of high-skilled workers in the regional workforce and the absence of low-skilled workers – appears to be the most robust support of growth in all types of regions. The effects of improvements in human capital also appear to last around five years.
- The third critical element is innovation, insofar as it can be measured by focusing mainly on the science and technology components of innovation for which data are available. Innovation appears to produce positive effects over a longer time span, approximately ten years.
- Economies of agglomeration also have a positive impact on growth, although they are neither necessary nor sufficient to ensure sustained growth rates. Both the fact that only 45% of metro regions grew faster than the national average during 1995-2005 and the trend towards divergence among urban regions implies that agglomerations as complex systems work more efficiently in some cases and less efficiently in others.

What is clear in these studies is the importance of endogenous elements for growth at the regional level, instead of depending on transfers and subsidies. A follow-up study (OECD, 2012) combining quantitative analysis and 23 qualitative case studies reinforces the earlier results and in addition it finds evidence highlighting the importance of policy and institutional factors. The evidence gathered in this publication confirms the benefits of the new regional paradigm to OECD member countries:

- Investing in less-developed regions makes good economic sense, given their growth potential. Policies targeted at less-developed regions should not merely be advocated on social grounds; these regions have a great deal to contribute to national growth as long as their own assets are nurtured.
- A pro-growth, rather than a subsidy-based, policy stance is the most beneficial and sustainable approach. In the long run, it also helps build a fairer society. It can avoid dependency, rent-seeking behaviour and high remedial costs in the future.

The combined analysis points to a number of policy levers to enhance the effectiveness of regional policy:

- Policies that increase the skills of low-skilled workers may be as important for growth as policies aimed at expanding higher education. The "drag" effect on growth of a large low-skilled population appears as one of the most critical factors in less-developed regions.
- Infrastructure does not appear to be the binding constraint for the great majority of regions. Thus polices targeting infrastructure are not usually the most effective tools for strengthening growth in underdeveloped regions. Yet, given that, the gains from improvements in infrastructure are higher (at the margin) in important instruments if they co-ordinate with other policies.
- Innovation is not a bottleneck for growth but appears to be a critical pillar for advanced regions.

Box 1.9. **Endogenous drivers of regional growth** (*continued*)

- How policy makers frame the challenges they face does matter. The case studies suggest that a self-conscious shift towards a growth-oriented policy framework is very often a part of the recipe for success. As long as policy makers focus on exogenous sources of support for a region ("levelling up" policies), growth is unlikely to take off and actors are likely to focus on the appropriation of rents from external sources.
- Institutional factors are also critical. Formal and informal institutions that facilitate negotiation and dialogue among key actors in order to mobilise and integrate them into the development process are vital, as are those that enhance policy continuity. At times, the challenge is to create institutions that strengthen the region's "voice" in dealing with other regions and countries and those that foster linkages among the private, public and education sectors.

In sum, this study calls for including geography and place-based factors into the structural policy agenda to increase the growth potential of countries. In addition to efficiency, place-based policies also have the capacity to create a more inclusive and fairer society through their ability to mobilise local actors and ensure they are involved and engaged in the development process.

Sources: OECD (2009), *How Regions Grow: Trends and Analysis*, http://dx.doi.org/10.1787/9789264039469-en; OECD (2012), *Promoting Growth in all Regions*, http://dx.doi.org/10.1787/9789264174634-en.

Figure 1.37. **Specialisation in mining and growth in gross value added**

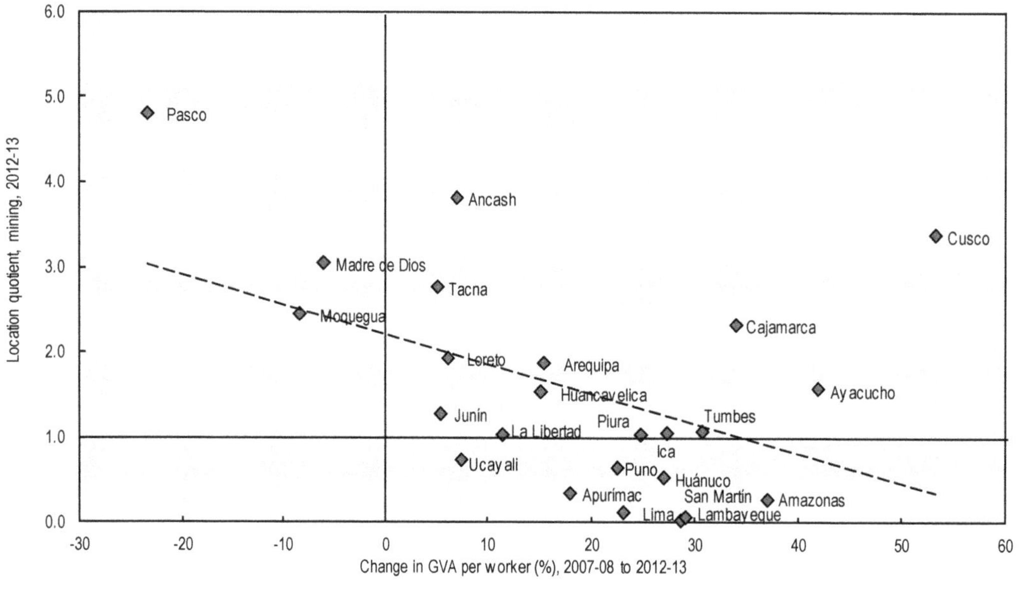

Notes: Mining includes mining oil and gas (*extracción de petróleo, gas y minerales*); specialisation is measured by the location quotient, that is the share of gross value added (GVA) in mining in the region divided by the share of GVA in mining in Peru. A value greater than 1 indicates relative specialisation in mining.

Source: OECD analysis based on data from INEI.

It is important to note that the mining industry is concentrated in fewer regions and is associated with more growth volatility due to different phases (investment and production), and changing market conditions. Some regions have also performed relatively poorly in spite of a higher concentration of mining activity and price increases.

Factors contributing to this might be less diversity in the local economy, the low amount of employment in the mining industry, the negative impact of mining on agriculture (e.g. competition for water resources) and the lack of integration of local firms into resource value chains.

Agriculture constitutes 6% of national GVA and is an important rural export industry. There is a positive relationship between the concentration of the agricultural sector in the regional economy in 2007 and the pattern of growth experience by the department between 2007 and 2013.

Figure 1.38. **Specialisation in agriculture and growth in gross value added**

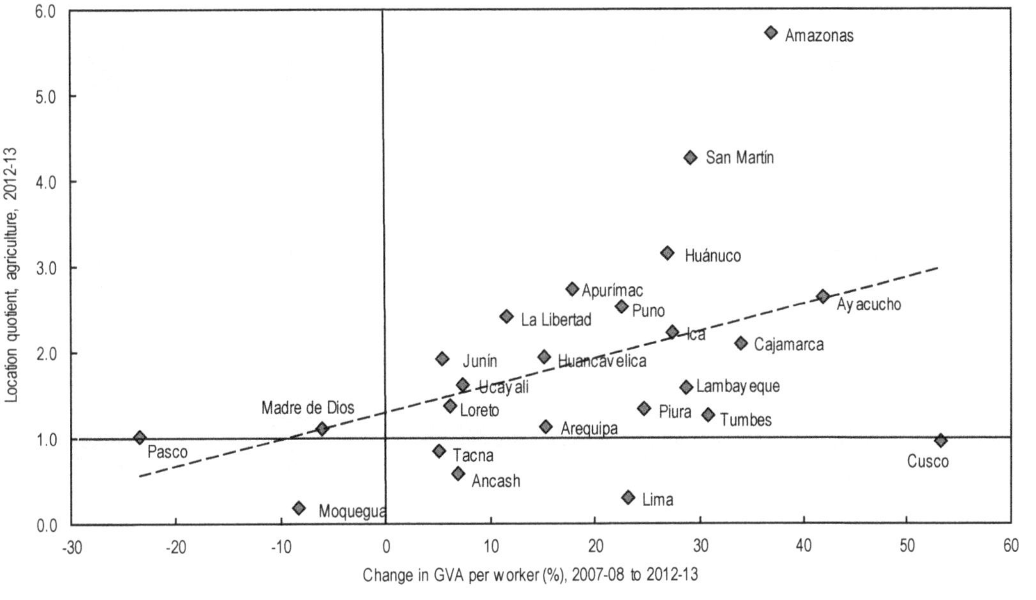

Notes: Agriculture includes agriculture, livestock, hunting and forestry (*agricultura, ganadería, caza y silvicultura*); specialisation is measured by the location quotient, that is the share of gross value added (GVA) in agriculture in the region divided by the share of GVA in agriculture in Peru. A value greater than 1 indicates relative specialisation in agriculture.

Source: OECD analysis based on data from INEI.

A stronger relationship is evident because agricultural production is spread across a broader range of regions within Peru. Over a quarter of the labour force is also employed in agriculture, which means the local economic impacts would likely be higher. Part of these trends might also be explained by the capacity of this industry to diversify its sub-sectoral composition. Over the last two decades, traditional agricultural commodities (cotton and sugar) have been replaced by an export-oriented non-traditional agriculture sector (comprising horticultural, fruits and specialty crops).

Poverty reduction is becoming more difficult, and the growth is not necessarily diffusing to disadvantaged groups and places

At the departmental level there is not a clear relationship between overall economic performance and change in poverty incidence. High economic growth at the department level does not necessarily translate into declines of poverty incidence. Departments like Huancavelica and Ucayali managed to reduce substantially the incidence of poverty with a relatively average increase in GVA. In contrast, departments such as Cajamarca, Amazonas and Ayacucho had a substantially smaller reduction in poverty in spite of better GVA growth performance.

Figure 1.39. **Economic growth and poverty change by department**

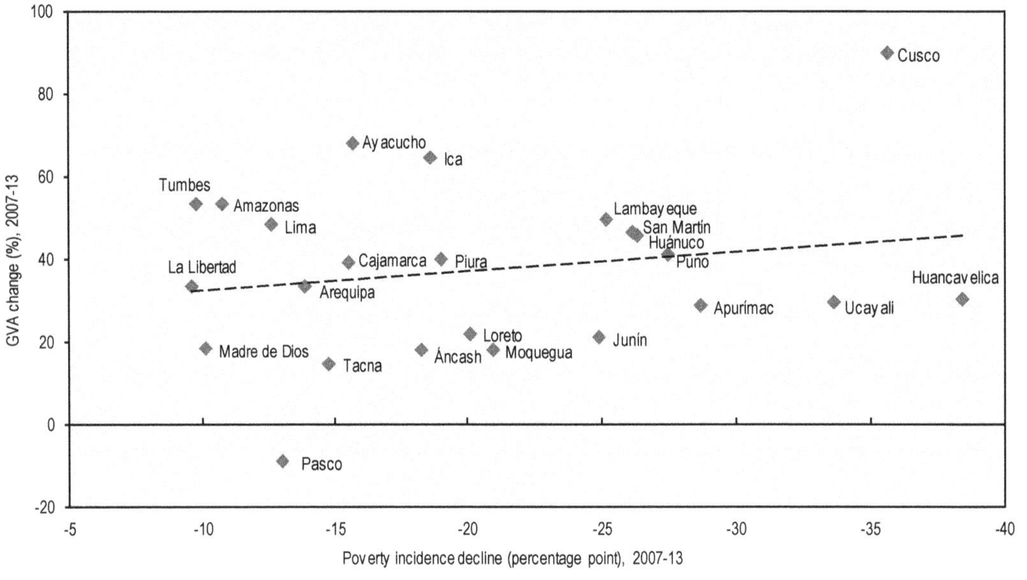

Notes: GVA growth (vertical axis) is computed as growth of gross value added (GVA) in constant terms between 2007 and 2013. Poverty decline (horizontal axis) is the percentage point difference between poverty incidence in 2013 and 2007. Callao is included in the department of Lima.

Source: OECD analysis based on data from INEI.

The relationship between increasing income levels and poverty reduction also seems to weaken as average incomes rise. At higher average income level (in current terms), the dispersion of poverty conditions increases, suggesting that beyond a certain limit changes in the average (income) are less likely to be diffuse across the population and specifically to reach the most disadvantage groups. For instance, in 2014, the seven departments with the highest average income (roughly between PEN 1 100 and PEN 1 850) had a poverty incidence fluctuating in the range of 15% to 7%. This may reflect the concentration of extreme poverty in population groups and places, and the complex barriers they face to participating in the economy.

Human capital development will be important for addressing the challenge of inclusive growth

Increasing educational attainment is associated with higher productivity at a country and regional level. Human capital appears to be the most important factor influencing the performance of OECD regions. Both the presence of highly skilled workers and the absence of low-skilled workers have a positive influence on regional growth. Education and skills is also important for inclusive growth and an important element in strategies to reduce poverty and inequality.

Figure 1.40. **Incidence of poverty and average employment income by department**

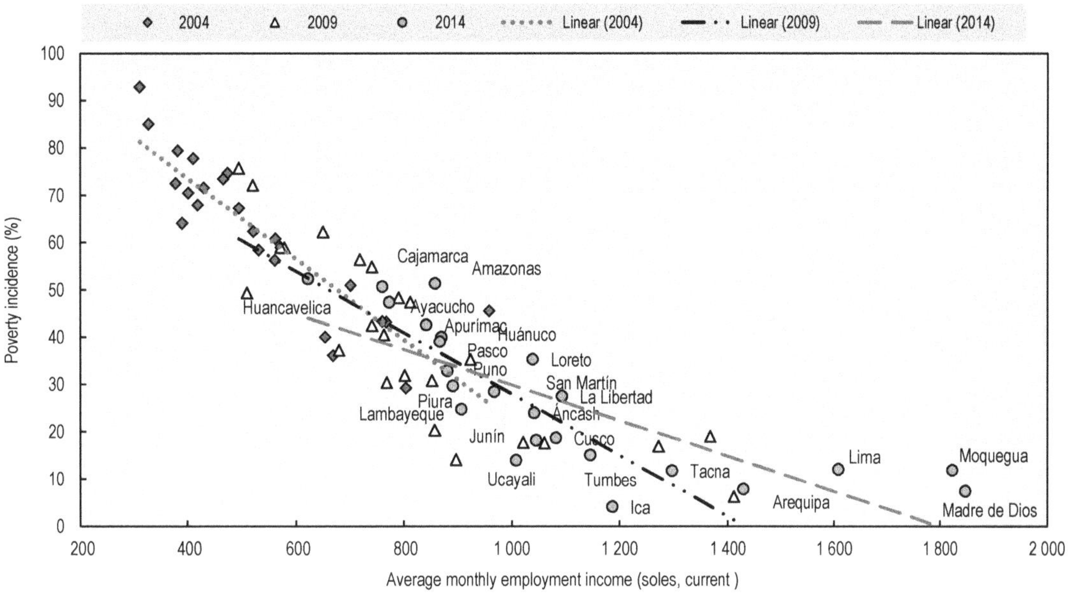

Notes: Departmental names are reported only for the reference year 2014 (blue circles). Lima includes the department of Lima and Callao. Income data refer to "*ingreso promedio mensual proveniente del trabajo*"; income is in current terms.

Source: OECD analysis based on data from INEI.

In terms of the low-skilled component of the workforce, the proportion of people aged over 15 who are illiterate varies significantly by region with five regions having twice the national average (Apurímac, Huancavelica, Ayacucho, Cajamarca and Huánuco). These poor outcomes are associated with higher levels of poverty and the proportion of the population living in rural areas. Individuals living in predominantly rural regions were nearly five times more likely to be illiterate than individuals living in predominantly urban regions. Predominantly rural regions in some departments are performing better than the average rural region or even predominantly urban and intermediate regions of other departments (for example, Ica and Tumbes, and to a lesser extent also Arequipa).

Figure 1.41. **Illiteracy rate by department, 2007**

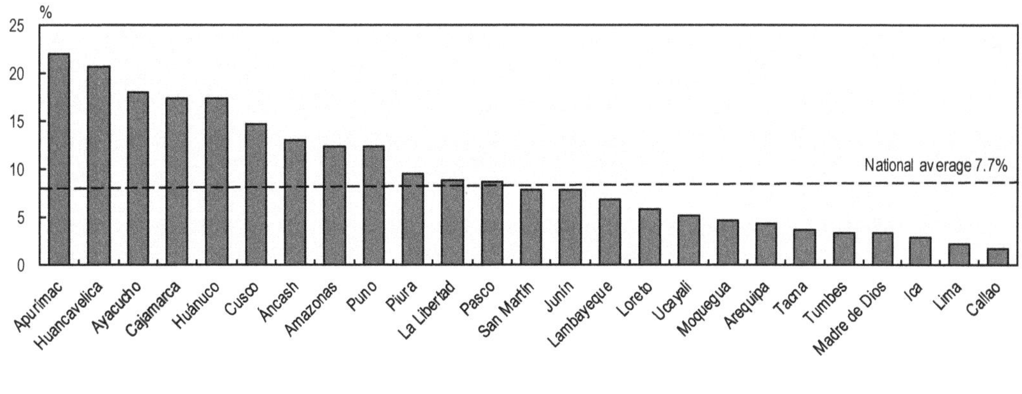

Source: OECD elaboration based on INEI data.

Table 1.7. **Illiteracy rate by department and OECD regional typology, 2007**

Department	Predominantly urban	Intermediate	Predominantly rural	Total
Amazonas	...	8.2%	13%	12.4%
Áncash	...	10.6%	13.4%	13%
Apurímac	...	13.8%	24.6%	22.1%
Arequipa	3.2%	...	7.3%	4.3%
Ayacucho	...	12.9%	21.2%	18.1%
Cajamarca	...	15.7%	18.6%	17.4%
Callao	1.6%	...	...	1.6%
Cusco	4%	...	19.6%	14.7%
Huancavelica	...	...	20.7%	20.7%
Huánuco	...	17%	17.4%	17.3%
Ica	...	2.9%	2.8%	2.9%
Junín	5.9%	8%	9%	7.8%
La Libertad	3.5%	6.7%	16%	8.8%
Lambayeque	4.8%	...	11.2%	6.8%
Lima	1.9%	5.8%	4.2%	2.1%
Loreto	...	...	5.9%	5.9%
Madre de Dios	...	...	3.3%	3.3%
Moquegua	2%	...	6.4%	4.7%
Pasco	...	...	8.7%	8.7%
Piura	...	7.1%	12.8%	9.6%
Puno	5.8%	11.9%	14.6%	12.4%
San Martín	3.6%	...	9.2%	7.9%
Tacna	...	...	3.7%	3.7%
Tumbes	3.8%	3.3%	3.6%	3.4%
Ucayali	...	...	5.1%	5.1%
Peru	2.6%	9.9%	12.5%	7.7%

Notes: ..: not available. Due to the availability of data, this table is based on total population counts instead of population 15 years and over. Hence, percentages are slightly lower than official rates.

Source: OECD analysis based on data from INEI.

At the departmental level, inequalities in illiteracy rates have persisted, and correlate with the incidence of poverty. The departments with a higher incidence of poverty (over 40%) are those showing the higher illiteracy rates (close to or above 10%). In contrast, departments with lower illiteracy rates generally have less than 20% poverty incidence.

Higher levels of GDP per capita and productivity are usually correlated with the share of highly educated workers. The regions with the highest proportion of people with higher educational attainment are also generally the regions with the highest GVA per worker. This includes the regions of Moquegua, Tacna, Arequipa, Lima, Madre de Dios and Ica. The exceptions are the regions of Pasco and Áncash. Both these regions benefit from other economic drivers, such as specialisation in mining activities and proximity to Lima.

The percentage of people with a higher education is typically larger in predominantly urban regions. This pattern is normally observed across OECD countries. However, the regional educational attainment differentials in Peru are large by OECD standards. Individuals living in predominantly urban regions were approximately three times more likely to report higher educational attainments than individuals living in predominantly rural regions.

Figure 1.42. **Illiteracy rate and poverty incidence by department, 2014**

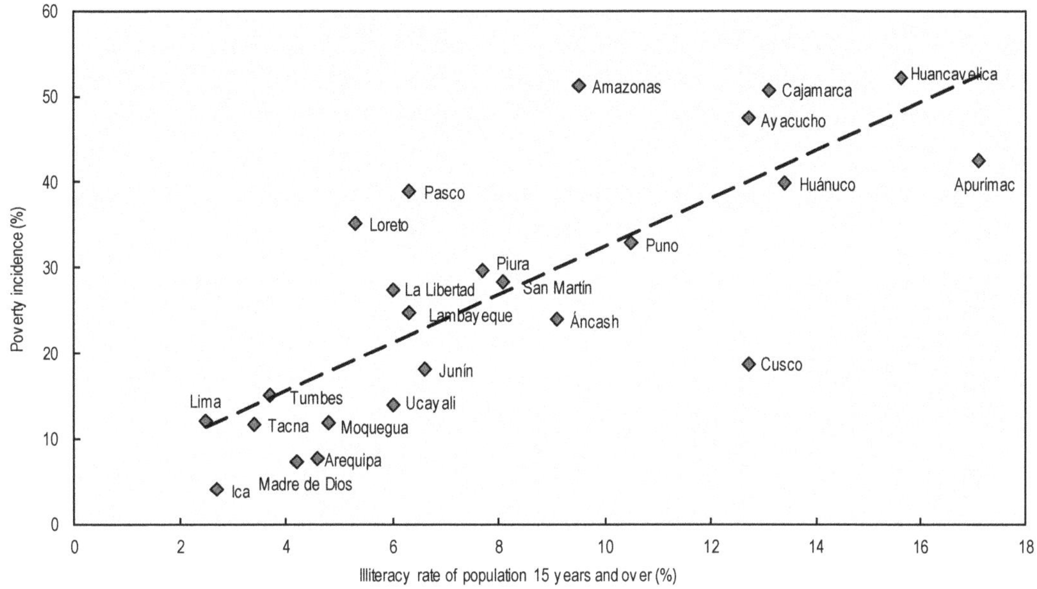

Source: OECD analysis based on data from INEI-ENAHO.

Box 1.10. **Informality is more prevalent in rural areas**

Peruvian regions generally perform well in relation to key labour market indicators. However, these statistics should be interpreted with caution as they include both formal and informal sectors. As a result, employment rates are high and unemployment is low. Estimated employment rates are generally over 95% across all departments, while unemployment rates are less than 4% in most departments. The exceptions are departments with the lowest shares of informal sector employment, such as Callao, Lima and Moquegua. These are also the departments that are generally performing better on most of the other economic indicators.

At a national level it is estimated that close to three-quarters of the labour force is engaged in informal employment. This percentage varies significantly across regions of Peru, with five departments reporting over 90% of informal employment (Apurímac 90.8%, Cajamarca 91%, Puno 91.3%, Ayacucho 91.6% and Huancavelica 94.6%) and six departments reporting less than 70% (Callao 57.1%, Lima 60.6%, Ica 63.9%, Arequipa 65.4%, Moquegua 66.5% and Tacna 69.4%).[1]

Table 1.8. **Informal employment trends in Peru's regions**

	2008	2009	2010	2011	2012	2013	% change
National	79.1%	77.2%	77.1%	75.0%	74.3%	73.7%	-6.84%
Lima metropolitan	60.4%	56.8%	58.0%	54.3%	54.6%	53.7%	-11.04%
Rest of country	88.6%	87.4%	86.8%	85.7%	84.6%	84.1%	-5.07%
Urban	72.1%	69.6%	69.9%	67.4%	66.8%	66.5%	-7.82%
Rural	96.5%	96.3%	96.1%	96.1%	95.9	95.4%	-1.17%

Rates of informality are much higher in rural areas with a higher proportion of the workforce in the agricultural and fishery sectors. The agricultural sector also has low productivity with a comparatively high proportion of the labour force employed in it. Initiatives to lift agricultural productivity and address informality will benefit the country in the longer term.

Note: 1. See: www.inei.gob.pe/media/MenuRecursivo/publicaciones_digitales/Est/Lib1154/index.html.

Sources: INEI (n.d.), http://www.inei.gob.pe; OECD (2015e), *Multi-dimensional Review of Peru: Volume 1. Initial Assessment*, http://dx.doi.org/10.1787/9789264243279-en.

As observed for illiteracy rates, however, some of the departments entirely or largely classified as predominantly rural regions (by OECD standards) outperform many of the intermediate or predominantly urban areas (within the same department or in another department). Ica, Arequipa and Moquegua are examples of this unique regional combination, suggesting that even smaller population centres can lead in terms educational attainments and human capital development.

Figure 1.43. **Proportion of the population with a higher education (*educación superior*) attainment, by department (2007)**

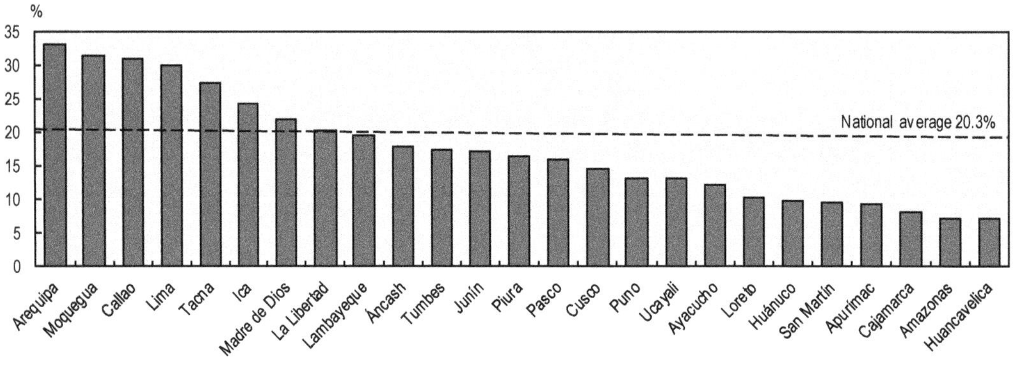

Source: OECD elaboration based on data from INEI.

Table 1.9. **Individuals with a higher education (*educación superior*)**

By department and OECD regional typology, 2007

Department	Predominantly urban	Intermediate	Predominantly rural	Total
Amazonas	...	14.8%	6.1%	7.2%
Áncash	...	25.3%	16.7%	17.9%
Apurímac	...	17.5%	6.9%	9.4%
Arequipa	37.2%	...	20.2%	33%
Ayacucho	...	18.8%	8%	12.1%
Cajamarca	...	12.4%	5.2%	8.2%
Callao	30.9%	...	...	30.9%
Cusco	31%	...	7.2%	14.6%
Huancavelica	...	...	7.2%	7.2%
Huánuco	...	15.9%	6.2%	9.7%
Ica	...	20.8%	27.2%	24.3%
Junín	25.2%	16%	12%	17.2%
La Libertad	29.3%	19.5%	9.1%	20.3%
Lambayeque	22.9%	...	11.7%	19.4%
Lima	30.8%	16.2%	20.2%	29.9%
Loreto	...	...	10.3%	10.3%
Madre de Dios	...	...	21.9%	21.9%
Moquegua	33.6%	...	29.9%	31.4%
Pasco	...	...	15.9%	15.9%
Piura	...	20.6%	10.7%	16.4%
Puno	21.6%	20%	7.8%	13.1%
San Martín	18.5%	...	7%	9.6%
Tacna	...	...	27.4%	27.4%
Tumbes	12.8%	19.1%	12.6%	17.3%
Ucayali	...	...	13.1%	13.1%
Peru	30.1%	18.3%	11.6%	20.8%

Notes: ..: not available. Percentages are computed using total population, instead of population 15 years of age or more.

Source: OECD analysis based on data from INEI.

At a departmental level, the relationship between higher educational attainments and poverty incidence mirrors that observed for illiteracy rates. The departments of Lima, Arequipa, Moquegua, Ica and Tacna are those presenting the largest share of population with a university education (above 18%) and are also the regions with a lower incidence of poverty in 2014.

Figure 1.44. **University education and poverty incidence by department, 2014**

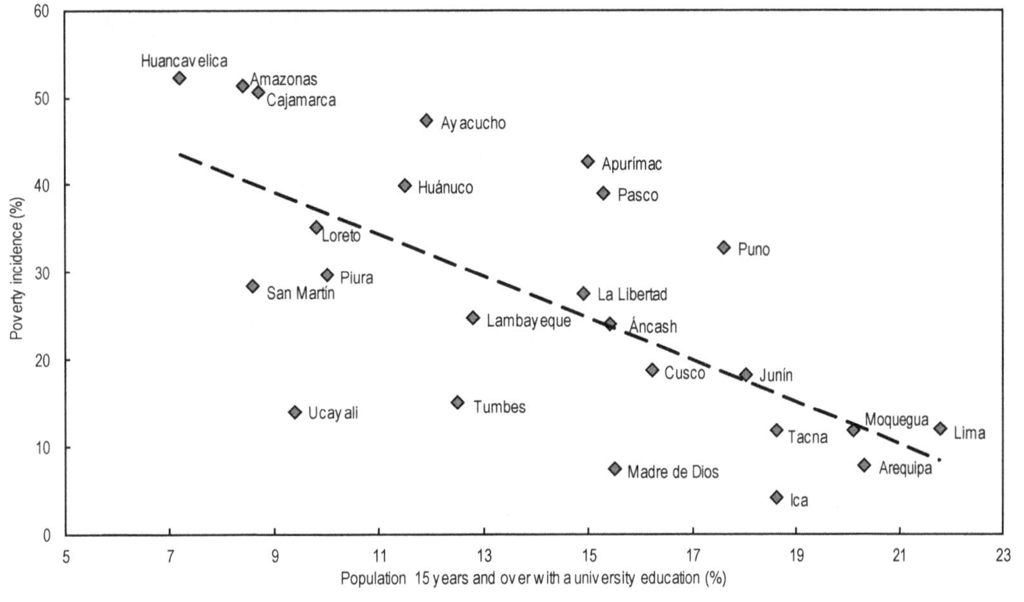

Source: Based on data from INEI-ENAHO.

Human capital development continues to be a challenge for Peru. Illiteracy rates are still high, associated with poverty and concentrated in the rural areas of a small number of regions (Apurímac, Huancavelica, Ayacucho, Cajamarca and Huánuco). These regions have also larger shares of indigenous population, mainly Quechua speaking, who tend to have lower educational attainment. Rural areas are also affected by higher levels of informality. This suggests there is a need to boost the productivity and competitiveness of rural industries, and in combination with strategies to develop skills, address informality and alleviate poverty. Highly skilled workers are a mirror image of these outcomes and are concentrated in predominantly urban areas and associated with higher productivity regions. Making Peru's cities work better will be crucial in delivering a high wage and value-added economy.

Lima is a major contributor to Peru's economy and is performing relatively well in an international context

The metropolitan area of Lima[5] dominates the urban system of Peru, and is critical to the performance of the national economy. Lima is a large city by OECD standards and is the ninth-largest when compared with OECD countries. Nearly one-third of the population of the country lives in the metropolitan area of Lima. Some OECD countries have a higher proportion, including Korea (Seoul-Icheon), Ireland (Dublin) and Denmark (Copenhagen), which represent between 49.5% and 40% of their national populations.

Figure 1.45. **Lima compared to the largest OECD metropolitan areas, 2014**

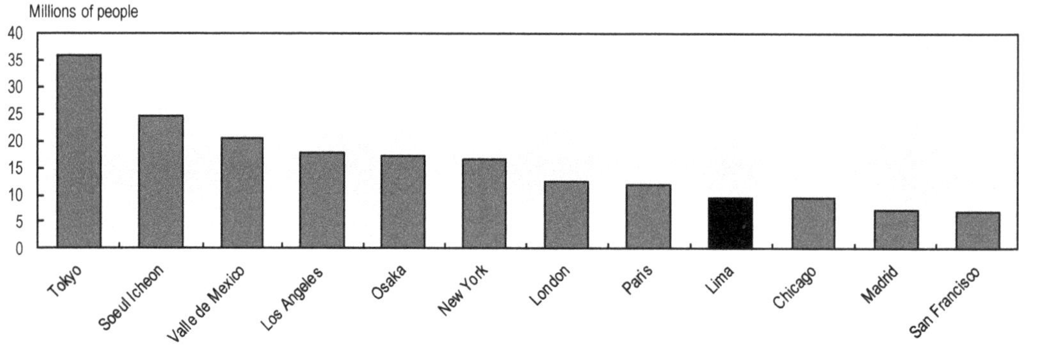

Source: OECD Metropolitan database, http://dx.doi.org/10.1787/region-data-en and World Bank, Population in largest city, http://databank.worldbank.org/data/reports.aspx?source=2&Topic=16.

Figure 1.46. **Percentage of the population of the largest metropolitan area of the national population, Peru compared to select OECD countries, 2014**

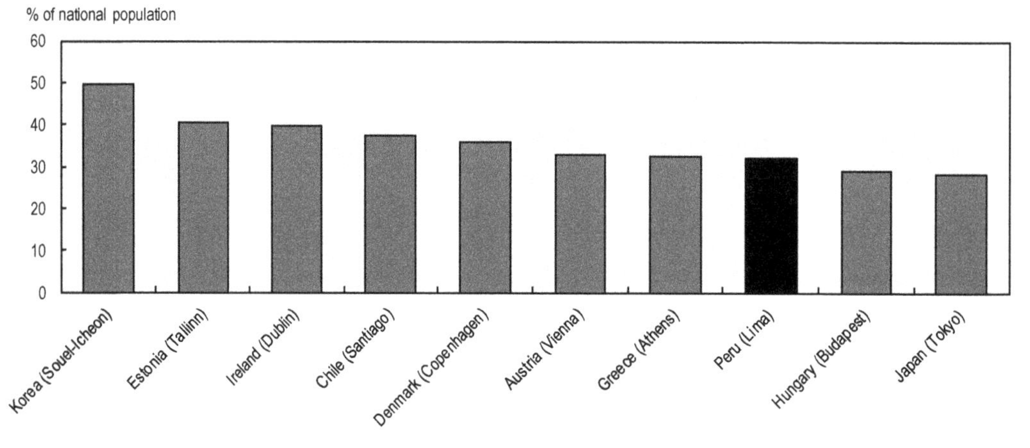

Source: OECD Metropolitan database, http://dx.doi.org/10.1787/region-data-en and World Bank, Population in largest city, http://databank.worldbank.org/data/reports.aspx?source=2&Topic=16.

Given that Lima concentrates a significant percentage of the country's population, it is not surprising that it also plays a significant role in the national economy. Lima has 34.4% of the country's jobs and 48.1% of GDP. This share of national GDP is similar to OECD countries such as Ireland (Dublin), Hungary (Budapest), Chile (Santiago), Greece (Athens) and Korea (Seoul-Incheon). In terms of the major city producing a higher share of GDP compared to the share of national population, Peru is performing better than Chile (Santiago), and similar to countries such as Ireland (Dublin) and Greece (Athens).

The concentration of high-value producer services in Lima is an important factor in explaining its contribution to the national economy. Compared to its share of the national economy (48%), Lima has a higher share of information and communications (68%); professional, scientific and technical (69%); and financial and insurance services (80%). This is reflective of the role that Lima plays in the national economy in terms of high-level business and administrative services, and transport and logistics.

Figure 1.47. **Largest city's percentage of national population, employment and GDP, 2010**

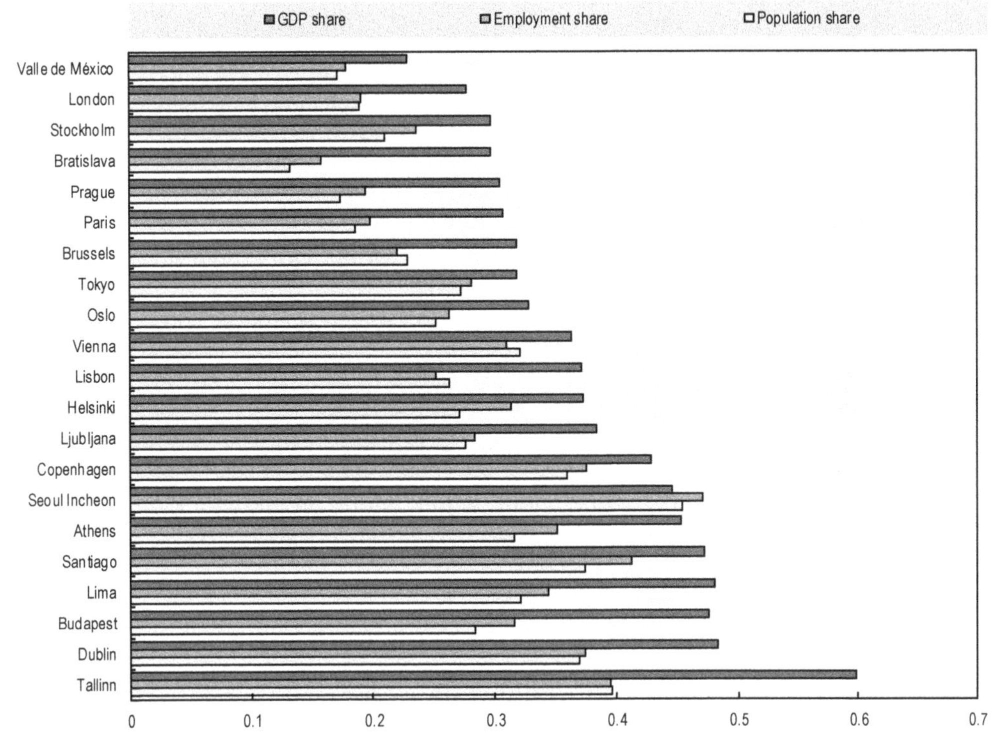

Notes: The data for Lima include the department of Lima and the Constitutional Province of Callao. The data are from 2013 and are gross value added.

Source: OECD Metropolitan database, http://dx.doi.org/10.1787/region-data-en and INEI, http://www.inei.gob.pe.

Figure 1.48. **Proportion of gross value added in Lima (by sector) compared to the contribution of Lima to the national economy**

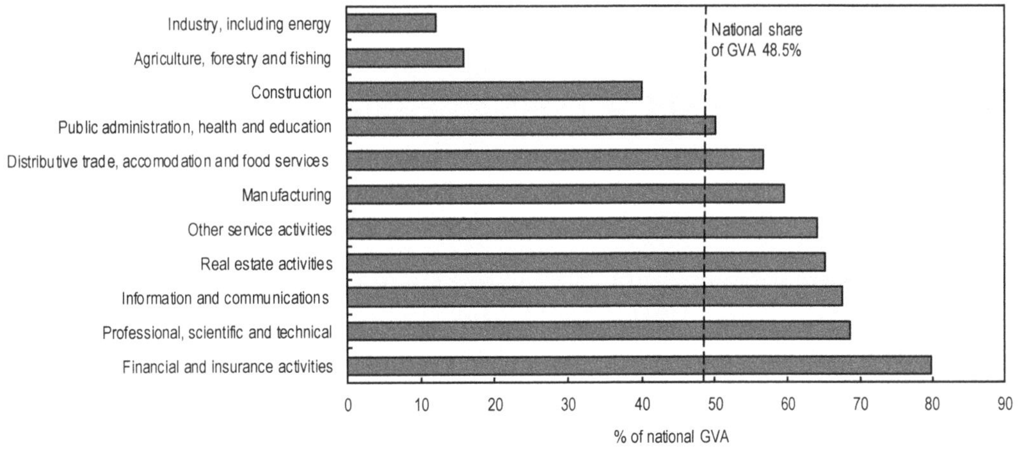

Source: OECD analysis based on data from INEI.

However, Lima also demonstrates higher productivity than other regions in Peru across the services sector. Differences in productivity between Lima and the rest of the country are apparent for high- and low-value services. In the period 2008-13, annual growth in GVA averaged 7% whilst growth in population averaged 1%, which indicates the relatively strong productivity performance of firms in Lima.

Figure 1.49. **Percentage difference in labour productivity for select services between Lima and the rest of the country, 2014**

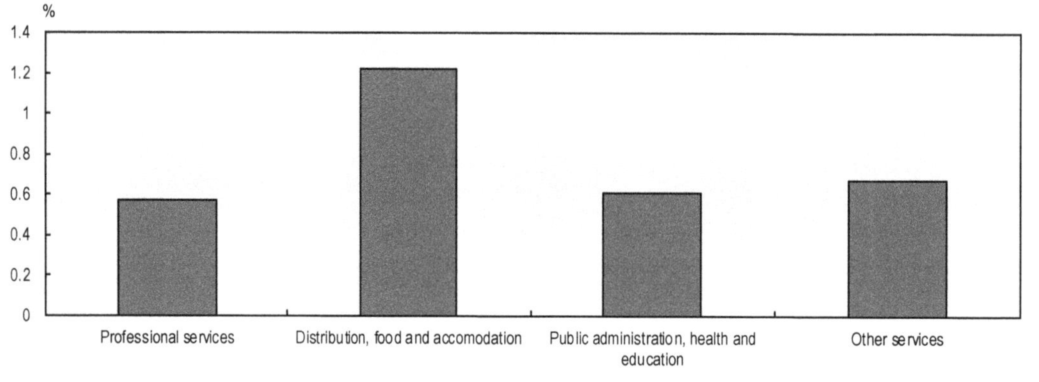

Source: OECD analysis based on data from INEI.

The economic performance of the Lima-Callao metropolitan area is critical to the growth of the national economy. It is the location of the vast majority of Peru's high-value services, which reflects its role as an international gateway for the country. The productivity of the services sector is significantly higher in Lima-Callao than in the rest of the country, and the economy of the city is performing relatively well internationally. Although these trends are positive, it also indicates weaknesses in other regions of the country, and most likely the underperformance of second-tier cities.

Infrastructure and accessibility are important for enhancing urban-rural linkages

Improvements to transport and telecommunications infrastructure can reduce transport costs for firms and workers. Infrastructure and accessibility – both internally and to external markets – are important for Peru. The country is large with a challenging topography with export gateways and population concentrated in Lima.

The backbone of the Peruvian transport infrastructure is the road network. The national highway network has improved in recent decades but in terms of quality and coverage still lags behind many other Latin American countries (IADB, 2006). Jorge Chavez International Airport is the main international gateway for passenger traffic with multiple destinations in North America and Europe, and extensive connections to destinations in Latin America. There are 22 other airports with mainly domestic services with key hubs including Arequipa, Cusco, Iquitos and Piura. Callao is the major port for the country with a number of smaller ports along the Pacific coast and the Amazon basin.

Since the early 1990s there has been increased investment by the national government and local municipalities in the road network. The national government has developed a network of paved national highways whilst local municipalities have developed local roads which are mainly unpaved. Between 1999 and 2012 the density of the road network increased by 80%, which has been a significant factor in improving accessibility for rural communities and reducing poverty (Webb, 2013).

Table 1.10. **Quality of the Peruvian road network**

	Proportion of the road network (%)	Proportion of paved roads (%)
Local roads	69.3	2
Regional roads	15.1	10
National roads	15.6	68

Source: Based on data from CEPLAN.

Improvements to the road network have been uneven, which reflects the size and physical geography of the region and proximity to urban centres. Loreto, Ucayali and Madre de Dios with the lowest level of road density are the three biggest regions of the country. The five regions with the lowest road density are also in the Amazon basin. Regions with high levels of poverty, such as Cajamarca, Huancavelica or Apurímac, have higher levels of road density although most of the network is unpaved.

Figure 1.50. **Regional density of road infrastructure, 2014**

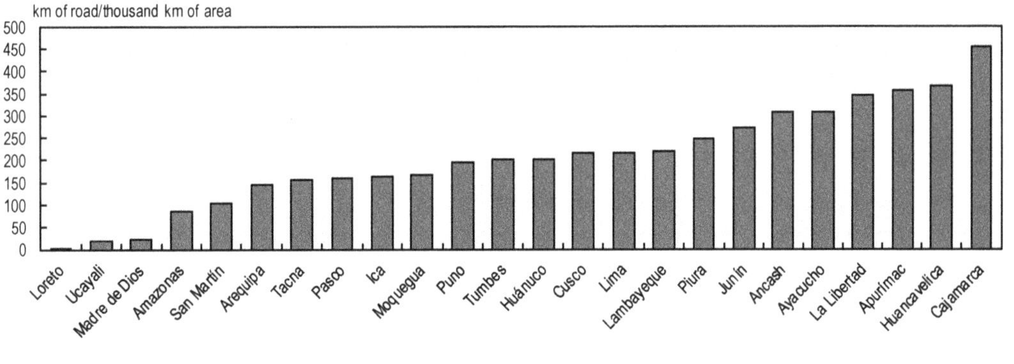

Source: OECD analysis based on data from the Ministry for Transport and Communications (Ministerio de Transportes y Comunicaciones- MTC), www.mtc.gob.pe.

Within the majority of regions, the road network linking district with provincial capitals is still largely made up of gravel roads (*camino carrozable*, or *carretera afirmada*). Only eight regions (excluding Callao) have more than 50% of district-provincial road connections made up of paved roads (*carretera asfaltada*). In the departments of Amazonas, Ayacucho, Cajamarca, Huancavelica, Huánuco and Pasco, gravel roads are still the most common type of road connection between smaller centres.

The quality of the transportation network improves in terms of connections between provincial capitals and departmental capitals. Across Peru, 16 departments have more than 50% of roads between the provincial and departmental capitals paved. Yet, in the departments of Apurímac, Ayacucho, Cajamarca, Huancavelica, Huánuco and Pasco a large part of this primary transportation network is made of gravel roads (*carretera afirmada*).

The quality of local and regional roads is reflected in average travel times and costs. In most departments, the cost (per unit of km) of travelling from district to provincial capitals is about twice as high as the cost of travelling from provincial to departmental capitals. The average speed of travel from district to provincial capital (average of 33 km/hour) is also much lower than the provincial to department travel time (average of

44.6 km/hour). These differences probably reflect the poorer quality of road connections, and less choice and competition in terms of transport modes.

Figure 1.51. **Transportation access between district and provincial capital by department, 2012**

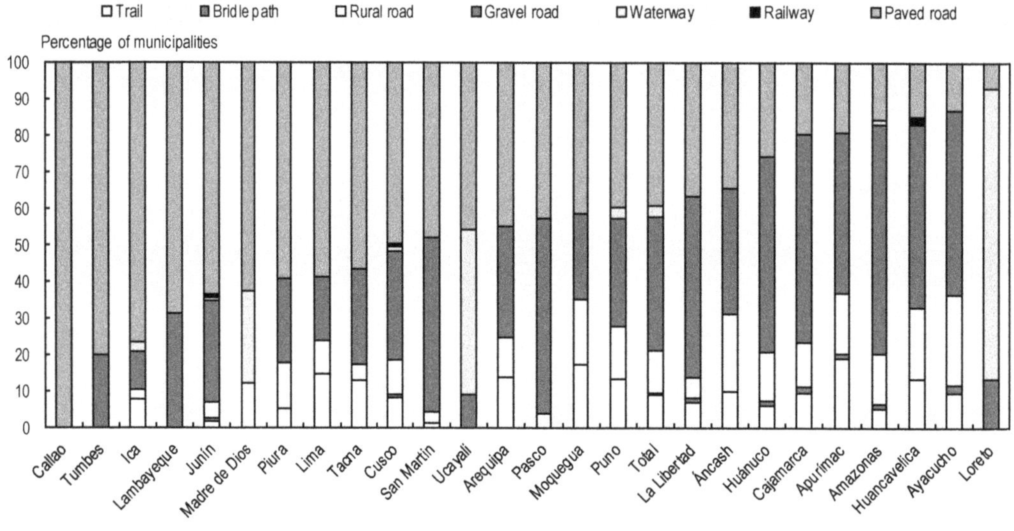

Note: Callao is omitted from the graph (reporting 100% of connection with paved roads).

Source: INEI (2012c), Registro Nacional de Municipalidades 2012.

Figure 1.52. **Transportation access between provincial and department capital by department, 2012**

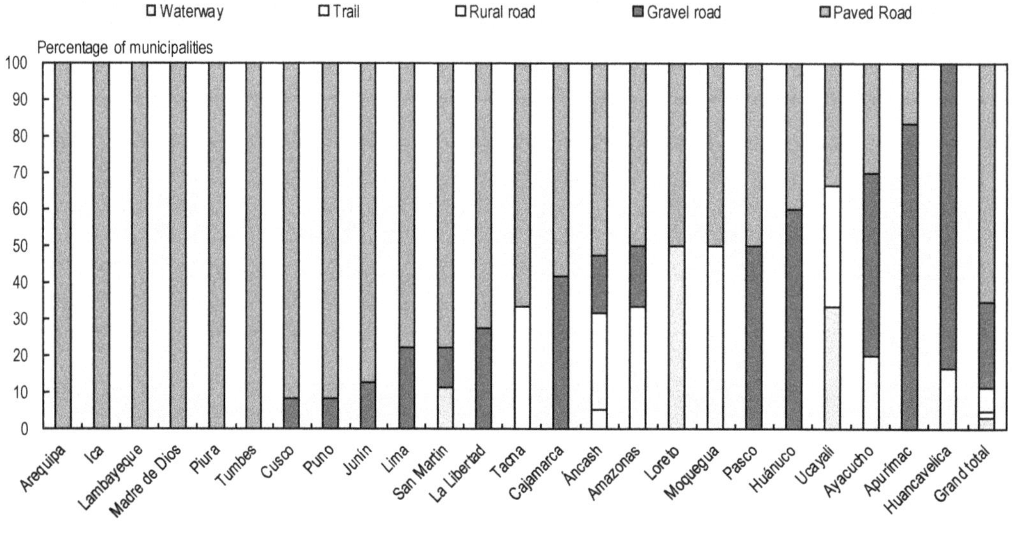

Source: INEI (2012c), Registro Nacional de Municipalidades 2012.

Since the early 2000s there have been rapid improvements in access to communications technologies. Over the past decade there has been a rapid expansion of cellular phone coverage and use (Webb, 2013). Available statistics confirm that today the majority of Peruvian households have access to a cellular phone. Specifically, between

2001 and 2014, the percentage of households with at least one member having a cellular phone went from less than 10% in all departments to well over 75% in almost all departments (INEI, 2015).

Table 1.11. **Transportation accessibility indicators at the municipal level by department, 2012**

Department	Travel from provincial to departmental capital			Travel from district to provincial capital		
	Municipality reporting	Average cost/km	Average km/hour	Municipality reporting	Average cost/km	Average km/hour
Amazonas	6	0.35	32.1	77	0.58	31.6
Áncash	19	0.15	40.0	146	0.35	28.0
Apurímac	6	0.17	34.2	73	0.25	27.0
Arequipa	7	0.11	50.6	101	0.23	34.6
Ayacucho	10	0.17	34.5	101	0.28	27.6
Cajamarca	12	0.13	41.8	114	0.34	30.3
Callao	...	...	...	5	0.13	39.0
Cusco	12	0.08	50.8	95	0.24	37.2
Huancavelica	6	0.23	33.6	88	0.33	29.3
Huánuco	10	0.24	32.6	66	0.41	32.4
Ica	4	0.06	69.7	38	0.30	38.1
Junín	8	0.16	34.7	114	0.24	32.9
La Libertad	11	0.13	39.0	71	0.26	31.4
Lambayeque	2	0.10	53.8	35	0.16	45.6
Lima	9	0.10	50.9	161	0.22	31.1
Loreto	4	0.25	43.4	43	0.34	25.7
Madre de Dios	2	0.17	46.6	8	0.45	50.9
Moquegua	2	0.07	49.2	17	0.37	36.1
Pasco	2	0.18	29.1	26	0.28	31.6
Piura	7	0.09	53.9	56	0.34	34.7
Puno	12	0.12	56.0	96	0.14	42.5
San Martín	9	0.17	61.5	67	0.36	41.7
Tacna	3	0.10	47.3	23	0.18	40.9
Tumbes	2	0.15	65.7	10	0.21	46.1
Ucayali	1	0.15	64.8	10	0.41	28.9
All municipalities	166	0.15	44.6	1641	0.29	33.0

Notes: ..: not available. The cost is computed from the approximate price of a trip (*precio aproximado del pasaje, Nuevos soles*), using the most common means of transportation. Averages exclude municipalities connected by airplane (*avioneta*).

Source: OECD analysis based on INEI (2012c), Registro Nacional de Municipalidades 2012.

Statistics on household Internet services indicates that this technology is still at an early stage of adoption, although it has rapidly expanded in the most urbanised departments and in recent years. In 2013, close to 40% of households in Lima and Callao had Internet services, and most of these households accessed this service between 2007 and 2013. This process of recent adoption is even more evident for the other departments: in each of them the current level of access is nearly equivalent to the change between 2007 and 2013. The current level of adoption of Internet remains particularly low (approximately 10% of households or less) in a group of 12 departments.

Efforts and improvements in that sense are being made. In recent years networks of optical fibre have increased, largely due to the construction of the National Fiber Optic Backbone (NFOB) and regional fibre optic networks, which initially include the connectivity of all provincial capitals and district capitals later. The NFOB should be completed in June 2016 and cover 180 of the 198 provincial capitals through the regional fibre optic networks, in 21 regions. As for the remaining four regions, it still needs to be completed.

Figure 1.53. **Fixed and mobile telephones per capita in 2013 and change between 2007 and 2013, by department**

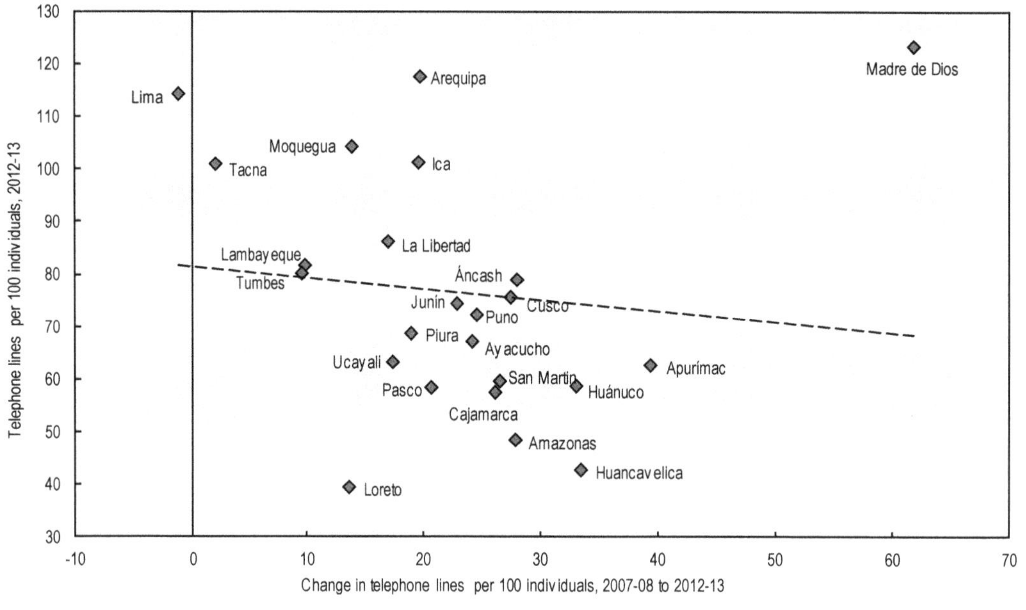

Notes: INEI notes that in both 2012 and 2013 approximately 6 million telephone lines (out of approximately 30 million) did not have a geographic code (*código de área de localización*, LAC). These lines are not included in the computations of this graph. Per capita level (vertical axis) is computed as average value for the years 2012 and 2013. Changes (horizontal axis) are computed using the 2012-13 average and the 2007-08 average. Two-year averages are used to smooth the effect of an unusually high or low value for one single year. Callao is included in the department of Lima.

Source: OECD analysis based on data from INEI.

Infrastructure and accessibility have improved significantly in Peru over the past two decades, and this has contributed to increasing economic activity and reducing poverty across different regions. However, these improvements have been uneven between and within regions. Infrastructure and accessibility outcomes are poorer for regions that are sparsely populated with desert and mountainous terrain (such as Pasco, Hanuco, Apurímac and Huancavelica). Rural areas continue to generally have lower quality infrastructure, which impacts on access to services and economic opportunities. Some of the most important development challenges for Peru are located in rural areas, and better connections with urban settlements will help address them. This suggests that a continued focus is required on improving the local road networks connecting rural areas with provincial and departmental capitals.

Innovation will be important for the productivity and competitiveness of tradeable sectors

Innovation is an important driver of regional growth. Indeed, for regions with high levels of income per capita and productivity (e.g. closer to the production possibility frontier), innovation appears to be one of the main determinants of growth. This factor will be less relevant for regions in Peru. However, innovation will play a role in lifting productivity and promoting economic diversification, particularly within the tradeable sector.

Figure 1.54. **Households with Internet services in 2013 and change between 2007 and 2013, by department**

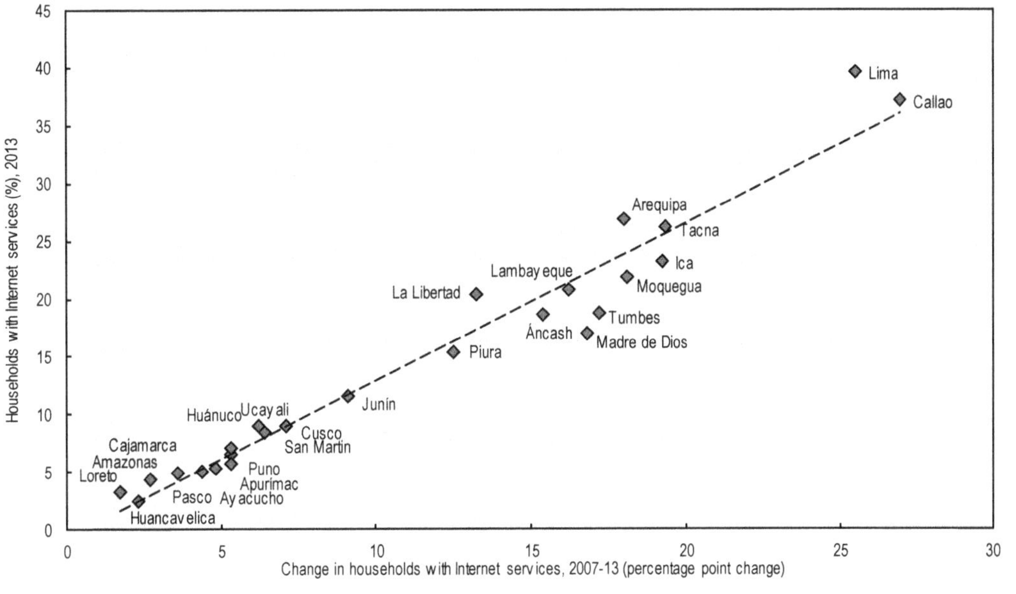

Source: OECD analysis based on data from INEI-ENAHO.

There are limited data related to innovation at a regional level in Peru. There are some data related to business demography which provide an indication about the type of businesses and their location across the country. The first key characteristic is that the overwhelming proportions of businesses are microenterprises, and these proportions do not vary greatly between departments (for further information see Chapter 2).

Table 1.12. **Proportion of businesses, by size, 2013**

Size of business	Proportion of total businesses (%)
Large	0.55
Medium	0.17
Small	4.6
Micro	94.6

Source: OECD elaboration based on INEI data.

The size of firms has a significant influence over innovation activity (OECD, 2011b). Microenterprises are much less likely to innovate, have short value chains and low-skilled workers with poorer quality products. Larger enterprises are more likely to be integrated into global value chains and are quicker to adopt new technologies and practices. Small and medium-sized enterprises tend to spend less on innovation activities and there seem to be limited spillovers to these firms from larger enterprises in Peru (OECD, 2011b).

Another key structural characteristic of innovation is differences between sectors. The location of these sectors also influences how innovation occurs and the design of policies to promote it. Agriculture and mining are predominantly located in rural areas whilst manufacturing is predominantly in urban areas. Mining tends to be undertaken by subsidiaries of large multinationals whereas locally owned firms are more important in the agriculture and manufacturing industries.

Table 1.13. **Innovation at a sectoral level in Peru**

Sector	Key characteristics
Agri-business (non-traditional)	– Products such as asparagus, mango, organic coffee and paprika – Strong export growth over three decades (2.5 times traditional agricultural exports) – Development and adoption of latest technologies (e.g. irrigation and crop management) – Characterised by strong interactions between local firms and with universities
Textile and clothing manufacturing	– Exports rose four-fold between the mid-1990s and 2008 – Free trade agreement with the United States (2006) important in terms of opening new export markets, and accelerating the adoption of new equipment and machinery – Government programmes to promote soft technology transfer (training and expert advice about products in international markets) have also been important
Mining	– Leading export industry and source of foreign direct investment – Characterised by subsidiaries of large multinationals using imported technologies and services – Lack of strong relationships with various actors, including local firms and universities

Source: OECD (2011b), *OECD Regional Outlook 2011: Building Resilient Regions for Stronger Economies*, http://dx.doi.org/10.1787/9789264120983-en.

Regional policies will have to account for these structural differences; for example, the development of collaborative networks between firms, universities and research institutes will be different for low-density economies. Efforts to promote innovation will also need to be accompanied by complementary policies to lift workforce skills and improve infrastructure at a regional level.

Citizens generally rate institutions poorly

Institutional factors are important to regional growth across the OECD. Formal and informal institutions that facilitate negotiation and dialogue among key actors in order to mobilise and integrate them into the development process are vital, as are those that enhance policy continuity. This co-operation is easier when citizens trust each other and expect reciprocity, and there is confidence in democratic institutions.

An integrated approach to regional development also depends upon effective co-ordination between levels of government, and different public agencies. Peru lags behind other countries in the co-ordination of public policies (OECD, 2015e). These problems are likely to be exacerbated at a regional and local level where governance capacities are lower (Muñoz, 2010).

The quality of institutions is perceived poorly by Peruvian citizens. Peru scores the lowest in government effectiveness and the rule of law, and marginally better than Mexico in terms of political stability and the control of corruption. The quality of governance is fundamental to creating a sound business environment and will need to be improved at a national and subnational level.

Participation in the democratic process through electoral vote is generally high across all departments of Peru. Voter turnouts from the 2001, 2006 and 2011 national elections show a high (well above 70%) voter turnout in all departments and a growing participation trend in most departments. The departments with the highest voter turnout are generally the most affluent and better performing on various dimensions, such as

Tacna, Ica, Arequipa, Lima and Callao; in these departments voter turnout has been generally between 85% and 90%, a percentage which is high by OECD standards.

Figure 1.55. **Quality of governance indicators, 2014**

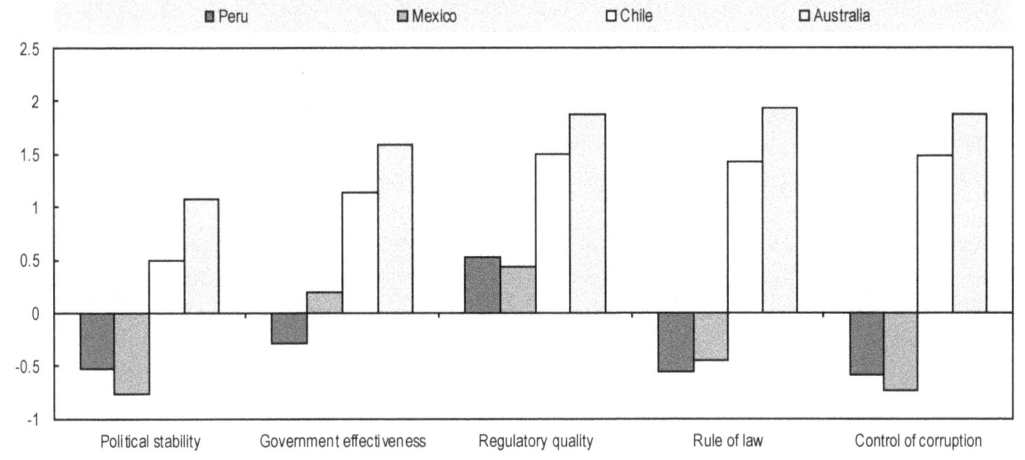

Source: World Bank (2016), Worldwide Governance Indicators, http://info.worldbank.org/governance/wgi/index.aspx#home.

Figure 1.56. **Voter turnout by department**

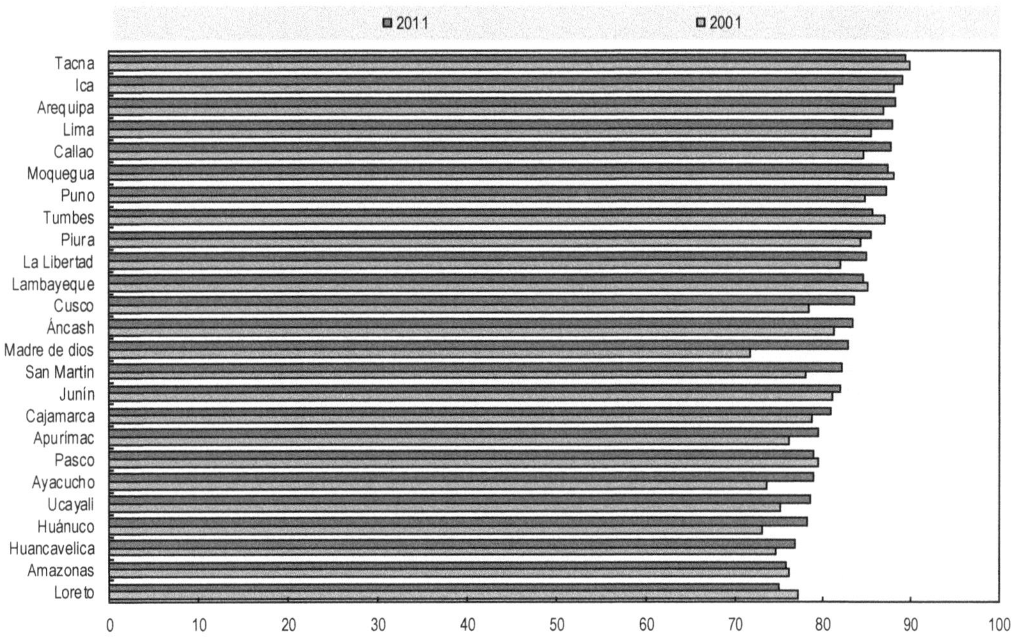

Source: Based on INEI data, http://www.inei.gob.pe.

Overall the quality of governance in Peru appears to be low and these issues are likely to be greater at a subnational level. Effective regional development policies depend upon including, and co-ordinating, a broad range of actors in the policy process. Competencies also need to exist at a regional level to ensure policies are tailored to address the development challenges and opportunities within that location. Chapter 4 will investigate these issues, further including the central role of regional governments in addressing the issues highlighted in this chapter.

Natural resources will need to be carefully managed to ensure the country's future well-being and competitiveness

There is an increasing recognition internationally that economic growth and development should occur in a way that reduces environmental damage and inefficient resource use (OECD, 2015a). Environmental assets such as forests, grasslands, wetlands and other natural assets located primarily in rural areas are important to well-being and the national development of Peru. In addition to generating private market opportunities, these assets can have recreational values, offer flood protection, purify drinking supplies, protect biodiversity and regulate the climate.

The physical geography of the country (categorised as the coast, highlands and rainforest) shapes the distribution of natural resources. Water resources are distributed unevenly with the majority in the Amazon basin. Natural water storages and flows in the highlands and coast are limited, and the coastal area has an arid climate. The soil along the coast and in the highlands is generally of poor quality. The interior is largely covered by forest. It is estimated that 37.8% of land is suitable for forestry production whilst 42.3% is protected.

Figure 1.57. **Loss of forest coverage, 2001-14**

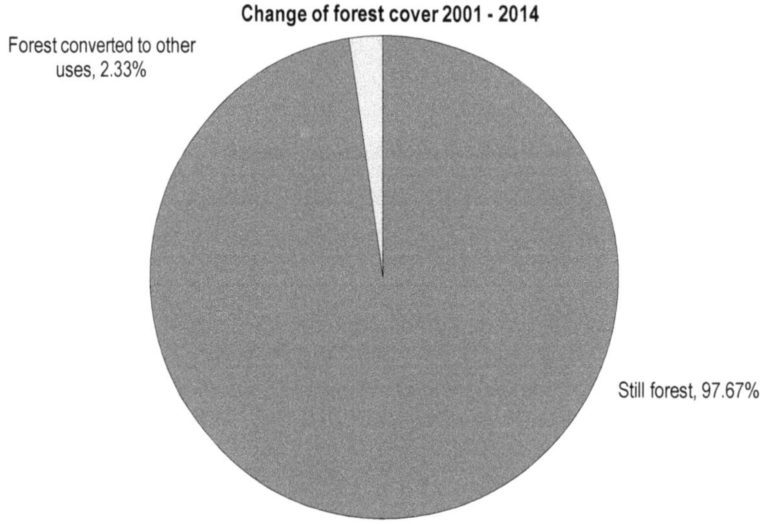

Source: Ministry of Agriculture and Irrigation (information generated in the framework of the ACTO project "Monitoring Deforestation, Forest Use and Land Use Change in the Pan-Amazonian Forests").

In terms of agricultural production, according to the Land Classification Study of Peru, 5.9% of land is suitable for crops and 13.9% for pasture. Agricultural production is important for the regions in the Amazon basin. However, production increases impact on forest through expanding the agricultural frontier. The Amazon has significant value to the global environment, and is also a potential source of economic growth through specialised crops, aquaculture, bio-medical applications and tourism. There are also opportunities to promote the sustainable development of the forestry industry.

Sea-based resources are also important, with fisheries exports valued at USD 2.4 billion in 2008 (FAO, 2015). Key catches include anchovy, mackerel, hake and squid. Overfishing and the impacts of El Niño events in the early 1970s and 1990s led to large declines in the fishing catch, and the introduction of measures such as quotas to address sustainability issues. Aquaculture has also grown in recent years in Peru and will need to be carefully managed in the context of water scarcity and biodiversity impacts.

The Peruvian Ministry of the Environment has developed an ecological footprint indicator which measures human demand for renewable resources.[6] The indicator has six components, which include the carbon footprint, farm areas, pasture areas, forest areas, fishing areas and urban areas.[7] Some of the regions with the slowest growing economies are also among those with the highest ecological footprint in 2013 (e.g. Madre de Dios, Tacna, Áncash and Moquegua). Some faster growing economies are also consuming higher rates of natural resources including Cusco, Ica and Lambayeque. In contrast, the only high-performing region which has managed to reduce its ecological footprint index is Tumbes.

Figure 1.58. **Ecological footprint per capita, by department**

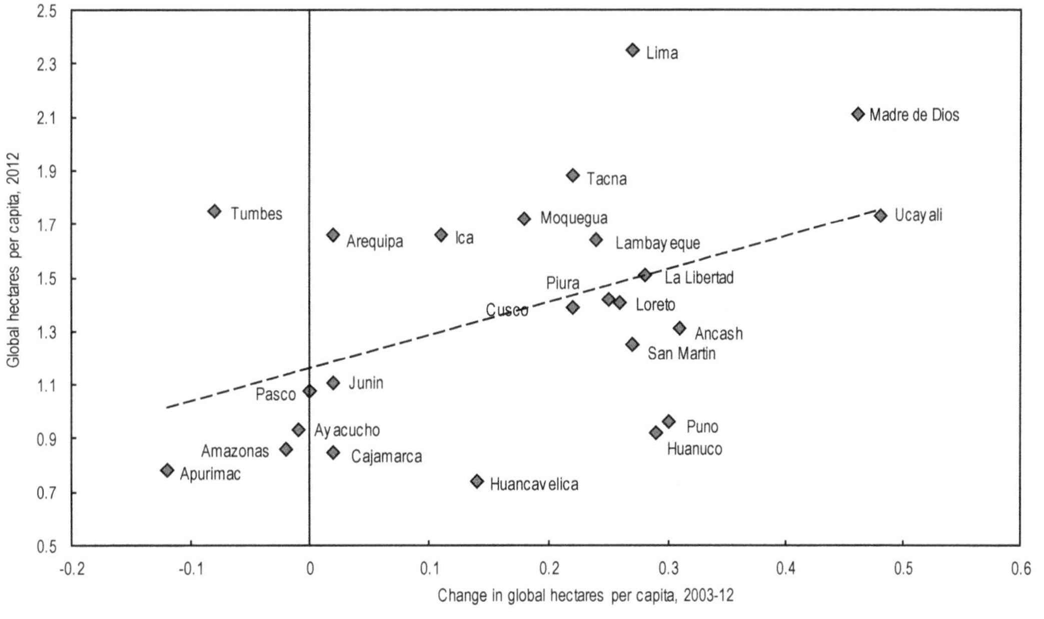

Note: For Ucayali the time frame 2003-11 is used.

Source: OECD analysis based on data from Ministry of Environment – National System of Environmental Information (Ministerio del Ambiente- Sistema Nacional de Información Ambiental) INAM-SINIA, http://sinia.minam.gob.pe.

Climate change also presents risks for Peru. Glaciers in the Andes lost a significant proportion of their ice volume over the 20th century. Further reductions in glacial runoffs would impact upon hydroelectricity production and the supply of water to agriculture and urban populations (World Bank, 2014a). Approximately half of Peru's population lives in the arid coastal region and depends upon water from the western slopes of the Andes. The likelihood of more extreme weather events associated with El Niño presents risks to Peru's rich fishing grounds, and economic damage caused by more frequent extreme heat and increased precipitation.

Given the importance of environmental issues, there is an opportunity for Peru to develop regional environmental indicators. In some case, this would require the integration of datasets form heterogeneous sources and/or the use of geospatial analysis. These data sources include:

- municipal level data, from the RENAMO, provide information on the major environmental challenges faced by each municipality
- other national information systems that focus on environment indicators include the SISFOR and OSINFOR on forestry resources and the Sistema Nacional de Gestión Ambiental (SNGA) of the Ministry of Environment
- land-use data are available from the national cadastre (*Catastro nacional*) and the updated urban Cadastre (*Catastro urbano actualizado*)
- the Ministry of Environment manages a Sistema de Información Geográfica para el Ordenamiento y Monitoreo del Territorio, which provides information related to land use, deforestation and vulnerability to natural disasters (which provides data on land-use changes and vegetation coverage every 15 days).

This should build upon existing initiatives such as the National Environmental Information System, which has already made some steps towards this by integrating environmental information to support processes of decision making and environmental management.

Notes

1. The comparison year has been chosen as 2004 due to a methodological change by INEI in collecting labour market statistics in that year.

2. There are a number of international definitions for informality, and depending on the definition, between half and two-thirds of individuals are employed informally. According to the legal definition of CEDLAS and the World Bank (i.e. an informal worker is one who does not have the right to a pension when retired), 49.9% of workers in Peru were in informal work in 2011, the latest year for which there are comparable data for our benchmark countries. When using the "productive" definition (i.e. an employee in a firm with five or fewer employees, a non-professional self-employed or a zero-income worker), 59.4% of workers fell into the informal category in 2012. The International Labour Organization's (ILO) non-agricultural

informal employment rate for Peru, 68.8% in 2012, was the highest share amongst all of the benchmark countries (OECD, 2015e).

3. The cornerstone for territorial demographic and socio-economic indicators is the Census of population. The most recent one conducted in Peru was undertaken in 2007; it was used for subsequent projections of the population (INEI, 2015).

4. INEI does not produce GDP data at the departmental level. The indicator used for departmental statistics is gross value added (GVA). The difference between GDP and GVA is given by *impuestos a la producción* and *derechos de importación*, these are only estimated at the national level. These two items represent approximately 8% of the national GDP; hence, departmental GVA is a close proxy for regional GDP. The methodology to generate gross value added by economic activity at a regional level was updated by INEI with a new data series released in 2007. This included improvements in data collection and methodological changes to better align with international standards. As a result, GVA data prior to 2007 has not been utilised in this report.

5. The statistics on "Lima" in this section refer to the metropolitan area of Lima, which (normally) includes the province of Lima and Callao.

6. For a detailed description of the methodology used to compute this index, see: http://sinia.minam.gob.pe/documentos/huella-ecologica-peru

7. To determine whether human demand for renewable resources and CO_2 uptake can be maintained, the ecological footprint is compared with the regenerative capacity of the planet or biocapacity, the total regenerative capacity available to meet demand represented by the footprint. Both the ecological footprint (which represents demand for resources) and biocapacity (which represents the availability of resources) are expressed in units called global hectares (gha), with 1 gha being the production capacity of 1 hectare of world average production.

Bibliography

AFIN (2015), *Plan Nacional de Infraestructura 2016-2025*, Universidad de Pacifico, Lima.

Aghion, P. and P. Howitt (2006), "Joseph Schumpeter lecture appropriate growth policy: A unifying framework", *Journal of the European Economic Association*, Vol. 4/2-3, pp. 269-314, http://dx.doi.org/10.1162/jeea.2006.4.2-3.269.

Ahrend, R. (2006), "How to sustain growth in a resource based economy?: The main concepts and their application to the Russian case", *OECD Economics Department Working Papers*, No. 478, OECD Publishing, Paris, http://dx.doi.org/10.1787/622880627053.

Barro and Lee (2010), "A new Data Set of Educational Attainment in the World, 1950-2010", Journal of Development Economics, vol. 104, pp. 184-198.

BCRP (2015), *Annual Series Database*, Banco Central de Reserva del Perú, https://estadisticas.bcrp.gob.pe/estadisticas/series/anuales.

CELDAS and World Bank (2014), *Socio-Economic Database for Latin America and the Caribbean* (SELDAC), Universidad Nacional de la Plata and The World Bank, http://sedlac.econo.unlp.edu.ar/eng/index.php.

FAO (2016) "Fishery and aquaculture country profiles: The Republic of Peru", Food and Agriculture Organization, Rome, www.fao.org/fishery/facp/PER/en.

Hausmann R. and B. Klinger (2008), "Growth diagnostics in Peru", CID Working Paper, No. 181, Center for International Development, Harvard Kennedy School, Cambridge, MA, https://research.hks.harvard.edu/publications/getFile.aspx?Id=435.

IADB (2006), "CCLIP: National highway system five-year Infrastructure Program and national highway system Serviceability Program loan proposal", Inter-American Development Bank, http://idbdocs.iadb.org/wsdocs/getdocument.aspx?docnum=865642.

ILO (2014), *Key Indicators of the Labour Market*, 8th Edition, International Labour Office, Geneva.

INEI (n.d.), http://www.inei.gob.pe.

INEI (2016), "Economía", www.inei.gob.pe/estadisticas/indice-tematico/economia.

INEI (2015), *Avance Económico y Social Departamental, Diciembre 2014*, Instituto Nacional de Estadística e Informática, Lima, www.inei.gob.pe/media/MenuRecursivo/publicaciones_digitales/Est/Lib1249/index.htm.

INEI (2014a), "Producción y empleo informal en el Perú. Cuenta satélite de la economía informal 2007-2012", Instituto Nacional de Estadística e Informática, Lima, www.inei.gob.pe/media/MenuRecursivo/publicaciones_digitales/Est/Lib1154/libro.pdf.

INEI (2014b), *Informe Técnico de Pobreza 2014*, Instituto Nacional de Estadística e Informática, Lima.

INEI (2014c), *Perú: Producto Bruto Interno por Departamentos 2007-2013: Año Base 2007*, Instituto Nacional de Estadística e Informática, Lima.

INEI (2014d), "Una mirada a Lima Metropolitana", Instituto Nacional de Estadística e Informática, Lima, www.inei.gob.pe/media/MenuRecursivo/publicaciones_digitales/Est/Lib1168/libro.pdf.

INEI (2014e), *Perú: Principales Indicadores Departamentales 2008-2014*, Instituto Nacional de Estadística e Informática, Lima, www.inei.gob.pe/media/MenuRecursivo/publicaciones_digitales/Est/Lib1205/index.html.

INEI (2014f), "Evolución de la pobreza monetaria 2009-2013", *Informe Técnico*, Instituto Nacional de Estadística e Informática, Lima, www.inei.gob.pe/media/cifras_de_pobreza/informetecnico.pdf.

INEI (2013a), *Perú Estadísticas de la Emigración Internacional de Peruanos e Inmigración de Extranjeros 1990-2012*, Instituto Nacional de Estadística e Informática, Lima, www.inei.gob.pe/media/MenuRecursivo/publicaciones_digitales/Est/Lib1102/libro.pdf.

INEI (2013b), Plan Estratégico Nacional para el Desarrollo Estadístico PENDES 2013-2017, Instituto Nacional de Estadística e Informática, Lima, www.inei.gob.pe/sistema-estadistico-nacional/#url.

INEI (2013c), Registro Nacional de Municipalidades 2013: Principales Resultados, CD-ROM, Instituto Nacional de Estadística e Informática, Lima.

INEI (2012a), "Condiciones de vida en el Perú", *Informe Técnico*, No. 3, September, Instituto Nacional de Estadística e Informática, Lima, www.inei.gob.pe/media/MenuRecursivo/boletines/17168.pdf.

INEI (2012b), "Evolución de la pobreza 2007-2011", *Informe Técnico*, May, Instituto Nacional de Estadística e Informática, Lima, www.inei.gob.pe/media/cifras_de_pobreza/pobreza_informetecnico.pdf.

INEI (2012c), Registro Nacional de Municipalidades 2012, Instituto Nacional de Estadística e Informática, Lima.

INEI (2009a), "Perú: Estimaciones y proyecciones de población urbana y rural por sexo y grupos quinquenales de edad, según departamentos, 2000-2015", *Boletín Especial*, No. 19, December, Instituto Nacional de Estadística e Informática, Lima, http://proyectos.inei.gob.pe/web/biblioineipub/bancopub/Est/Lib0844/index.htm.

INEI (2009b), *IV Censo Nacional Económico del 2008*, Instituto Nacional de Estadística e Informática, Lima, http://censos.inei.gob.pe/cenec2008.

INEI (2006), "Condiciones de vida en el Perú: Evolución 1997-2004", Instituto Nacional de Estadística e Informática, Lima.

INEI (2000-2010), Encuesta Nacional de Hogares (ENAHO), Instituto Nacional de Estadística e Informática, Lima.

INEI (2016), "Economía", www.inei.gob.pe/estadisticas/indice-tematico/economia.

Ministry for Transport and Communications (Ministerio de Transportes y Communicaciones- MTC), www.mtc.gob.pe.

Muñoz (2010), "¿La Política Importa? Los Determinantes Políticos de la Eficiencia del Gasto Municipal", CIES, SER (Asociación Servicios Educativos Rurales), Lima, www.cies.org.pe/es/investigaciones/descentralizacion-y-modernizacion-del-estado/lapolitica-importa-los-determinantes.

Natural Resource Governance Institute (2015), "Local level resource curse: The 'cholo disease' in Peru", Revenue Watch Institute, www.resourcegovernance.org/sites/default/files/SubnationalresourcecurseresearchDRAFT.pdf.

OECD (2016a), *Regions at a Glance*, OECD Publishing, Paris, http://dx.doi.org/10.1787/reg_glance-2016-en.

OECD (2016b), "The productivity-equality nexus: A concept paper", 7th New Approaches to Economic Challenges (NAEC) Group Meeting, OECD, Paris.

OECD (2015a), *Towards Green Growth?: Tracking Progress*, OECD Green Growth Studies, OECD Publishing, Paris, http://dx.doi.org/10.1787/9789264234437-en.

OECD (2015b), *Economic Policy Reforms: Going for Growth*, OECD Publishing, Paris, http://dx.doi.org/10.1787/growth-2015-en.

OECD (2015c), *All on Board: Making Inclusive Growth Happen*, OECD Publishing, Paris, http://dx.doi.org/10.1787/9789264218512-en.

OECD (2015d), *The Future of Productivity*, OECD Publishing, Paris, http://dx.doi.org/10.1787/9789264248533-en.

OECD (2015e), *Multi-dimensional Review of Peru: Volume 1. Initial Assessment*, OECD Development Pathways, OECD Publishing, Paris, http://dx.doi.org/10.1787/9789264243279-en.

OECD (2015f), *Main Science and Technology Indicators Database*, www.oecd.org/sti/msti.

OECD (2014a), *OECD Regional Outlook 2014: Regions and Cities, Where Policies and People Meet*, OECD Publishing, Paris, http://dx.doi.org/10.1787/9789264201415-en.

OECD (2014b), *OECD Rural Policy Reviews: Chile 2014*, OECD Publishing, Paris, http://dx.doi.org/10.1787/9789264222892-en.

OECD (2013a), *OECD Regions at a Glance 2013*, OECD Publishing, Paris, http://dx.doi.org/10.1787/reg_glance-2013-en.

OECD (2013b), *OECD Metropolitan Database*, http://dx.doi.org/10.1787/region-data-en.

OECD (2012), *Promoting Growth in all Regions*, OECD Publishing, Paris, http://dx.doi.org/10.1787/9789264174634-en.

OECD (2011a), *OECD Reviews of Innovation Policy: Peru 2011*, OECD Publishing, Paris, http://dx.doi.org/10.1787/9789264128392-en.

OECD (2011b), *OECD Regional Outlook 2011: Building Resilient Regions for Stronger Economies*, OECD Publishing, Paris, http://dx.doi.org/10.1787/9789264120983-en.

OECD (2009), *How Regions Grow: Trends and Analysis*, OECD Publishing, Paris, http://dx.doi.org/10.1787/9789264039469-en.

OECD (2016), *OECD Patent Database*, www.oecd.org/sti/inno/oecdpatentdatabases.htm.

Perales, J. and E. Morón (2010), *La Economía Política del Tratado de Libre Comercio entre Perú y Estados Unidos*, Woodrow Wilson International Center Scholars, Washington, DC, www.wilsoncenter.org/sites/default/files/Peru_US.pdf.

RICYT (2015), Network for Science and Technology Indicators –Ibero-American and Inter-American website, www.ricyt.org/homeenglish (accessed on 1 August 2015).UNESCO/UIS (2015), *UNESCO Institute for Statistics Database*, www.uis.unesco.org/Pages/default.aspx.

Webb, R. (2013), "Conexión y despegue rural", Instituto del Perú, Universidad de San Martín de Porres, www.lampadia.com/assets/uploads_librosdigitales/2f207-cdr.pdf.

WEF (2014), *The Global Competitiveness Report 2014-2015*, World Economic Forum, Geneva, www3.weforum.org/docs/WEF_GlobalCompetitivenessReport_2014-15.pdf.

World Bank (2016), Worldwide Governance Indicators, http://info.worldbank.org/governance/wgi/index.aspx#home.

World Bank (2015a), "Exports of goods and services (% of GDP)", http://data.worldbank.org/indicator/NE.EXP.GNFS.ZS.

World Bank (2015b), "GDP at market prices (constant 2010 US$)", http://data.worldbank.org/indicator/NY.GDP.MKTP.KD/countries?display=graph.

World Bank (2015c), "GDP per capita (current USD)", http://data.worldbank.org/indicator/NY.GDP.PCAP.CD.

World Bank (2015d), "GDP per person employed (constant 2011 PPP $)", http://data.worldbank.org/indicator/SL.GDP.PCAP.EM.KD.

World Bank (2015e), "Peru", http://data.worldbank.org/country/peru.

World Bank (2014a), *Turn Down the Heat: Confronting a New Climate Normal*, The World Bank, Washington, DC, https://openknowledge.worldbank.org/handle/10986/20595.

World Bank (2014b), Logistics Performance Index 2014, http://lpi.worldbank.org.

World Bank (2014c), *Socio-Economic Database for Latin America and the Caribbean* (SELDAC) (database), http://sedlac.econo.unlp.edu.ar/eng/index.php.

Annex 1.A1.
Peru's administrative and statistical definitions

Peru's territorial definitions

For the purpose of statistical dissemination, the National Institute of Statistics and Informatics (Instituto Nacional de Estadística e Informática, INEI) has established a set of territorial definitions, which, to a large extent, reflects the administrative structure of the country. Table 1.A1.1 presents the territorial units most frequently used for the purpose of statistical dissemination of census, survey and other administrative data. In addition, INEI maintains a system of georeferenced statistics that permits territorial indicators for specific types of infrastructure or establishments (such as educational and health facilities) to be produced.

Table 1.A1.1. **Subnational territorial units of Peru**

Territorial unit	Count	Statistical	Administrative
Department	25	Yes, nearly all territorial indicators are produced or can be rolled up at this geographic level	Yes, referred to as a region. Elected regional government (governor), every four years
Province	195	Yes, some statistics are available at this geographic level	Yes, provincial municipality
District	1 854	Yes, mainly census and census-like administrative data	Yes, district municipality
Population centre	65 535	Yes, census data	Some have municipal responsibility and structure
Macro regions	3	Yes, nearly all territorial indicators are produced or can be rolled up at this geographic level	No

Annex 1.A2.
Geographic Concentration Index

The Geographic Concentration index of population and gross domestic product (GDP) is defined as:

$$\left(\sum_{i=1}^{N} \left| p_i - a_i \right| \Big/ 2 \right) * 100$$

where p_i is the population and GDP share of region i, a_i is the area of region i as a percentage of the country area, N stands for the number of regions and $| \ |$ indicates the absolute value.

The index lies between 0 (no concentration) and 1 (maximum concentration) in all countries and is suitable for international comparisons of geographic concentration.

Chapter 2.

Implementing a regional approach to national economic development

This chapter discusses how to implement a regional approach to sectoral and innovation policies. The chapter is divided into four main parts. The first section focuses on assessing regional policies in Peru, including alignment with the contemporary OECD approach to regional policy. The second section discusses macroeconomic policies and their impacts on regions, including an overview of the productive fabric of the country. The third section discusses the importance of integrating sectoral and innovation policies with a regional agenda. Finally, the fourth section draws some conclusions and sums up key recommendations.

Key findings and recommendations

Key findings

- Peru is made up of regions that strongly differ in their performance and growth rates. Although a small number of regions generally contribute disproportionately to growth, previous OECD work on regional growth has shown that there is potential for growth in all regions. Regional level factors yield significant differences in productivity and consequently income levels among regions. Influencing these factors requires a shift towards a "place-based" approach that integrates infrastructure, skills and innovation policies.
- Regional development is an important national policy priority for Peru; however, it would benefit from a shift towards a place-based approach based on regional competitiveness and unlocking growth potential. The concerted regional development plans are an important innovation and provide a platform for strengthening the role of regions in the design and delivery of national sectoral policies. However, these plans do not appear to be effectively linked or integrated with fiscal frameworks.
- Peru's sectoral and innovation policies have a focus on diversifying the economy and increasing the complexity of the country's export basket. These are primarily designed and executed at a national level. The rise of global value chains (GVCs), the increasing importance of networks and technological platforms to innovation, and dynamic processes of entrepreneurial self-discovery all point toward the need for a more bottom-up strategy. The smart specialisation strategy currently being implemented by the European Union, combined with new mechanisms to co-ordinate policies and build capability at a subnational level, can provide a platform to develop this place-based approach.

Key recommendations

3. Consider the establishment of more effective and strategic institutional support capacity that can facilitate a partnership-based approach to regional development between departments and the national government. Two strategic options to achieve this outcome are: 1) deconcentrated agencies of the Presidency of the Council of Ministers (PCM) and the Ministry of Economy and Finance (MEF) that can work in partnership at a macro-regional level; and 2) regional development agencies (RDA) that are constituted as a partnership between departments and the national government.
   - developing the skills and technical capacity of regional governments (departments) in areas such as policy development and evaluation, strategic planning, procurement, and project/programme delivery
   - providing support to departments and municipal governments to better integrate strategic plans with fiscal frameworks and investment strategies
   - communicating strategic priorities of the departments to the national government, identifying opportunities for strategic alignment between departments, and ensuring these priorities inform the national budget and planning cycle
   - ensuring that national policies and priorities are considered and reflected in departmental planning
   - co-ordinating investments and programme delivery at a regional and inter-regional scale
   - evaluating and monitoring departmental and municipal level planning to ensure plans are effective and aligned with the national system of strategic planning.

Key findings and recommendations (*continued*)

4. Improve the quality and effectiveness of concerted regional development plans by:
   - ensuring that within the next two years all departments have an endorsed concerted regional development plan.
   - requesting that the regional governor submit the draft concerted regional development plan for consideration and response by the relevant national ministries (co-ordinated by the deconcentrated agency or RDA model)
   - mandating a formal review of the implementation of concerted regional development plans every three years, synchronised with other regions, and which is publicly available (co-ordinated by the deconcentrated agency or RDA model)
   - mandating publicly available annual reporting on progress in implementing the concerted regional development plan by the regional governor (which also includes a summary of the activities and achievements of the regional co-ordination councils)
   - strengthening the economic analysis within these plans, for example, incorporating further analysis of the industry and business structure within regions at the scale of functional economic areas (including at a macro-regional scale), including how regional businesses are integrated with GVCs, and the identification of key bottlenecks and growth opportunities at these scales
   - creating opportunities for policy makers at a departmental level to learn from each other, and good practices nationally and internationally (e.g. through targeted training, and a bi-annual conference on regional planning and investment).
5. Better integrate regional planning with the fiscal framework by:
   - Introducing competitive-based funding programmes that are designed to encourage innovation, infrastructure and skills initiatives at a regional level. Ensure that the criteria for prioritising funding includes demonstrating alignment with concerted regional development plans, and co-contributions from regions, different municipalities, business and other actors.
   - Tasking the National Centre for Strategic Planning (CEPLAN; through the RDA or deconcentrated agency) to work in partnership with departments to identify and prioritise medium-term (three to five years) capital investment programmes in the concerted regional development plans to deliver on strategic priorities in the territory (derived from the national and subnational plans and programmes). Through the RDA the Ministry of Economy and Finances should also contribute to the development of these investment programmes.
   - Including the annual report on progress in implementing the concerted regional development plan in the department's budget and plans, demonstrating alignment with budget instruments.

Introduction

Across the OECD, it is increasingly recognised that regional development policies are a key part of improving aggregate growth performance. There are strong differences in the economic performance between regions and these differences tend to persist over time due to regional factors. These factors can be influenced by integrated and tailored investments in skills, infrastructure and innovation that are designed to unlock regional growth potential. Tailoring these policy interventions is important because drivers of growth vary between regions depending on their level of development, institutional arrangements, resource endowments, and population size and density. Opportunities for growth exist in all types of regions and these places can be assisted to reach their growth potential endogenously through "place-based" approaches to regional development (OECD, 2011a).

A key element of this contemporary approach to regional policy is enabling the identification and development of new economic activities, which build upon and combine existing strengths. These processes of innovation are generated through facilitating collaboration between businesses, higher and vocational education, and public and private R&D at a regional level. The analysis in this chapter shows that "one-size fits all" national industrial strategies which focus on export sectors are unlikely to succeed due to factors such as the complexity of Peru's economic geography, and the increasing importance of global value chains (GVCs) to how businesses organise production. Shifting toward this place-based approach to sectoral and innovation policies will require Peru to strengthen co-ordination mechanisms and build governance capability at a subnational level.

Peru already has a planning and institutional architecture that can provide the foundation for this place-based approach. Peru has established a national planning system across levels of government, which includes concerted regional development plans. However, national ministries are not effectively engaged in the design and implementation of these plans, and they are not integrated with the fiscal framework. In addition, there is significant variation in capabilities between regional governments, and a lack of consistency and depth in measures to build these capabilities. There are a range of lessons from across the OECD which Peru can learn from in addressing these issues, some of which build on existing practices such as results-based budgeting. This includes the use of regional development agencies (RDAs) to encourage a partnership-based approach to regional development, and mutually agreed contracts to align budgeting across different levels of government toward shared outcomes.

The OECD regional approach and assessing Peru's regional policy framework

Peru, like many other countries, is made up of regions that strongly differ in their performance and growth rates. Across the OECD, these differences persist over time, suggesting that regional level factors yield significant differences in productivity and consequently income levels among regions (Garcilazo and Oliveira Martins, 2013). Although a small number of large cities contribute disproportionately to growth, there are many smaller and lagging regions that also make important contributions to national growth. A decomposition of the latter in OECD countries shows that between 1995 and 2007, less-developed regions made a vital contribution to aggregate growth, since they accounted for 43% of aggregate OECD growth. Previous OECD work on regional growth has shown that there is potential for growth in all regions, and that the determinants of growth can be addressed by public policies (OECD, 2009a; 2011a).

This growing body of evidence has been accompanied by a shift in how OECD countries approach regional policies. In the past, these policies tended to focus on addressing disparities between regions through the provision of subsidies to compensate regions for lower incomes. Policies were designed by central governments through departments of state that delivered narrowly defined economic development programmes.

This approach was seen as increasingly ineffective and not sustainable from a fiscal point of view. The new approach to regional policies emphasises a focus on competitiveness and working with regions to unlock growth potential. This approach has significant implications for how government works. Governments need to work in a more integrated way at a regional and local level. This "place-based" approach is outlined in Table 2.1.

Table 2.1. **The paradigm shift in regional policy**

	Traditional regional policies	New paradigm
Objectives	Balancing economic performance by temporary compensation for regional disparities	Tapping underutilised regional potential for competitiveness
Strategies	Sectoral approach	Integrated development projects
Tools	Subsidies and state aid	Soft and hard infrastructure
Actors	Central government	Different levels of government
Unit of analysis	Administrative regions	Functional regions
→	Redistributing from leading to lagging regions	Building competitive regions to bring together actors and targeting key local assets

Source: OECD (2009b), *Regions Matter: Economic Recovery, Innovation and Sustainable Growth*, http://dx.doi.org/10.1787/9789264076525-en.

Growth drivers vary across different types of regions, which emphasises the importance of a "place-based" approach

In the OECD as in the entire world economy, a handful of regions (the big "hubs") account for a disproportionate share of aggregate growth: typically, around 4% of regions generate about one-third of a country's total growth. The remainder of growth comes from all the other regions combined, which although not contributing much individually, they have a high collective impact (OECD, 2012c). There are two key implications for policy makers of these findings:

1. policy makers are right in being concerned about getting the performance of their big regional hub right, since their individual impact on growth is high
2. given that the biggest share of growth comes from the other regions, neglecting them and solely focusing on the frontier regions may have significant negative impacts on aggregate growth.

A broader based growth provides benefits to the overall economy in terms of national resilience, equity and fiscal heath (OECD, 2012c). Broader regionally based growth is likely to be more diversified, in turn making the economy more resilient to external shocks. "Catch-up" driven growth in poorer regions is also likely to strongly reduce inequalities and economic opportunities across regions and individuals. Finally, lifting regions from under-performance limits the cost of fiscal equalisation transfers to those regions and strengthens national cohesion.

Drivers of growth vary across levels of development. The barriers to growth that regions must overcome vary widely across regions and levels of development. Successful performance therefore requires more than "one-size fits all" economy-wide policies: a place-based approach is needed. The OECD has developed a taxonomy of regions based on their performance against national averages, and then against both national and OECD averages. Regions were grouped depending on their starting point in 1995 (in gross domestic product [GDP] per capita) and their growth rates between 1995 and 2007. This approach allows for identifying commonalities among regions with similar levels of development or distance to a production possibility frontier (Aghion and Howitt, 2006).

The taxonomy was used to find the key drivers of growth at each level of development and their impact on aggregate output. This taxonomy defined regions as follows:

- regions with large catching-up potential
- regions with catching-up potential
- advanced regions.

The main factors of growth vary between these different types of regions based on their stage of development (OECD, 2009a; 2012c) (Table 2.2).

Table 2.2. **Drivers of regional growth vary according to their stage of development**

Type of region	Main factors of growth
Regions with large catching-up potential	– Lower-income regions *ceteris paribus* tend to grow faster, implying that there is a process of income convergence within this group. However, the latter do not appear to be strong. – Human capital has a positive impact on growth. The most important effect appears at the bottom of the skill distribution: the negative impact of a large share of the workforce with very low skills appears to be a more important factor than the positive impact of a large share with tertiary qualifications. This result has important policy implications. – Population density is not associated with higher growth, reinforcing the impression created by the benchmarking exercise that there is more to generating agglomeration economies than simply putting large numbers of people in close proximity to one another. – Regions with low employment rates can generate growth by increasing labour force participation.
Regions with catching-up potential	– Human capital – measured in terms of both the absence of workers with no more than a primary educational attainment in the labour force and the presence of workers with a tertiary education – has a positive impact on growth. – Mobilisation of the labour force brings growth in intermediate regions. – Some innovation-related indicators appear to have an impact on growth in certain models (e.g. business R&D and government R&D expenditures) but the results are not stable.
Advanced regions	– Conditional convergence is weaker among leading regions than among intermediate regions. Agglomeration economies play a larger role in leading regions, and agglomeration economies tend to work against convergence. The logic of agglomeration would lead one to expect divergence of regional performance over time, with the leading regions pulling further ahead. So the results for this group reflect the contradictory impact of the forces of convergence and agglomeration. – Infrastructure density is not a key factor. That is related to the expectable diminishing returns to investments in infrastructure and the fact that advanced regions would tend to already have good connective infrastructure. – Human capital has a positive impact on growth. Again, it is the share of individuals with very low skills that is significant in every model, suggesting the degree to which large groups of unskilled or low-skilled workers can act as a drag on growth. – Innovation has a positive impact on growth.

Source: OECD (2009a), *How Regions Grow: Trends and Analysis*, http://dx.doi.org/10.1787/9789264039469-en; OECD (2012c) *Promoting Growth in All Regions*, http://dx.doi.org/10.1787/9789264174634-en.

For policy makers, these findings suggest a small number of key growth bottlenecks which vary across different types of regions. Skills are particularly important across all types of regions, particularly the share of the workforce with very low skills. Infrastructure is generally not a binding constraint, and innovation is more important at more advanced stages of development. Across all regions the quality of government is an important factor, particularly for less-developed regions. The key message for policy makers is the importance of integrated approaches which combine these different policy areas, and ensuring they are adapted to the needs and circumstances of different regions.

In this sense, policy complementarities are critical. Without effective co-ordination there is a cost associated with isolated interventions and "unbalanced" policy packages. Improving regional performance has less to do with executing a sequence of individual steps than with identifying a feasible strategy for addressing a number of policy challenges in a co-ordinated fashion. Seeking to individually improve parts of the policies may cause negative effects if reforms are not considered in a comprehensive way.

Table 2.3. **Growth bottlenecks per level of development**

Growth drivers/bottlenecks	Relative level of development		
	Lagging (>75% of national average per capita GDP)	Intermediate (75-100% of national average per capita GDP)	Leading (>100% of national average per capita GDP)
Human capital/skills: presence of very low skilled	√√	√	√√
Human capital/skills: presence of highly skilled	√	√	√√
Labour force mobilisation: participation/employment rates		√	√√
Innovation activity: patents, R&D spending, employment in knowledge-intensive sectors	√	√	√√√
Agglomeration effects: density of population, density of GDP			√
Quality of government	√√	√	√

Notes: √ = somewhat important; √√ = very important; √√√ = critical factor.

Source: Based on results in OECD (2012c), *Promoting Growth in All Regions*, http://dx.doi.org/10.1787/9789264174634-en.

Effective public investment across levels of government

The implementation of these policies depends upon governance and fiscal reforms that can enable an integrated place-based approach to public investment. Investments that are poorly designed and executed not only imply high opportunity costs but may also directly hamper growth. Subnational governments in Peru and across the OECD are the biggest providers of public investments (see Chapter 4), thereby efficiency in public investments requires strong co-ordination across levels of government and governance capacities to design and implement policies.

Subnational governments generally play a strong role in addressing the key growth bottlenecks discussed in the previous section. Across the OECD, regions invest 37% of their budget in economic affairs (transport, communications, economic development, energy, etc.). Another 23% of their investments go to education, which will in turn impact the levels of skills of the workforce. Subnational governments also play an important co-ordinating role, in helping to align and co-ordinate investments between national and local governments.

As discussed, the paradigm shift in regional policies has important implications for how government works. Policies should be adapted to the needs and circumstances (social, economic, cultural, geographic, environmental, etc.) of different regions. Policies should also be integrated to help realise complementarities between them. Tailoring policies in this way requires new ways of working and organising which are challenging for traditional forms of public administration and fiscal management. To help countries address these challenges, the OECD has developed the Principles on Effective Public Investment across Levels of Government. The purpose of these principles is to help governments at all levels assess the strengths and weaknesses of their public investment capacity using a whole-of-government approach, and set priorities for improvement. The principles are grouped into three pillars, which represent systemic multi-level governance challenges for public investment:

Box 2.1. Subnational governments invest in building critical capacities for sustainable growth across the OECD

Most of subnational public investment goes to areas of critical importance for future economic growth, sustainable development and citizens' well-being (Figure 2.1). In terms of total investment by subnational governments across the OECD, 37% is allocated to economic affairs (transport, communications, economic development, energy, construction, etc.). Approximately 23% of public investment is used for education, which helps determine the quality of the future labour force. A further 11% is dedicated to housing and community amenities. Healthcare and environmental protection are also major areas of investment for subnational governments, in particular in Nordic countries for health or Eastern European countries for the environment.

Many policy areas instrumental for inclusive growth and sustainable development are mainly in the hands of subnational governments. The policy areas in which subnational governments have the highest share of the investment spending as a share of general government spending are housing and community amenities (with 96% of direct investment done at the subnational level in the OECD-26), recreation and culture (87%), environmental protection and education (around 80%), social protection (64%), economic affairs (53%), public order and safety (51%), and health (38%).

Figure 2.1. **Subnational public investment is a potential driver of competitiveness**

Share of direct public investment by economic function undertaken by subnational governments, 2011

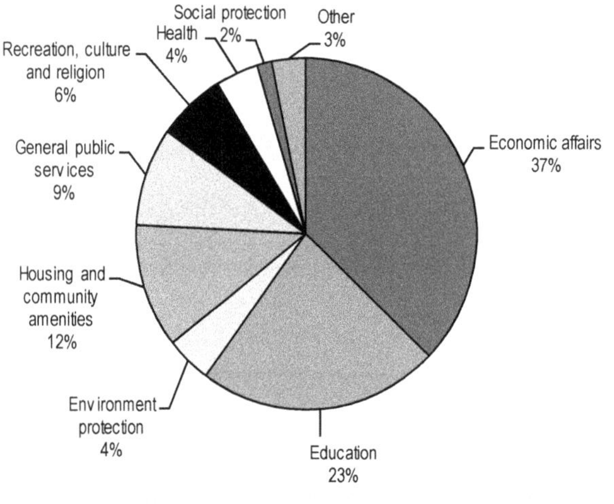

Source: OECD (2013c), OECD Regions at a Glance 2013, OECD Publishing, Paris, http://dx.doi.org/10.1787/reg_glance-2013-en.

Public investments also have direct impacts today given the large share spent on maintaining existing infrastructure. In EU countries, around 70% of public investment is actually for maintenance costs associated with past infrastructure investments. In the United States, for the transport and water sectors, they account for 52% of public spending, with subnational governments responsible for nearly 90% of that maintenance spending. Deferred maintenance is a common strategy in times of budget pressures. However, the result is that quality of critical public infrastructure will continue to degrade, which can cause problems such as unusable school buildings or hospital facilities as well as closed bridges and road congestion. Asset values also erode with a long-term disinvestment. Therefore, the lack of needed maintenance investments can also lead to problems for today's well-being and competitiveness.

Source: OECD (2014a), *OECD Regional Outlook 2014: Regions and Cities: Where Policies and People Meet*, http://dx.doi.org/10.1787/9789264201415-en.

- Co-ordination challenges: cross-sector, cross-jurisdictional and intergovernmental co-ordination are necessary, but difficult in practice. Moreover, the constellation of actors involved in public investment is large and their interests may need to be aligned.
- Capacity challenges: where the capacities to design and implement investment strategies are weak, policies may fail to achieve their objectives. Evidence suggests the public investment and growth outcomes are correlated to the quality of government, including at the subnational level.
- Challenges in framework conditions: good practices in budgeting, procurement and regulatory quality are integral to successful investment, but not always robust or consistent across levels of government.

Box 2.2. OECD Principles on Effective Public Investment across Levels of Government

The OECD instrument groups 12 principles under 3 pillars: co-ordination, capacities and framework conditions.

- Pillar 1: Co-ordinate across governments and policy areas
    1. Invest using an integrated strategy tailored to different places.
    2. Adopt effective co-ordination instruments across levels of government.
    3. Co-ordinate across subnational governments to invest at the relevant scale.
- Pillar 2: Strengthen capacities and promote policy learning across levels of government
    4. Assess upfront long-term impacts and risks.
    5. Encourage stakeholder involvement throughout the investment cycle.
    6. Mobilise private actors and financing institutions.
    7. Reinforce the expertise of public officials and institutions.
    8. Focus on results and promote learning.
- Pillar 3: Ensure sound framework conditions at all levels of government
    9. Develop a fiscal framework adapted to the objectives pursued.
    10. Require sound, transparent financial management.
    11. Promote transparency and strategic use of procurement.
    12. Strive for quality and consistency in regulatory systems across levels of government

Source: OECD (2014c), Effective Public Investment Across Levels of Government Toolkit, www.oecd.org/effective-public-investment-toolkit.

The first pillar focuses on co-ordination, which tends to include complex interactions between public and private actors. This complexity can generate gaps and duplication in investment between levels of government (Charbit and Michalun, 2009). In adapting the new regional paradigm for Peru, co-ordination mechanisms will need to be taken into account. OECD countries have set up a range of different mechanisms to co-ordinate investment at a regional level. This will be important for Peru as adapting national diversification policies to the place where they are applied strongly increases the chances of them working. Canada and France have both introduced place-based approaches to the delivery of industry and innovation policies.

Box 2.3. Investing using an integrated strategy tailored to different places: The cases of Canada and France

Canada

Regional development agencies (RDAs) across Canada help to address key economic challenges by providing regionally tailored programmes, services, knowledge and expertise that: 1) build on regional and local economic assets and strengths; 2) support business growth, productivity and innovation; 3) help small and medium-sized enterprises (SMEs) effectively compete in the global marketplace; 4) provide adjustment assistance in response to economic downturns and crises; and 5) support communities.

The RDAs continue to promote the importance of innovation and skills for regional development. For example:

- Western Economic Diversification Canada launched the Western Innovation Initiative (WINN), a CAD 100 million five-year federal initiative that offers repayable contributions for SMEs to move their new and innovative technologies from the later stages of research and development to the marketplace.
- Federal Economic Development Agency for Southern Ontario's (FedDev Ontario) Southern Ontario Prosperity Initiatives focus on innovation, productivity and economic diversification; additionally, the agency's Advanced Manufacturing Fund is a USD 200 million fund to support product and process innovation in the manufacturing sector.
- Atlantic Canada Opportunities Agency provides approximately CAD 90 million annually to support innovation and commercialisation under its current programmes, including the Atlantic Innovation Fund and the Business Development Program.

France

France introduced competitiveness poles in 2004. A *pôle de compétitivité* brings together large and small firms, research laboratories and educational establishments, all working together in a specific region to develop synergies and co-operative efforts. Other partners may be brought in, such as public authorities, either local or national, as well as firms providing business services. Although there are 71 poles, including 5 designated in 2007, project selection has channelled most funding to relatively few. Sixteen poles are of international rank, while the rest have a national or regional focus.

In an evaluation report in June 2008, the networking, SME involvement and visibility of the poles were viewed positively, but there were some concerns about their different performances. Responding to this concern, it was recommended that 39 poles be extended unconditionally for 3 years, 19 be extended for 3 years but subject to a funding review after 18 months, and 13 be evaluated after one year. The strategic approach to the poles will be consolidated via new "performance contracts" and the new calls in the field of eco-technologies.

Sources: OECD (2007a), *Linking Regions and Central Governments: Contracts for Regional Development*, http://dx.doi.org/10.1787/9789264008755-en; www.feddevontario.gc.ca/eic/site/723.nsf/eng/01690.html; OECD (2014a), *OECD Regional Outlook 2014: Regions and Cities, Where Policies and People Meet*, http://dx.doi.org/10.1787/9789264201415-en; OECD (2010c), *Regional Development Policies in OECD Countries*, http://dx.doi.org/10.1787/9789264087255-en; and www.datar.gouv.fr.

The second pillar of the principles focuses on core capacities for public investment, notably at subnational level, and the need to promote policy learning at all levels of government. Co-ordination is a necessary condition but not sufficient to achieve successful public investments. If capacities to design and implement investment strategies are weak, co-ordination mechanisms will not be sufficient to produce good outcomes. A key element for Peru will be how to more effectively engage the private sector and other non-governmental actors throughout the policy and investment cycle. This will help to build continuity in policies, and capability at a subnational level.

Box 2.4. Encouraging stakeholder involvement throughout the investment cycle: The cases of Denmark and Slovenia

Denmark

In 2007, Denmark sought to promote greater efficiency as well as a more regional approach through municipal reform. Fourteen counties were restructured into 5 regions, and 271 municipalities reduced to 98. As part of the reform process, each region was required to appoint at least one regional growth forum to guide regional business development strategies and the use of associated regional and EU Structural Funds. By law, the 20-member public-private boards include regional and municipal elected officials, business persons, representatives of the higher education and research community, and trade unions. Members are appointed by the regional council upon recommendation by the municipalities and social partners. They meet four to six times a year and are supported by the regional administration.

Slovenia

In 2011, Slovenia enhanced the participation of stakeholders in Development Regional Council. The 2011 law reorganised regional development councils and regional councils, which are combined to form a development region council in order to rationalise their activities and costs. Membership consists of representatives of municipalities (40%), economic associations – such as chambers of commerce or craft (30%), and non-governmental organisations (30%).

Sources: OECD (2012b), *OECD Reviews of Regional Innovation: Central and Southern Denmark 2012*, http://dx.doi.org/10.1787/9789264178748-en; OECD (2011c), *OECD Territorial Reviews: Slovenia 2011*, http://dx.doi.org/10.1787/9789264120587-en.

The third pillar of the principles provides a macro perspective on the key framework governance conditions for public investment. Strong framework conditions are pre-requisites for good investments. If framework conditions are weak, efforts to strengthen co-ordination and (subnational) capacities may miss part of their targets. Many of the framework conditions for effective public investment are usually largely the responsibility of national governments, but not solely, as in many cases subnational governments have an explicit role (OECD, 2014a). Lessons for improving the overall system of public investments could be drawn from countries such as Australia or Sweden (Box 2.5).

Assessing the Peruvian framework for regional development

The analysis in the previous section highlights some important insights and lessons from good practices across the OECD for Peru. The first is that regions are important to national growth and there is variation in the drivers of growth at a regional level. Secondly, regions are increasingly important to the design and execution of sectoral and innovation policies. Thirdly, this depends on reforms to public governance and fiscal arrangements, particularly at a subnational level. This includes how policies are co-ordinated, capabilities are built and the adaptation of fiscal frameworks to policy goals. This section assesses how these elements are reflected in the national policy framework for regional development.

Box 2.5. Developing a fiscal framework adjusted to the objectives perused: The cases of Australia and Sweden

Australia

In 2008, the Council of Australian Governments (COAG) agreed to a new Intergovernmental Agreement on Federal Financial Relations. This agreement increased the financial autonomy of the states, moving from input control to the monitoring of outputs, and rationalising the payments made to the state into five broad areas (health, affordable housing, early childhood and schools, vocational education and training, and disability services). Each of these payment areas are funded by a special purpose payment, distributed to the states on an equal per capita basis (there is no need to adapt the amounts to the needs and costs of each state, as this is done by the Commonwealth Grants Commission). For each of these payment areas, a mutually agreed national agreement clarifies the roles and responsibilities that will guide the Commonwealth and the states in the delivery of services across the relevant sectors and covers the objectives, outcomes, outputs and performance indicators for each special purpose payment. The performance of all governments in achieving mutually agreed outcomes and benchmarks specified in each special purpose payment is then monitored by the independent COAG Reform Council (CRC) and publicly reported on an annual basis

Sweden

The National Reform Programme connected to the Europe 2020 targets emphasises a growth friendly fiscal policy while preserving sound public finances. Returning to surplus is vital for protecting jobs and welfare in a small open economy such as Sweden's. The 290 municipalities throughout Sweden also work on many fronts and within many of their core activities on measures that can be linked to the Europe 2020 objectives. In a majority of regional councils, municipalities have also integrated the targets of the strategy into their operational plans and budgets and defined measurable indicators.

Local governments have recently developed new fiscal instruments to better support environmental objectives – and indirectly regional development, through increased focus on public transport. Sweden is one of the few countries with carbon emissions below the level recorded in 1990. One of the best-known examples is Stockholm's congestion tax, implemented in 2007, which has decreased traffic to and from the city centre by 20%. Combined with many other proactive policies to combat climate change, this has made Stockholm one of the most advanced cities in terms of climate change policies; it was named European Green Capital 2010.

Sources: OECD (2010a), *OECD Reviews of Regulatory Reform: Australia 2010*, http://dx.doi.org/10.1787/9789264067189-en; OECD (2014c), Effective Public Investment Across Levels of Government Toolkit, www.oecd.org/effective-public-investment-toolkit; OECD (2010b), *OECD Territorial Reviews: Sweden 2010*, http://dx.doi.org/10.1787/9789264081888-en.

Peru has established a national planning system across levels of government, however, it is not effectively integrated with the fiscal framework and measures to build the capability of subnational governments

Over the last decade the Peruvian government has invested in improving its strategic planning capabilities. In 2008, the National Strategic Planning System (SINAPLAN) and its National Strategic Planning Centre (CEPLAN) as its governing and guiding body were created. CEPLAN is integrated within the Presidency of the Council of Ministers (PCM), and its role is codified in the Law on the Creation of the National System of Strategic Planning (SINAPLAN) and CEPLAN (Legislative Decree 1088). Under this law, the two main functions of CEPLAN are to:

1. formulate and disseminate a shared vision of the future of the country in the different levels and sectors of the general government, through the elaboration and update of the National Strategic Development Plan (PEDN in Spanish)
2. regulate the strategic planning process in all public sector entities.

Box 2.6. Importance of planning to national growth and development

It is widely accepted that the quality of public institutions is a key factor in explaining long-term differences in productivity and GDP per capita (see McLean, 2013; Gill et al., 2014). These institutions provide the foundation for implementing sound fiscal policies to manage the risks such as price fluctuations associated with resource-based economies (Ahrend, 2006). Other key institutional factors include the effectiveness of regulation, and the quality of public services and infrastructure.

Delivering these outcomes requires public institutions which can prioritise and co-ordinate a range of different policy instruments. In this sense, the capability to develop clear policy frameworks and having the mechanisms to link them to legislative and budgetary instruments is essential for economic growth and diversification.

The development experience across several OECD countries has shown that strategic planning at a national level can be important to the development process. Countries at certain levels of economic development can benefit from planning specially in the provision of basic public services and those that are essential for growth and diversification, such as schooling, infrastructure and creating the right framework for investments in innovation, as it has been the case for many years in France with the Commissariat au Plan.

Effective strategic planning can help solve co-ordination issues, externality issues, reduce asymmetries of information, socialise part of the costs of discovery, contribute to the better functioning of markets, and create new markets where there are no markets. The two latter elements contribute improvements in the allocation of resources once markets function. Planning agencies have also shown to be successful at increasing production levels and productivity in certain sectors such as agriculture, as was the case, for example, in India with the Green Revolution during the 1950s and 1960s.

In terms of its regulatory role, CEPLAN undertakes a number different advisory and capability building functions. These roles focus on building strategic planning capability across different levels of government. However, CEPLAN does not have the capacity to enforce rules or use incentives to improve and align strategic planning across the national government, or with subnational governments. CEPLAN's current functions in relation to its regulatory role focus on the provision of technical advice:

- advising government entities (especially the PCM) and regional and local governments in the definition, monitoring and evaluation of policies and strategic development plans, to ensure coherency with the objectives of the PEDN
- developing methodologies and technical tools to ensure consistency in planning; it works to ensure the harmonious and sustained development of the country and strengthen democratic governance
- supporting professional development and technical training of specialists in strategic planning, forecasting, and in the definition and evaluation of public policies and plans at the three levels of government, including in higher education institutions
- monitoring and evaluating the government's strategic management capabilities and outcomes.

The strategic planning methodology established by CEPLAN utilises foresight techniques to establish scenarios and link them to clear objectives, progress measures and actions. This methodology is used to develop medium-term strategic policy frameworks at a national, regional and sectoral level. In turn, these are translated into shorter term organisational level planning. This methodology includes a result-based approach to planning. The different phases of the planning process are outlined in Box 2.7.

Box 2.7. Phases of the planning process established by CEPLAN

- Prospective analysis (foresight/horizon scanning): a conceptual model is defined in the directive to enable an understanding of the evolution of a sector or territory over a medium-term planning horizon. The environment is analysed to identify trends and other external factors; variables are identified, analysed and prioritised on the basis of which scenarios are built; an analysis of risks and opportunities is carried out. This generates futures scenarios for the National Strategic Development Plan's (PEDN) vision framed by a medium-term planning horizon. This activity is conducted using different tools:
  - definition of a conceptual model for understanding the sector or territory
  - environmental analysis identifying trends for the PEDN timeframe and other external factors
  - identification of variables through discussions with experts
  - prioritisation of strategic variables
  - diagnosis of variables and/or analysis of facts, for scenario building
  - analysis of risks and opportunities: definition of scenarios.
- Strategic phase: a central scenario for the PEDN timeframe is defined, with the vision, mission, strategic objectives, indicators actions and goals. Furthermore, articulation mechanisms are developed at the level of objectives and chain of strategic plans.
- Institutional phase: the institutional mission and strategic objectives are determined, together with their corresponding indicators and goals. Additionally, institutional strategic actions are identified, broken down into activities and linked to the public budgeting system.
- Monitoring phase: continuous monitoring of the pursuit of strategic objectives is performed through indicators in order to provide feedback to the planning process for the anticipation of risks and delays.

Source: Based on information from CEPLAN.

CEPLAN has also established a hierarchy which links national development planning to sectoral and regional plans. Each ministry is required to develop a sector-specific strategic plan (PESEM) which has a five-year planning horizon. Subnational governments are also required to develop the following strategic planning frameworks:

- Concerted regional development plan (PDRC): this document is prepared by the regional governments, using an eight-year planning horizon. It is put together during the strategic phase, taking into account the PEDN and PESEM objectives and the multi-year macroeconomic framework.
- Concerted local development plan: this document is prepared by local governments, also using an eight-year planning horizon. It is also put together during the strategic phase, taking into account the PEDN and PESEM objectives and the multi-year macroeconomic framework.

In terms of operationalising these planning frameworks, subnational governments are required to develop institutional plans which link strategic and organisation planning. The institutional strategic plan (PEI) has a three-year timeframe and is developed during the institutional phase of the planning process (as set out in Box 2.7). It develops the entity's strategic actions to achieve the goals set in the PDRC and/or in the PESEM. The institutional operational plan (POI) is also prepared by the public entities every year. It contributes to the management of the entity to achieve its strategic objectives.

This planning architecture establishes a framework to better align and co-ordinate national and regional planning, and link it with operational planning at an organisational level. The role of CEPLAN focuses on monitoring and evaluating these subnational planning frameworks in terms of their alignment with national and sectoral planning frameworks, and the articulation between objectives, indicators and targets within each plan. Although this quality assurance and advisory role is important, there is a gap between these plans and the fiscal framework.

One way to address this gap is by using outcomes set at a national or regional level to guide budget strategy and prioritisation. For example, New Zealand has gone down this reform path through its Better Services Initiative. This sets high-level results and targets for ministers and departments, which provide the basis for setting budget priorities and reporting progress. A rationale is provided for each of these result areas to explain why it is important to the country's future development, and each has a key indicator to monitor progress.

Another way is to embed longer term infrastructure planning into the fiscal framework. This can include requiring ministries and lower levels of government to complete capital investment and asset management plans. Asset management covers the life cycle of public investment and includes the planning, acquisition, operation and disposal of assets. Given the medium-term nature of public investment decisions, these plans should have a five- to ten-year time horizon. The completion of these plans can then be made a condition of allocating public funds for infrastructure.

Some jurisdictions have also developed mutually agreed funding agreements at a regional or city scale. For example, UK City Deals are used to link new spending to city productivity and growth, give local government greater autonomy and revenue-raising capacity, and incentivise governance reforms. Colombia has also gone down this reform path through its *contratos plans* (Box 2.8).

Peru has begun to develop mechanisms to better link public investment with outcomes. Traditionally, public budgeting across the OECD has been based on defined inputs (amount of capital investment or recurrent expenditure) with recent shifts over the past two decades toward accountability for specific outputs (e.g. the quantity and quality of services to be delivered). There has been a recent shift across the OECD toward budgeting for outcomes, for example, in terms of improving educational performance and reducing crime (Webber, 2004). The Results-Based Budgeting Initiative in Peru is consistent with these reform directions. However, it is a tool that focuses on individual budgeting programmes. A logical next step is to develop mechanisms to better link strategic planning with budget strategy and resource allocation (as outlined above).

Box 2.8. *Contratos plan* in Colombia

Colombia's *contratos plan* is a governance tool that helps align investment agendas at the national and local level, improving accountability and transparency and providing subnational authorities with capacity building. The contract is a binding agreement between the central government and a department, a group of departments or a group of municipalities. The parties commit to co-ordinate their investment agendas among sectors and across tiers of governments. In addition, they agree to deliver their interventions within a given timeline.

Colombia's negotiated territorial development is part of a broader national strategy whose aim is to create institutions and capacity that can support development policies. Contracts were introduced in 2012 by the national Law on Land Use (Ley Orgánica de Ordenamiento Territorial, LOOT) and by the National Development Plan 2010-14, *Prosperidad para Todos*. The LOOT is a key achievement for Colombia because it demonstrates that public authorities have regained control of the national territory after decades of conflict. Its intent is to improve Colombia's multi-level governance, and provides public authorities with flexible governance instruments to deliver policy interventions where they are needed the most. The *contrato plan* was instituted as a result of the 2011 reform of royalty payments. This important reform distributes revenues generated by extractive activities to all departments in the country. Subnational authorities can use this additional revenue to co-finance interventions listed in the contracts. Finally, contracts also connect with innovative approaches to rural development that seek to improve service delivery to poor households in remote communities.

As of 2013, seven *contrato plans* had been signed in Colombia, for a total (anticipated) investment of USD 6.7 billion, over five years. The policy affects almost 6 million citizens, most of whom live in rural/remote areas in nine departments. The contracts identify infrastructure, and in particular road connectivity, as their main objective. Basic services such as healthcare, education and water sanitation are also priorities. While these objectives are supported by national transfers earmarked by the central government to all departments and municipalities, the contracts add flexibility to the policy and allow subnational authorities to tailor action to their specific needs. In short, departments and municipalities have more funds, the possibility of co-ordinating different sources of investment from different levels of government (co-financing mechanisms) and improved capacity to promote development and fight poverty. Contracts are not a panacea in the Colombian context, but they have generated some positive results.

For instance, they have "reactivated" development planning at the department level. Department plans, in fact, identify measures to be taken within the contracts. Another key advantage is the opportunity for learning that the contracts provide departmental governments. They offer subnational authorities the possibility of working with national representatives as they execute the measures, including large infrastructure projects. In general, contracts are a first attempt in Colombia to connect spatial planning with development policy.

Source: OECD (2014b), *OECD Territorial Reviews: Colombia 2014*, http://dx.doi.org/10.1787/9789264224551-en.

The Ministry for Development and Social Inclusion (MIIDIS) has also followed that path with the elaboration of causal models – results chains, including both intermediate and immediate, and products that the state must deliver to achieve the results of each priority – based on evidence. These are important steps towards an intersectoral and intergovernmental articulated framework.

In order to make this link, the quality and consistency of strategic planning at a subnational level will need to be improved. Subnational planning frameworks are in their early days of development and implementation. To date, only twelve concerted regional development plans (in Amazonas, Ancash, Puno, Ayacucho, Ica, San Martín, Tacna, Ucayali, Huancavelica, Junín, Loreto and Moquegua) have been developed – with the methodology of developed by CEPLAN to articulate plans development plans.. No concerted local development plans have yet been developed. This indicates the early stage of implementation, and also variations in capability between different regional governments, and the lack of incentives for subnational governments to complete these plans.

Box 2.9. Results-oriented budgeting

Under the responsibility of the Ministry of Economy and Finance (MEF), results-oriented budgeting is being adopted to maintain fiscal discipline, improve efficiency in the distribution of resources and the quality of public spending, and ensure the operational effectiveness and efficiency of all entities and agencies.

According to General Law of the National Budget System, the results-oriented budget (PpR) is a public management strategy that links the allocation of resources to measurable outputs and outcomes in favour of the population. This is implemented by the MEF's Director General of the National Budget (DGPP) in four progressive stages: budget programmes, performance monitoring, independent evaluations and management incentives.

The directive distinguishes between two types of results:

- Specific result: change that solves an identified problem for the targeted population, which contributes to the achievement of the final result. Each budget programme only has one specific result.
- Final result: change in the conditions, quality or features inherent of an identified population, its environment or in the organisations that serve it. It corresponds with a national policy objective. It is worthwhile to note that the change in the final result may be influenced by exogenous factors and not only by the public policy.

In 2015, the DGPP approved the Directive 001-2015-EF on budget programme for the 2016 budget, which included an objective to improve the territorial articulation of the budget programmes.

A gradual and asymmetric approach (such as presented in Chapter 4) to integrating strategic planning and the fiscal framework must be taken, in order to build competencies at the subnational level and enable successful implementation. The task force (presented in Chapter 4) as well as the creation of institutional support capacity at macro-regional level could help subnational governments build more coherent plans with the national level that could be articulated to the budget. Linking strategic planning with the fiscal framework would create a greater incentive to produce coherent and actionable plans, and to develop a more strategic approach to public investment.

In addition, CEPLAN will need to be better resourced and have strengthened capacities to ensure co-ordination in the implementation of the National Strategic Planning System. There is a high degree of complexity associated with this system with strategic, operational and institutional plans at a national, sectoral, regional and local scale. It will be important to ensure planning cycles are aligned and feedback loops are in place, that plans are actionable and respond to changing circumstances. This also relates to ensuring the development of a more strategic role for the PCM as outlined in the OECD's *Public Governance Review of Peru* (OECD, 2016).

National planning provides a framework for regional policy in Peru, which is mainly associated with the old paradigm of regional policy

Approved in 2011 by Supreme Decree 054-PCM, the Plan Estratégico de Desarrollo Nacional (PEDN) is the long-term national development plan establishing priorities and progress measures over the next decade. It was conceived as an open and flexible tool, subject to ongoing improvement and updating. The PEDN reflects a participative process involving all levels of government, institutions and stakeholders, including public, online consultation and workshops.

In the context of the update of the PEDN, CEPLAN published a Methodological Guideline for the Update Process of the PEDN in 2014, with four specific issues:

1. the consolidation of growth with democracy and social inclusion
2. alignment of equal rights opportunities and social goals with the UN Millennium Goals
3. achievement of economic and social co-operation at the regional and local levels
4. attainment of an historical encounter with rural Peru.

The updated PEDN is organised around six pillars which each have a national strategic objective and corresponding indicator and target (Table 2.4).

Table 2.4. **The pillars of the national strategic plan**

Pillar	National strategic objective	Lead indicator	Source	Baseline	2016 target	2021 target
1	Effective exercise of human rights and dignity of persons with social inclusion from the poorest and most vulnerable part of the population	Human Development Indicator (HDI)	UNDP	0.737 (2013)	0.739	0.764
2	Guaranteeing access to quality services that will allow for the full development of the capacities and rights of the people, under fair and sustainable conditions	Multidimensional Poverty Indicator	UNDP	0.043 (2012)	0.040	0.018
3	Development and consolidation of democratic governance and of strong public institutions*	Government Effectiveness Indicator	World Bank	2.73 (2014)	2.90	3.03
4	Development of a diversified and sophisticated economy with sustainable growth in a decentralised structure, generating decent jobs	Per capita GDP	World Bank	9 875 (2014)	10 412	12 852
5	Territory knitted and organised in sustainable cities with guaranteed provision of quality infrastructure	Share in the departmental gross value added (except for Lima) *vis-à-vis* the total value	INEI	50.84 (2014)	50.71	51.30
6	Offers a global vision of the environmental performance of the country, efficient, responsible and sustainable use of biological diversity, ensuring adequate environmental quality for a healthy life of the people and a sustainable development of the country	Environmental Performance Indicator (EPI)**	Yale University	45.05 (2012)	46.37	49.06

Note: * The indicator has a range of values between -2.5 and 2.5. This has been rescaled to a range between 0 and 5: the lower value implies worse performance in this indicator, while 5 refers to the best performance.

Source: CEPLAN (2016), Proyecto del Plan estratégico de Desarrollo Nacional: Plan Bicentenario: El Perú hacia el 2021. Actualizado, http://www.ceplan.gob.pe/wp-content/uploads/2016/07/caratula-y-primeras-paginas.pdf.

The fifth objective of the PEDN is to pursue balanced regional development with the right infrastructure. This pillar of the plan is based on the realisation that there are disparities in population, poverty, economic activities and infrastructure within and between regions. The plan has led to the establishment of three priorities: 1) fostering investments in productive infrastructure and services required by the regions; 2) investing in activities that transform primary regional production, in a sustainable and competitive manner while creating jobs; and 3) reducing the dispersal of the population. The plan is then divided into four objectives declined in indicators and strategic actions. The four objectives are:

1. sufficient and adapted economic and productive decentralised public infrastructure in the macro-regional planning areas
2. diversified and high value-added production in the agrarian, fishery, mining and tourism sectors based on the comparative and competitive advantages of each region
3. strengthen job-creating decentralised private investments focused on responding to national and international demand
4. regroup rural population in rural intermediary cities established on the basis of planned population centres.

This regional development objective has introduced several elements of the new paradigm, such as planning based more on economic functional areas rather than on administrative regions, although the three macro-regions do not match the five economic corridors previously identified in the document. The PEDN also puts emphasis on the identification of regional assets, and focuses more on enabling factors rather than on the provision of sectoral subsidies or grants.

Despite the inclusion of these elements, the basis of the analysis that sets the focus for the policy strategies is still shaped by the old paradigm of compensating regions for disparities in income and well-being. Pursuing an objective of more balanced growth is difficult as disparities and inequalities in income and jobs tend to persist over time. The key is ensuring each region can maximise its endogenous growth potential by focusing on competitiveness and improving framework conditions.

The indicators and targets set by the PEDN also do not always seem to match the objective that they have been set to analyse, nor is there necessarily a strong link between the actions and the indicator. For example, the only indicator to measure the attainment of the third objective, that of "strengthening job-creating decentralised private investments", is the number of workers outside of Lima affiliated to the pension system. Although this indicator does encapsulate some important elements, such as the number of formal jobs created, it does not take into account the quality of employment, its productivity, whether it contributes to productive diversification, the place of the production in GVCs and the potential spillovers of these investments. Also, it removes Lima from the calculation, which, given its weight in the economy, should not be neglected, although it should probably be considered separately.

Another element of the old paradigm in this pillar of the PEDN is the weight given to hard infrastructure, and the lack of focus on soft infrastructure and its adaptation to the needs and circumstances of different regions. Furthermore, the indicators used to assess the advancement in the completion of the plan are related to the construction of infrastructure per se rather than its actual use and impact on the economic functions of the country. For example, more emphasis should be put on the connectivity and quality of the transport network.

Finally, although the plan seems to place a strong emphasis on the regional aspects, some governance instruments seem to be missing. For example, the plan mentions the three economic macro-regions, but when it comes to the strategic actions, their implementation seems to be based more on the administrative divisions of the country rather than on the potential economic corridors of the country or on the functional economic areas. Also, the realisation of the plan relies on national programmes, which have a strong top-down bias while also lacking an integrated approach. The new regional development paradigm puts strong emphasis on the need to provide both an integrated and bottom-up approach to realise the full benefits of public investments.

As mentioned above, the plan is also not clearly integrated in a systemic way with the fiscal framework at a national or subnational level. There are some linkages through the development of sectoral and institutional plans; however, these are designed at an organisational level, which would incentivise a fragmented approach to programme design and investment. There is a need for mechanisms that can link planning priorities to a programme of investment at a territorial scale, which involves multiple institutional actors. This approach is a key feature of the EU Cohesion Funds.

Box 2.10. **EU Cohesion Funds and integrated territorial investments**

Achieving more balanced and sustainable territorial development is a core objective of the European Union (EU). The overarching objective of European cohesion policy is to promote the harmonious development of the EU and its regions. It makes an important contribution to the strategic objectives of the Europe 2020 Strategy:

- smart growth, by increasing competitiveness, especially in less-developed regions
- inclusive growth, by promoting employment and improving people's well-being
- green growth, by protecting and enhancing environmental quality.

There are a number of different funds which support these objectives, including the European Regional Development Fund (ERDF), the European Social Fund (ESF) – the two "Structural Funds" – and the Cohesion Fund. The distribution of these funds is conditional upon regions developing strategies with clear performance and outcome measures.

Integrated territorial investments have recently been introduced as a governance instrument which allows EU member states to bundle funding from one or more EU programmes to ensure the implementation of an integrated strategy for a specific territory. This instrument provides a way of better linking planning with budgeting, and recognises that investments in infrastructure must be combined in an integrated way with investments in skills, innovation and economic development.

Source: European Urban Knowledge Network (2016), www.eukn.eu/events/policy-labs/integrated-territorial-approach/policies/eu-policies-and-tools-in-the-field-of-integrated-territorial-and-urban-strategies.

Concerted regional development plans are an important public policy innovation but require better integration at the national level and with fiscal frameworks

Concerted regional development plans are developed by the regional governments and are traditionally divided into five principal pillars, of which both an analysis of the current situation and based on those findings set priorities, objectives, targets, strategies and indicators. The five pillars are: social aspects (demography, poverty, education and health), environment, economy, infrastructure, and institutional management and governance.

Regional governments are required to involve local governments and civil society actors in the development of these plans. In the case of San Martín, these were the representatives of:

- the ten provincial municipalities of the region, the heads of specific projects (for example the Proyecto Especial Alto Mayo, the Proyecto Especial Huallaga Central Bajo Mayo and PROCEJA)
- "strategic allies" (GIZ, USAID-ProDecentralización) and national ministries and agencies (the MEF and INEI)
- representatives of the civil society (research centres and think tanks, non-governmental organisations, indigenous groups).

The inclusion of different levels of government, particularly the MEF (although it is not clear how this regional participation of the MEF is then co-ordinated centrally), is important in improving alignment and co-ordination. However, it is unclear how other ministries are integrated into these regional planning processes, and what role the PCM and CEPLAN play in terms of whole-of-government co-ordination. The co-ordinating role of these central agencies is important because it ensures input from all ministries.

The participation of members of the civil society is also good practice. Nonetheless, in that same example, there are no representatives of the business community on the planning committee, which is an important input, particularly to understand the bottlenecks and potential unexploited assets of the region. This has also been the case in the drafting of other concerted regional development plans, such as the one in Huancavelica. Business representation can be achieved through including representatives of industry associations in the decision-making process (such as chambers of commerce), and/or using workshops and surveys to engage directly with business owners.

The concerted regional development plans display different levels of quality and detail with some degree of alignment to contemporary OECD practices. Prioritising and executing policies based on functional economic areas is an important element of the new regional paradigm. Some plans, such as the one in San Martín, have identified economic corridors within the region. The region has identified natural and cultural resources, economic activities and human capital resources within each of these corridors. This analysis could be further improved with a more detailed assessment of the industry and business structure within these corridors and their position within global, national or regional value chains. This information would assist in designing initiatives to improve conditions for the private sector in the region.

Another feature that can be found in some of the plans is the use of SWOT analysis. Some of the plans have been able to identify the interdependencies between different pillars which may cause positive or negative externalities that need to be managed. This is important in terms of identifying policy complementarities and encouraging an integrated approach to regional development. Some elements of other pillars are also identified as influencing outcomes across different pillars, showing a more integrated vision of public policies. Nonetheless, this analysis is not applied consistently across the plans.

Despite showing slightly higher levels of integration in certain cases, most of the plans do not take into account the different sectoral plans and programmes of the national government. Furthermore, sectoral plans at a national level do not consistently account for the regional concerted plans. There is also a lack of consistency in how spatial issues are treated across these national planning frameworks. This is likely to reduce the scope for co-ordination between levels of government across different sectoral policies. Very few of the plans articulate how different levels of government will work together in an integrated way to achieve regional planning objectives.

There also appears to be a lack of collaboration and joint planning between different regional governments. The interdependencies between regions are not strongly identified, and the plans generally do not articulate how different regions will collaborate to achieve development objectives. This is particularly important in terms of planning in relation to supply chains, and also leveraging assets such as universities in neighbouring regions.

Much like in the case of the PEDN developed by CEPLAN, there are a certain number of mismatches between the chosen indicators to assess progress, the objectives that have been set, and the policies and programmes to be deployed in order to reach those objectives. Policies and initiatives identified in these plans tend to focus on individual policy areas, and very few are organised around broader outcomes that would require collaboration across different agencies and levels of government. It is also not clear how these planning priorities are considered systemically in the budget process at a regional, local or national level.

The concerted regional development plans also tend to have a bias towards the production of hard rather than soft infrastructure. A more inclusive process with national policy makers and the business community would assist in broadening the focus to other issues including skills development, market access and innovation.

Despite these issues concerted regional development plans are an important public policy innovation for Peru. They provide a platform for the further evolution of a contemporary approach to regional development policy. Some measures to improve the quality and effectives of these plans include:

- building the capability of regional governments to improve the quality of regional planning, and its integration with budgeting and resource allocation
- consideration of reforms to budgeting processes to enable a more integrated and multi-year approach to public investment at a regional scale (including linking transfers to regional and local planning frameworks)
- inclusion of a broader range of policy actors in the planning process (including national ministries, the private sector and other regions
- further analysis of the industry and business structure within regions at the scale of functional economic areas
- adjusting performance indicators so they better align with desired outcomes
- better integration of regional plans in the national planning cycle (and vice versa).

In sum, regional development is an important national policy priority; however, it is still largely informed by a logic of compensating regions for inequalities in income and well-being. The policy framework would benefit from a shift toward an approach based on regional competitiveness and unlocking growth potential. The concerted regional development plans are an important innovation and provide a platform for strengthening the role of regions in the design and delivery of national sectoral policies. However, these plans do not appear to be effectively linked or integrated with fiscal frameworks. The following section will assess national economic and industry policies and identify ways to improve this alignment and integration.

Macroeconomic policies and their impacts on regions

Peru has demonstrated a commitment to sound fiscal, monetary and trade policies over the past two decades

As outlined in Chapter 1, Peru has experienced strong economic growth and made significant advances in reducing poverty over the past two decades. This good performance was driven by a strong reform of both the fiscal and monetary framework since the 1990s, including the independence of the central bank in maintaining price stability, a commitment to fiscal discipline and open trade policies. These changes have been maintained across four different governments since 1990, despite strong ideological differences, showing a broad-based consensus over the need for good fiscal and monetary policies. These policy settings have allowed Peru to make the most of the favourable external conditions for its commodity-based industries, and the growth of the economy.

The improvement of the fiscal framework lies upon four important regulations. First, the 1993 law voted in Congress prohibiting the central bank from lending money to the central government, which limits the potential for over expansionary monetary policy. Second, the approval of the pension reform allowed to strongly limit fiscal gaps. Third, the Fiscal Responsibility Law voted in 1999 introduced controls over the public deficits. Finally, the 2013 approval of the new macro-fiscal framework inserting medium-term objectives in the fiscal framework limited the pro-cyclical effect of public spending over the cycle.

As a result, public deficits have been contained since the early 1990s. Since 1994, fiscal deficits have almost consistently been maintained below 3% of GDP, and since 2007 – aside from the 2008-09 period – Peru has achieved a fiscal surplus. This fiscal management has allowed Peru to significantly reduce its public debt levels as a proportion of GDP, which has allowed it to obtain an investment rating and to issue bonds in the national currency in international markets.

Figure 2.2. **Evolution of general government net debt, Peru and select countries**

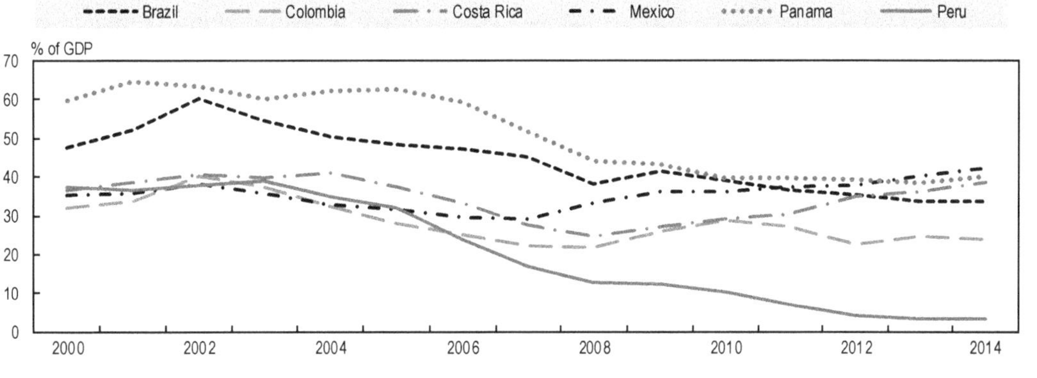

Source: OECD (2015a), *Multi-dimensional Review of Peru: Volume 1. Initial Assessment*, http://dx.doi.org/10.1787/9789264243279-en.

These fiscal reforms have been accompanied by a broad-based commitment to trade openness (Calero, 2006). Peru unilaterally removed tariff protections that were further progressed within the framework of the Uruguay Round of trade liberalisation during the 1990s (Reynoso, in Lengyel et al., 2003). In 1990, average tariff barriers were set at 66%

and applied rates ranged from 0% to 110% with a standard deviation of 25%. By 1997, the average tariff rate had dropped to 13.2%, the standard deviation remained at 3% and the effective rate of protection was estimated to be at around 15%. All restrictions to exports, export subsidies and export taxes were removed in 1991. Only a 15% drawback was installed for exported products. These policies have continued since the early 2000s with bilateral free trade agreements and further reductions in trade barriers (De la Flor in Perales and Morón, 2010).

In addition to reducing barriers to trade, the government has funded programmes to attract investment and facilitate access to markets. This includes the Commission for the Promotion of Exports (2006), and two export processing zones (Reynoso, in Lengyel et al., 2003 and UNCTAD, 2000). Fiscal benefits have been provided to attract investments and to support exports via COFIDE, which is Peru's development bank. Other significant changes came from the creation of PROINVERSION in 2002, a governmental body in charge of attracting foreign direct investment (FDI), and also of government export support agencies such as Sierra Exportadora (see Chapter 3).

Economic openness has enabled the diversification of exports and the further development of an internal market

These policies have helped Peru to diversify its export basket both in terms of products and destination. New products such as chemicals, new agricultural types of exports or metal-mechanic, that are considered as non-traditional export (all products that were not exported before the 1990s) have increased at a faster rate than traditional exports (from a low base). Agricultural goods have managed to diversify (including the development of the so-called "non-traditional" agricultural exports – see Chapter 3) and significantly increase in real terms. The other main beneficiary has been the textile industry, despite its relatively low weight, real term values have gone from USD 0.4 billion to almost USD 2 billion. Finally, despite their small size, some new types of exports, such as chemicals, have emerged.

Nonetheless, the evolution remains very slow compared to the weight of traditional exports in the overall basket (Illescas and Jaramillo, 2011). This is a particularly relevant point because export diversification has been associated in the literature with increased growth levels, and higher investment levels due to the reduction of income instability (Gutierrez de Piñeres and Ferrantino, 2000; Haussmann, 2008).

Furthermore, the diversification of the export basket is not only very limited, but it is concentrated in products with very low sophistication levels. In 2013, 9% of the exports were low-technology products and only 3% were medium-technology products. The complexity of the export basket, computed by the economy complexity indicator (ECI),[1] remains low. Moreover, it participates in GVCs at the lower end of supply chains, mainly by providing primary products to other countries (OECD, 2015a).

In terms of the domestic market, private consumption has been one of the fundamental drivers of Peruvian growth over the past decade. This is closely related to the development and strengthening a new middle class (OECD, 2015a; Ernst & Young, 2014). During the 2002-05 period, exports also acted as a locomotive, strongly contributing to GDP growth. Nonetheless, since 2006, their contribution to growth has been negative for several years and investments have provided the main driver. The decreased contribution of exports to growth is due to the fall in commodity prices, but also, and most importantly, to the fact that imports have continued growing faster than exports. Since then, investments have been driven both by public sector investments, namely related to the royalty system of the country, but also to attraction of both national and foreign direct investments in the mining, construction and service sectors. However, this investment is still related to the commodity price cycle, and decoupling the two will ensure more sustainable growth in the future, which relates back to the need to continue to grow the internal market.

Figure 2.3. **Economic complexity indicator (ECI)**

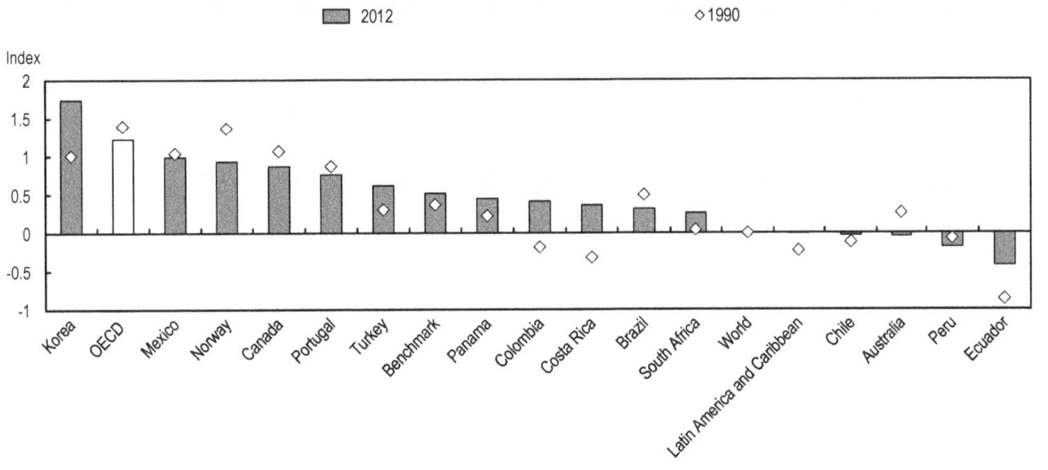

Source: OECD (2015a) based on Hausmann, R. et al. (2012), *The Atlas of Economic Complexity*.

Peru's geography is complex and these macroeconomic policies have different impacts across the economic landscape

These macroeconomic and trade policies have enabled Peru's economy to focus on core areas of comparative advantage and specialisation in terms of commodity production and associated manufacturing. In addition, this flow of income into the economy has seen the expansion and growth of the services sector. These policies have not been spatially neutral, and would have different regional impacts. A better understanding of Peru's economic geography and integrating this with macroeconomic and sectoral policies would help maximise the endogenous growth potential of Peru's regions. The following section provides an overview of Peru's industrial geography and draws some initial conclusions about the productive fabric of the country.

Regions specialise in different tradeable activities, with manufacturing and mining concentrated in a small number of places

Locational quotients can be used to reveal sectoral specialisations between regions by comparing a region's business composition to the national level. A number higher than one indicates a specialisation in a particular economic activity. The analysis of employment in key tradeable sectors reveals a number of key patterns:

- Agriculture is an important industry to a majority of regions with 14 having a specialisation in this sector in terms of employment. It is particularly important to some of the poorest regions in Peru in the highlands and rainforest. Fishing is an important industry for regions in the coastal areas and the rainforest (Loreto, Madre de Dios and Ucayali).

- As outlined in Chapter 1, the GVA of the mining industry is concentrated in a small number of regions (with Áncash, Arequipa, Cajamarca and Cusco producing slightly over 50% of the national GVA in mining). Nine regions indicate a specialisation in mining employment, and this does not include Áncash and Cajamarca, which may indicate the presence of informal mining in some of these areas.
- Manufacturing employment is concentrated in relatively fewer areas. Only four regions indicate a specialisation in this activity: Callao, Lima, Arequipa and La Libertad. These are all coastal regions with larger urban areas.

Table 2.5. **Regional specialisation, key traded sectors, 2013 (employment)**

Department	Agriculture	Fishing	Mining	Manufacturing
Amazonas	2.4	0.2	0.4	0.4
Áncash	1.5	2.7	0.7	0.7
Apurímac	2.4	0.0	0.7	0.2
Arequipa	0.5	1.2	3.2	1.2
Ayacucho	2.2	...	0.4	0.4
Cajamarca	2.3	...	1.0	0.9
Callao	0.0	0.7	0.5	1.6
Cusco	1.6	0.0	0.5	0.8
Huancavelica	2.7	0.7	2.2	0.3
Huánuco	2.1	...	0.5	0.6
Ica	0.7	2.2	1.5	1.0
Junín	1.5	0.0	2.1	0.9
La Libertad	1.0	0.3	1.2	1.2
Lambayeque	0.9	3.0	0.2	0.9
Lima	0.1	0.2	0.5	1.4
Loreto	1.1	4.7	0.2	0.5
Madre de Dios	0.9	1.3	5.1	0.6
Moquegua	1.0	2.5	2.2	0.7
Pasco	1.8	0.3	4.1	0.4
Piura	1.1	3.8	0.6	0.9
Puno	1.7	0.3	3.5	0.9
San Martín	1.9	0.2	0.2	0.5
Tacna	0.6	1.0	0.9	0.6
Tumbes	0.4	7.8	0.0	0.7
Ucayali	0.9	2.5	0.4	1.0

Source: OECD elaboration based on data from INEI.

This analysis is useful for understanding the relative importance of these industries at a regional level. However, it does not indicate the contribution that these industries make to the national economy. The relative contribution that different areas make to total industry value added generates a different picture about the economic geography of the country, and reveals the significant inequalities and differences between regions.

In terms of manufacturing, Lima and Callao contributed 59% national GVA for this sector in 2013. Five regions in the coastal regions with larger cities (Ica, Piura, Moquegua, La Libertad and Arequipa) contributed another quarter of national manufacturing GVA. The remaining 15% is spread across 18 regions.

Figure 2.4. **Regional contribution to manufacturing value added, 2013**

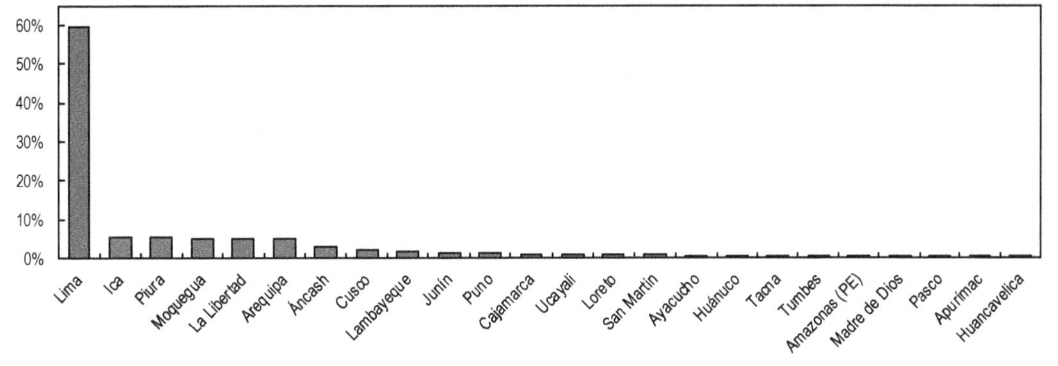

Source: INEI (n.d), http://www.inei.gob.pe.

In relation to agriculture, forestry and fishing, the distribution is more even, which indicates the role that rural regions also play in this sector. Lima is still the largest contributor to national GVA in this sector with 16%. Another 30% comes from the contribution of the coastal regions of La Libertad, Piura, Ica and Arequipa. However, there are a number of rural regions which also make a significant contribution given their relative share of the national population and economy. This includes Puno (6%), Cajamarca (5%) and Junín (5%).

Figure 2.5. **Regional contribution to agriculture, forestry and fishing value added, 2013**

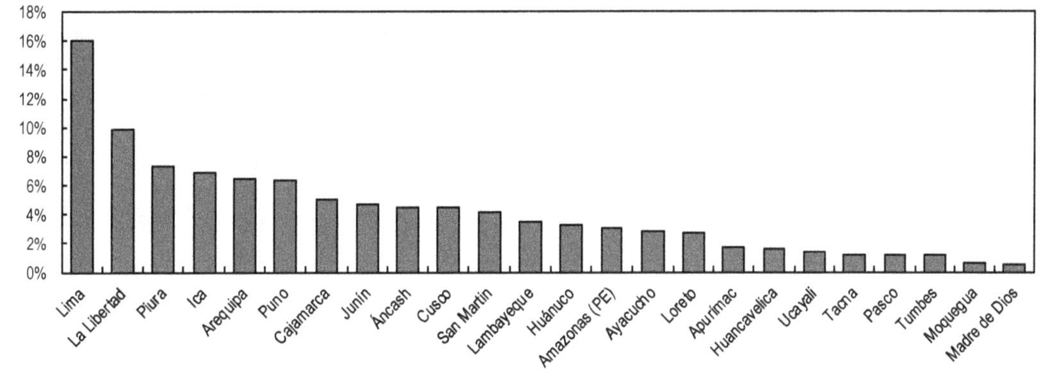

Source: INEI (n.d), http://www.inei.gob.pe.

In relation to mining, the proportion of the overall labour force employed in this activity is low (under 1.5% nationally). However, mining can have an important impact in terms of related activities such as construction, accommodation and food services, equipment and maintenance, and transportation. In Peru, an important aspect is economic activity associated with the construction phase of mining projects, with large differences at different time periods between regions.

The non-traded sector is more evenly spread across regions, with the vast proportion of high value-added activities located in Lima

The services sector, which is predominantly non-traded, will become more important to the economic development of Peru as the economy transitions away from a growth dynamic driven by high commodity prices. These services sectors are relatively evenly distributed, with the exception of "real estate and rental services" and "other services", which are relatively more important for Lima-Callao and the secondary city of Arequipa. Hotels and restaurants is a key sector because it is also associated with the tourism industry, and is relatively more important for the coastal regions of Arequipa, Ica, Tacna and Tumbes; and the rainforest regions of Madre de Dios, Ucayali and Loreto.

Box 2.11. The importance of mining investments at a regional level

The previous section has shown the importance of the contribution of investments for Peru's growth in recent times. These investments are particularly significant contributors for growth, at least in the short term in regions where they take place. Cusco, Arequipa and Apurímac attracted the biggest share of mining investments in 2014 but flows of investments per region show significant levels of volatility. Also, some regions have been deeply hit by social unrest because of mining projects, such as Conga. Those regions have seen decreasing levels of investment in the mining sector. The question of the long-term positive impact of these investments for the regions and municipalities where they take place still remains in most cases due to the lack of connection of the mining firms with the local economy (Natural Resource Governance Institute, 2015).

Table 2.6. **Investments in mining per region**

Million USD

Region	2005	2006	2007	2008	2009	2010	2011	2012	2013	2014	Total
Arequipa	338	649	208	229	566	559	484	745	1 395	2 024	7 197
Amazonas	1	3	13	1	2	8	13	7	9	2	59
Áncash	47	64	56	100	137	464	823	914	732	493	3 830
Apurímac	22	32	34	8	18	12	838	1 056	1 745	1 677	5 442
Ayacucho	0	2	10	9	37	70	93	103	89	63	476
Cajamarca	4	149	274	361	283	555	1 437	1 303	579	349	5 294
Callao	0	0	0	0	0	0	0	0	0	0	0
Cusco	183	248	282	331	367	684	681	460	1 173	1 312	5 721
Huancavelica	25	30	42	81	72	96	107	138	101	65	757
Huánuco	0	0	0	0	5	9	26	26	24	19	109
Ica	5	2	1	42	19	38	110	179	98	97	591
Junín	16	19	21	46	80	143	960	1 469	1 524	688	4 966
La Libertad	65	81	83	114	210	270	399	679	632	523	3 056
Lambayeque	0	0	0	0	0	0	0	0	2	0	2
Lima	35	46	50	79	270	309	289	286	299	318	1 981
Madre de Dios	0	0	0	0	1	2	4	17	19	1	44
Moquegua	261	197	62	88	74	128	240	309	373	363	2 095
Pasco	20	32	47	123	270	359	319	381	572	367	2 490
Piura	0	0	0	2	263	226	167	71	49	41	819
Puno	3	0	1	9	30	50	100	149	102	75	519
San Martín	0	0	0	0	0	0	0	0	0	0	0
Tacna	61	57	65	86	116	88	152	210	207	174	1 216
Total	1 086	1 610	1 249	1 708	2 822	4 069	7 243	8 503	9 727	8 654	46 671

Source: Ministerio de Energía y Minas (2015), Anuario Estadístico Minero 2014, http://www.mem.gob.gt/wp-content/uploads/2015/06/ANUARIO-ESTAD%C3%8DSTICO-MINERO-2014.pdf.

Table 2.7. **Regional specialisation, select non-traded sectors, 2013 (employment)**

Department	Construction	Hotels and restaurants	Real estate and rental	Transport and communications	Education	Other services
Amazonas	0.8	0.4	0.3	0.6	1.1	0.5
Áncash	1.1	0.9	0.5	0.9	1.1	0.6
Apurímac	0.7	0.6	0.2	0.4	1.0	0.4
Arequipa	1.4	1.4	1.1	1.0	1.1	1.0
Ayacucho	0.7	0.8	0.2	0.5	0.9	0.5
Cajamarca	0.8	0.5	0.3	0.5	0.9	0.4
Callao	1.2	1.0	2.1	1.5	1.2	1.5
Cusco	0.8	1.0	0.5	0.6	0.9	0.6
Huancavelica	0.4	0.5	0.1	0.2	0.6	0.3
Huánuco	0.7	0.8	0.3	0.8	1.0	0.6
Ica	1.2	1.3	0.9	1.3	1.0	1.0
Junín	0.8	1.0	0.7	0.8	0.9	0.7
La Libertad	1.2	1.1	0.9	0.9	0.9	0.9
Lambayeque	1.0	1.1	0.6	1.3	1.0	1.1
Lima	1.1	1.1	1.9	1.3	1.2	1.5
Loreto	0.9	1.4	0.6	1.1	1.0	0.9
Madre de Dios	0.8	1.6	0.6	1.4	0.7	0.7
Moquegua	1.3	1.0	0.9	0.9	1.1	0.7
Pasco	1.1	0.7	0.6	0.5	1.0	0.7
Piura	0.8	0.9	0.6	1.0	0.8	0.9
Puno	0.8	0.6	0.4	0.7	0.8	0.6
San Martín	0.9	0.9	0.3	0.7	1.0	0.7
Tacna	1.1	1.2	0.9	1.0	1.1	0.9
Tumbes	0.9	1.4	0.9	1.8	1.1	1.0
Ucayali	0.9	1.7	0.5	1.3	0.9	0.8

Source: OECD analysis based on data from INEI.

The relative dominance and the economic role and functions of Lima and Callao are revealed in the contribution that these regions make to national GVA in select service sectors. Lima and Callao contributed close to half (48%) of total national industry GVA in 2013. These regions contributed 57% to the distributive trade, transport, accommodation and food services sector in 2013, which indicates the important transport and logistics role of the capital in the national economy. Lima is also a key financial and business service centre for the country. The vast majority of value added from the financial and insurance sector (80%) and professional services (69%) are generated in the capital.

A key feature of business clustering in Peru is the diversity across different regions

In recent years, substantial policy attention has been placed on the development of business clusters (Consorcio Cluster Development 2013 – *Directorio Nacional de Empresas Manufactureras* 2012 de PRODUCE). Supporters of a cluster-based approach view it as a tool to encourage value-added upgrading within existing clusters, to promote spillovers and synergies to upgrade local economies, to attract FDI and facilitate integration with the global economy, and to engage the private sector in more effective collaboration with government at the national and regional level (Porter, 2009).

Figure 2.6. **Regional contribution to distributive trade, transport, accommodation and food services value added, 2013**

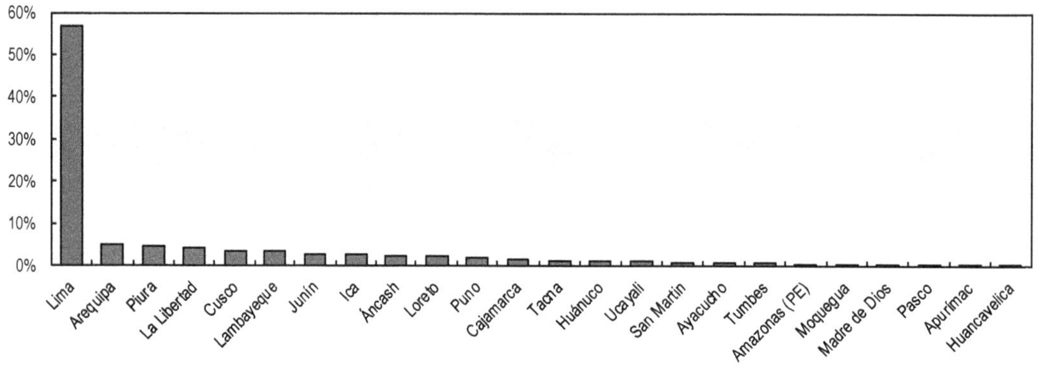

Source: OECD analysis based on data from INEI.

Figure 2.7. **Proportion of key business services located in Lima-Callao, 2013 (value added)**

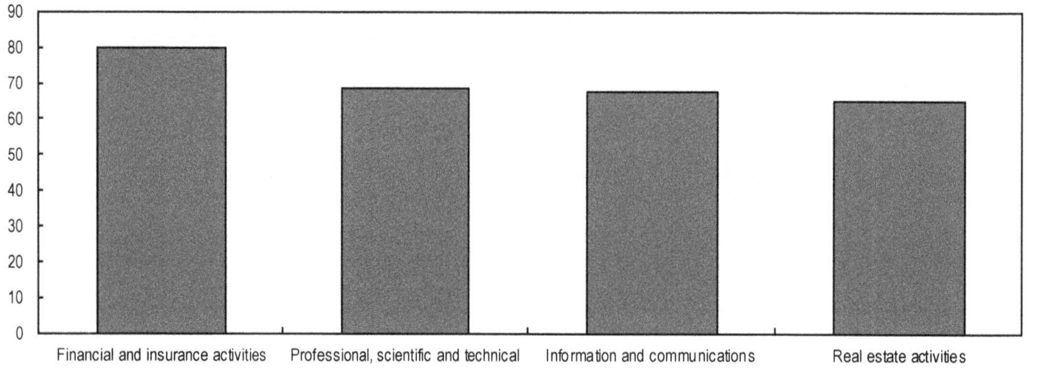

Source: OECD analysis based on data from INEI.

An analysis of clusters, however, is limited by the lack of quality and timely business statistics and business performance indicators. Addressing this information gap would improve the quality of strategic planning and programme design at a national and regional level in Peru. This information gap is not surprising as the geolocation of business micro data and implementation of consistent business demography statistics remains a major challenge across OECD countries.

In 2013, the total number of businesses (*empresas*) including large, medium, small and micro businesses was estimated at nearly 1.5 million (SUNAT/PRODUCE – DIGECOMTE). In Peru, microenterprises are defined as having 1-10 employees, small ones 11-50 employees, medium ones 51-200 employees and large ones 200 or more (IFC, 2016).

Compared to OECD averages, Peru has a slightly higher proportion of microenterprises (94.6% in Peru compared with 92.4% across the OECD), and a slightly lower proportion of small and medium-sized businesses (4.8% in Peru compared with 7% in the OECD; OECD, 2015a). Nearly half of all businesses (47.9%) are concentrated in the department of Lima, which reflects its share of the economy. Lima also has a higher proportion of large business (0.82% compared to the national average of 0.55%). This pattern is not repeated for secondary cities (except for Piura), which again reinforces the relative importance of Lima to the national economy.

Table 2.8. **Business by size and department, 2013**

In percent

	Large	Medium	Small	Micro
Amazonas	0.19	0.17	3.4	96.2
Áncash	0.18	0.08	3.6	96.1
Apurímac	0.15	0.08	2.7	97.0
Arequipa	0.33	0.12	3.9	95.6
Ayacucho	0.20	0.07	3.5	96.2
Cajamarca	0.24	0.12	3.8	95.8
Cusco	0.19	0.06	2.7	97.0
Huancavelica	0.08	0.02	2.1	97.8
Huánuco	0.24	0.08	3.3	96.4
Ica	0.34	0.09	4.1	95.5
Junín	0.18	0.09	2.7	97.0
La Libertad	0.28	0.11	3.8	95.8
Amazonas	0.24	0.10	3.1	96.6
Lambayeque	0.46	0.14	5.1	94.3
Lima	0.82	0.23	5.8	93.2
Loreto	0.61	0.19	4.4	94.8
Madre de Dios	0.19	0.05	2.4	97.3
Moquegua	0.14	0.06	3.4	96.4
Pasco	0.30	0.10	3.7	95.9
Piura	0.72	0.17	4.5	94.6
Puno	0.28	0.10	3.4	96.2
San Martín	0.27	0.09	3.7	95.9
Tacna	0.24	0.09	2.9	96.8
Tumbes	0.22	0.12	3.0	96.6
Ucayali	0.42	0.21	4.7	94.7
Peru	0.55	0.17	4.6	94.6

Source: OECD analysis based on data from INEI.

Data from the national household survey (ENAHO) suggest that the share of employment in larger enterprises (with 51 employees or more) has grown over time. This growth was countered by a progressive decline of employment in smaller enterprises. There are eight regions that have increased the proportion of employment in larger businesses, including some predominantly rural and poorer regions. These regions are: Amazonas, Apurímac, Cajamarca, Ica, Huánuco, Cusco, San Martín and La Libertad.

The number and type of businesses are distributed unevenly across departments, reflecting specialisation in different sectors and the scale of the regional economy. These data reveal the relative importance of clusters of businesses for different regions, such as fishing in Áncash and Pasco; mining in Loreto and Arequipa; and manufacturing in Lima, Arequipa and Junín.

In sum, the analysis reveals the diversity of economic specialisation between regions, and the importance of clusters of small firms to industry performance in Peru. The key feature of Peru's industrial geography is the dominant role of Lima in the national economy. In terms of the export sector, the majority of the country's manufacturing sector is located in the capital. Lima is also the major transport and logistics hub of the country through which most of the goods and services essential for the economy flow. Lima also plays a key role in terms of providing high-value business services to other sectors in terms of finance, insurance, professional, scientific and technical services. The analysis also reveals that there are other urban hubs in the country which also play this role at a much smaller scale, in particular within the regions of Arequipa, Cusco, La Libertad and Piura.

Table 2.9. **Distribution of enterprises by major sector and department, 2013**

In percent

	Agriculture	Fishing	Mining	Construction	Manufacturing	Commerce	Services	Total
Amazonas	1.0	0.2	0.3	**1.2**	0.4	0.5	0.6	0.6
Áncash	**3.8**	**11.1**	**3.9**	**9.4**	1.9	2.7	2.8	2.9
Apurímac	0.7	0.1	**1.1**	0.5	0.6	0.7	1.0	0.8
Arequipa	**7.8**	1.4	**9.3**	4.4	**5.9**	**5.8**	5.4	5.6
Ayacucho	0.7	0.8	0.5	**1.6**	0.6	0.9	**1.4**	1.1
Cajamarca	**2.6**	0.3	1.0	**4.6**	1.7	2.0	**2.2**	2.1
Callao	2.7	0.4	1.9	2.1	3.0	**4.0**	**4.2**	3.9
Cusco	0.4	**0.5**	**0.8**	**1.1**	0.3	0.4	0.4	0.4
Huancavelica	**2.0**	0.3	**1.4**	**2.4**	1.2	**1.4**	1.2	1.3
Huánuco	**3.4**	2.3	**5.1**	**3.0**	1.4	**2.9**	2.3	2.6
Ica	**4.6**	1.7	**3.7**	**4.8**	3.1	**3.7**	3.5	3.6
Junín	**8.1**	1.9	**7.2**	8.6	**5.4**	5.4	4.6	5.2
La Libertad	**5.6**	**5.5**	0.6	2.1	2.8	3.8	3.3	3.5
Lima	22.4	26.3	36.7	36.8	**56.3**	47.1	**49.0**	47.9
Lambayeque	**5.2**	**2.6**	0.6	2.2	1.2	**1.8**	1.7	1.7
Loreto	5.6	0.3	13.5	0.1	0.4	0.6	0.5	0.7
Madre de Dios	0.2	1.1	0.6	0.4	0.4	0.7	0.8	0.7
Moquegua	1.5	0.5	1.5	2.3	0.4	0.6	0.6	0.6
Pasco	4.1	4.2	1.5	3.8	2.7	4.1	3.8	3.9
Piura	0.6	27.5	0.8	1.6	3.2	3.0	3.8	3.2
Puno	1.1	3.4	5.9	1.3	2.7	2.0	2.0	2.0
San Martín	3.5	1.2	0.8	1.7	1.5	2.0	1.7	1.8
Tacna	1.1	0.7	0.9	0.8	1.5	2.0	1.4	1.7
Tumbes	1.1	5.0	0.1	1.4	0.3	0.8	0.6	0.7
Ucayali	10.1	0.6	0.3	1.7	1.0	1.4	1.2	1.5
Peru	100.0	100.0	100.0	100.0	100.0	100.0	100.0	100.0

Note: The bolded numbers indicate where the share of enterprises in each sector is higher than the share of enterprises in the region for the country as a whole.

Source: OECD analysis based on data from INEI.

Rural areas still play a key role in the national economy. The export sector, which has been such as important driver of Peru's growth, is primarily located in rural areas. Agriculture is an important industry for a majority of regions whereas mining is concentrated in fewer places. The structure and distribution of both industries is influenced by differing levels of informality. For example, the higher value commercial scale and export-orientated agriculture and fishing tends to be located in the coastal regions. Mining employment is important for a number of different regions; however, only four of these regions produce over 50% of value added. The employment analysis shows that tourism is an important diversification strategy for some regions in the coastal and rainforest areas, which is both an urban and rural phenomenon.

In terms of business demography, the key feature of Peruvian industry is the higher proportion of microenterprises and lower proportion of small and medium-sized enterprises compared to OECD averages, particularly outside of the capital and secondary cities. This may be due to the level of informality in the economy, and the lack of incentives and support for microenterprises to grow and expand. The analysis of business by economic activity reveals the relative importance of clusters of business to different regions. These findings have important implications for the design of industry and innovation programmes, and the importance of a "place-based" approach.

Overall, this analysis enables us to build a picture about the complexity and interdependencies between different regions of the country. Many of Peru's key comparative advantages – in terms of minerals, fresh water and fertile soils, fishing grounds, biodiversity, mountains and landscapes – are located in rural areas. These provide the foundation for industries such as mining and agriculture, where Peru is competitive in international markets. The capacity to move these goods to market and add value to them is dependent upon relationships with cities, and in particular the movements of goods and services through Lima-Callao. These cities are also key hubs for manufacturing and services which add value to Peru's exports and imports. It is important that this territorial diversity and the interdependencies between regions are considered in the design and delivery of national sectoral and innovation policies.

Better linking national sectoral and innovation policies with a regional development agenda

Key considerations in relation to contemporary industry policy and product diversification strategies

In recent years, the national government has had a strong policy focus on promoting diversification of the country's export basket. Diversifying the economy of a country, regardless of the specific challenges of Peru, is a complex issue which requires proactive and well-designed public policies (Haussmann and Rodrik, 2003). In the post-war period, many proactive approaches to industry policy have not achieved their desired objectives.

Modern industrial strategies have built upon Haussmann and Klinger's (2007)[2] product space and the need to socialising part of the cost of innovation to foster "self-discovery" (Hausmann et al., 2003).[3] Others such as Porter (2009) have placed emphasis on the need for the creation of development clusters which would allow full utilisation capacity of the comparative advantages of an economy in a self-enforcing cycle.

One of the factors of complexity of economic development is that experience has shown that it goes against the traditional logic of mere competitive advantages. Indeed, countries show changing levels of diversification depending on their level of wealth. As countries get richer they tend to have stronger sectoral and employment diversification, while beyond a high level of development – equivalent to Ireland's current GDP per capita – they tend to have concentration patterns in their economy and labour force (Imbs and Wacziarg, 2003). Klinger and Lederman (2004) find this same U-curve phenomenon in the diversification of new exports.

Box 2.12. Diversification strategies currently being explored by Peru

Peru, via CONCYTEC, and in partnership with the Harvard Center for International Development, is currently undertaking a study on growth diversification. The approach is based on productive diversification strategies based on the product space map developed by Hausmann and Klinger. The rationale behind the argument is that the economic complexity index –computed based on the type of exported products – would be a better predictor of the income of a country than education variables, governance variables and competitiveness variables. Based on this argument, the objective would be to diversify the economy via product diversification, and complexification of the production by "jumping" across the product space towards more complex products, which would entail lower costs of self-discovery and lower co-ordination failures in the markets.

Preliminary findings of that study show that compared to other countries Peru has diversified its economy very little since 1962 (compared with other benchmark countries such as Mexico). Exported products are mainly to be found in products with low levels of complexity and in products that have few links with products at the centre of the product space which have higher complexity levels. According to this framework, Peru would be in situation with a relatively low complexity outlook and a low complexity index. In that sense, the policy advice would be to target strategic sectors that facilitate shifts toward the centre of the product space.

This analysis shows several interesting points and many lessons can be drawn from it. It presents a sharp and detailed vision of the productive fabric of the country, and puts emphasis on essential elements for product diversification such as co-ordination failures, and the accumulation of capacities in a sector that allows easier diversification to nearby products. The level of diversification and complexity of an economy is also associated with higher incomes. Therefore, productive diversification would be a great asset to lead Peru towards higher development levels.

Nonetheless, the relative significance of these findings and the direction of causation are not clear, particularly when analysing the contribution to per capita income growth of elements such as education, governance and competiveness. Some of these elements may not be the biggest constraint depending on the level of development of a region, but gain importance as the development advances. Also, higher income countries tend to have themselves higher levels of education – and lower levels of the active population with little or no education, competitiveness and governance capacities. As discussed elsewhere in the report, lifting productivity across the economy is the key to the long-term sustainable growth of Peru.

Heterodox policies face two constraining issues. First, the information gaps, as it is difficult to know if new industries would be competitive given the cost structures of an economy. The market prices of an economy reveal little about the potential profitability of a reallocation of resources (Rodrick, 2004). Second, and this is particularly the case for small and open economies like Peru, entrepreneurs in new economic sectors face competition from other firms already installed in that sector. In order to become competitive, firms in these new sectors have to quickly reach critical mass and/or attain the levels of productivity of their competitors abroad before being able to take off.

Given that set of circumstances, it may be argued that seeking a productive diversification in the non-tradeable sector may be counter-intuitive. Nonetheless, the risk for a country like Peru to rely on a small base of capital-intensive and highly volatile resource-extractive industries is risky in the medium term – as shown by the issues generated by the recent decrease in the price of minerals – but also a constraint for long-term growth since linkages of the extractive industry with the manufacturing sector may not be sufficient to develop a large base of highly productive employment to continue to improve per capita incomes.

Nonetheless, in its attempt to develop a broader base productive fabric, Peru must bear in mind a series of lessons, which it has in some cases experienced itself. Strong interventions of the state in choosing winners and losers have often failed to deliver (Barca, 2001; OECD, 2014a, 2014b). They tend to create state capture by private interests, misallocation and over-sizing of investments, and generate rent-seeking behaviour. Furthermore, when directed by central governments, they lack information and knowledge on the opportunities available.

Specialisation and complexity in production is also increasingly shaped and constrained by global value chains, which also reduces the importance of focusing solely on particular exporting sectors. Indeed, recent OECD studies have shown that much more important than the actual exports of a country are their place in the GVCs. In that sense, it is not so much what the country exports rather than value added and the types of imports used in exported products.

Box 2.13. Global value chains

Industry policies need to be adapted to the increasing importance of global value chains (GVCs). Globalisation and advances in ICT allow firms to fragment their production across GVCs. As a result, the relevant unit analysis is not the industry or sector, but the "business function" or "activity" along the supply chain (e.g. design, R&D, procurement, operations, marketing and customer services). Countries tend to specialise in specific "business functions" or "activities" rather than specific industries (e.g. assembly operations for the People's Republic of China or business services for India). Specialisation no longer takes place solely in industries, but rather in functions or activities of the value chain (OECD, 2012b).

Multinational corporations account for over 80% of international trade, and they have both complex vertical and horizontal supply and value chains. In that sense, when accounting for exports, a better measure is the value added and the level of technological input produced in a country. There are several examples across OECD countries showing this phenomenon. For instance, a country such as Mexico has an important number of "*maquiladoras*" close to its US border, some states produce helicopters, important numbers of cars and other high value-added products. Nonetheless, a deeper analysis of the value added in those border states of Mexico shows that the latter are specialised in the assembly of high value-added components, with limited value adding and spillovers.

Territorial approaches can help in strategies to increase participation and value adding within GVCs, and enable the shift toward the public sector providing a range of integrated and specialised public goods, services and infrastructure to business. Place-based policies help identify the local potential for specialisation in the GVCs and help provide the right set of public goods to maximise that potential. The challenge in the age of globalisation is less to pick sectors to back on the international stage, as countries once sought to do, than to integrate into global value chains at whatever levels their endowments make them competitive (Baldwin, 2006; OECD, 2013c).

Furthermore, the focus on tradeable goods is indeed important, but the development of such products will also depend strongly on the real exchange rate. Two mechanisms may affect the competiveness of the tradeable goods sector. The first is that of the Dutch Disease due to a rising exchange rate, as discussed in Chapter 1. The other effect, which may be coupled with the Dutch Disease – if it is at play – is more related to an inverted Balassa-Samuelson effect, whereby the too high prices in the non-tradeable goods sector crowd-out production factors of the tradeable good market thereby decreasing their competitiveness. Monetary policy and fiscal policy are in that sense relevant for the diversification of production in a country.

Box 2.14. Real multilateral exchange rate

The competitiveness Peru's exports and opportunities for diversification are also shaped by the evolution of the real multilateral exchange rate. Higher prices relative to other economies reduces the competitiveness of the tradeable sector, and shapes the scope, trajectory and pace of export diversification. This is particularly true for resource-based economies, which can be demonstrated by the increase in the real multilateral exchange rate for Peru during the commodities boom in the 2000s.

Figure 2.8. **Peru's real multilateral exchange rate (2009=100)**

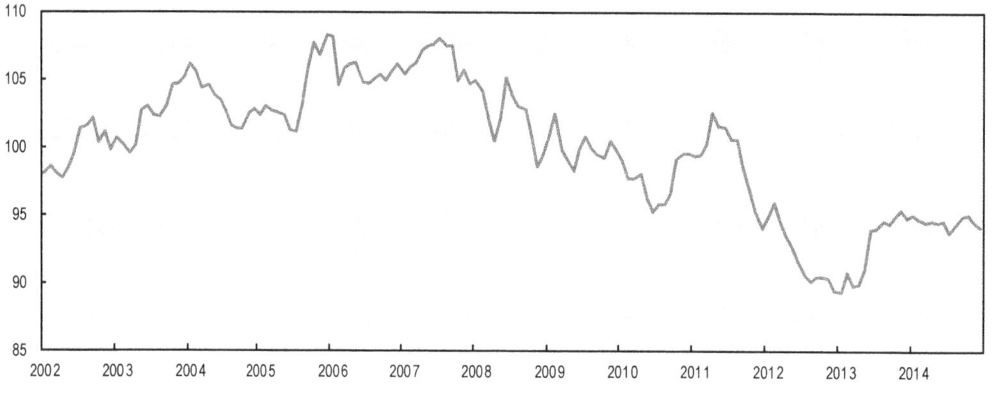

Source: BCRP (2015), Banco Central de Reserva del Perú, http://www. bcrp.gob.pe.

In a more general way, the objective of productive diversification cannot be pursed without taking into account the need to enhance productivity in other sectors already present in the economy. Significant benefits can come from policies destined to increase productivity in currently low productive sectors. For instance, there is significant scope to increase productivity in agriculture and services, which will have important territorial implications.

Strong state interventions in industrial policies for productive diversification are based on the principle of the presence of "Marshallian externalities", which implies that knowledge spillovers, labour pooling and supplier specialisation can arise from a concentration of production, which would in turn increase productivity in the sector. This could indeed be the case in some places, but these externalities may also not appear depending on the stages of development and the presence of growth constraints such as the ones mentioned above. Also, benefits from clustering may not appear unless the economy enjoys a comparative advantage in the sector. As pointed out by Rodríguez-Clare (2005), industrial policies should not be targeted at creating comparative advantages but rather at achieving high productivity where competitive advantages already exist.

Box 2.15. Productivity in the agricultural and services sector

Increasing agricultural productivity will decrease the employment rate in that sector. As shown in Chapter 1, close to one-quarter of the Peruvian labour force is employed in agriculture, whereas in advanced OECD countries, the labour forced employed in agricultural production is generally lower than 5%. Nevertheless, this is a significant opportunity for Peru, given its age profile and population growth. Active labour policies, skills policies, and the development of governance mechanisms and enhancing rural-urban linkages will help manage these issues and allow Peru to take full advantage of this shift.

Finally, and consistent with the findings of Chapter 3, 60% of the labour force is in services, with most of this activity located in cities. "Getting the cities right" is fundamental to increase the productivity of services and the performance of the national economy. Services such as finance or software development and/or adaption can be important assets for the tradeable goods sector. As such, increases in productivity in services can have beneficial effects on the growth and diversification of the tradeable goods sector.

In that same line of analysis, the process of discovery matters often more than the outcome, since the outcome is by nature unknown. Policies that tend to focus on the discovery of underlying costs and opportunities via the creation of incentives for firms and governments tend to provide better outcomes (OECD, 2014b). Discovery processes tend to come with a corollary of a high number of mistakes, policies that incentivise discovery should allow mistakes to happen and not provide open-ended support for activities that do not take off. Focus therefore should be put on avoiding persisting in mistakes rather than on avoiding mistakes.

Box 2.16. How experimentation provides unexpected but positive surprises: The case of Finland

The emphasis on experimentation points to a final and very important conclusion: the outcomes of successful diversification policies will be difficult to predict. Policy makers should resist the temptation to try to define the production structure in the direction they believe the economy should evolve. Markets will always produce surprises, as Hayek (1988) famously observed.

The example of Finland is instructive. Its comparative advantage in forestry products is long-standing and obvious, but most of its other competitive strengths are not: not even the most well-informed economist could have foreseen its development of strong comparative advantages in such products as lifts, satellite navigation equipment, off-shore drilling equipment or – to name the most famous of all – cellular telecommunications. In 1990, the last of these products would hardly have merited a mention in any industrial strategy for Finland; ten years later, they were a cornerstone of Finnish growth, and a decade after that, the country as a whole felt the fallout from the rise of the iPhone, the eclipse of Nokia being as unexpected as its rise.

Yet new sources of growth rapidly began to emerge based on the human capital and infrastructure associated with the telecommunications sector. Finland thus continues to adjust, its success a product not of anyone's ability to predict, let alone direct, the productive structure of the economy, but of a set of transversal, sectorial and regional policies that create conditions favourable to innovation and entrepreneurship.

Source: OECD (2014b), *OECD Territorial Reviews: Colombia 2014*, http://dx.doi.org/10.1787/9789264224551-en.

This analysis shows that "one-size fits all" industry strategies are unlikely to succeed. Peru is a territorially diverse country with quite different socio-economic and institutional conditions between regions. Self-discovery is of necessity a bottom-up process, so there should be advantages in being able to address the co-ordination and information externalities closer to where they occur. While it is true that national governments are typically better equipped to intervene, in terms of resources and authority, the information needed for effective action is often local. Place-based approaches are an important element in contemporary sectoral and innovation policies.

Place-based approaches are central to new sectoral and innovation policies

This shift in sectoral and innovation policies is consistent with the paradigm shift in regional policies outlined at the beginning of this chapter. Whereas the old approach to industrial policy is characterised by governments providing subsidies to national champions, the contemporary role of government is as a facilitator in the face of complexity and uncertainty, enabling closer co-ordination between individual economic agents as well as greater experimentation in the economy (OECD, 2015b). By comparison with the earlier historical experience of industrial policy, so-called "new industrial policy" might be characterised as exhibiting some or all of the following characteristics (Warwick, 2013; Warwick and Nolan, 2014):

- greater emphasis on building networks, improving co-ordination and promoting awareness
- less reliance on direct support in the form of state aid and (market-failure correcting) subsidies
- greater emphasis on strategic (rather than defensive) industrial policy
- a shift away from sector-based strategies and towards certain technologies and activities.

These characteristics have shifted industrial policy closer to innovation policies, due to the perceived links between technological development and structural change in the economy. At the same time there has been greater recognition of the importance of ensuring that government only bears risk which is "proportionate", e.g. enough to matter, not too much to lead to moral hazard. Policy makers are also increasingly cognisant of the need to plan for exit from the policy, and to make these plans known in order to help resist pressure from firms for the retention of government support and benefits.

One element of the emergence of new industrial policy is smart specialisation, which involves regional (and national) governments encouraging investments in domains that leverage endogenous assets to create future domestic capability and interregional comparative advantage (Foray et al., 2009). What distinguishes smart specialisation from traditional industry and innovation policies is mainly the process defined as "entrepreneurial discovery" – an interactive process in which market forces and the private sector are discovering and producing information about new activities and the government assesses the outcomes and empowers those actors most capable of realising the potential (Hausmann and Rodrik, 2003). As a result, smart specialisation strategies are much more bottom-up than traditional industrial policies.

Like traditional industrial policy, smart specialisation strategies aim to address market/systems and co-ordination failures. But traditional industrial policies required significant levels of information to justify subsidy support and they tended to be implemented in vertically integrated sectors with stable technological paradigms. In contrast, smart specialisation – as well as new industrial policies – recognises the lack of perfect information, the level of advancement of a given activity and the relative risks for policy. It focuses on helping entrepreneurs identify their knowledge-based strengths at the regional level and in a more exploratory approach in which public decision makers listen to market signals using a range of assessment tools (e.g. SWOT analysis, surveys) and mechanisms such as public-private partnerships, technology foresight and road mapping. A recent OECD report on smart specialisation identified the following key policy messages (OECD, 2013a):

- Policies for entrepreneurial discovery. The smart specialisation approach calls for an "entrepreneurial selection" of market opportunities (e.g. to minimise failures and to avoid ill-informed policy decisions). While successful companies will constitute the new specialisation of the country/region (self-discovery), the role for policy is to develop a flexible strategy focusing on measurable intermediate goals, identifying bottlenecks and market failures and ensuring feedback into policy learning processes. The approach includes incentives to strengthen entrepreneurship and encourage agglomeration.
- Promoting general purpose technology platforms and networks. Given the range of applications of general purpose technologies, technology platforms involving public and private actors but also standards settings organisation can help increase productivity in existing sectors and help identify sectors in which to concentrate resources.
- Diagnostic and indicator-based tools and infrastructure. Smart specialisation requires regions and countries to maintain an infrastructure and indicator base to monitor and evaluate performance and policies.
- Strategic governance for smart specialisation. Good governance and the development of local capabilities are key to identifying local strengths, aligning policy actions, building critical mass, developing a vision and implementing a sound strategy. See below for a further discussion on governance.
- Openness to other regions. The specialisation strategy of regions should take into account that other regions are also involved in knowledge-creating activities and that duplication might lead to lower effectiveness and finally failure. Hence, co-operation with other regions with complementary capabilities and strategies is important.

Assessment of national industry policies

Peru has more than 60 productive development programmes led by different public entities, without an articulated strategy. This lack of co-ordination could generate overlap of programmes (beneficiaries, territories), unattended sectors and geographical areas, different approaches in the provision of services, difficulties in the monitoring and impact evaluation process, among others. Thus, the National Centre for Strategic Planning (CEPLAN), the Ministry of Production (PRODUCE) and the National Competition Council (CNC) along with other ministries related to productive development are guiding the strategic direction that Peru is taking with regard to industrial policy and enhancing competitiveness in territories. Moreover, the National Council for Science, Technology and Innovation (CONCYTEC), has taken the lead in addressing the country's agenda for growing innovation.

Box 2.17. Smart specialisation: What does it mean?

The European Union has adopted the principle of smart specialisation as the basis for its territorial development policies in its Europe 2020 strategy, which defines a ten-year growth strategy for its member countries. The idea of smart specialisation emerged out of work by the European Union, the OECD and other intergovernmental bodies on the drivers of territorial development. This work found that regional economic policy was most effective when focused on supporting a limited number of sectors with global innovative potential that also drew on existing related regional economic strengths. From 2014, all European operational programmes for Structural Funds are required to be based on an RIS3 (Research and Innovation for Smart Specialisation Strategy) as a prior condition for the grant of funding.

The main principles of the EU's smart specialisation framework can be summarised as follows:

- Concentration of public investments in R&D and knowledge on particular activities is crucial for regions/countries that are not leaders in any of the major science or technology domains. Past policies tended to spread "knowledge investment" too thinly (e.g. higher education and vocational training, public and private R&D), not making much of an impact in any one area. However, concentration in the smart specialisation context is about focusing knowledge investments on activities – business functions carried out by firms which range from the conception of a product to its end use and beyond (e.g. design, production, marketing, distribution and support to the final consumer) (Porter, 1986; Gereffi and Kaplinsky, 2001). These activities (e.g. goods or services) may be undertaken by a single firm or divided among different (supplier) firms and be concentrated within one location or spread out over global value chains (OECD, 2012b). The emerging feature of many of these activities is that they increasingly cut across established sectors and industries.
- Smart specialisation relies on an entrepreneurial process of discovery that can reveal domains of economic activity where a country or region excels or has the potential to excel in the future. It empowers entrepreneurs who are able to combine the necessary knowledge about science, technology and engineering with knowledge of market growth and potential in order to identify the most promising activities. In this learning process, entrepreneurial actors have to play the leading role in discovering promising areas of future specialisation, because the needed adaptations to local skills, materials, environmental conditions and market access conditions are unlikely to be able to draw on codified, publicly shared knowledge, and instead will entail gathering localised information and the formation of social capital assets. One implication for policy makers is that this requires ensuring policy tools to collect the entrepreneurial knowledge embedded in the region to transform it into policy priorities. In this context, entrepreneurial actors are not only the people creating new companies, but also innovators in established companies, in academia or in the public sector.
- Specialised diversification: specialisation in selected activities that provide comparative advantage based on differentiation of their operations and products in global markets.
- The specific properties of general purpose technologies (GPTs) underlie the logic of smart specialisation. Invention of a GPT extends the frontier of invention possibilities for the whole economy, while the "co-invention of applications" changes the production function of a particular sector. GPTs are important for upgrading upstream and downstream of the value chain. The leading regions invest in the invention of a GPT or the combination of different GPTs (e.g. bioinformatics). Regions do not need to "lead" in these technologies to benefit. In fact, follower regions often are better advised to invest in the "co-invention of applications" around a GPT. Benefiting from GPTs generally also requires alignment with education and training policies in order to build capacity.

Box 2.17. **Smart specialisation: What does it mean?** (*continued*)

- Smart specialisation strategies are interlinked through complementary activities at horizontal level and require horizontal policy co-ordination. But they are in particular co-defined by the "vertical" alignment of entrepreneurial activity, partnering in clusters, regional development strategy and interregional and international arrangements that all are part of a multi-level governance structure for smart specialisation. Setting common goals therefore constitutes a powerful governance mechanism for the vertical alignment of these strategies, without jeopardising a market-oriented process of resource allocation. This multi-level governance co-ordination requires the synchronisation of both national strategies with regional strategies and the synchronisation of different regional strategies (e.g. innovation strategies, research strategies, industrial strategies), to support regional priorities.
- Structural change is a driver of economic growth. Smart specialisation aims to accelerate structural change by encouraging the transformation of economic activities from a structural perspective. It may in some cases mean modernising existing industries or enabling lagging sectors to improve their competitiveness through the adoption of ICTs, but for front-runner countries it can also mean developing new areas at the edge of the technological frontier.

Source: OECD (2014), OECD Territorial Reviews: Netherlands, OECD Publishing: Paris, http://dx.doi.org/10.1787/9789264209527-en.

CEPLAN and the Bicentennial Plan

CEPLAN is Peru's central planning agency responsible for guiding and co-ordinating the National System of Strategic Planning. CEPLAN has elaborated a "Bicentennial Plan: Peru Until 2021", which sets out the roadmap and goals for 2021, when Peru will celebrate the bicentennial of its independence. One of the six priorities of the plan is "economy, competitiveness and employment". This includes a focus on stimulating the production of high value-added exports by establishing a logistics and information chain for international trade, supporting exporting SMEs, and promoting public-private alliances for greater infrastructure investment.

From this general policy direction, two priority objectives are being formulated, which have strong alignment with ideas associated with the product space. The first one focuses on developing a diversified productive structure that is competitive, sustainable and of high value and productivity. A second objective relates to increasing and diversifying exports, and accessing to new markets. A number of strategic actions are defined to achieve these objectives, including:

- creating a specific entity in charge of promoting new economic activities that are internationally competitive
- establishing support mechanisms for the development of productive chains
- developing industrial parks with a national, regional and local focus
- promoting the development of businesses and export chains
- linking SMEs with large enterprises and elaborating export-promotion schemes.

Closely linked to competitiveness, some of the plan's other objectives target the science, technology and innovation sector and the promotion of knowledge and technology diffusion for business innovation. Most of the actions defined for those are embedded in the National Council for Science, Technology and Technological Innovation's core strategy.

Ministry of Production and strategies to diversify production and exports

The Ministry of Production is responsible for designing, implementing and overseeing the development of industrial, microenterprise, SME and fishery policies developed as part of the National Production Diversification Plan (PNDP). The PNDP's objective is to increase Peru's growth in the medium and long term by relying on a greater productive capacity, the diversification of its production and a reduction in its dependence on the price of raw materials.

The PNDP is developed around three pillars, each foreseeing multiple lines of intervention:

1. the promotion of production diversification
2. the adaptation of regulations and administrative simplification
3. the expansion of productivity.

A Multi-sectoral Commission for Productive Diversification chaired by the Minister of Production has been established to implement the PNDP. The Multi-sectoral Commission also includes the President of the Council of Ministers, the Minister for Economy and Finance, the Minister for Foreign Trade and Tourism, the Minister for Agriculture and Irrigation, the Minister for Energy and Mining, and four representatives of business associations. The commission should help provide co-ordination between the different actions of the different ministries as well as identify synergies between programmes. The inclusion of the private sector should also allow priorities and programmes to be better matched with business needs.

The PNDP is operationalised through a number of different mechanisms, which include

- infrastructure and skills programmes (e.g. clusters, industrial parks, training schemes)
- funds for innovation and entrepreneurship (Innovate Peru and Start up Perú)
- service delivery platforms such as the network of centres for technological innovation (CITES)
- methodological instruments (e.g. economic research, information systems)
- working groups aligned with each of these pillars which are composed of national and regional government officials as well as representatives from the private sector and academia
- sectoral working groups comprised of members of academia and from the private and public sectors (four have been created so far: forestry, creative industries, textile and aquaculture).

The PNDP has sought to develop a holistic approach whereby it sees its action not only as part of an overall national strategy where co-ordination with other ministries such as education or agriculture is fundamental for certain of its actions. There are programmes of articulated interventions including the Ministry of Production, the Ministry of Development and Social Inclusion (MIDIS) and the Ministry of Agriculture and

Irrigation, showing positive steps towards cross-sectoral articulation of social policies with productive policies.

One of the most interesting elements for the strategy is the role of the CITES. The CITES provide several functions that have shown to be particularly useful for the development of industries such as Pisco (a brandy based on distilling grapes). This includes assistance to businesses in terms of demand development, technological transfers, research and innovation, the provision of technical classes, and test trial laboratories. Incentives could be set for further implication of regional governments in the CITES in order to provide both a further bottom-up approach and better local knowledge. For example, funding for innovation, which is currently allocated from the *canon*, could be directed through the CITES to maximise these synergies (see Chapter 4).

Box 2.18. Network of centres for technological innovation (CITES)

Role of the CITEs

The CITEs are probably the most representative intermediary institutions in the Peruvian innovation system. They were created in 2000 by the Ministry of Production (PRODUCE) to enhance the innovation capabilities of small and medium-sized enterprises (SMEs), foster their productivity and improve their ability to comply with international standards. They are essentially institutions engaged in technology diffusion and the provision of technical, certification, testing and training services for producers' associations in the sectors of activity in which they operate. They can also act as "knowledge brokers" between firms and other sources of expertise and technologies (universities, research institutes, consultants, international technical co-operation).

CITES have either a public or a private status and are accredited by PRODUCE. Public CITEs receive institutional funding from this ministry and other revenues from the sale of their services to enterprises or producer associations or from project-related grants from international co-operation agencies (public or non-governmental organisations). Private CITEs are not funded by the ministry. CITEs' activities are overseen and co-ordinated by OTCIT, an office of PRODUCE, which provides assistance for the diffusion of technological information, project development and management. OTCIT is also involved in the certification of new CITEs.

As of 2011 there were 14 active CITEs (3 public and 11 private) operating in industries with previously well-organised conglomerates of SMEs. They cover nearly 6 000 SMEs and have very broad coverage in terms of programmes or instruments in the field of innovation in Peru. From 2006 to 2009, the number of enterprises assisted was quite stable, but more than doubled in 2010; the number of trained persons rose substantially; and the average annual number of transactions involving technological services was over 17 000. The largest increase in CITEs' activities concerned the agro-industrial sector, owing to the need to increase productivity and develop innovative products for fast-growing external markets.

Private sector representatives and users, who pay for the services and thus contribute to the centres' revenues, positively evaluate CITEs' actions. They recognise their impact and important role in helping SMEs to increase their productivity, export potential and product quality, at least in the first or less sophisticated stages, by facilitating the adoption of better technologies and practices and helping to increase their collaborative capacity and improve their social capital. However, as firms grow and begin demanding more sophisticated technological services, the CITEs seem to be less effective and cannot always meet their needs, mainly owing to capability and budget constraints that prevent CITEs from engaging in R&D, upgrading services and hiring highly skilled personnel.

Box 2.18. **Network of centres for technological innovation (CITES)** *(continued)*

The case of a successful CITE: CITE-Vid and the Peruvian Pisco

The development of the pisco industry during the 2000s, with exports increasing tenfold to USD 1 million in 2007, illustrates the positive impact of CITE-Vid, an intermediary institution which, along with private investment, improved co-ordination among the different actors in the pisco production chain and contributed to a move towards a more export-driven and innovation centred strategy.

CITE-Vid, the technological innovation centre for the pisco and wine industry, was created in 2000, based on the Spanish technological institutes. Its objective is to improve quality, productivity, information and innovation in the pisco and wine-making production chain and to support the domestic and international promotion of pisco. CITE-Vid played an important role in improving the organisation of small producers of pisco. It promoted their first consortium and provides technical assistance and infrastructure for wine and pisco producers in order to improve and standardise the quality of pisco, while preserving the essence of the traditional production process. In particular, it has facilitated closer links between the pisco industry and training and research institutions and universities, to a level that is quite unusual for Peru. This has led to the provision of diverse services and facilities, such as: training services, standardisation, technical assistance and technology transfer (from Argentina and Spain), laboratory testing services and market information linked to Conapisco action in the exploration and development of foreign markets. Revenue from sales of services increased nearly tenfold (from 2001 to 2007) and users evaluated positively the services provided by CITE-Vid, whose main contribution has been in raising pisco quality and developing new markets.

Further development

Based on their successful experience, the network of CITEs has the potential to develop further in various directions:

- First, although CITEs have steadily increased the number of firms they serve, their coverage is still rather limited compared to the number of firms that could benefit. Scaling up the CITE model to increase the coverage of SMEs and industrial sectors would help to accelerate the catching-up process and increase productivity in a wider base of the SME pyramid ready to engage in innovation activities as they upgrade their technological capacity to meet the demand of more advanced enterprises or export consumer markets. Such an expansion may be accomplished through the development of a new sort of CITE that would be neither a private nor a public institution but a public-private one. Cost sharing may help to draw more producers' associations into the CITE scheme.
- Second, as the technological capacities of enterprises served by the CITEs increase, they require more sophisticated services. To respond to this demand, the CITEs would have to develop their own applied research and technological development capabilities. Here again, in order to ensure a good match between supply and demand, the most effective model would probably be one that involves the private sector in the governance of the CITES in more intensive in applied research activities. Such centres could be public-private, with a share of their resources coming from performance-based institutional funding from budgetary allocations. Alternatively, they could be private, with applied research activities financed by revenues from research and technological services to producers (individuals or associations) and by competitive innovation funds such as FINCYT and FIDECOM. This model, with a gradual upgrading of applied research capacities and public support, has been successfully adopted in a number of countries and regions.

Box 2.18. **Network of centres for technological innovation (CITES)** (*continued*)

- Third, by increasing their S&T capacity, private CITEs would be in a better position to engage in mutually beneficial S&T co-operation with public research institutions and universities. As CITEs mainly operate at regional or local level, joint projects with regional universities might benefit from *canon* resources for their investment in R&D and technological development activities, including S&T equipment. This would apply to both public and private CITEs.

Finally, to boost overall productivity in the industries in which CITEs operate, it is necessary to complement their work with programmes to create links between SMEs and large firms, either through productive chain programmes (see below) or initiatives for cluster development in fields in which Peru has sound comparative advantages (mining, fishing, agribusiness, tourism, jewellery and apparel).

Source: OECD (2011b), *OECD Reviews of Innovation Policy: Peru 2011*, http://dx.doi.org/10.1787/9789264128392-en.

National Competitiveness Council and the Ministry of Economy and Finance

The National Competitiveness Council (CNC) was created in 2002 as a co-ordinating commission for competitiveness issues. The CNC is composed of a Technical Secretariat, a Board of Directors which includes 5 ministries (Presidency of the Council of Ministers, Ministry of Economy and Finance, Ministry of Production, Ministry of Foreign Trade and Tourism, Ministry of Agriculture and Irrigation), representative members of the private sector, and local and regional governments. The Competitiveness Agenda (2012-13 and 2014-18) was prepared by the CNC's Technical Secretariat in co-ordination with several sectors (public and private) and approved by its Board of Directors. This agenda defines the strategic objectives and priority targets of the country in order to improve its competitiveness and has 8 strategic lines of action with 65 goals. These strategic lines of actions are: 1) production and business development; 2) science, technology and innovation; 3) internationalisation; 4) logistics and transport infrastructure; 5) information technology and communications; 6) human capital; 7) business facilitation; 8) natural resources and energy. This agenda provides a framework to prioritise and co-ordinate efforts to increase Peru's productivity and competitiveness.

The Competitiveness Agenda is highly aligned to the National Plan of Productive Diversification (Ministry of Production), the National Policy for the Development of STI (National Council of Science, Technology and Technological Innovation), the National Strategic Export Plan (Ministry of Trade and Tourism). Through this agenda the CNC seeks to emphasise the most important aspects of these plans and integrate them into its initiatives and projects. In addition, the CNC seeks to co-ordinate with subnational governments to increase their competitiveness and attract investment. As outcomes, these activities have led to improvements in business facilitation at the regional and local level.

In 2013, the National Competitiveness Council, as part of the Productive and Business Development strategic line, promoted the clusters mapping exercise intended to generate information for the national policy of clusters and the Clusters Support Programme. This programme was established in co-ordination with ministries and entities in charge of the productive sector (Ministry of Production, Ministry of Foreign Trade and Tourism, Ministry of Agriculture and Irrigation, National Strategic Planning Centre, National Council for Science, Technology and Innovation, among others). The clusters were studied according to the criteria shown in Table 2.10. Forty-one criteria were identified as a result of this exercise. Subnational governments were not involved in the selection of these clusters, which would be important for future policy directions. Some of these clusters would benefit from a greater level of specificity, for example, by drawing on the business demography data presented in the previous section of this chapter.

Table 2.10. **Objectives and criteria to analyse clusters**

Objectives	Criteria for analysis of the clusters
Measuring the growth potential based on the productive offer and market demand	– Competitive advantage of the cluster – Growth potential of the business
Measuring the importance of the cluster at the country and regional levels	– Dragging effect of the chain in terms of businesses, occupation and technology – Business critical mass
Measuring the level of effort necessary to respond to challenges	– Feasibility of the cluster initiative

Table 2.11. **Top clusters and ranking identified – National Competitiveness Council**

Clusters	General ranking
Mining, centre, auxiliary mining, Lima and Arequipa	1
Prêt-à-porter/fashion, Lima	2
Cultural tourism, Cusco	3
Wool fibre, Arequipa – Cusco – Puno	4
Logistics, Callao	5
Construction, Lima	6
Fishing: Flower and fish oil, coast	7
Fishing: Frozen fish and canned, coast	8
Gastronomy and food service, Lima	9
Coffee, north	10
Health, Lima	11
Software, Lima	12
Auxiliary agro-food, Lima	13
Fruits and vegetables, coast	14
Meat, Lima	15
Mango, Valle de San Lorenzo and Chulucanas (Piura)	16

Clusters are a common strategy across OECD countries to organise policies for promoting innovation (OECD, 2011a). However, there are a number of risks that need to be considered when designing and delivering these initiatives, including the risk of locking in dependency relationships with the public sector, and "wishful thinking" clusters that seek to replicate success elsewhere and do not build upon existing assets and strengths.

The management of natural resource and energy supply – namely water and electricity supply – has also been included in the national Competitiveness Agenda. The CNC is working with the National Water Authority (ANA) and the Ministry for Agriculture and Irrigation on the development of the National Irrigation Plan and the National Water Information System Resources. As far as access is concerned, the Competitiveness Agenda 2014-2018 sets two goals: the creation of new hydroelectric plants (providing an additional 2 480 MW to the system) and the expansion of transmission lines (for an investment of USD 1.25 billion). In collaboration with the Ministry of Energy and the private sector, it is seeking to develop a mechanism to increase the financing capacity of the electricity distribution companies of the government.[4]

Box 2.19. Implementing cluster policies: Key lessons from across the OECD

- Identify explicitly what the national level's interests are, what the barriers to achieving those goals are, and how a cluster approach can help overcome these problems. Goals are often vague (enhancing competitiveness, promoting innovation).
- Determine a cross-ministerial strategy for national level intervention. The proliferation of national programmes promoting clusters makes this increasingly important.
- Work together with regional levels in programme development for capacity building, coherence and complementarity.
- Structure the programme to minimise the associated risks, such as picking winners and lock-in. The public sector is not well placed to predict sectoral trends and evolutions in business strategy.
- Ensure sufficient private sector engagement, as its motivation is required for long-term partnerships and its skills for reactivity to market changes. The private sector must see the benefits of the instruments available.
- Be clear about what the targets are and realistic with respect to funding and programme duration.
- Ensure that programmes have a range of instruments for adaptation across the targets (cluster types, region types, etc.). A national level programme requires even greater flexibility.
- Set outcome measures, even if it is difficult to evaluate the causal relationship of public policy on private action. This serves to clarify programme goals and feasibility.

Source: OECD (2007b) Competitive Regional Clusters: National Policy Approaches: OECD Publishing: Paris, http://dx.doi.org/10.1787/9789264031838-en.

The Ministry of Economy and Finances and support to productive competitiveness

The MEF has also established the Law of Support to Productive Competitiveness (Ley de Apoyo a la Competitividad Productiva, PROCOMPITE) as an arrangement in support of productive competitiveness in the jurisdictions of regional and local governments through offices for programming investment (*oficina de programacion de inversiones*). The offices are in charge of authorising each initiative of Support to Productive Competitiveness, the so-called PROCOMPITE.

The objective of PROCOMPITE is to improve the competitiveness of productive chains through the development, adaptation, improvement or transfer of technology in zones where private investment is insufficient to achieve the competitive and sustainable development of the productive chains. PROCOMPITE is primarily aimed at business initiatives that rely on high technology and innovations to improve their productive capacity for goods or services. One of the pre-requisites for the implementation of PROCOMPITE in regional and local governments is to prioritise areas for intervention.

Regional and local governments have an important role to play in the execution of the development strategy of PROCOMPITE. In addition to identifying local and regional priorities, their responsibilities include resource management, the organisation of the competition process, the financing of business initiatives, and the execution of investments and the phase down of public support to the business.

To cope with such a large set of responsibilities, regional and local governments can dedicate up to 10% of budgetary resources for project spending, with the exception of resources coming from funding sources of official credit operations, donations and transfers. In March 2015, 17 programmes were implemented in regional governments, 64 in provincial municipalities and 130 in district municipalities.

Table 2.12. **Number of subnational governments engaged in PROCOMPITE, 2009-15**

Regional government/municipality	Dedicated resources, (million PEN)	Approved funding	Executed funding
Regional governments	18	15	15
Provincial municipalities	66	38	36
District municipalities	136	93	83
Total	220	146	134

Figure 2.9. **Distribution of funding from PROMCOMPITE, by region, 2009-14**

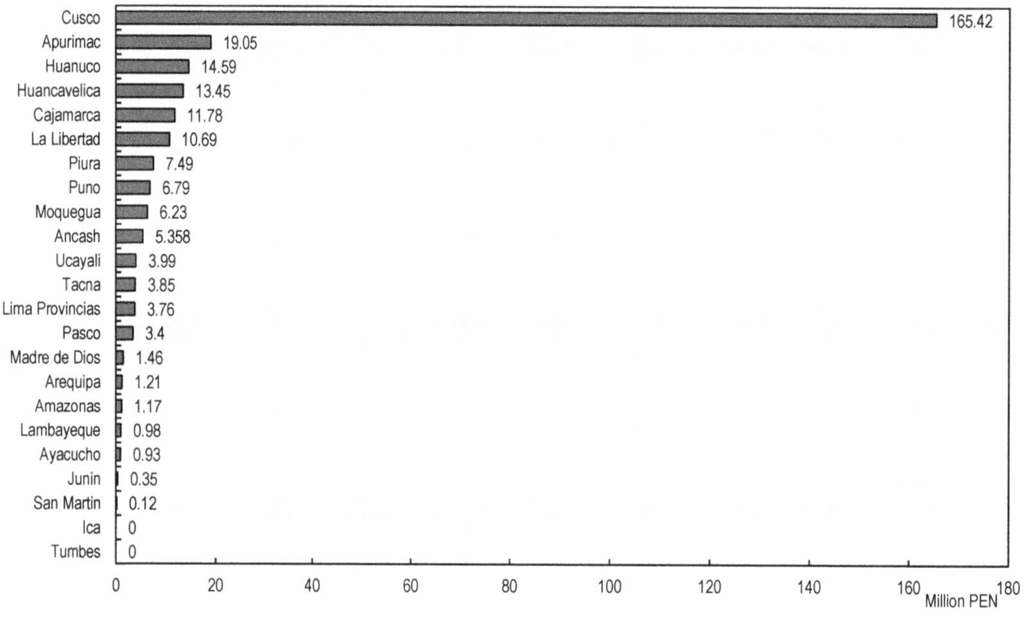

Source: Data from the Ministry of Economy and Finances.

This initiative is particularly interesting because of the role of subnational governments in identifying priorities and delivering the programme. However, an evaluation of the programme found little positive impacts because it acts as a subsidy to micro-businesses rather than a fund providing seed capital. There is little or no evidence that the fund helps provide better life expectancy to business once public funding has been withdrawn. In addition, the distribution of the fund has been uneven, which indicates the need for complementary initiatives to improve the skills and capacities of regions to identify priorities and deliver the programme. There is also an opportunity to redesign the fund so that it has a greater focus on co-investment and growth potential (Box 2.20).

Box 2.20. Core regional growth areas in Brandenburg (Germany)

Brandenburg is a region which was part of the former German Democratic Republic (GDR). After reunification, like many areas in the former GDR, the region experienced a restructuring of its industrial base, and received significant subsidies and support from the national government.

In recent years, the region has experienced a shift in its development approach from a mentality dominated by subsidies and transfers towards one more focused on growth potential. Since unification, the regional and local authorities have put tremendous efforts into mobilising local actors and firms to take part in the development process with the gradual phasing out of subsidies in 1995 as part of the Solidarity Pact.

With these goals in mind, the region established a new policy identifying 15 core regional growth areas with high growth potential in 2004. These "growth poles" receive preferential financing, which is conditional upon them displaying endogenous growth potential. The growth poles are also required to design integrated development strategies which are integrated with the region's overall development strategy. Additionally, growth poles are required to spread some of their benefits to other territories.

This policy has been an important element shifting the mentality in the region, resulting in a new spirit of competiveness. The policy deliberately targeted enough growth poles to create a diverse development pattern and induce other areas in the region to focus on their own growth potential and potentially also become growth poles. The 15 growth poles are home to 35% of the population and have so far generated positive initiatives of co-operation between towns. The growth poles have been a key element in supporting the economic transition and growth of the region.

Source: Advice provided by Land Brandenburg (2011), http://www.brandenburg.de/cms/list.php/bbstart.

National Council for Science, Technology and Innovation

CONCYTEC's National Strategic Plan for the Development of Science, Technology and Technological Innovation for Competitiveness and Human Development (2006-2021) (PNCTI) places science, technology and innovation (STI) as a key component of the national product diversification strategy. The plan aims at ensuring the co-ordination of the actors of the National System of Sciences, Technology and Innovation (SINACYT) to address the technological demands of the prioritised strategic areas in the country. Although it has a sectoral focus, the PNCTI is aligned with the new industrial policy approach and focuses on building capabilities in science and technology, and technological transfers and diffusion to enhance competitiveness and increase value-added creation. The priorities set by the plan are:

- promote the development and transference of innovation technologies to firms, increasing their competitiveness and added value based on economic and environmental sustainability criteria
- propel scientific and technological research oriented to solve problems and meet demands from prioritised strategic areas of the country
- improve qualitative and quantitative human capabilities in STI, emphasising capacity building through post-graduate studies and specialised fields
- foster the creation and strengthening of efficient and sustainable mechanisms of co-ordination, information sharing and decentralisation of STI.

Later, the National Policy for the Development of Science, Technology and Technological Innovation was set as the first STI policy in 2016. The policy has six priority objectives:

1. promote the generation and transference of scientific and technological knowledge, aligning research results to the needs of the country (defined by the priority sectors)
2. promote and develop new incentives that stimulate and increase STI activities by the actors of SINACYT
3. promote the generation of properly qualified human capital for STI
4. improve the quality of research and technological development centres
5. generate information of quality about the development of the actors of SINACYT
6. strengthen the institutional framework for STI.

This national policy will be supported by a suite of existing sectoral or transversal programmes which provide incentives for the private sector to collaborate with researchers. Sectoral programmes focus on 12 key areas, which include, among others: agriculture, medicinal plants, fishing, health and mining. On the other hand, transversal programmes correspond to the scientific and technological specialisation areas connected to the sectoral programmes. The latter focus on six key areas:

1. Program for the Appraisal of Biodiversity
2. Program of Biotechnology
3. Program of Science and Materials Technology
4. Program of Science and Environmental Technology
5. Program Information and Communication Technologies
6. Program for Basic Research.

As part of this policy, CONCYTEC will support the elaboration of "regional agendas for innovation" (RAI) to provide a territorial application of this policy. It aims to promote a regional approach to STI policies, programmes and projects as well as to strengthen the institutional capacity of regions to implement innovation strategies and generate their own policies. Piura and Arequipa will be the first regions to develop their RAIs, following the RIS3 methodology.[5] This is an important policy direction and signals a greater role for regions in sectoral and innovation policies. To serve its mission, CONCYTEC has been assigned the National Fund for the Development of Science, Technology and Technological Innovation (FONDECYT). It is also, with INEI, elaborating the first National Census for Research and Innovation.

There needs to be a stronger role for regions in national sectoral and innovation policies

There is strong alignment between the different strategic plans which have a joint focus on increasing the diversity and complexity of Peru's export base. However, the design and execution of these plans is led by national agencies and reflects a top-down approach to industrial policy. Central government actors have led the design of each of the above-mentioned plans and the strategic actions they encompass, including the definition of sectoral agendas. Addressing Peru's competitiveness challenges only from the lens of the central government may limit the country's economic transition.

For example, the priority clusters mapping exercise, led by the National Competitiveness Council, is designed to inform the development of national policies to support cluster development. This exercise involved seven central government agencies, three of which are the leading co-ordinators of the Clusters Programme developed as a result of the priority mapping exercise. While in many countries regional governments would take a leading role in identifying and developing the clusters, the role played by regional governments in Peru remains unclear.

Regional governments and other local actors such as representatives of the private sector are central to the development of sound industrial and innovation strategies. Their knowledge of local assets provides them with the advantage of better identifying policy complementarities and place-based opportunities. Their involvement can significantly improve policy integration across sectors based on the different needs and competitive advantages of their regions.

The Policy Strategy for Territorial Innovation and the Regional Strategy for Innovation are important in terms of shifting toward a smart specialisation strategy for Peru. Unlike traditional industrial and innovation policies, smart specialisation strategies rely on a bottom-up process of "entrepreneurial discovery" driven by the private sector. Instead, Peru is engaging in a framework led by the central government, which is responsible for defining the country's strategic sectorial directions without the extensive involvement of regions in agenda setting.

Partnerships with regions will need to be developed in an asymmetric way which recognises the territorial diversity of the country. Peru's regions are at different stages of development, possess local assets of different competitive value and have different institutional capacities. The overall lack of a regional focus in sectoral and innovation policies is likely to result in diminished impacts depending on the regions, with better performing regions continuing to perform well and engaging in greater product diversification, while the potential of other regions is not being exploited. The list of priority clusters and their regions identified as part of the Clusters Programme may illustrate this point as Lima is over-represented and no strategy is put in place to best take advantage of under-represented regions' untapped resources.

Another key point for Peru will be improving the underlying framework conditions in terms of the quality of institutions, infrastructure and skills. Product diversification is likely to happen in regions with higher levels of quality human capital. Policies that seek to increase the quality of education and provide training in fields of relevance for the different regions could significantly contribute to the development of competitive regions and the better exploitation of local assets. Integrating national sectoral policies with regional strategies should allow Peru to support not only a more harmonised regional growth, but also more competitive industrial development across the whole of its territory.

Providing better institutional support capacity for regional development

In order to deliver a regional approach to industrial policies, key considerations for Peru will be better co-ordination and alignment between levels of government, and measures to build capacity to design and execute these policies at a regional level. In terms of mechanisms to strengthen vertical co-ordination, OECD member countries employ various mechanisms. These mechanisms include a mix of national strategies with clearly defined goals for public investment, national territorial representatives, nationally funded regional development agencies, contracts and formal agreements between levels of government (OECD, 2007), co-financing, formal consultation processes, platforms for regular inter-governmental dialogue, and *ad hoc* co-ordination arrangements. Their application depends on the national context, the issues to be addressed and the objectives to be realised.

Box 2.21. Key vertical co-ordination mechanisms for regional development

- Co-financing of public investment is among the most basic forms of national/subnational co-ordination. It brings together the commitment of national and subnational actors to the success of a project. National co-financing to ensure that national priorities are reflected in regional development projects, and conversely, regional priorities can be reflected in the design and execution of projects undertaken by the national government. It can also be an important mechanism for risk-sharing on particular investment projects. A pre-requisite is of course that there are ample funds at the subnational level to co-finance.
- Special conditions ("conditionalities") are often associated with co-ordination for public investment. There may be conflicting or complementary agendas for the purpose of the investment depending on the perspective at each level of government. For example, construction of major new transport infrastructure may be seen by the national government as a tool to facilitate trade flows. The region, by contrast, may be more concerned with using its procurement activities associated with the project to promote the development of local small and medium-sized enterprises. And local authorities may be chiefly concerned with minimising the noise and other negative local externalities. That is why higher levels of government often include particular conditions in the financing or co-financing of different public investments.
- Contracts are the formalised arrangements that are generally used to co-ordinate investment between national and subnational governments. In most cases this implies some form of co-financing and conditionalities. They are quite powerful instruments for cross-governmental co-ordination: they are frequently concluded by high-level political actors and they often include both dedicated budgets to ensure implementation and clearly defined mechanisms to resolve any conflicts that arise.[1] They are used in around half of OECD countries (OECD, 2013a) and are common in federal as well as unitary countries contexts (e.g. Canada, France, Italy, Portugal, Spain). Contracts are often designed with high-level engagement and specifically dedicated multi-year budgets. They can help foster partnership rather than a top-down approach, and contribute to capacity building. They can also provide a flexible, tailor-made framework that can clarify assignment of responsibilities across levels of government that are otherwise often imperfect.
- Subnational forums are also utilised with most federal countries creating platforms to exchange information on policy objectives between the different levels of government. In Germany, for example, there are so-called "conferences" or "joint tasks" in specific sectors, like science or regional development, in which different levels of government regularly gather to determine policy priorities. In the United States, several bodies exist, including the White House Rural Council and regional commissions. In addition, national level investment planning relies on investment plans drawn up at the subnational level. In Canada, there are two instruments: one horizontal and the other vertical. The provinces meet amongst themselves to determine investment priorities, while federal arms of the government are represented in the provinces, via structures such as the regional federal councils or the regional development agencies. Their interests lie not only in representing the central government's priorities in the provinces but also in conveying provincial preferences to the federal authorities.

Note: 1. The typology of contracts identified in earlier OECD work lends itself to distinguishing contracts according to their programme or project nature. "Transactional" contracting involves an *ex ante* determination of the complete set of binding and enforceable rights and duties of the parties. By contrast, "relational" contracting involves parties committing to co-operate *ex post* (after the signing of the agreement) and supervision of compliance with the agreement tends to be project-based, bilateral, relying on a co-operative spirit. In practice, most contracts are characterised by both transactional and relational elements and fall somewhere on a continuum from being pure transactional to pure relational contracts (OECD, 2007).

Source: OECD (2014a), *OECD Regional Outlook 2014: Regions and Cities, Where Policies and People Meet*, http://dx.doi.org/10.1787/9789264201415-en.

In the case of Peru there are a number of different levels of co-ordination required in terms of sectoral and innovation policies. National ministers responsible for key policies will need to work together more effectively. There is a large variation in economic conditions and governance capability across the country, and a need to better integrate these national policies at a regional level. This vertical co-ordination needs to occur within a complex governance system. The national government will need to better co-ordinate with a large number of subnational governments (24 regions, 196 provinces and 1 854 districts) in an efficient way which accounts for this diversity and differences in capability.

Peru already has a number of mechanisms in place to facilitate intergovernmental co-ordination in the context of the decentralisation process. This includes the Inter-governmental Coordination Council, which aims to co-ordinate and promote recommendations on policies, strategies and actions related to the decentralisation process, and inter-governmental commissions, which have been established on a sectorial basis (e.g. health, education) to facilitate collaboration between national and subnational governments. However, these existing institutions are not equipped to address challenges related to the effective delivery of regional policies. These challenges are:

- gaps in critical skills and capabilities at a subnational level, including policy development and evaluation, strategic planning, procurement, and project/programme delivery
- lack of co-ordination in how priorities of the national ministries are included in the planning and policy cycle at a subnational level (and vice versa)
- gaps between strategic plans and fiscal frameworks at a national and subnational level
- fragmentation of public investment and services at a regional and local level
- variations in the quality and implementation of key planning instruments
- lack of systemic co-operation between regions.

It is important that these challenges are addressed in partnership between the national and subnational governments (in particular the regional level). This institutional support would have an overarching focus on ensuring better co-ordination and alignment of policies, and improving skills and capabilities at a subnational level. One option for this institutional support is to create a deconcentrated agency of the Presidency of the Council of Ministers/Ministry of Economy and Finances. This would involve both entities jointly establishing an administrative office in each region or at a macro-regional level, and working in partnership to execute functions which are designed to address the challenges outlined above.

Another option for the national government may be establishing regional development agencies (RDAs) which include the regions in the governance of this entity. There are a number of key policy choices and issues in considering these options. RDAs and deconcentrated agencies of different forms are common in OECD countries and focus on delivering integrated approaches to regional policies (OECD, 2015c). While regions may have authority to initiate at their own discretion, the choice for central government action is nested in a set of alternatives, many of which may be used simultaneously (Figure 2.10).

Figure 2.10. **Choices for central government action: Regional development agencies and alternatives**

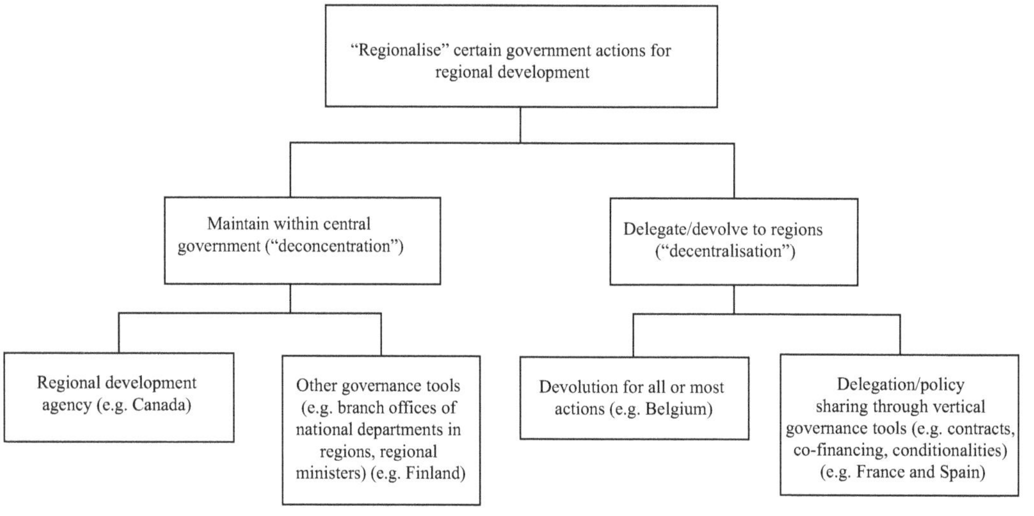

Source: OECD (2015c), *Regional Development Agencies (RDA): a tool for regional development*, Paper for the 33rd Session of the Regional Development Policy Committee.

A central government may create a network of RDAs as a tool for implementing its regional development policy and/or building regional capacity. Alternatively, RDAs may be created by an intermediate tier of government (regions, states, provinces, groupings of municipalities, etc.). The national model of RDAs has a more active role in bridging national actions or funding with regional needs. The board to which it is accountable may be composed of regional stakeholders and not include the central government, but the central government may still play a fundamental role via funding or other forms of oversight. In a more decentralised context, it may be the choice of individual regions to establish an arm's-length entity to deliver on a regional economic development strategy, and in some cases to help shape the strategy itself.

In most OECD countries with a national RDA network, the impetus for creation was to build capacity at the regional level in a centralised country context. The institution of RDAs or structures of a similar purpose has been driven in many OECD countries by the EU accession process, notably for countries in Eastern Europe, such as Hungary. The creation of these national networks of regional agencies is designed to map to statistical areas that would receive EU regional policy funds. EU engagement with Turkey was one of the drivers, among others, behind the development of its national model. The Inter-American Development Bank co-financed the development of Chile's national network of 15 RDAs. In several of these examples, the central government has worked to embed these agencies in the regions over time for a greater sense of regional "ownership", albeit Hungary has chosen to recentralise its network.

RDA networks tend to enable a more targeted approach focusing on business development. Several national RDA models are actually not multi-sectoral, with a focus on several policy sectors (business development, skills, rural or urban issues, etc.). The models in Chile, the Czech Republic, Iceland, New Zealand and Turkey, for example, address one or more of the following: business support, cluster development, innovation programmes and investment attraction. They therefore do not actually address this goal of complementarity, but are rather more focused on action as a one-stop shop for firms to get information on programmes delivered by the agency itself or other sources.

Another goal may be for the RDAs to conduct some form of "regional proofing" of policies as they arise. Depending on the design of the RDA feedback mechanisms to central government, the RDA may, or may not, be the ideal tool to achieve this goal. In Canada, following the last elections, RDAs are now part of the portfolio of the Minister of Innovation, Science and Economic Development along with the Department of Innovation, Science and Economic Development. In this way, Canada has an RDA minister that represents regional perspectives at various Cabinet committees, which is an integral element to the RDA design. This allows the ministers to raise regional considerations/issues when policies are being discussed. The former RDA model in England had ties to regional ministers, albeit much less institutionalised than in Canada. Regional ministers and other tools such as a central government unit to "proof" policies, before they are fully conceived and implemented, may be better able to represent regional interests in national policy-making processes than an RDA per se.

The choice of an agency model may be used to address greater accountability, such as through performance indicators. The English RDAs were subject to extensive review, including four generations of performance indicator monitoring in the just over a decade of their existence (OECD, 2009a). Canada's RDAs are subject to performance monitoring, as are other federal departments and agencies. Turkey is in the process of developing a performance indicator system for its RDAs. The national culture of performance monitoring, or obligations from another level of government (such as the EU for its Investment Funds), are likely the most important factors, irrespective of the choice of an agency model or other institutional form. Certain aspects of accountability can be addressed outside of an agency structure, through performance management in general or through co-financing arrangements and contracts that stipulate the goals to achieve and the sanctions or rewards with respect to performance.

The RDA tool may be used to deliver policy at a more adapted spatial scale when there is no regional tier or it is too small a scale. The Turkish model corresponds to statistical regions that don't match a full-fledged regional government. In contrast, the Canadian RDAs are not specifically designed to cover a functional region directly; rather, for the most part, they are assigned a coverage area that is typically significantly larger than a potential functional region. In other country examples, the national RDAs are assigned to cover an administrative region. An alternative to a national RDA policy is a set of incentives for inter-regional collaboration when the regions are not of sufficient scale. For example, Switzerland's cantons are in several cases at a scale that is perhaps too small for certain aspects of regional development. To address this challenge, the federal government's New Regional Policy offers incentives for cantons to collaborate to access funding to achieve actions at a more relevant scale than would have been achieved otherwise.

In practice, several countries combine the use of an RDA with other governance tools. As mentioned above, one of the most powerful elements of the Canadian model is the fact that the RDA minister represents regional perspectives at various Cabinet committees. Turkey's RDAs were created along with 100-member regional development councils. The purpose of these councils is to build a culture of public-private interaction for regional strategy building and it is an integral part of the efforts to build capacity at subnational level. The English RDAs were complemented by the pre-existing Government Offices with central government representation covering the same regions, as well as regional ministers. The choice to develop an RDA network therefore does not stop with the RDA itself, but also concerns the design of the model and the complementary governance tools.

Box 2.22. Turkey's new national regional development agency model

Background

The current network of regional development agencies (RDAs) in Turkey was established between 2007 and 2009. Among other factors, alignment with EU approaches to regional policy was an important factor to their establishment. The initial phases of the RDAs focused on establishing the institutions themselves and building institutional capacity at subnational level. The Ministry of Development oversees the agencies and the Higher Council of Regional Development approves the regional development plans the RDAs are tasked with developing.

The 26 agencies cover the country's 81 provinces, with coverage ranging from 1 to 6 provinces depending on the region. The 26 "regions" correspond to the NUTS II level statistical unit principles used by the European Union. The National Development Plan (2014-2018) has a stated goal of strengthening the connections across the RDA network.

Roles and responsibilities

These RDAs have three key functions: 1) planning, research and analysis; 2) conducting grant programmes for profit and not-for-profit institutions; 3) promoting and supporting investments and promoting their region. They also play capacity-building and service delivery roles. Capacity building includes: technical support for local authority planning studies; capacity improvements for rural and local development; improving co-operation between the public, private and non-profit sectors; and ensuring research on the resources and opportunities of regions. Business support roles include promotion of business and investment facilities, supporting the administrative process for investors in the regions, supporting small and medium-sized enterprises and start-ups, and supporting other activities to ensure implementation of the regional plan.

Ministerial linkages

The State Planning Organisation is responsible for co-ordination of the agencies. They are under the line authority of the Ministry of Development for final approval of the regional development strategies and corresponding work programmes. In addition to the Ministry of Development, the RDAs are also increasingly taking on roles on behalf of other national ministries such as the Ministry of Economy (for delivery of incentive programmes for selected industries, investment programmes, R&D incentives, etc.). There is tendency for the RDAs to increasingly serve as a one-stop shop for firms to access different national programmes.

Oversight and management

Agencies comprise a Development Council as well as the RDA Administrative Board and General Secretariat. The Development Council is a public-private platform to include (maximum of 100) local authorities, private sector representatives, non-governmental organisations (NGOs), universities, etc. This body can make recommendations to the RDA in an advisory role via its feedback in meetings (at least twice per year). While some regions have tested *ad hoc* working groups within the development councils, in the future some form of leadership group within the development councils may be established to facilitate an increasing role in RDA oversight. The Administrative Board is the decision-making body composed of the provincial governors, the mayors of metropolitan or provincial municipalities, chairmen of the provincial councils, and chairmen of the chambers of commerce and/or industry. The Administrative Board Chairman represents the agency and is always a provincial governor; rotating on an annual basis if the RDA covers more than one province. The Administrative Board is supported by a Secretary General and the Secretariat that implements decisions of the Administrative Board and prepares the work plans, manages finances, supports projects and provides technical assistance.

Funding

The resources are grouped into a single pot. Funding includes mainly appropriations by the High Planning Council (based on population, level of development and performance of each agency), international funds (including the European Union), funds from own activities, 1% of yearly revenues of the special provincial administrations, 0.5% of yearly revenues of the municipalities, and 1% of yearly revenues of the chambers of industry and commerce. Since 2008, the central government has provided EUR 630 million (67%) and local institutions (municipalities, special provincial administrations, chambers of commerce and industry) EUR 310 million (33%) to RDAs.

Box 2.22. Turkey's new national regional development agency model (*continued*)

Instruments

Within the context of national rules regarding requests for proposals, the RDAs may adapt some of their programmes for local needs within a set of common instruments across the country. The variations may include the sectors for support or the types of organisations (in some cases this may be an NGO), etc. Any RDA actions must be in compliance with national policy and international agreements, therefore support to certain sectors may be restricted. In addition to business support-related measures, RDAs also have an explicit technical assistance role (see description of mission above). Local institutions may apply for training, human resource development or other capacity-building needs. The RDA can either provide services directly or contract out those services. The RDA may also support certain infrastructure investments for innovation and business development. RDAs also provide promotion of business and investment facilities, supporting administrative processes for investors through investment support offices established in each province. Since 2008, RDAs have supported more than 12 000 projects, through all modalities, by allocating nearly EUR 770 million.

Performance monitoring

The original law does not specify any overarching performance targets/indicators of RDAs, but does require performance evaluation by the Ministry of Development and an evaluation/impact evaluation by RDAs of their own programmes after two years. The Turkish government is looking into the development of a performance evaluation system. To facilitate evaluation of individual programmes, the national government has provided all RDAs with a standardised management information system. This harmonised tracking tool for all entities supported by the RDAs and implemented across the country facilitates evaluations of specific programmes and their impact on recipients. The system is recognised by the OECD Observatory of Public Sector Innovation (OPSI).

Source: OECD (2015a), *Multi-dimensional Review of Peru: Volume 1. Initial Assessment*, http://dx.doi.org/10.1787/9789264243279-en.

Box 2.23. Canada's long-standing regional development agency model

Background

Canada's active regional development efforts at federal level began several decades ago. The Department of Regional Economic Expansion was created in 1969 at the federal level given concerns about inter-regional disparities. To respond to critiques of the initial model, general development agreements were developed to increase co-operation with provinces. In 1982, the entity was reoriented to become the Department of Regional Industrial Expansion and a Ministry of State for Economic and Regional Development was created.

It was in the late 1980s that the model for national efforts grew more decentralised with the creation of the first four regional development agencies (RDAs). Among the rationales for this new approach was greater interaction with sub-national governments and a greater flexibility to adapt to regional needs. That model has not only remained in place for almost four decades, but was expanded in 2009 to cover the entire territory with two additional RDAs. The RDAs were actively used in the delivery of the 2009 Federal Stimulus Package, for example.

Description

Coverage: The network of six RDAs was built over time to now cover the entire country (Table 2.13). Four of the agencies cover multiple provinces or territories, one agency maps to a province, and one province has two agencies. Most of the agencies have additional satellite offices within their coverage area as well as the national capital.

Box 2.23. Canada's long-standing regional development agency model (*continued*)

Table 2.13. Canada's six regional development agencies

Regional development agency	Year founded	Coverage area
Atlantic Canada Opportunities Agency (ACOA)	1987	Multiple provinces
Western Economic Diversification Canada (WED)	1987	Multiple provinces
Federal Economic Development Initiative in Northern Ontario (FedNor)	1987	Partial province
Canadian Economic Development for Quebec Regions (CED)	1991	Province
Federal Economic Development Agency for Southern Ontario (FedDev)	2009	Partial province
Canadian Northern Economic Development (CanNor)	2009	Multiple territories

Mission: Each RDA has a different status and mandate based on its respective enabling legislation. The mandates all generally refer to the importance of economic development and diversification in their coverage areas.

Ministerial linkages: The RDAs' minister represents regional perspectives at various Cabinet meetings. In addition, the RDAs work with line departments, particularly for sectors of economic interest in their coverage area such as agriculture, health, natural resources, as well as public companies ("Crown corporations"). There are six regional federal councils, chaired by the respective RDA Deputy Minister. The councils' mandate is focused on communicating and collaborating on horizontal, federal government-wide priorities.

Oversight and management: The President of each RDA is a Deputy Minister in the federal government, giving high-level oversight to their actions.[1] Furthermore, RDAs as federal agencies are subject to many of the similar reporting requirements of other federal departments. This includes: reports on plans and priorities and departmental performance reports (presented to parliament annually), as well as programme evaluations (see below).[2]

Funding: In total, the RDAs received 0.4% of the government of Canada's total programme expenses (almost CAD 1 billion) in 2013-14. This represented 0.05% of the country's 2014 gross domestic product.

Strategy development and capacity building: Through different programmes implemented across all RDAs and by individual RDA initiatives, there are efforts to build capacity through support to community development organisations, including in some locations with Aboriginal communities.

Instruments: RDAs currently have the flexibility to adapt the types of instruments and investments according to regional assets and needs. They may directly deliver programmes or finance intermediaries in the region to do so. A couple of federal programmes are administered in all RDAs (i.e. Community Futures Program to support community futures development corporations in rural areas and the Economic Development Initiative for language minority communities). All RDAs address some form of business development, whether through specific innovation funds, such as ACOA's Atlantic Innovation Fund or the WED's Western Innovation Initiative. Some have programmes focusing on manufacturing industries, such as the FedDev Advanced Manufacturing Fund or FedNor's Targeted Manufacturing Initiative. Other programmes may have a broader economic development and community outreach mission, such as the CED's Quebec Economic Development Program or the CanNor's Northern Aboriginal Economic Opportunities programmes.

Performance monitoring: In addition to the annual reporting to parliament, federal programmes are all subject to a performance measurement framework. This includes evaluations every five years and the development of a management action plan to respond to evaluation results. Furthermore, per the Policy on Management, Resources and Results Structure, government and parliament must receive both financial and non-financial performance information.

Notes: 1. With the exception of FedNor, which is part of Industry Canada. 2. Idem.

Source: OECD (2015a), *Multi-dimensional Review of Peru: Volume 1. Initial Assessment*, http://dx.doi.org/10.1787/9789264243279-en.

Recommendations

Over the past two decades Peru has demonstrated a commitment to sound macroeconomic policies, which has enabled the growth and diversification of exports. Peru's sectoral and innovation policies, which are primarily designed and executed at a national level, have focused on further diversifying the economy and increasing the complexity of the country's export basket. Capabilities have been built within national ministries to design and deliver these policies, and constituencies have been built with key private and public sector stakeholders around these core ideas. Measures have been developed to develop a territorial dimension to these policies, including the Policy Strategy for Territorial Innovation.

In recent times, Peru has also made significant advances in improving its system of strategic planning and policy development. The National System of Strategic Planning establishes a clear and consistent framework for policy and organisational planning for public sector agencies at a national and subnational scale. The co-ordinating and advisory roles of CEPLAN, if appropriately resourced and executed, will raise the quality and improve the alignment of national policies over time. The PEDN establishes a framework for national policy priorities, and concerted regional development plans provide a complementary framework for priority setting at a regional level.

Within the context of these policy improvements, the analysis shows there are three core challenges that will need to be addressed. The first is in terms of the further incorporation of contemporary policy ideas which recognise the increasing importance of regions in sectoral and innovation policies. This includes organising policies at the scale of functional economic areas, recognising the importance of skills and innovation to regional development, and enabling processes of "entrepreneurial self-discovery". The second challenge is in terms of how these policies are integrated with fiscal frameworks, which can enable a more strategic and multi-year approach to resource allocation. The third challenge is related to how to better co-ordinate policies at a regional level, and build the capability of regional governments to shape and deliver economic development policies. Policy recommendations which respond to these core challenges are outlined below.

Improve alignment between industry and innovation policies at a national and regional level

A key to improving sectoral and innovation policies in Peru will be updating and strengthening alignment with policies at a regional level, which should build upon existing mechanisms such as the concerted regional development plans. Measures to improve the quality and effectives of these plans are:

- ensuring that within the next two years that all departments have an endorsed concerted regional development plan
- requesting that the regional governor submit the draft concerted regional development plan for consideration and response by relevant national ministries (co-ordinated by the deconcentrated agency or RDA model)
- mandating a formal review of the implementation of concerted regional development plans every three years, synchronised with other regions, and which is publicly available (co-ordinated by the deconcentrated agency or RDA model)

- mandating publicly available annual reporting on progress in implementing the concerted regional development plan by the regional governor (which also includes a summary of the activities and achievements of the regional co-ordination councils)
- strengthening the economic analysis within these plans, for example incorporating further analysis of the industry and business structure within regions at the scale of functional economic areas (including at a macro-regional scale), including how regional businesses are integrated with GVCs, and the identification of key bottlenecks and growth opportunities at these scales
- creating opportunities for policy makers at a departmental level to learn from each other, and good practices nationally and internationally (e.g. through targeted training and a bi-annual conference on regional planning and investment).

Strengthen co-ordinating and capacity-building mechanisms to implement a regional approach to economic development

Peru could consider the establishment of more effective and strategic institutional support capacity that can facilitate a partnership-based approach to regional development between departments and the national government. Two strategic options to achieve this outcome are: 1) deconcentrated agencies of the Presidency of the Council of Ministers (PCM) and the Ministry of Economy and Finance (MEF) that can work in partnership at a macro-regional level; and 2) regional development agencies (RDA) that are constituted as a partnership between departments and the national government.

- developing the skills and technical capacity of regional governments (departments) in areas such as policy development and evaluation, strategic planning, procurement, and project/programme delivery
- providing support to departments and municipal governments to better integrate strategic plans with fiscal frameworks and investment strategies
- communicating the strategic priorities of the departments to the national government, identifying opportunities for strategic alignment between departments, and ensuring these priorities inform the national budget and planning cycle
- ensuring that national policies and priorities are considered and reflected in departmental planning
- co-ordinating investments and programme delivery at a regional and inter-regional scale
- evaluating and monitoring departmental and municipal level planning to ensure plans are effective and aligned with the national system of strategic planning.

Better integrating national and regional planning with the fiscal framework

The government should consider how to better integrate regional planning with the fiscal framework by:

- Introducing competitive-based funding programmes that are designed to encourage innovation, infrastructure and skills initiatives at a regional level. Ensure that the criteria for prioritising funding includes demonstrating alignment with concerted regional development plans, and co-contributions from regions, different municipalities, business and other actors.

- Tasking CEPLAN (through the RDA or deconcentrated agency) to work in partnership with departments to identify and prioritise medium term (three- to five-year) capital investment programmes in the regional concerted development plans to deliver on strategic priorities in the territory (derived from the national and subnational plans and programmes). Through the RDA the MEF should also contribute to the development of these investment programmes.
- Including the annual report on progress in implementing the concerted regional development plan in the department's budget and plans, demonstrating alignment with budget instruments.

Notes

1. The economic complexity indicator measures the amount of different products exported by the country, and the number of countries to which it exports.
2. The product space maps the intensity of links between types of products. The products that are deemed to be close are those closely linked in terms of technological requirements, types of machines used, human capital requirements or types of regulations. Haussmann and Klinger's argument is that it is much easier to develop a new type of product closely related to an already produced product. Productive diversification is easier when the production structure of an economy is more concentrated in the centre of the map, since jumps are easier to other products. In the case of Peru, the prevalence of mining and agricultural products, which are distant from other products, make it harder to "jump" to the productions of products that would have positive implications on growth, namely sophisticated products (Hausmann, Hwang and Rodrik, 2005).
3. Haussmann et al. (2003) have also provided evidence of the importance of socialising part of the private cost of innovating into new products, in order to achieve a process of development as "self-discovery". The argument behind the socialisation of some of the costs of innovation lies behind the fact that the cost of innovation may be a too strong deterrent to do so while the benefits are widely spread across society.
4. Legislative Decree No. 1208 and No. 1221.
5. RIS3 stands for Research and Innovation Strategies for Smart Specialisations and are "integrated, place-based economic transformation agendas" developed by the European Union as a strategy for 2020 with the goal to ensure knowledge- and technological-based development at a national and regional level.

Bibliography

Acemoglu, D., S. Johnson and J.A. Robinson (2005), "Institutions as the fundamental cause of long-run growth", in: Aghion, P. and S. Durlafu (eds.), *Handbook of Economic Growth*, Elsevier, Amsterdam, Netherlands.

Acemoglu, D., Johnson and J.A. Robinson (2001), "The colonial origins of comparative development: An empirical investigation", *American Economic Review*, Vol. 91/5, pp. 1 369-1 401, http://dx.doi.org/10.1257/aer.91.5.1369.

Aghion and Howitt (2006), "Joseph Schumpeter Lecture: Appropriate Policy Growth: A Unifying Framework," Journal of the European Economic Association 4, pp. 269-314.

Ahrend, R. (2006), "How to sustain growth in a resource based economy? The main concepts and their application to the Russian case", *OECD Economics Department Working Papers*, No. 478, OECD Publishing, Paris, http://dx.doi.org/10.1787/622880627053, published as "Kak podderzhivat' ekonomicheskii rost v resursno-zavisimoi ekonomike?", *Voprosy Ekonomiki*.

Baldwin, R. (2006), "Globalisation: The great unbundling(s)", Prime Minister's Office, Economic Council of Finland, 20 September, http://graduateinstitute.ch/files/live/sites/iheid/files/sites/ctei/shared/CTEI/Baldwin/Publications/Chapters/Globalization/Baldwin_06-09-20.pdf.

Barca, F. (2001), "Cooperation and knowledge pooling in clusters: Designing a new policy for territorial competitiveness", presented at the seminar "The Influence of Co-operations, Networks and Institutions on Regional Innovation Systems", Max-Planck-Institute for Research into Economic Systems, 8-10 February 2001, Jena, Germany.

Bassanini, A. and R. Duval (2006), "The determinants of unemployment across OECD countries: Reassessing the role of policies and institutions", *OECD Economic Studies*, Vol. 2006/1, OECD Publishing, Paris, http://dx.doi.org/10.1787/eco_studies-v2006-art2-en.

BCRP (2015), Banco Central de Reserva del Perú, http://www. bcrp.gob.pe.

Botero, J. et al. (2012), "Education and the quality of government", *NBER Working Papers*, No. 18 119, National Bureau of Economic Research, Cambridge, Massachusetts, http://dx.doi.org/10.3386/w18119.

Calero, J.P. (2006), *La politique commercial du Pérou: De la communauté andine au libre-échange avec les Etats-Unis – 1ère partie : La dépendance envers le modèle exportateur primaire*, Cahiers de Recherche – CEIM, Centre Études internationales et Mondialisation, Institut d'études internationales de Montréal, Université de Québec, Montreal, Canada, www.ieim.uqam.ca/IMG/pdf/CaleroJean-Paul_RegardSurLHistoireDeLaPolitiqueCommerciale.pdf.

Castells, M. and P. Hall (1994), *Technopoles of the World: The Making of Twenty-First Century Industrial Complexes*, Routledge, London and New York.

CEPLAN (2016), Proyecto del Plan estratégico de Desarrollo Nacional: Plan Bicentenario: El Perú hacia el 2021. Actualizado

CEPLAN (2015), "Background report for the National Territorial Review of Peru", unpublished.

CEPLAN (2011), "Plan bicentenario: El Peru hacia el 2021", National Center for Strategic Planning, Peru, www.ceplan.gob.pe/plan-bicentenario.

Charbit, C. and M. Michalun (2009), "Mind the gaps: Managing mutual dependence in relations among levels of government", *OECD Working Papers on Public Governance*, No. 14, OECD Publishing, Paris, http://dx.doi.org/10.1787/221253707200.

Consorcio Cluster Development-Metis Gaia-Javier D'Avila Quevedo (2013), *Elaboración de un Mapeo de Clusters en el Perú*, Consejo Nacional de Competitividad, Lima, www.cnc.gob.pe/images/upload/paginaweb/archivo/25/Informe%20Final%20Mapeo%20Clusters.pdf.

Corden, W.M. and J.P. Neary (1982), "Booming sector and de-industrialisation in a small open economy", *The Economic Journal*, Vol. 92/368, pp. 825-848, December, http://dx.doi.org/10.2307/2232670.

Dahl, R. (1971), *Polyarchy: Participation and Opposition*, Yale University Press, New Haven, Connecticut.

Dollar, D. and A. Kraay (2003), "Institutions, trade, and growth: Revisiting the evidence", *Policy Research Working Paper Series*, No. 3 004, The World Bank, Washington, DC, http://dx.doi.org/10.1596/1813-9450-3004.

Duranton, G. and D. Puga (2000), "Diversity and specialisation in cities: Why, where and when does it matter?", *Urban Studies*, Vol. 37/3, pp. 533-555, http://dx.doi.org/10.1080/0042098002104.

Easterly, W. and R. Levine (2003), "Tropics, germs, and crops: How endowments influence economic development", *Journal of Monetary Economics*, Vol. 50/1, pp. 41-47, http://dx.doi.org/10.1016/S0304-3932(02)00199-X.

Ernst & Young (2014), "Peru's business and investment guide 2014/2015", Ernst & Young, www.ey.com/Publication/vwLUAssets/Peru-Business-and-Investment-guide-2014-15/$FILE/Peru%C2%B4s%20Business%20and%20investment%20guide%202014-2015-2.pdf.

European Urban Knowledge Network (2016), "EU policies and tools in the field of integrated territorial and urban strategies", www.eukn.eu/events/policy-labs/integrated-territorial-approach/policies/eu-policies-and-tools-in-the-field-of-integrated-territorial-and-urban-strategies.

Fairlie Reynoso, A. (2004), "Peru: Trade policy and international negotiations", in: Lengyel, M. and V. Ventura-Dias, *Trade policy reforms in Latin America*, pp. 168-190, Palgrave Macmillan, New York, http://dx.doi.org/10.1057/9780230523760_8.

Foray et al. (2009), Smart Specialisation – the concept, http://ec.europa.eu/invest-in-research/pdf/download_en/kfg_policy_brief_no9.pdf.

Garcilazo, E. and J. Oliveira Martins (2013), "The contribution of regions to aggregate growth in the OECD", *OECD Regional Development Working Papers*, No. 2013/28, OECD Publishing, Paris, http://dx.doi.org/10.1787/5k3tt0zzp932-en.

Gereffi, G. and R. Kaplinsky (eds.) (2001), "The value of value chains", *IDS Bulletin*, Vol. 32/3, special issue.

Gill, I.S. et al. (2014), *Diversified Development: Making the Most of Natural Resources in Eurasia*, The World Bank, Washington, DC, www.worldbank.org/content/dam/Worldbank/Feature%20Story/ECA/diversified-development-eurasia-full-report.pdf.

Gutierrez de Pineres, S.A. and M.J. Ferrantino (2000), *Export Dynamics and Economic Growth in Latin America: A Comparative Perspective*, Vermont.

Hadenius, A. (1992), *Democracy and Development*, Cambridge University Press, Cambridge, Massachusetts.

Hausmann, R. and B. Klinger (2008), "Growth diagnostics in Peru", *Faculty Research Working Paper Series*, No. 181, Center for International Development, Harvard University, Cambridge, Massachusetts, https://research.hks.harvard.edu/publications/getFile.aspx?Id=435.

Hausmann, R. and B. Klinger (2007), "The structure of the product space and the evolution of comparative advantage", *CID Working Paper*, No. 146, Center for International Development, Harvard University, Cambridge, Massachusetts, www.hks.harvard.edu/centers/cid/publications/faculty-working-papers/cid-working-paper-no.-146.

Hausmann, R. and D. Rodrik (2003), "Economic development as self-discovery", *Journal of Development Economics*, Vol. 72/2, pp. 603-633, http://dx.doi.org/10.1016/S0304-3878(03)00124-X.

Hausmann, R., J. Hwang and R. Rodrik (2005), "What you export matters", *CID Working Paper*, No. 123, December, Center for International Development, Harvard University, Cambridge, Massachusetts, www.hks.harvard.edu/content/download/69336/1250154/version/1/file/123.pdf.

Hausmann, R. et al. (2012), *The Atlas of Economic Complexity*, Puritan Press, Cambridge, Massachusetts.

Hausmann et al. (2003), "Economic Development as self-discovery", *Journal of Development Economics*, Vol. 72:2, http://www.sciencedirect.com/science/article/pii/S030438780300124X.

Hayek, F.A. (1988), *The Fatal Conceit: The Errors of Socialism*, in: Bartley, W.W. III (ed.), Routledge, London.

Helliwell, J. (1994), "Empirical linkages between democracy and economic growth", *British Journal of Political Science*, Vol. 24/2, pp. 225-248, www.jstor.org/stable/194169.

IFC (2016), "How do economies define micro, small and medium enterprises?", http://www.ifc.org/wps/wcm/connect/624b8f804a17abc5b4acfddd29332b51/msme-ci-note.pdf?mod=ajperes.

Illescas, J. and C.F. Jaramillo (2011), "Export growth and diversification: The case of Peru", *Policy Research Working Papers*, The World Bank, Washington, DC, http://dx.doi.org/10.1596/1813-9450-5868.

Imbs, J. and R. Wacziarg (2003), "Stages of diversification", *American Economic Review*, Vol. 93/1, pp. 63-86, http://dx.doi.org/10.1257/000282803321455160.

Klinger, B. and D. Lederman (2004), "Discovery and development: An empirical exploration of 'new' products", *World Bank Policy Research Working Papers*, No. 3 450, The World Bank, Washington, DC, http://dx.doi.org/10.1596/1813-9450-3450.

Kose, M.A. (2002), "Explaining business cycles in small open economies: How much do world prices matter?", *Journal of International Economics*, Vol. 56/2, pp. 299-327, http://dx.doi.org/10.1016/S0022-1996(01)00120-9.

Koske, I., J.M. Fournier and I. Wanner (2012), "Less income inequality and more growth – Are they compatible? Part 2. The distribution of labour income", *OECD Economics Department Working Papers*, No. 925, OECD Publishing, Paris, http://dx.doi.org/10.1787/5k9h2975rhhf-en.

Land Brandenburg (2011), http://www.brandenburg.de/cms/list.php/bbstart.

Lengyel, M. and Ventura-Dias, V. (Eds.) (2004). Trade policy reforms in Latin America. (New York: Palgrave Macmillan).

Lester, R.K. and M.J. Piore (2004), *Innovation – The Missing Dimension*, Harvard University Press, Cambridge, Massachusetts.

Lychagin, S. et al. (2010), "Spillovers in space: Does geography matter?", *CEPR Discussion Papers*, No. 7 928, July.

McLean, I.W (2013), *Why Australia Prospered: The Shifting Sources of Economic Growth*, Princeton University Press.

Mendoza, E. (1995), "The terms of trade, the real exchange rate, and economic fluctuations", *International Economic Review*, Vol. 36/1, pp. 101-37, http://dx.doi.org/10.2307/2527429.

Ministerio de Energía y Minas (2015), Anuario Estadístico Minero 2014, http://www.mem.gob.gt/wp-content/uploads/2015/06/ANUARIO-ESTAD%C3%8DSTICO-MINERO-2014.pdf.

Ministry of Economy and Finances (n.d.), https://www.mef.gob.pe.

Mukand, S. and D. Rodrik (2002), "In search of the holy grail: Policy convergence, experimentation and economic performance", *NBER Working Papers*, No. 9 134, National Bureau of Economic Research, Cambridge, Massachusetts, http://www.nber.org/papers/w9134.

Natural Resource Governance Institute (2015), "Local level resource curse: The 'cholo disease' in Peru", Revenue Watch Institute, www.resourcegovernance.org/sites/default/files/SubnationalresourcecurseresearchDRAFT.pdf.

North, D. (1990), *Institutions, Institutional Change and Economic Performance*, Cambridge University Press, Cambridge, Massachusetts.

OECD (2015a), *Multi-dimensional Review of Peru: Volume 1. Initial Assessment*, OECD Development Pathways, OECD Publishing, Paris, http://dx.doi.org/10.1787/9789264243279-en.

OECD (2015b), "Review of entrepreneurship issues and policies in Israel: Draft report", OECD, Paris.

OECD (2015c) *Regional Development Agencies (RDA): a tool for regional development*, Paper for the 33rd session of the Regional Development Policy Committee, OECD.

OECD (2014a), *OECD Regional Outlook 2014: Regions and Cities, Where Policies and People Meet*, OECD Publishing, Paris, http://dx.doi.org/10.1787/9789264201415-en.

OECD (2014b), *OECD Territorial Reviews: Colombia 2014*, OECD Publishing, Paris, http://dx.doi.org/10.1787/9789264224551-en.

OECD (2014c), Effective Public Investment Across Levels of Government Toolkit, OECD, Paris, www.oecd.org/effective-public-investment-toolkit.

OECD (2013a), *Investing Together: Working Effectively across Levels of Government*, OECD Publishing, Paris, http://dx.doi.org/10.1787/9789264197022-en.

OECD (2013b), *Interconnected Economies: Benefiting from Global Value Chains*, OECD Publishing, Paris, http://dx.doi.org/10.1787/9789264189560-en.

OECD (2013c), OECD Regions at a Glance 2013, OECD Publishing, Paris, http://dx.doi.org/10.1787/reg_glance-2013-en.

OECD (2012a), "OECD draft synthesis report on innovation-driven growth in regions: The role of smart specialisation", OECD, Paris, https://www.oecd.org/innovation/inno/smart-specialisation.pdf.

OECD (2012b), *OECD Reviews of Regional Innovation: Central and Southern Denmark 2012*, OECD Reviews of Regional Innovation, OECD Publishing, Paris, http://dx.doi.org/10.1787/9789264178748-en.

OECD (2012c), *Promoting Growth in all Regions*, OECD Publishing, Paris, http://dx.doi.org/10.1787/9789264174634-en.

OECD (2011a), *OECD Regional Outlook 2011: Building Resilient Regions for Stronger Economies*, OECD Publishing, Paris, http://dx.doi.org/10.1787/9789264120983-en.

OECD (2011b), *OECD Reviews of Innovation Policy: Peru 2011*, OECD Publishing, Paris, http://dx.doi.org/10.1787/9789264128392-en.

OECD (2011c), *OECD Territorial Reviews: Slovenia 2011*, OECD Publishing, Paris, http://dx.doi.org/10.1787/9789264120587-en.

OECD (2010a), *OECD Reviews of Regulatory Reform: Australia 2010: Towards a Seamless National Economy*, OECD Publishing, Paris, http://dx.doi.org/10.1787/9789264067189-en.

OECD (2010b), *OECD Territorial Reviews: Sweden 2010*, OECD Publishing, Paris, http://dx.doi.org/10.1787/9789264081888-en.

OECD (2010c), *Regional Development Policies in OECD Countries*, OECD Publishing, Paris, http://dx.doi.org/10.1787/9789264087255-en.

OECD (2009a), *How Regions Grow: Trends and Analysis*, OECD Publishing, Paris, http://dx.doi.org/10.1787/9789264039469-en.

OECD (2009b), *Regions Matter: Economic Recovery, Innovation and Sustainable Growth*, OECD Publishing, Paris, http://dx.doi.org/10.1787/9789264076525-en.

OECD (2007a), *Linking Regions and Central Governments: Contracts for Regional Development*, OECD Publishing, Paris, http://dx.doi.org/10.1787/9789264008755-en.

OECD (2007b) Competitive Regional Clusters: National Policy Approaches: OECD Publishing: Paris, http://dx.doi.org/10.1787/9789264031838-en.

Pack, H. and L.E. Westphal (1986), "Industrial strategy and technological change: Theory versus reality", *Journal of Development Economics*, Vol. 22/1, pp. 87-128, http://dx.doi.org/10.1016/0304-3878(86)90053-2.

Perales, J.R. and E. Morón (eds.), (2010), *La Economía Política del Tratado de Libre Comercio entre Perú y Estados Unidos*, Woodrow Wilson Center Reports on the Americas, No. 25, www.wilsoncenter.org/sites/default/files/Peru_US.pdf.

Porter, M. (2009), "Competitiveness: A new economic strategy for Peru", PowerPoint presentation, www.hbs.edu/faculty/Publication%20Files/20091130_Peru_7abdf2f2-94cc-4f45-b262-347e24423ddf.pdf.

Porter, M.E. (ed.) (1986), *Competition in Global Industries*, Harvard Business School Press.

Rodríguez-Clare, A. (2005), "Clusters and comparative advantage: Implications for industrial policy", *Latin American Research Network Working Papers*, No. 523, Inter-American Development Bank, Washington, DC, December, www.iadb.org/en/research-and-data/publication-details,3169.html?pub_id=wp-523.

Rodrik, D. (2004), "Industrial policy for the twenty-first century", *Faculty Research Working Papers Series*, John F. Kennedy School of Government, Harvard University, Cambridge, Massachusetts, https://research.hks.harvard.edu/publications/getFile.aspx?Id=146.

Rodrik, D. (1996), "Why do more open economies have bigger governments?", *NBER Working Papers*, No. 5 537, National Bureau of Economic Research, Cambridge, Massachusetts, www.nber.org/papers/w5537.

Rodrik, D. et al. (2004), "Institutions rule: The primacy of institutions over geography and integration in economic development", *Journal of Economic Growth*, Vol. 9/2, pp. 131-165, http://dx.doi.org/10.1023/B:JOEG.0000031425.72248.85.

UNCTAD (2000), "Trade policy review – Peru – Report by the Secretariat", UNCTAD, Geneva.

Warwick, K. (2013), "Beyond industrial policy: Emerging issues and new trends", *OECD Science, Technology and Industry Policy Papers*, No. 2, OECD Publishing, Paris, http://dx.doi.org/10.1787/5k4869clw0xp-en.

Warwick, K. and A. Nolan (2014), "Evaluation of industrial policy: Methodological issues and policy lessons", *OECD Science, Technology and Industry Policy Papers*, No. 16, OECD Publishing, Paris, http://dx.doi.org/10.1787/5jz181jh0j5k-en.

Webber, D. (2004), "Managing the public's money: From outputs to outcomes – and beyond", *OECD Journal on Budgeting*, Vol. 4/2, pp. 101-121, OECD Publishing, Paris, www.oecd.org/gov/budgeting/43488736.pdf.

Chapter 3.

Urban and rural development policies

This chapter discusses urban and rural policies in Peru. It suggests how to design better urban and rural policies to improve regional development outcomes. The chapter is divided into three main parts. The first section focuses on urban development, and in particular steps that will need to be taken in terms of policy development and implementation, to develop a comprehensive urban policy framework for Peru. The second section discusses rural policies, and identifies principles and lessons for a rural development policy that can better link economic and social objectives. Finally, the third section draws some conclusions and sums up key recommendations.

Key findings and recommendations

Key findings

- The urban system in Peru is characterised by the dominance of Lima, which is performing comparatively strongly, and a number of intermediate and smaller cities with mixed performance outcomes. Regardless of these mixed outcomes, people living in cities generally have higher standards of living, which indicates that access to services are an important factor shaping urban-rural migration. Urban growth and development is shaped by the issue of informality, which makes the funding and co-ordination of infrastructure and service provision more difficult. Informal settlements constitute approximately 70% of the land area of Lima.
- Rural areas are a key source of wealth and income for the country, and exports from rural areas have diversified over the past decade. Although many of these rural areas are rich in resources, the people living there are generally poorer. Poverty is becoming more concentrated in fewer and predominantly rural places. In half of Peru's provinces, over 20% of children below five suffer from chronic malnutrition. Growth policies which can better link the endogenous assets of these places to employment and business development opportunities are needed.
- The institutional framework for urban and rural policies is fragmented and there is a lack of effective mechanisms to co-ordinate and align planning and resource allocation. Policy and planning frameworks which have been developed are not connected to resource allocation decisions in a co-ordinated way, and their implementation is not consistently monitored and evaluated. There is significant variation in how policies are implemented at a subnational level, and a lack of alignment between different levels of government. Regions are largely bypassed, which reduces incentives for collaboration between provincial and district municipalities.

Key recommendations

6. The Peruvian government should develop a comprehensive approach to urban policy which builds upon the lessons of the National Urban Development Plan (NUDP) 2006-2015, and encompasses the following elements:
   - clear policy objectives and indicators, which are outcomes-based, and monitored and evaluated
   - leadership of the Presidency of the Council of Ministers and the Ministry of Economy and Finances to ensure co-ordination in urban policies across national ministries (in particular Housing, Construction and Sanitation, Transport and Communications, Environment, and Production)
   - incentives and technical assistance for provincial and district municipalities to implement planning instruments and systems for land management (land-use zoning, development approvals and cadastre)
   - enforcement of laws to protect public land and property rights, which is currently lacking
   - the incorporation of strategic spatial planning into the fiscal framework (for example funding proposals for infrastructure should be required to demonstrate alignment with strategic spatial plans)
   - incentives to encourage the matching and co-ordination of policies at the scale of functional urban areas

Key findings and recommendations *(continued)*

– an articulation of how cities can contribute to national strategies to lift productivity and promote economic diversification, and an identification of the economic roles and functions of cities within Peru's urban system.

7. In parallel with this work, the government should also work with key stakeholders to identify options for improving the governance of land use and infrastructure for functional urban areas. This includes ensuring each city has an endorsed strategic spatial plan and urban plans, and there is a co-ordinated process for linking this with investment decisions about infrastructure at a subnational and national level. The government should prioritise reforms for the metropolitan region of Lima, which will then provide lessons for improving planning and governance arrangements in intermediate cities.

8. The development of a pro-growth rural agenda can be achieved in the following ways:

   – ensuring that the vision, objectives and priorities for rural development have a strong focus on productivity and diversification and are included in relevant policies across government (the centre of government – Presidency of the Council of Ministers and the Ministry of Economy and Finances – should work in partnership to ensure buy-in and commitment from different national ministries to this policy agenda)

   – prioritise the development of initiatives which are designed to enhance productivity and diversification opportunities for rural communities (e.g. mining, agriculture, fisheries and tourism)

   – adapt existing social programmes such as *Juntos* and better link clients with opportunities for skills development, employment and entrepreneurship (this will provide a platform to make further inroads into poverty reduction, and reduce reliance on transfers over time)

   – strengthen the role of regions in the planning and co-ordination of rural development initiatives by ensuring concerted regional development plans include a strong focus on rural economic development.

Introduction

Peru is a territorially diverse country and cities and regions play differing roles in the country's future development. To lift the productivity of the services sector, Lima and secondary cities will need to work better. With Lima playing such a dominant role in the economy, the productivity and well-being of the city is a national policy issue. More can be done to foster a system of cities by increasing connectivity and improving integration with rural areas. Rural areas are a key driver for the national economy with the vast majority of Peru's exports coming from mining and agriculture. However, people living in rural areas are poorer, and low levels of human capital constrain the potential of these places to fully utilise their assets. Urban and rural policies will play a key role in harnessing the growth potential of Peru's cities and regions.

Increasingly across OECD countries it is recognised that national governments should play a more proactive role in urban policy. Three-quarters of the population in OECD countries live in cities, and if their development is managed effectively, they can be an important source of technological development and productivity growth. Effective urban policy requires clear differentiation and alignment between the roles of different levels of government, and mechanisms to co-ordinate "city shaping" land-use, infrastructure and environmental policies. As urban policy tends to involve trade-offs between different policy options, citizen engagement is also important to the design and implementation of policies at a metropolitan and local scale.

The national government is beginning to take a greater role in urban policy through the National Urban Development Plan (NUDP) (2006), which was developed by the Ministry of Housing, Construction and Sanitation. It has also sought to provide support for more effective planning and governance for metropolitan Lima. However, there is still very little co-ordination between the different levels of government.[1] Urban policy in Peru is designed and executed within a complex institutional landscape involving all levels of government to differing degrees. There is a need to better co-ordinate policies, and ensure they are linked to regulatory and budget instruments. These are common issues across OECD countries, and OECD principles and practices present some lessons and insights for policy makers in Peru as they move toward a more comprehensive urban policy for the country.

Over the past 20 years OECD countries have shifted toward a place-based approach to rural policy to better mobilise the varied assets and potential of different rural areas. This approach has a number of key features. The first is the recognition of the varied potential of different rural places linked to agriculture, tourism, extractive industries and environmental services. The second is that mobilising this potential depends on a development strategy that can influence the different factors that shape the performance of local firms (e.g. infrastructure, skills and innovation). The third is that government needs to play an enabling role by empowering local actors to design and deliver place-based rural development strategies.

These lessons can provide insights for rural policy makers in Peru in crafting a rural development agenda for the country. There currently is no clear whole-of-government policy framework or co-ordinating mechanism for rural development policies in Peru. There are many different programmes with significant resources that are designed to address poverty in rural areas, and a smaller number focused on improving agricultural productivity and natural resource use. These programmes have been able to build various constituencies of interested stakeholders and a vast network of clients receiving direct transfers. However, these resources are not effectively linked at national, regional and local level. The contemporary approach to rural development outlined in this chapter provides ideas and lessons for addressing these issues.

Urban development and policies

Levels of urbanisation have converged to the OECD average

Peru is a highly urbanised country when compared to other countries with similar gross domestic product (GDP) per capita. According to official definitions, 78.3% of the population lives in urban areas. The level of urbanisation has increased significantly over the past 50 years, from 46.8% in 1960 to 76.9% in 2010.

It is important to note that increasing urbanisation is not necessarily related to development. Indeed, the increasing rate of urbanisation over the past 50 years in Peru is not associated with significant advances in per capita income. While virtually all high-income countries have fairly high levels of urbanisation, not all urbanised countries have achieved high levels of income (Henderson, 2010). Unfortunately, Latin American countries are prominent among those that urbanised faster than they developed (OECD, 2014c).

Figure 3.1. **Urban population as a percentage of the national population: Peru compared to countries with similar per capita incomes, 2014**

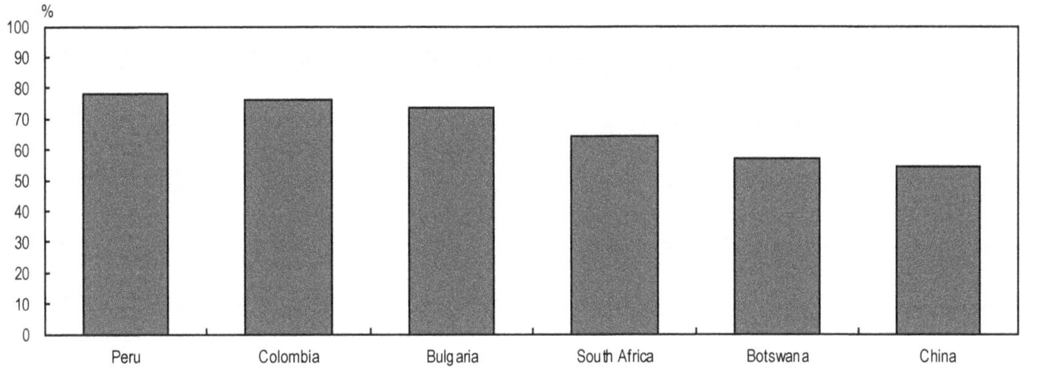

Source: World Bank (2015), "International tourism, number of arrivals", http://data.worldbank.org/indicator/ST.INT.ARVL?page=4.

Figure 3.2. **Urban population as a percentage of the national population: Peru compared with OECD and Latin American and Caribbean countries**

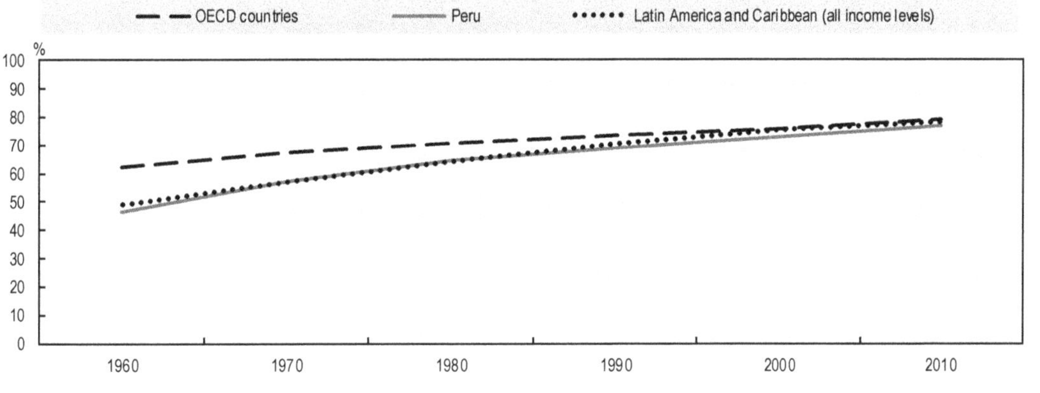

Note: Urban population refers to people living in urban areas as defined by national statistical offices.

Source: World Bank (2015), "International tourism, number of arrivals", http://data.worldbank.org/indicator/ST.INT.ARVL?page=4.

In the case of Peru, the concentration of growth in Lima is also due to a mix of historical, political and institutional factors. This includes the historical dominance of Lima in the economic and political system of Peru, and the likelihood that migration toward Lima was shaped by non-economic factors (particularly access to services). It is probably also a reflection of the lack of strategic planning and management in the growth of urban areas across the country.

The metropolitan area of Lima-Callao dominates the urban system

The key feature of the urban system of Peru is the dominance of the metropolitan area of Lima-Callao with approximately 30% of the national population. Prior to European settlement, the area of Lima was an important religious and agricultural-based settlement for indigenous people. Lima was settled by the Spanish in 1535 and as the capital of the Viceroy became one of the most important cities in the Spanish empire. The key political and administrative functions for governing Latin America were located in Lima, and it was an important economic and trading centre as mineral resources from the interior were transported through the city. The critical role and functions that Lima plays in the national economy evolved from these initial conditions.

Figure 3.3. **Urbanisation and convergence in the world**

Real GDP per capita (as a percent of US GDP/capita) and level of urbanisation, selected countries

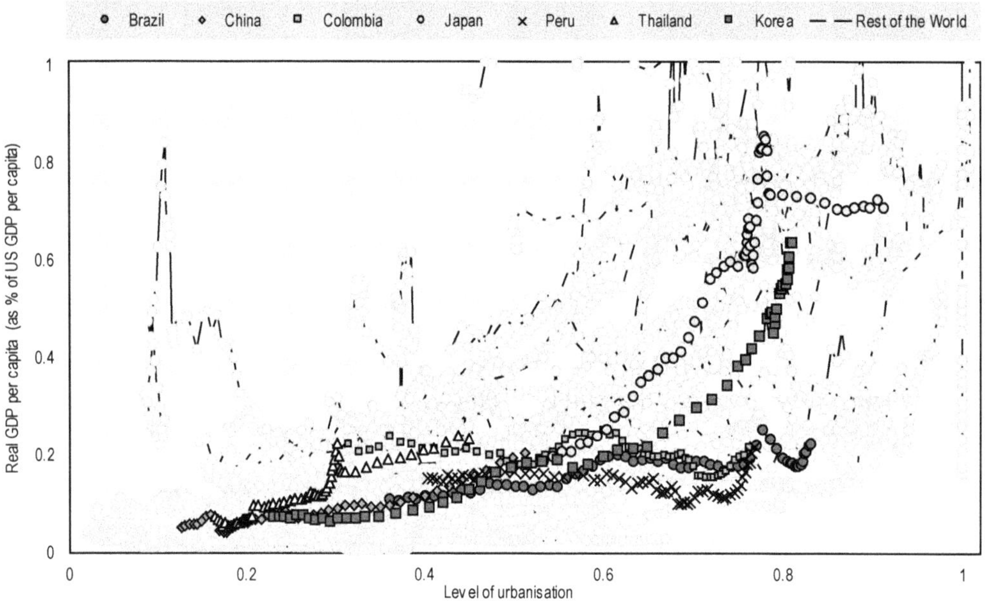

Source: Feenstra, R.C., R. Inklaar and M.P. Timmer (2015), "The next generation of the Penn World table", www.ggdc.net/pwt; United Nations, Department of Economic and Social Affairs, Population Division (2014), *World Urbanization Prospects: The 2014 Revision*, https://esa.un.org/unpd/wup/CD-ROM.

The dominance of Lima in the urban system was also shaped by the topography of the country. Among cities with a population over 100 000, 10 are located on the coast (*costa*), 6 in the highlands (*sierra*) and only 2 in the rainforest (*selva*) (Ministry of Housing, Construction and Sanitation, 2006). These coastal cities developed because of their proximity to natural resources, and the capacity to access Lima and international markets. The fewer cities which did develop in the highlands and the rainforest were due to proximity to natural resources and key trading routes (such as Arequipa).

Detailed analysis of the urban structure of Peru is limited by the availability of descriptive statistics at the city level. The main unit of analysis is the district/municipality level drawing from the 2007 census. This data limitation reinforces the importance of improving the country's system of territorial statistics as outlined in Chapter 1. The 2007 census accounts for 93 districts with a population greater than 50 000, with 40 located in Lima-Callao, which have a total population of 8.4 million.

The dominance of the metropolitan area of Lima-Callao is revealed when assessing the distribution of districts with a population over 50 000. The total population of these districts in Peru is 13.8 million, and 60.9% of the population living within them is located in 40 districts within Lima-Callao. The next three most-urbanised regions are Piura and La Libertad in the north of the country on the coast, and Arequipa in the south which includes both coastal and highland areas. There are 18 districts within these regions with a population over 50 000, and the total population of these districts is 1.9 million.

Figure 3.4.: **Log population sizes and ranks of Peruvian cities above 50 000 inhabitants**

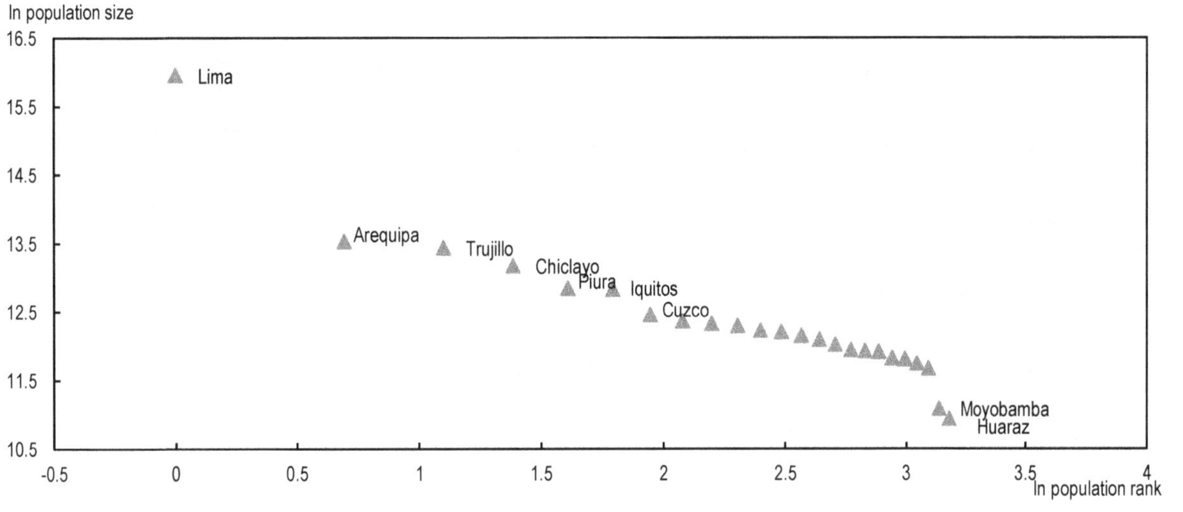

Source: OECD elaboration.

Peru's urban structure with a single dominant city is similar to other countries in Latin America including Argentina, Chile and Uruguay. However, a key feature of Peru's urban system is the lack of secondary cities, with no other cities above 1 million people. There are two key implications of this in terms of national development:

1. The complexity and costs of improving infrastructure and services within Lima, particularly addressing investments to address overcrowding and better connecting informal settlements to the metropolitan transport network. This is likely to become more of an issue as the country's per capita income increases and the policy focus shifts to more inclusive growth.

2. Because other cities of sufficient size have not emerged, there is a lack of alternative locations for rural migration, or the capacity for a number of cities to develop different specialisations in services and manufacturing. This is a characteristic of many other countries, and as further economic activity concentrates in Lima it is likely to be further affected by overcrowding and diseconomies of scale.

Table 3.1. **Regional distribution of districts with a population over 50 000, 2007***

Department	Number of districts > 50 000	Total population
Lima and Callao	40	8 431 147
Piura	5	647 517
La Libertad	4	642 820
Arequipa	9	624 848
Lambayeque	3	496 683
Loreto	4	360 314
Puno	2	333 993
Junín	3	323 054
Cusco	4	319 257
Áncash	2	305 408
Ica	4	286 983
Cajamarca	2	213 405
Ucayali	2	202 936
Tacna	2	154 953
Huánuco	2	129 303
Ayacucho	1	97 390
Tumbes	1	91 365
San Martín	1	67 362
Moquega	1	58 649
Madre de Dios	1	56 382
Total	93	13 843 769

Note: * Last census, population projections can be found at: http://proyectos.inei.gob.pe/web/biblioineipub/bancopub/Est/Lib1010/index.htm.

Source: CEPLAN (2015), "Background report for National Territorial Review of Peru", unpublished.

As a result, policy makers need to primarily consider Lima as a separate case in designing national policies. This also emphasises the importance of improving the growth planning and management of other cities in Peru, and examining ways to better link these cities with the metropolitan area of Lima-Callao. Through better connections these cities can benefit more from the agglomeration effects generated by the capital.

Although the proportions are still rather small compared to Lima, some secondary cities such as Arequipa, Trujillo or Chiclayo have been capturing some of the rural migration. An important number of the latter nonetheless end up moving to Lima, and those that stay do so in cities that have not planned their growth and often in informal settlements, as it has been the case in Lima.

People living in urban areas enjoy higher standards of living but cities are not performing to their potential

In terms of labour productivity (measured by regional gross value added [GVA] per worker), urban areas are not performing strongly. Five out of the nine regions above the national average do not have significant urban agglomerations within them (Moquegua, Ica, Madre de Dios, Tacna and Pasco). In terms of regions with larger urban populations, Lambayeque, Loreto, Puno and Junín performed poorly. Although Lima is the third-best performer, it is not performing that well considering the size of its population and the industry mix. This reinforces the point that the sources of Peru's growth are largely exogenous through the demand and price for commodities. The drivers of growth are far less urban than the level and scale of urban populations, and the structure of employment and activity would suggest.

Box 3.1. Connectivity and fostering a system of cities

Because cities do not exist in isolation, connectivity at all scales is increasingly important to the performance of national urban systems. This, too, is an area where national policies matter. A number of national governments have considered improving transport both within and among metropolitan areas to boost development potential. National decisions about major infrastructure networks can have a tremendous impact on cities' competitiveness and growth potential, particularly in countries where decision-making authority over national infrastructure is held tightly at central government level. In many OECD countries, for example, the location of airports remains a matter for national governments. Inter-city road and rail networks are likewise generally planned by senior governments.

Much depends on how governments assess potential investments in new infrastructure. In the United Kingdom, for example, critics have long argued that the kinds of cost-benefit analysis typically employed focus too much on resolving immediate constraints and too little on growth potential. The result is that in the most recent period, as much as 80% of major transport infrastructure spending was earmarked for London and the South-East, compared to just 6% for the North (NEFC, 2012; HM Treasury, 2011).

National governments also play a major role in intra-urban transport. This is the case partly because their financial support is often required for major infrastructure investments and partly because higher level governments sometimes have to step in to assure co-ordination of transport networks at metropolitan or regional scales, which transcend the boundaries of individual municipalities.

Some governments foster systems of cities by establishing stronger links between cities of varying sizes, particularly through transport. Governments may set targets for cities to fulfil different roles (e.g. "Innovation Cities", "Enterprise Cities", "Eco-Towns") or increase linkages between metropolitan areas and smaller cities within a larger region (e.g. proposals for the Seine valley axis between Paris and Le Havre). National governments can also support the development of urban transport networks in metropolitan areas. In 2008, the French government's proposal to boost the economic competitiveness of the Paris metro region through the Greater Paris Plan (*Grand Paris*) centred on the development of a new high-speed underground transport line to connect Paris' suburbs (Kamal-Chaoui and Plouin, 2012).

Source: OECD (2014a), *OECD Regional Outlook 2014: Regions and Cities, Where Policies and People Meet*, http://dx.doi.org/10.1787/9789264201415-en.

Figure 3.5. **GVA per worker: Peru's regions, 2013**

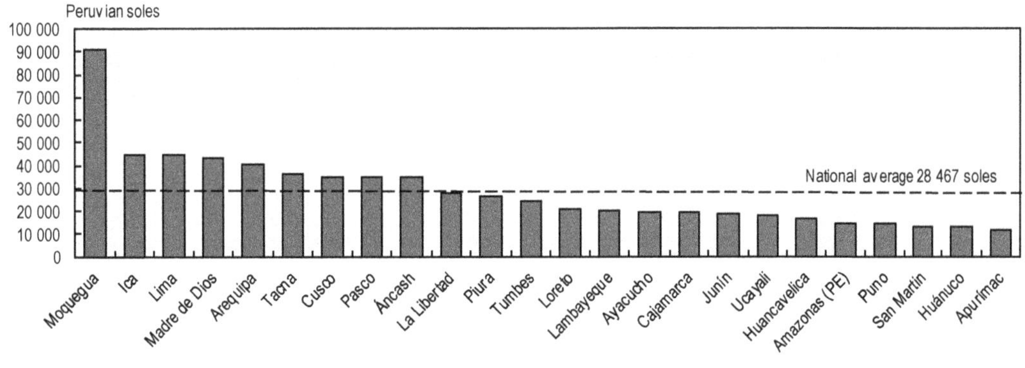

Source: OECD analysis based on data from INEI.

Cities are also not performing strongly in terms of their rate of economic growth. In the period 2007-13, the more urbanised regional economies of Cusco (11%), Ica (9%) and Lambayque (7%) performed well above the national average of 5% average annual growth rate in GVA. Lima also performed relatively strongly with an annual average growth rate of 7%. Other regions with larger urban populations performed at or below the national average: La Libertad (5%), Arequipa (5%), Loreto (3%), Junín (3%) and Áncash (3%). Regions with a smaller urban population such as Ayacucho (9%), Tumbes (8%), Huánuco (7%) and San Martín (7%) also performed strongly. Although rural-based industries are important to regional economic performance, these findings also suggest that some of the secondary cities in Peru are also underperforming.

Figure 3.6. **Average annual growth (GVA) for regions compared to the national average, ranked by total population in urban districts**

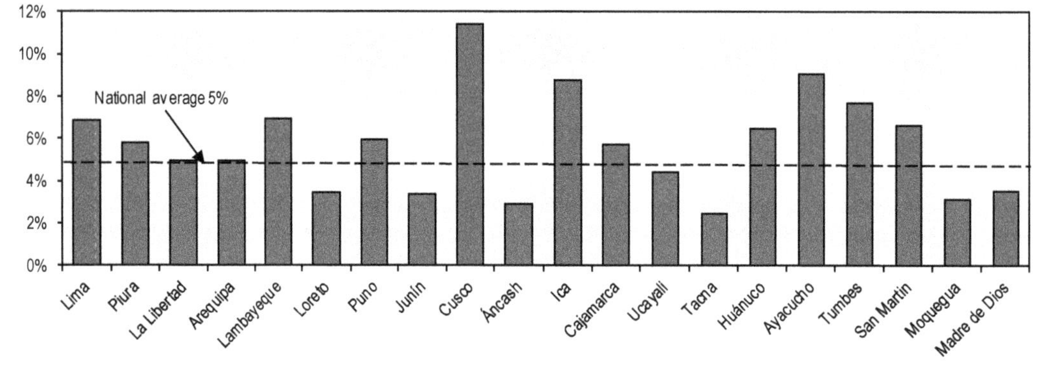

Source: OECD analysis based on data from INEI.

Regardless of this mixed performance, people living in urban areas generally experience higher standards of living. This is apparent in differences between urban and rural areas in terms of access to basic services and levels of poverty. These differences also suggest that access to public services and infrastructure has been an important factor in shaping migration trends in Peru.

Figure 3.7. **Access to improved water sources, urban and rural areas, Peru, 2015**

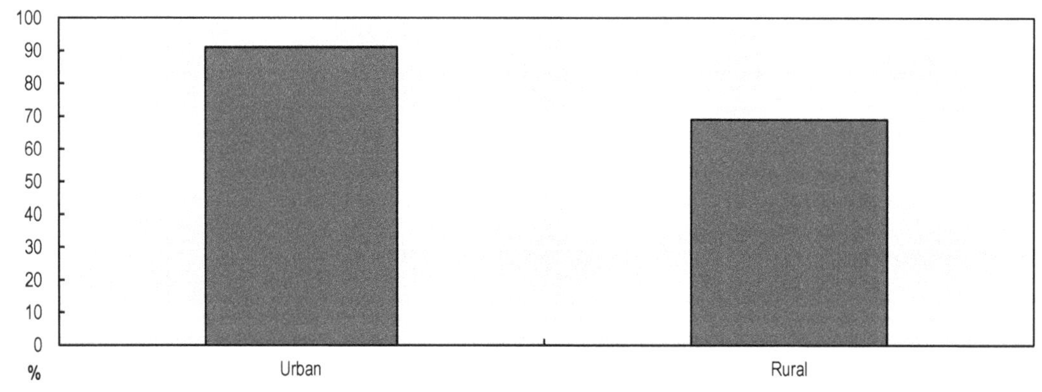

Source: World Bank (2016a), Improved water source, urban and rural (% population with access), http://databank.worldbank.org/data/reports.aspx?source=2&series=SH.H2O.SAFE.UR.ZS&country=.

Figure 3.8. **Percentage of the population living below national poverty lines, 2014**

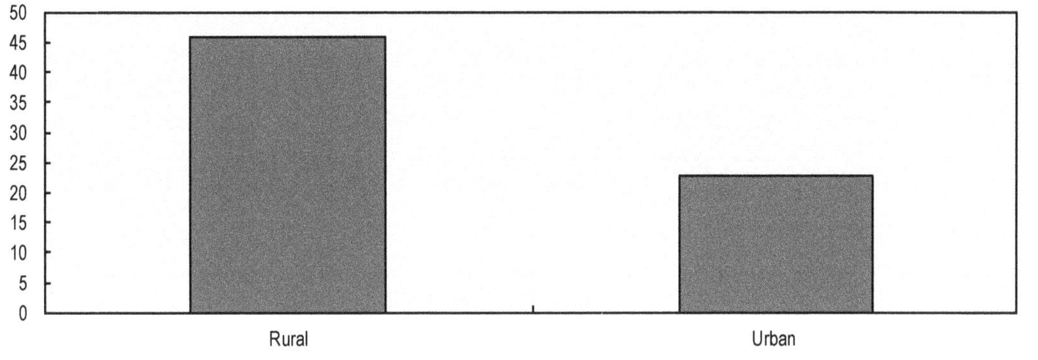

Source: World Bank (2016 b). Rural poverty headcount at national poverty lines (% of rural/urban populations) http://databank.worldbank.org/data/reports.aspx?source=2&Topic=11.

As the economy continues to transition, the productivity performance of Lima and other cities will become more important to aggregate growth. Cities are important to productivity growth, particularly in terms of the services sector, because they can enable easier interactions between firms and workers (OECD, 2014a). The ease of these interactions depends, in turn, on how cities are organised and the functioning of the transport network.

Box 3.2. **Agglomeration economies**

Economic activity is not naturally dispersed; rather it tends to concentrate in some places rather than others, mainly owing to the benefits associated with economies of agglomeration. People want to live where firms – and therefore job opportunities – are concentrated, and firms want to locate where demand – and therefore population – is large. Agglomeration economies occur when firms enjoy increasing returns to scale (IRS) in a particular place. Some of these IRS effects are internal to the firm while others are externalities. Often, these external effects are reciprocal, at least to some degree – that is, agents are not compensated for the benefits they generate for their neighbours, but neither do they have to compensate others when they themselves benefit from positive externalities. The reciprocal effects are one of the main reasons why clusters form and flourish.

IRS could arise in a place because of the presence of natural advantages (i.e. natural resources, location, etc.), monopolistic protection, political factors (e.g. the decision to create a capital city or administrative centre) or some other reason. The presence of IRS also induces other firms to locate there, as people come in search of higher wages, a wider range of job opportunities, and better/more varied amenities and consumption opportunities. Part of the advantage of large cities thus stems from their attraction for high productivity firms and for individuals with high levels of human capital; in other words, a selection effect is at work. However, there is clear evidence that this selection process is magnified by agglomeration dynamics: other things being equal, individuals and firms become more productive in denser places. This reflects the opportunities that cities afford for sharing assets, improving matches on the labour market and knowledge diffusion . The result of these combined selection effects and agglomeration dynamics is that cities tend to be more productive, on average, than non-urban places (the major exceptions tend to be resource-rich rural regions). They have higher incomes and higher GDP per capita. Three main mechanisms work to produce agglomeration economies:

Box 3.2. **Agglomeration economies** (*continued*)

1. Mechanisms that deal with sharing of:

- Indivisible facilities such as local public goods or facilities that serve several individuals or firms. Some examples, other than public goods, are facilities such as laboratories, universities and other large goods that do not belong to a particular agent but where some exclusion is implicit in providing them.
- The gains from the wider range of input suppliers that can be sustained by a larger final goods industry. In other words, the presence of increasing returns to scale, along with forward and backward linkages, allow firms to purchase intermediate inputs at lower costs. While the literature has tended to focus on the variety of inputs available, a variety of potential suppliers is also good for firms, in that it is likely to lead to lower prices (more competition) and less risk of disruption if an upstream firm is distressed (redundancy in markets). The latter issue is particularly relevant in low-density places, where long supply chains and a lack of such redundancy can render firms vulnerable – and may in some cases prompt greater vertical integration than would be efficient in a denser place.
- The gains from the narrower specialisation that can be sustained with higher production levels. Several firms specialise in producing complementary products, reducing overall production costs.
- Risks. This refers to the idea that an industry gains from having a constant market for skills. If there are market shocks, firms can adjust to changes in demand if they have access to a deep and broad labour market that allows them to expand or contract their demand for labour.

2. Matching mechanisms by which:

- Agglomeration improves the expected quality of matches between firms and workers, so both are better able to find a good match for their needs.
- An increase in the number of agents trying to match in the labour market also improves the probability of matching.
- Delays are alleviated. Contractual problems arising from renegotiation among buyers and suppliers can potentially result in one of the parties losing out to the other party in a renegotiation. However, if the agglomeration is extensive enough, agents can find an alternative partner.

3. Learning mechanisms based on the generation, diffusion and accumulation of knowledge. This refers not only to the learning of technologies, but also the acquisition of skills.

OECD metropolitan regions benefit from agglomeration effects and thus tend to display higher levels of productivity, higher rates of employment and higher levels of GDP per capita than other regions. These benefits, however, are limited by congestion costs, diseconomies of scale and oversupply of labour, among other potential negative elements, and many metro regions have in recent decades tended to underperform national economies.

Source: OECD (2014c), *OECD Territorial Reviews: Colombia 2014*, http://dx.doi.org/10.1787/9789264224551-en.

Reshaping cities to realise these agglomeration benefits depends upon effective co-ordination between land use and infrastructure policies across levels of government

(OECD, 2014c). A larger number of stakeholders can increase the degree of complexity in policy co-ordination, and small municipalities can also fail to account for metropolitan-wide benefits in decision making about land use and infrastructure (OECD, 2015). These complexities can generate costs and empirical evidence suggests that administrative fragmentation can reduce productivity (Ahrend et al., 2014).

The governance landscape in Lima is complex. There are a number of national ministries which have responsibility for urban infrastructure and land-use policies including the Ministry of Housing, Construction and Sanitation; the Ministry of Development and Social Inclusion; the Ministry of Transport and Communications; and the Ministry of Production. The municipality of metropolitan Lima has the third-largest administrative area of any city in Latin America and includes 43 municipal districts. Callao is functionally integrated with Lima and is overseen by a different provincial government. There are also different entities involved in the planning, construction and operation of different elements of the transport network.

Table 3.2. **Land area of Latin American cities**

City	Land area (km^2)
Sucre (Bolivia)	11 800
Brasilia (Brazil)	5 802
Lima (Peru)	2 670
Mexico City (Mexico)	1 485
Caracas (Venezuela)	777
Bogota (Colombia)	776
Santiago (Chile)	641
Quito (Ecuador)	352
Buenos Aries (Argentina)	202
Montevideo (Uruguay)	200
Asuncion (Paraguay)	117

Source: Data from Municipalidad Metropolitana de Lima.

Issues related to a lack of effective co-ordination between land use and infrastructure is apparent in patterns of urban growth within the metropolitan area of Lima. Lack of clarity in land use, infrastructure and housing policies has resulted in the development of an unequal city with insufficient provision of public infrastructure and services for a significant proportion of the population. Informal settlements constitute approximately 70% of the urban land area of the metropolitan region (DCC and MEF, 2014). People living in these informal settlements lack access to basic services, which creates barriers for participation in economic and social participation. Due to lack of land availability, the formal city is increasing in density, and this is placing further pressures on water and sewerage systems, and the transport network.

Table 3.3. **Service gap in informal settlements**

Availability of public services	Service gap
Drinkable water	62.2%
Rain drainage	12.9%
Sewage system	61.1%
Domestic/public lighting	73.1%
Street paving	16.0%
Phone coverage	94.9%
Internet coverage	60.7%

Source: CEPLAN (2015), "Background report for National Territorial Review of Peru", unpublished.

Box 3.3. The price of administrative fragmentation in metropolitan areas

Metropolitan areas frequently contain more than 100 local governments. This degree of administrative fragmentation might create positive outcomes. Improvements can arise if competition among local administrations results in better services provided by the local governments or reduces the costs paid by residents through local taxes. But administrative fragmentation also adds a degree of complexity to the design and implementation of policies that require co-ordination, which can stymie the productivity of urban agglomerations. Particularly fields that require co-ordination at the metropolitan scale, such as land-use or transport planning, or economic policies that create externalities across administrative borders, are adversely affected by administrative fragmentation and result in a "price" that metropolitan areas have to pay when their administrative boundaries differ strongly from their economic realities.

Ahrend et al. (2014) quantify the impact of administrative fragmentation. Using a two-step estimation procedure, they first estimate the relative productivity of functional urban areas (FUAs) from micro-data on employees' earnings. These differentials indicate how much more (or less) a worker with the same characteristics earns in different FUAs. Assuming that labour markets are competitive, these differentials capture how much productivity differs across FUAs. In the second step, the productivity differentials are explained by characteristics of FUAs that influence the productivity of the workforce. These characteristics include the FUA's size (to capture agglomeration benefits), its industrial structure and degree of specialisation, and an indicator for capital cities and port cities, Crucially, Ahrend et al. (2014) also control for the degree of administrative fragmentation and the presence of a metropolitan governance body.

Ahrend et al. (2014) find a strong negative impact of administrative fragmentation on productivity. Their results also show that metropolitan governance bodies, which are present in many OECD metropolitan areas, can help alleviate the "price". The empirical results indicate that for two metropolitan areas of similar size and population composition in terms of observable characteristics, but with one having twice the number of municipalities, the productivity in the more fragmented metropolitan area is about 6% lower. Governance bodies are estimated to reduce the penalty to about half its size.

Figure 3.9. **Administrative fragmentation and productivity**

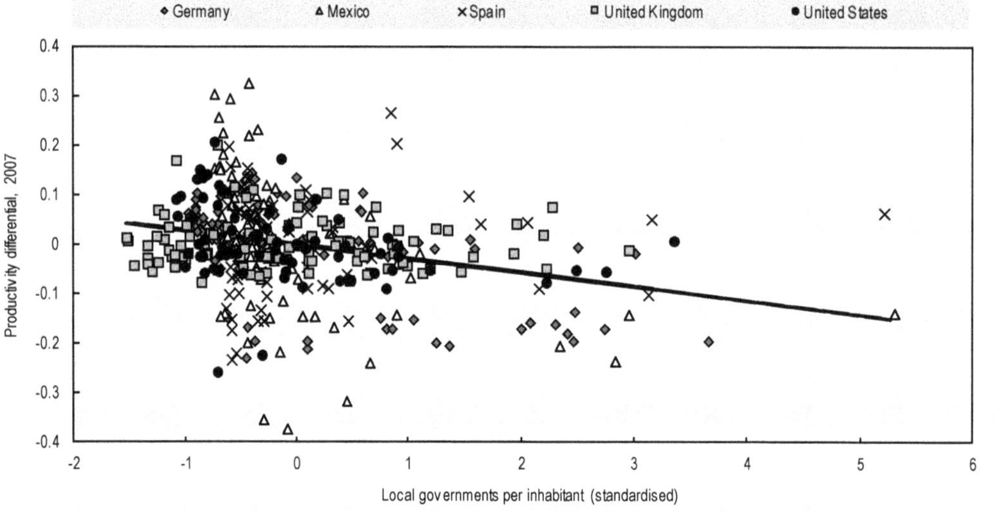

It is important to note that these results are not the same for rural areas. Reducing administrative fragmentation in rural areas tends to produce no or detrimental results in terms of economic growth. This is due to the increased distances required to administer and deliver public infrastructure and services in low density areas.

Sources: Ahrend, R. et al. (2014), "What makes cities more productive? Evidence on the role of urban governance from five OECD countries", http://dx.doi.org/10.1787/5jz432cf2d8p-en; Bartolini, D. (forthcoming), "Fiscal decentralisation and regional disparities: The role of fiscal vertical imbalances".

These *ad hoc* patterns of urban growth and development have also led to an increasing problem of traffic congestion, which is impacting upon the productivity and liveability of Lima-Callao. Between 1989 and 2012, annual motorised trips increased by 10 million, and there has been an increase from 1.1 trips per inhabitant to almost 2 trips per inhabitant (OECD, 2016). This increase in car use and mobility is generating negative externalities. It is reducing accessibility to jobs by increasing travel times (on average by 20% between 2004 and 2012); higher levels of pollution which is presenting public health risks; and deaths, injuries and disabilities caused by traffic accidents (OECD, 2016). Better integration of land use and transport planning to encourage a more efficient and sustainable urban form for Lima-Callao is a key challenge.

National governments have an important role in shaping urban development outcomes

There is no single definition for urban policies, and how these policies are conceived and delivered differs between countries. In the post-war period, many OECD countries developed national spatial planning frameworks to address inequities in the distribution of economic activity and welfare between regions. There has been a general trend toward urban policies which are more orientated toward the growth and competitiveness of cities, rather than distributional outcomes between cities and regions (OECD, 2006). Cities have developed strategic planning frameworks, which provide guidance for decisions about the location of businesses, housing, public services and transport infrastructure. There has been a growing recognition about the importance of how cities are organised to productivity, environmental sustainability and inclusive growth (OECD, 2015).

National governments play an important role in urban development policy. Their first role is establishing the ground rules for cities (OECD, 2014a). National legislation typically defines cities' responsibilities, powers and revenue sources. This basic legislative framework is overlooked and the main elements are outlined below.

- Tax and budgetary frameworks, which may create powerful incentives that contradict other national policy priorities, such as promoting urban sprawl. For example, property tax systems can make greenfield development more attractive to cities than infill (Merk et al., 2012). Where property taxes are levied chiefly on buildings and other improvements rather than land values, as is the case across much of the OECD, those who hold good sites for infill but do not use them are taxed very little and it is often more profitable for new developments to take place on greenfield sites.
- Fiscal frameworks can also reinforce urban inequalities. In Chile, for instance, rules governing subnational governments' access to credit for capital investment projects require municipalities to demonstrate an ability to reimburse the credit within a specified timeframe. This favours wealthier municipalities and increases inequalities in service provision within and across metro areas (OECD, 2013a). More generally, mechanisms like performance-based grants, which are used in many OECD countries, can reinforce inter-municipal inequalities by ensuring that those with more resources and better capacities are better able to "play the game" (Steffensen, 2010).
- National policies also define to a great extent the terms on which inter-jurisdictional competition takes place. Some forms of competition are healthy and can drive cities to improve services and amenities in an effort to attract firms and households (Tiebout, 1956). Others, though, are undesirable and

can encourage attempts to externalise tax burdens, to entrench spatial inequalities or to engage in a regulatory "race to the bottom" (Spink, Ward and Wilson, 2012).

Secondly, national governments are responsible for sectoral policies that impact urban development (e.g. education, transport and health), and also develop explicit urban policies. Many national urban policies tend to focus on problems rather than potential (OECD, 2014a). They are frequently conceived in response to specific urban problems, such as social exclusion, infrastructure bottlenecks or a deliberate desire to steer settlement patterns across the national territory (Le Galés, 2007). The broader needs of cities are thus overlooked by a problem-focused concept of urban policies and a lack of recognition of other policies with important urban impacts.

Table 3.4. **Complementarities among selected policies in urban areas**

Policy	Impact		
	Land-use zoning	Transportation	Natural resources
Land-use zoning *Land-use zoning determines the density, height of buildings and proportion of undeveloped land on each property.*		Segregation of land uses impacts travel distances and frequency; transit-oriented development zones encourage use of mass transportation.	Zoning designates natural resource areas that may be set aside to reduce vulnerability to flooding or urban heat island effects.
Transportation *Transportation policies determine the development and extension of road and mass transportation networks.*	Transportation infrastructure policies shape demand for land and acceptance of density increases.		Transportation systems impact natural resources and preserved zones.
Natural resources *Natural resource policies determine which areas are preserved from development and what uses are acceptable on them.*	Natural resource policies determine the limits of developed land-use zones and can improve quality of high-density zones.	Natural resource policies affect the placement of road and mass transportation infrastructure.	

Source: Based on Kamal-Chaoui, L. and A. Robert (2009), "Competitive cities and climate change", http://dx.doi.org/10.1787/218830433146.

Thirdly, higher levels of government can play an important role in terms of encouraging co-ordination amongst subnational governments. There has been increasing attention in recent years to the benefits of governing cities as functional economies rather than administrative units (OECD, 2014a). The greater Chicago tri-state area in the United States, for example, is home to no fewer than 1 700 municipalities and other special purpose governmental authorities. Even relatively modest-sized urban agglomerations are often quite fragmented. The evidence suggests that leadership from higher levels of government is often required to bring about the cross-jurisdictional co-operation among municipalities that is needed in complex metropolitan areas (OECD, 2013c).

National urban policies are designed and executed within a complex institutional landscape

In Peru, there are nine national ministries which have competencies related to the provision of infrastructure and the use of land, and therefore have a direct impact upon the form and structure of urban areas. This is comparable to OECD countries where the average government had 6.7 ministries or national level departments or agencies with explicit urban policy functions (OECD, 2014a). Some of these national ministries in Peru potentially have overlapping or closely related responsibilities in terms of:

- strategic spatial planning (Housing, Construction and Sanitation, and Environment with the PCM-CEPLAN playing a key role in national and regional development planning which also relates to cities)
- the regulation of land use (Ministries of Housing, Construction and Sanitation; Environment; Agriculture and Irrigation; and Culture)
- infrastructure planning and regulation (Ministries of Transport and Communications, Education, Health).

These policy areas have important complementarities that need to be considered systematically by policy makers.

Table 3.5. **Roles and responsibilities of national ministries in relation to urban policy**

National ministry	Roles and responsibilities
Housing, Construction and Sanitation	– Policies related to housing, construction, sanitation, public buildings and urban property – National urban policy guidelines and planning legislation (*ordenamiento urbano*)
Ministry of Economy and Finance	– National budgeting responsibilities – Instruments to assess subnational performance and investment proposals (SNIP) – Oversight of public private-partnerships (PPPs)
Environment	– National land-use planning guidelines and regulations (*ordenamiento territorial*) – National environmental planning and regulation – Guidance and technical tools for environmental planning at regional and municipal levels
Presidency of the Council of Ministers (CEPLAN)	– National development planning, and guidance and tools for the development of concerted regional development plans
Transport and Communications	– National policies regulating transport and communications – Management of the national highway network
Culture	– Management of cultural heritage
Agriculture and Irrigation	– Soil management, regulation and use
Education	– Policies and programmes related to the provision of education infrastructure
Health	– Regulations and provisions related to water supply, sewerage and solid waste disposal
Defence	– Reservation of land for defence purposes

Source: OECD analysis based on information provided by CEPLAN.

In addition, the MEF has a responsibility for assessing budgetary proposals from national ministries and subnational governments. Several other ministries have sectoral policies, regulatory responsibilities and programmes that also impact upon cities. This includes the Ministry for Social Inclusion and Development, the Ministry of Production, the National Council for Competitiveness, and, with more cross-cutting responsibilities, the Decentralization Secretariat of the Presidency of the Council of Ministers (PCM). Overall, this emphasises the importance of co-ordination amongst national ministries to ensure policies are complementary for working toward common urban development policy objectives.

Co-ordination and alignment between levels of government is essential for delivering urban policies (OECD, 2014a). This is especially true for Peru in terms of co-ordination between provincial and district municipalities, which both play an important role in developing land-use plans and infrastructure at a local level. Each provincial municipality has the role of developing a spatial plan for their territory and supervising regulatory provisions related to it. District municipalities also prepare local plans, and have responsibility for administrating regulatory instruments related to land use, building and infrastructure. There is also scope for district municipalities to co-operate a project level through *mancomunidades*, which is a legal instrument that enables inter-municipal co-operation and joint ventures. In turn, this raises the importance of co-ordination and alignment with the regional and national level, particularly when considering there are 196 provinces and 1 867 district municipalities in Peru.

Table 3.6. **Roles and responsibilities of provincial municipalities in relation to urban policy**

Functions of provincial and district governments	Roles and responsibilities
Exclusive functions of the provincial level	–Territorial Conditioning Plan that identifies areas for urban and rural land use, areas of protection or security from natural hazards, agricultural areas and areas of environmental conservation. – Approve the plans of metropolitan development and of urban development, the Rural Development Plan, the zoning scheme urban areas, the Development Plan on Human Settlements and other specific plans in accordance with the Territorial Conditioning Plan. – Supervision of the district municipalities in regards to regulatory approvals related to these plans including land use, building and environmental assessment.
Functions shared by the provincial level	– Co-ordination of infrastructure works that impact upon multiple district or provincial municipalities. – Design and promote the implementation of municipal housing programmes for low-income families.

Source: OECD analysis based on information provided by CEPLAN.

Table 3.7. **Roles and responsibilities of district municipalities in relation to urban policy**

Exclusive functions of the district level	– Approve the urban or rural district plan, as appropriate, subject to approvals from the provincial municipality for regulations they are responsible for. – Authorise and oversee the implementation of the plan of works for public and private services ensuring compliance with the rules on environmental impact. – Develop and maintain the district land register. – Promote the development and formalisation of human settlements. – Regulatory approvals related to building, land use, communications and infrastructure.
Functions shared by the district level	– Provision of urban and rural infrastructure essential for the development of the district, in co-ordination with the respective provincial municipality. – Identify dilapidated property and land in which urban renewal tasks be carried out in co-ordination with the provincial municipality and the regional government. – In consolidating rural property, the Commission to Formalise Informal Property will act as a technical advisory body of local governments, for which the respective agreements will be signed.

Source: OECD analysis based on information provided by CEPLAN.

The regional level of government has a smaller role than other levels of government in urban policy matters. Regions are required to prepare concerted regional development plans, which provide an overarching policy framework for the development of the region. They also have a role in the implementation of regional infrastructure and economic development initiatives. However, regional governments do not endorse or monitor planning frameworks at a provincial level, and lack the financial resources that would provide incentives for collaboration. The national government also allocates and distributes resources directly to provinces and municipalities, which bypasses the regional level.

In sum, urban policies in Peru are designed and executed within a complex institutional environment which emphasises the importance of co-ordination and alignment between sectoral policies and levels of government. At a national level there are shared responsibilities for strategic spatial planning and infrastructure provision which directly affects the development of cities. In this context, co-ordination between different national ministries, alignment of policy objectives and consistency in how these policies are administered at the subnational level is important. Provincial governments have important roles related to their strategic, supervisory and co-ordinating functions with districts that have a key implementation role. At the local level, co-ordination and alignment will also be important to achieving urban policy outcomes. The regional level of government is largely absent from urban policy matters, and there are not effective mechanisms in place to co-ordinate planning and investment at this scale. The following sections will examine how urban policies are operationalised within this complex institutional environment.

The implementation of national urban policies depends upon effective multi-level governance and capacity at a subnational level, which is lacking

The national government has begun to take steps to develop a better policy framework for managing urban growth and development. The NUDP (2006-15) provides broad policy guidance in relation to the development of policies to manage the growth of cities. It describes the urban system of Peru as: 1 national metropolis (Lima); 3 regional metropolises; and 33 intermediate cities with populations greater than 50 000. It is important to note that only two cities (Lima and Arequipa) currently have metropolitan plans.

The NUDP identifies four broad principles for urban development: 1) governance and governability; 2) connectivity, networks and fluxes; 3) productive specialisation, articulation and innovation; and 4) sustainability and competitiveness. The strategies set out in the NUDP also focus on guidance and tools related to planning at a subnational level. This includes the development of feasibility studies, and departmental or provincial plans required by law, and training and capacity-building initiatives associated with delivering them. The cost estimate at the time for implementing these initiatives was approximately USD 80 million.

One of the key issues related to these planning frameworks and tools is the capacity of subnational governments to design and implement them. The implementation of planning frameworks at a subnational level has been inconsistent. The budget attached to the NUDP earmarked close to USD 17 million for the technical formulation of 80 urban development plans in larger districts (population above 20 000) and 194 provincial plans (*planes de acondicionamento/ordenamiento territorial*). However, these planning frameworks have only been partially implemented.

An evaluation of planning frameworks at a local level reveals these implementation problems. Concerted development plans (*planes de desarrollo concertado*) are required to access fiscal transfers and the vast majority (94%) of districts with a population over 50 000 has one. However, the proportion of these districts implementing planning frameworks which guide land use and infrastructure is much lower. For example, over half (53%) of districts with a population over 50 000 do not have an urban development plan (*plan de desarrollo urbano*) as the main tool in regulating, among other things, the crucial issues of zoning and land use.

These implementation problems are also apparent at a provincial level. Territorial conditioning plans (*plan de acondicioneamento territorial*) are important because they provide a basis for land-use planning at a provincial level, and the co-ordination of planning and decisions about land use at a district level. However, only 22% of districts have completed these plans. Arequipa is one city which prevented districts from enacting planning functions until their provincial development plan was completed, although given this analysis, it is unlikely this is occurring across other areas in Peru.

Table 3.8. **Proportion of districts with a population over 50 000 that have implemented urban development plans**

Department	Number of districts > 50 000	Concerted municipal development plan	Urban development plan	Road plan	Plan of territorial conditioning
Áncash	2	50%	50%	50%	0%
Arequipa	9	100%	56%	22%	11%
Ayacucho	1	100%	100%	0%	100%
Cajamarca	2	100%	50%	50%	50%
Callao	4	75%	50%	50%	0%
Cusco	4	100%	100%	0%	75%
Huánuco	2	100%	0%	50%	0%
Ica	4	75%	50%	50%	25%
Junín	3	100%	33%	33%	0%
La Libertad	4	100%	50%	0%	0%
Lambayeque	3	100%	33%	0%	0%
Lima	36	94%	31%	33%	19%
Loreto	4	75%	50%	25%	0%
Madre de Dios	1	100%	100%	100%	0%
Moquegua	1	100%	100%	0%	100%
Piura	5	100%	40%	20%	20%
Puno	2	100%	100%	50%	0%
San Martín	1	100%	100%	0%	100%
Tacna	2	100%	50%	0%	50%
Tumbes	1	100%	100%	100%	100%
Ucayali	2	100%	100%	50%	0%
Total	93	94%	47%	30%	20%

Source: CEPLAN data.

Given the importance of Lima to the national economy, it is important to understand how these issues are playing out in the capital. The governance of the metropolitan region of Lima (or the functional urban area) is complex. The contiguous urban area of Lima incorporates a large proportion of the region of Lima, and the constitutional province of Callao, which also has the status of a region. The provincial municipality of Lima incorporates 43 districts within this urban area. Lima Metropolitana has been established to provide improved co-ordination in relation to urban planning and economic development and covers the constitutional province of Callao and the province of Lima.

Although Lima has a metropolitan plan, less than 30% of the main Lima districts (representing only 25% of the 7.6 million of their population) have developed and approved an urban development plan. The lack of these basic land management tools contributes, among other things, to inefficient land markets and overcrowding of public infrastructure and services.

There are also a number of barriers and limitations related to metropolitan-scale planning and decision making. The implementation of the Lima-Callao Metropolitan Development Plan 1990-2010 (extended to 2012) provides some lessons in relation to these problems. The new planning document that inherited its legacy (*Plan Regional de Desarrollo Concertado de Lima 2012-2025*), identifies a number of factors that affected implementation.

- the recentralisation of decision making to the national government, which continued until the early 2000s

- the retention of key competencies and functions in urban and territorial development, such as water management; state-owned and agricultural land management; mass transport systems; fiscal and legal management of informal settlements
- Decree No. 776 approved in 2002 that distributed the FONCOMUN redirected funds from provincial municipalities directly to districts, weakening the financial and administrative functioning of the provincial municipalities
- the failure to reorganise urban growth and city management according to the "polycentric city" paradigm, conceived for Lima more than 20 years ago
- the absence of effective decision-making capability at a metropolitan scale, which would allow governing and co-ordinating municipal districts on matters and competencies of metropolitan relevance.

Figure 3.10. **Availability of urban development plans in Lima's main districts**

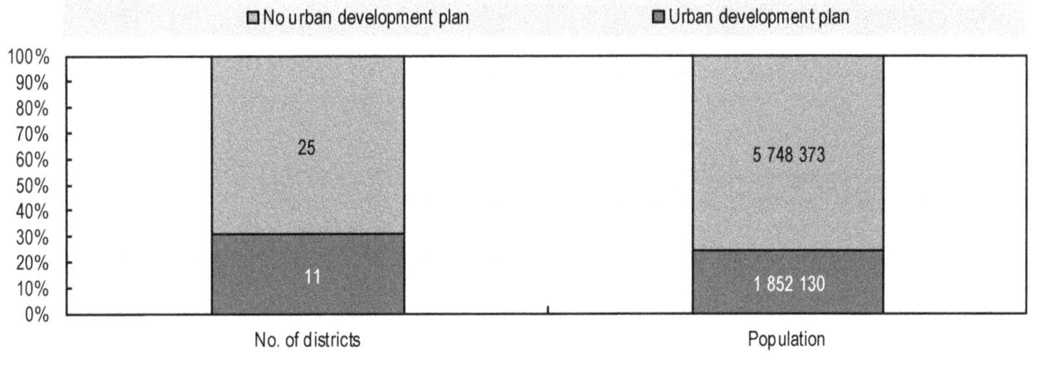

Source: Elaboration based on data from the Ministry of Economy and Finance (2014).

The effective delivery of Lima's new Metropolitan Plan will require a high level of co-ordination and alignment between different policy actors. The plan is based around a broad set of economic, social and environmental objectives. They are: inclusivity and equity, patrimonial and creative, sustainable, safe and resilient, compact, integrated, polycentric, and competitive and dynamic – positioning Peru as a global player (Municipalidad Metropolitana de Lima, 2016). The plan sets out a vision for the future urban structure of Lima in terms of transport, land use, open space, and energy and water infrastructure. These policy areas cut across the responsibilities of all levels of government in Peru.

There are a number of problems with existing governance arrangements that will need to be overcome to realise this urban development vision. The first is lack of effective mechanisms to ensure systemic co-ordination of planning and investment decision making between the region of Lima and the Constitutional Province of Callao. The second is the lack of fiscal resources and incentives for Lima Metropolitana to effectively co-ordinate urban districts within the department of Lima. Although Lima Metropolitana is responsible for metropolitan-scale planning, investment decisions are taken at the local level, and there are not any mechanisms to ensure alignment of decision making. The third is the problems at the district level where the implementation of key planning instruments is inconsistent.

Box 3.4. Metropolitan governance

Governance arrangements are central to the effectiveness of contemporary urban policies. Shaping the spatial form and structure of cities requires co-ordination between different policy areas, in particular land use, housing and transport policies. There are also other policy areas where spatial impacts are not traditionally considered (such as tax, higher education and innovation, and industry and regulatory policies), which shape the location of housing and public goods. These policy areas are also often the exclusive or shared competencies of different levels of government. The development of governance models that enable better co-ordination of policy actors at a metropolitan scale is an important trend across OECD countries (OECD, 2006; 2015).

Table 3.9. Four common approaches to metropolitan governance

Dots represent a municipality or other form of local government

1) Informal/soft co-ordination. Often found in metropolitan areas with multiple urban centres, lightly institutionalised platforms for information sharing and consultation are relatively easy both to implement and to undo. They typically lack enforcement tools and their relationship with other levels of government tends to remain minimal.	
2) Inter-municipal authorities. When established for a single purpose, such authorities aim at sharing costs and responsibilities across member municipalities – sometimes with the participation of other levels of government and sectoral organisations. Multi-purpose authorities embrace a defined range of key policies for urban development such as land use, transport and infrastructure.	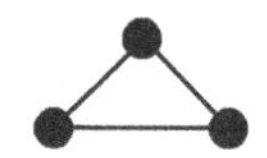
3) Supra-municipal authorities. An additional layer above municipalities can be introduced either by creating a directly elected metropolitan government or with the upper governments setting down a non-elected metropolitan structure. The extent of municipal involvement and financial capacity often determine the effectiveness of a supra-municipal authority.	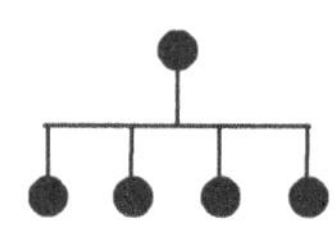
4) Special status of "metropolitan cities". Cities that exceed a legally defined population threshold can be upgraded into a special status as "metropolitan cities", which puts them on the same footing as the next upper level of government and gives them broader competencies.	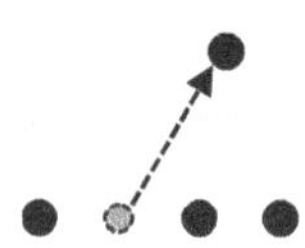

Source: OECD (2014a), *OECD Regional Outlook 2014: Regions and Cities, Where Policies and People Meet*, http://dx.doi.org/10.1787/9789264201415-en.

There is a growing interest across OECD countries in creating and reforming metropolitan governance bodies (OECD, 2014a). The type of institution depends on the particular context and is best determined on a case-by-case basis. However, there are some common lessons that can be drawn from creating and reforming these bodies, and the types of functions that are best suited at the metropolitan scale. Land-use planning and transport have a particularly important impact on the form and organisation of cities, and integrating them at a metropolitan scale is important because:

- The impacts of local decisions at a metropolitan scale. Failures in co-ordinating individual municipalities' transport and land-use policies generates substantial costs at the metropolitan scale in terms of congestion, duplication of investment, and under-use or misuse of land.
- Public sector versus private sector leadership. Transport systems are an important tool for public authorities to shape urban development. Land development is largely driven by the private sector, and the influence of public regulations on market choices may sometimes be marginal. It is important that publicly provided

transport infrastructure and privately led urban development is co-ordinated at a metropolitan scale.

- Long-term versus short-term time horizons. Land-use decisions may sometimes be implemented rapidly, whereas large-scale transport projects are typically carried out over a medium- to long-term period. The benefits of integrating land use and transport are usually not visible until ten or more years have elapsed, in contrast to local political mandates, which are likely to require visible short-term gains, such as job creation.

Table 3.10. **Effective metropolitan governance reforms: Lessons from OECD countries**

Lesson	Description	Example
Identify a common cause for collaboration and build on (as well as communicate) successful collaboration outcomes	Starting with small-scale and concrete projects can sometimes help rally forces and progressively lead to setting a "big picture", as success breeds success and trust.	In Barcelona, three sectoral inter-municipal authorities (transport, environment and planning) were created in 1987. After participating in the elaboration of the Metropolitan Strategic Plan with the municipality of Barcelona in 1999, a metropolitan authority of Barcelona was set up in 2011.
Develop metropolitan leadership and/or ownership	A relevant personality and/or institution often plays a pivotal role in steering change and creating and maintaining momentum for reform. The reform needs a strong advocate as the engine of the process. Such clear demand for reform may stem from different constituencies.	In France, impetus towards governance reforms in the three largest metropolitan areas has been largely (albeit not exclusively) driven by the central government in Paris; local governments in Lyon (municipalities and *départements*); and the private sector as well as the central government in Marseille.
Empower and engage stakeholders at an early stage, and ensure accountability and transparency	Those who are the ultimate recipients of governance/policy (and have the continuity that political bodies do not) – such as citizens, businesses and universities – need to be brought on board at the very beginning of the process. Policy makers, citizens and relevant parties require clear information both on short- and long-term gains/losses.	The Montreal Metropolitan Community created a mixed committee of elected officials and citizens to jointly organise a biennial set of debates among elected officials and civil society to discuss the implementation of the Strategic Metropolitan Plan 2031. The first series of debates took place in February and March 2013.
Strengthen the evidence base and track progress	Solid background research and scrutiny from unbiased experts can help create and sustain credibility for the reform. Strong, reliable instruments for monitoring and evaluation contribute to fostering continuous improvement.	In Canada, the Greater Toronto Civic Action Alliance convened all three levels of government with business, labour, academic and non-profit sectors since its diagnostic report "Enough talk: An action plan for the Toronto Region" (2003). It convenes a Greater Toronto Summit every four years to drive collective action on pressing issues such as transport, energy and socio-economic inclusion.
Provide (or secure) sources of financing	Metropolitan public finance is often the nexus of political resistance as governments are torn between the search for fiscal autonomy and dissuasive taxation. Securing an appropriate stream of financial resources helps to avoid unfunded mandates and often determines effective collaboration. In addition to traditional fiscal tools (e.g. own taxes, grants and transfers, fees), strategic partnerships with the business and financial community can be instrumental in gathering additional resources for public investment.	Former Mayor of London Ken Livingstone built a close relationship with the London Chamber of Commerce and Industry, the local branch of the Confederation of Business Industry, and London First – he then invited them to sit on the newly created London Business Board (2000) and convened them frequently.
Balance clear time frames and flexibility	Providing visibility on the short and long term will allow actors to anticipate next steps of the process while leaving room for trial and error as well as midway adjustments.	In Sweden, governance reforms have first been tested in a few pilot regions (Västra Götaland around Gothenburg, and Skåne around Malmö) with a multiannual timeline and evaluation mechanisms, before extending the possibility to other interested regions).

Source: OECD (2014a), *OECD Regional Outlook 2014: Regions and Cities, Where Policies and People Meet*, http://dx.doi.org/10.1787/9789264201415-en.

In sum, the NUDP (2006-15), led by the Ministry of Housing, has not accomplished its goal of serving as guide and catalyst for the development of Peruvian cities. However, it is important that an urban policy framework has been developed, which provides a platform to develop a national urban policy for Peru. A revised national urban policy framework for Peru would need to better identify the different roles and functions of Peru's cities, and provide a diagnosis of the challenges and opportunities they are facing. It would also need to move beyond broad policy principles, and develop measureable policy outcomes or performance measures to guide planning and resource allocation, and assess how different cities are tracking against them.

Reforms will also be required to more effectively link urban policy with investment decision making at a national level. Mechanisms to link urban policies with resource allocation at a national level are lacking, which means that the NUDP has not unlocked the investment required to support urban development objectives. Importantly, this is also about ensuring that investments are delivered at the right time, in the right location and in the right sequence (e.g. the co-ordinated delivery of economic and social infrastructure to support the development of new urban areas). This is not occurring consistently because urban policy objectives are not considered systematically by national ministries.

The regional level is missing from urban policy. The national government largely bypasses the regional level in relation to investment in urban infrastructure. There is also a lack of effective mechanisms for regions to co-ordinate planning and investment with the provincial and district levels. In addition, there is a lack of governance arrangements and co-ordination at the scale of functional urban areas. Regions could play an important intermediary role in urban policy, for example, in terms of increasing economies of scale in infrastructure investment, and supporting the integration of urban and rural areas.

There is a well-developed urban planning framework at a provincial and district level; however, it has not been implemented consistency across the country. These inconsistencies in implementation reinforce the point that there are not effective mechanisms in place to co-ordinate and align the various actors involved in urban policy. It also indicates differences in capacity between different provinces and district municipalities, and a lack of effective monitoring and evaluation of performance at regional and national levels. Even larger districts and provinces, which are likely to be better resourced, have low rates of implementation for key planning instruments. It is likely that other instruments, such as the cadastre, are also not updated or properly implemented, which in turn impacts upon the revenue-raising capacities of districts and provinces.

Towards a comprehensive national urban policy for Peru

Cities are important to the future development of Peru and they are not performing to their potential. Lima dominates the urban system, it is the key international gateway and is the location of high-value services. However, the metropolitan area is affected by inequalities with a significant proportion of the population without proper access to basic services. Peru's secondary cities are comparatively small and there is variable performance amongst them. They have not provided a buffer to the growth of Lima, or a growth engine for other areas of the country.

In part, these problems are due to the lack of effective institutions to manage urban development. There is a complex institutional context for urban policy in Peru and mechanisms to effectively co-ordinate decision making have not been adequately developed. National ministries do not systemically consider urban policy objectives in decision making, and these problems flow through to a subnational level. There is inconsistent implementation of planning instruments at a subnational level, and a lack of enforceable rules and incentives to ensure co-ordination between different policy actors at the appropriate spatial scale.

A growing number of OECD countries are adopting national frameworks, visions or strategies for cities (OECD, 2014a). This reflects increasing awareness of the need for policy co-ordination for cities. While 18 OECD countries still had no overall framework in place in mid-2013, a number were under preparation and urban policy in a number of other countries was encompassed in broader regional or spatial development strategies. This is a further indication of governments' desire for a more integrated, coherent approach to urban policies.

Designing national urban policy frameworks to improve co-ordination and policy coherence requires:

- identifying policies that have a particularly strong effect on urban development, even if they are not explicitly designated as "urban"
- analysing the interactions between these policies with a view to avoiding incoherence and, where possible, identifying potential synergies among them.

An assessment of national urban policies should consider five broad issues: money, place, connections, people and institutions. These areas should be considered as a system, rather than as policy "silos" to be managed in isolation. The critical question is: to what extent are the approaches adopted in the five domains coherent with one another? Two of the five – money and institutions – are effectively transversal, influencing all of the others. The other three concern the central issues around which sectoral policies must cohere (Figure 3.11).

Figure 3.11. **Five broad issues for assessing urban policy**

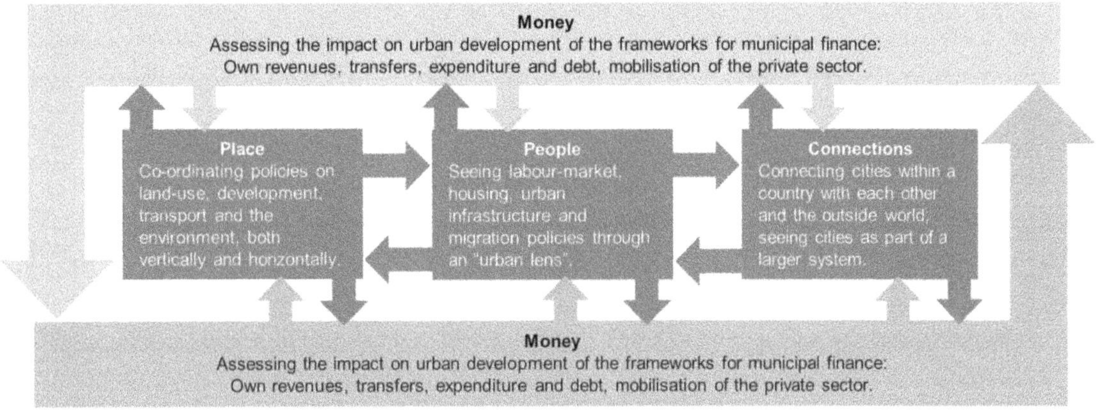

Source: OECD (2014a), *OECD Regional Outlook 2014: Regions and Cities, Where Policies and People Meet*, http://dx.doi.org/10.1787/9789264201415-en.

These policy implications provide a starting point for national policy makers to assess urban policies in Peru. The key priorities for Peru will be addressing the basic framework conditions for urban policy in terms of fiscal and institutional arrangements. These will be covered in greater depth in Chapter 4 and some initial guidance in relation to urban policies is provided below. A comprehensive review would also need to include an assessment of policies affecting the structure and form of cities (particularly land use, transport and the environment), connectivity between cities, and areas where urban policies can help achieve social policy objectives (and vice versa). Some initial guidance for national policy makers in reviewing urban policies in Peru is provided below.

Box 3.5. Policy implications related to the thematic pillars for assessing urban policy

A recent diagnosis of urban policies across OECD countries suggests the following policy implications related to these five thematic pillars (see Figure 3.10).

1. Money: Fiscal systems that determine urban finance are typically overlooked in the considerations of urban policy and governance. Policy makers therefore need to carefully examine the incentives provided by their fiscal systems for actions taken at the level of cities and their surroundings.
2. Institutions: The need for greater alignment of policy approaches also implies adapted governance arrangements to ensure that existing or new structures can sustain policy co-ordination for urban development across sectors, jurisdictions and levels of government.
3. Places: Spatial planning and land use, among other considerations, have far-reaching consequences for the way cities and their hinterlands develop. These policies, which help to determine urban form, are particularly important to co-ordinate together at the level of a functional urban area.
4. Connectivity: The nature of transport systems for people and goods both within and across urban areas has growth implications as well as environmental and social consequences. Connectivity is increasingly important for the performance of national urban systems.
5. People: Many urban policies are actually social policies. However, policy makers need to consider a wider range of policies for people that have a particularly important impact on cities, such as for labour market policy, affordable housing policy or policies for specific demographic groups such as immigrants.

Source: OECD (2014a), *OECD Regional Outlook 2014: Regions and Cities, Where Policies and People Meet*, http://dx.doi.org/10.1787/9789264201415-en.

Rural development and policies

Peru's economy has developed fast, but 50% of rural people live below the poverty line. Rural poverty contributes to generating migration flows to cities and to Lima, in particular. So dealing with rural development would also yield better conditions in cities. Rural regions have been a key contributor to Peru's international competitiveness. The good economic performance that has characterised the past two decades depends on the increasing capacity of the country to capitalise on rural assets, including oil, minerals and agricultural products. Also, rural regions in Peru attract an increasing number of tourists every year. The international image of Peru does not depend upon on its capital city, but rather understandably on its mountains and jungle.

Table 3.11. **Initial guidance to national policy makers in assessing urban policies in Peru**

OECD recommendations	Guidance for national policy makers in Peru
Money: Fiscal systems that determine urban finance are typically overlooked in the considerations of urban policy and governance. Policy makers therefore need to carefully examine the incentives provided by their fiscal systems for actions taken at the level of cities and their surroundings.	A review of urban policies should begin with a rigorous analysis of the four facets of the fiscal framework as it affects cities: own revenues, expenditures, transfers and debt. This includes creating reliable local tax revenues that enable investment in local services, incentives to improve governance and co-ordination at the scale of functional urban areas, and ensuring that subnational governments have the funds to carry out their competencies.
Institutions: The need for greater alignment of policy approaches also implies adapted governance arrangements to ensure that existing or new structures can sustain policy co-ordination for urban development across sectors, jurisdictions and levels of government.	Focus on how institutional capacity can be strengthened and co-ordination improved to give greater coherence to national policies at an urban level. This includes assessing the role of the Presidency of the Council of Ministers and the Ministry of Economy and Finance in co-ordinating at a national level, the role of regions in better managing urban-rural linkages, and how to build partnerships between levels of government.
Places: Spatial planning and land use, among other considerations, have far-reaching consequences for the way cities and their hinterlands develop. These policies, which help to determine urban form, are particularly important to co-ordinate together at the level of a functional urban area.	An assessment of policies affecting the spatial dimension of urban development (land-use policies, property rights and land registries, urban transport, and environment) should focus on the coherence of different policies and addressing variations in how they are implemented for different cities.
Connectivity: The nature of transport systems for people and goods both within and across urban areas has growth implications as well as environmental and social consequences. Connectivity is increasingly important for the performance of national urban systems.	Policy makers will need to consider these important connections as part of the urban policy framework. An assessment of national infrastructure policies will need to consider how to foster a system of cities by establishing stronger linkages between them.
People: Many urban policies are actually social policies. However, policy makers need to consider a wider range of policies for people that have a particularly important impact on cities, such as for labour market policy, affordable housing policy or policies for specific demographic groups such as immigrants.	An integrated approach to housing and urban infrastructure provision will be required to address informality with Peru's cities. An assessment should also investigate how urban policies can assist in improving skills, particularly through the provision of labour market information and the better matching of training at the scale of functional urban areas.

However, despite the importance of rural assets within the national economy, rural development is not within the top priorities of the government, and this for at least four reasons.

1. Rural is not properly defined. Peru's current regional taxonomy is a very basic (binary) one, which defines rural in terms of non-urban status. Almost any cluster of housing and people is considered "urban", accordingly there is no room to adopt modern – holistic – approaches to rural development that also take into account accessibility to services and urban-rural interaction, for example.

2. Rural development policy is associated by government authorities with providing subsidies to agriculture, skills and capacity building, and diffusing technologies. There is little knowledge of international good practices and this impinges on the possibility to put in place a holistic approach to rural development.[2] Rural Peru's economic base is potentially very diverse, and agriculture is able to compete on international markets quite successfully.

3. Rural is not considered as a growth opportunity. This challenge depends on several factors. First, there is a disconnect between assets and people; the former contribute to national wealth, the latter are mostly poor. Second, most ethnic minorities – who are the poorest among the poor – live in the mountains or in the Amazonas. Third, several rural regions used to be home to the Shining Path, a Maoist organisation which caused instability in the country till the early 1990s. In

this context, in which rural and poverty are considered as synonymous, policy does not aim to promote investment and growth. Rather, it focuses on providing poor people with short-term relief, before they migrate to a city.

4. Rapid urbanisation is seen as a driver of growth and then as the main solution to poverty in the country. Rural-to-urban migration has become a diaspora that converges to the informal settlements surrounding Lima, the *asentamientos humanos*. This large-scale migration does not depend on the transition to a new economic system; rural citizens do not abandon their communities of origin to be absorbed by manufacturing and earn higher wages. Rather, they go to cities to access basic services such as education for their children and healthcare. Rural people do not have the skill-set to get formal jobs in cities and are drafted in the army of informal workers. As a result, the rural diaspora generates a misallocation of human capital that contributes to dragging Peru's growth down.

The following sections will assess the challenges and opportunities facing rural areas, strengths and weaknesses of the current approach to rural policies, and relevant lessons from across the OECD.

Rural areas make an important contribution to the national economy

Exports from rural areas have had a significant influence on the historical performance of the Peruvian economy (Haussmann and Klinger, 2008). As shown in Chapter 1, three-quarters of Peru's exports is composed of mining, hydrocarbons and agriculture. The share these sectors make to Peru's export basket has not shifted significantly in the last 40 years (Haussmann and Klinger, 2008). Although there have been some compositional shifts within them, with the decreasing relative importance of hydrocarbons and agriculture and the increasing importance of mining and non-traditional agricultural exports.

Tradeable sectors are also important for the development of rural economies. Growth in the tradeable sector attracts income into the region. New consumption is generated through some of this income and local businesses spend part of this and generate additional local consumption. These effects multiply the initial effect and generate new jobs, investment and value added. In addition, the tradeable sector is generally more productive, which leads to the introduction of new technologies into local supply chains.

Over the past decade agriculture has made an increasing contribution to the country's exports within the framework of the numerous free trade agreements that the country has signed over this period. Agriculture contributes to the "non-traditional exports", which have become important contributors to the national wealth.[3] In Peru, non-traditional exports are defined to include sectors such as agriculture, fishing, metal-mechanic and chemical. The country has been able to specialise in a number of higher value agricultural products.

In particular, in 2012, Peru ranked as the world's top producer of fresh asparagus (USD 408 million exported as of December 2013), paprika and organic bananas; the world's second-largest producer of artichokes (USD 85 million exported as of December 2013) and fresh grapes (USD 428 million as of December 2013); the sixth-largest producer in the world of coffee (USD 1.013 billion exported in 2012); and the seventh-largest producer of avocado (USD 137 million exported in 2012). Mango exports grew by 8.0% between 2012 and 2013, totalling USD 127 million. During 2013, exports of quinoa and its by-products totalled USD 72.2 million, representing a 132% increase over 2012 (Ernst & Young, 2014: 7).

As outlined in Chapter 1, mining plays a critical role in the national economy. Mining accounts for 12% of GDP and half of the country's exports. Peru is one of the world's leading producers of zinc, tin, copper and silver, and has development potential in copper, gold and iron ore. Mining accounted for a quarter of Peru's foreign direct investment in 2013, and large multinationals such as Xstrata, Glencore, Rio Tinto and Anglo American have a significant presence in the country (Ernst & Young, 2014).

However, there are some challenges related to mining in rural areas. Mining only accounts for 1.5% of total employment in Peru. Although there are important indirect relationships (e.g. to manufacturing and services), the direct employment benefits to producer regions tend to be low. There are also difficulties associated with managing environmental impacts and achieving a social license to operate. There have been notable examples of mining projects generating conflicts with agricultural producers, and local opposition to development.

Tourism is also a significant source of growth potential for rural areas. International visitation to Peru increased from 479 000 in 1995 to 3.2 million in 2013 (World Bank, 2015). Tourism is estimated to make a direct and indirect contribution of 12% to Peru's GDP (World Economic Forum, 2013). A significant part of Peru's international tourism offer – in terms of landscapes, mountains, diverse flora and fauna, and world-famous cultural attractions – is located in rural areas. The main tourism destinations are in the regions of Cusco and Madre de Dios, which are far from the capital. There are a number of challenges to fostering the growth of the tourism industry which have a particular rural dimension, including high transport costs, poor sanitation, access to broadband and degradation of environmental assets (World Economic Forum, 2013).

Although rural areas generate significant wealth, the people living there are generally poor, particularly indigenous populations

Despite the fact that most of the national wealth generates from rural territories, 50% of rural people live below the poverty line. In 2014, less than one-third of the country's population lived below the national poverty line. In the same year, however, the national rural poverty rate was greater than 50%. For instance, departments with low population density and low regional accessibility like Huancavelica, Cajamarca, Huánuco and Apurímac are akin to those of severely underdeveloped economies in which poverty goes hand in hand with hunger and malnutrition (Figure 3.12). In Huancavelica, for example, 35% of children aged 5 and under suffered from chronic malnutrition in 2014. Similarly, in 2012, 42% of households in Cajamarca were exposed to caloric deficits (Table 3.12).

There is an important ethnic component that affects the possibility for rural people to be poor. Poverty rates are higher in the mountains and in the jungle area; those in which ethnic minorities are more numerous. Rural regions are especially impoverished: 17% of the population in rural Sierra, for example, was considered extremely poor in 2014. This compares with relatively low levels along the coast, and especially in the area of Lima. The poorest Peruvians are found in the arid Andean highlands that are home to a large majority of the indigenous *Quechua* and *Aymara*, many of which live below the poverty line.

Figure 3.12. **Regions exposed to extreme poverty also suffer from food insecurity**

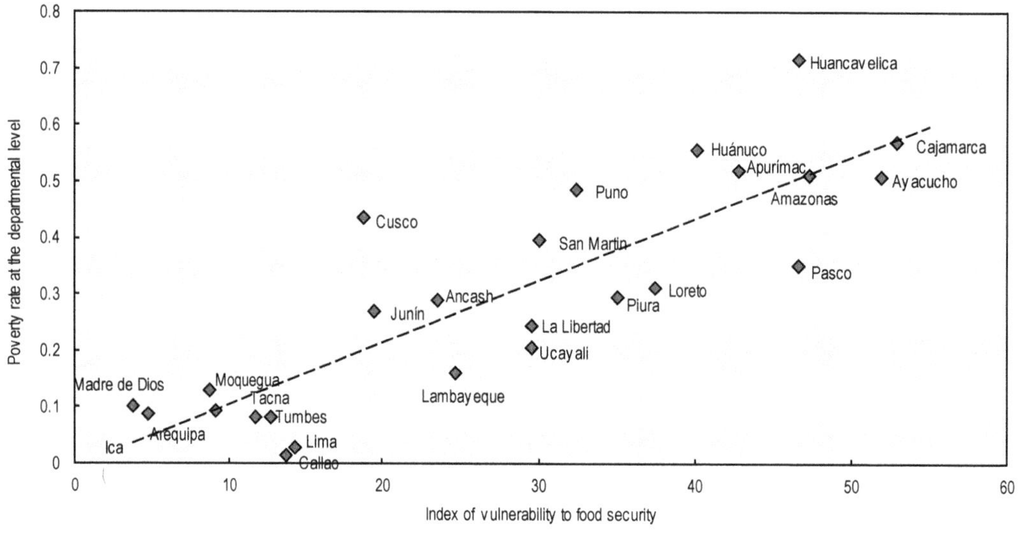

Source: OECD analysis based on data from INEI.

Table 3.12. **Selected indicators of extreme rural poverty at the department level, 2012 and 2014**

Department	Poverty rates at the department level, 2013	Index of vulnerability to food insecurity, 2012[1]	Children below 5 suffering from chronic malnutrition, 2012-14[2]	Households with a deficit in calories, 2012[3]
Huancavelica	46.6%	0.7163	35.0%	23.7%
Cajamarca	52.9%	0.5688	32.2%	42.0%
Huánuco	40.1%	0.5549	24.8%	34.6%
Apurímac	42.8%	0.5183	27.3%	42.1%
Amazonas	47.3%	0.5117	30.8%	27.3%
Ayacucho	51.9%	0.5075	26.3%	38.1%
Puno	32.4%	0.4865	17.9%	33.6%
Cusco	18.8%	0.4358	18.2%	22.8%
San Martín	30.0%	0.3948	16.0%	22.1%
Pasco	46.6%	0.3522	24.9%	55.7%
Loreto	37.4%	0.3124	24.6%	30.1%
Piura	35.1%	0.2962	21.7%	22.9%
Áncash	23.5%	0.2898	20.5%	29.2%
Junín	19.5%	0.2696	22.1%	34.4%
La Libertad	29.5%	0.2436	19.9%	25.3%
Ucayali	29.5%	0.2061	26.1%	6.7%
Lambayeque	24.7%	0.1589	14.3%	15.0%
Moquegua	8.7%	0.1281	4.2%	19.7%
Madre de Dios	3.8%	0.1002	9.8%	7.7%
Arequipa	9.1%	0.0931	7.3%	26.6%
Ica	4.7%	0.0869	6.9%	8.7%
Tacna	11.8%	0.0825	3.7%	14.5%
Tumbes	12.7%	0.0815	8.3%	17.2%
Lima	14.3%	0.0270	4.6%	17.2%
Callao	13.7%	0.0138	7.0%	15.0%

Sources: 1. Normalised for population; Mapa de vulnerabilidad a la inseguridad alimentaria, 2012. Ministerio de Desarrollo e Inclusión Social (MIDIS) & Programa Mundial de Alimentos (PMA). 2. INEI – Encuesta Demográfica y de Salud Familiar (ENDES). 3. Encuesta Nacional de Hogares (ENAHO).

Figure 3.13. **Distribution of poverty in a selection of urban and rural areas**

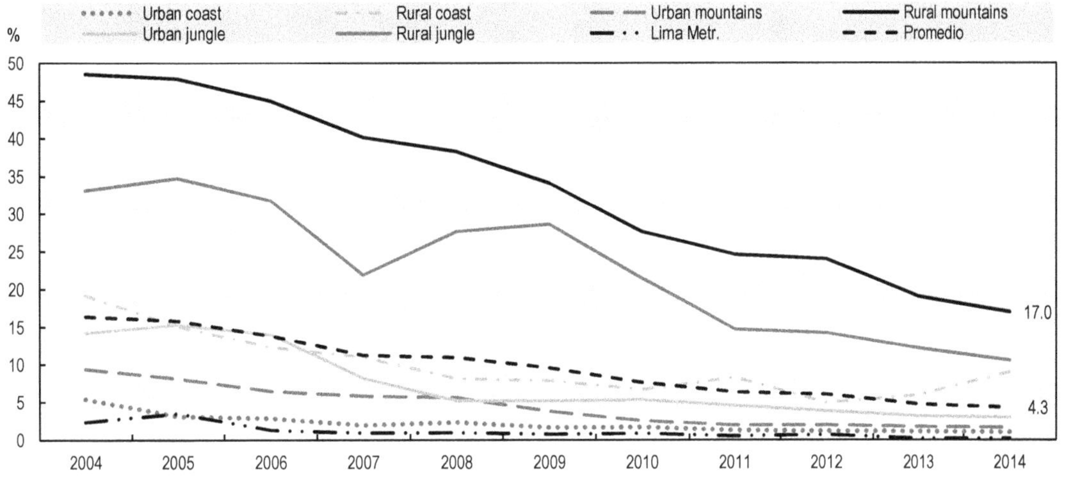

Source: INEI (2004; 2014), Encuesta Nacional de Hogares, http://webinei.inei.gob.pe/anda_inei/index.php/catalog/195.

These outcomes are mirrored in OECD countries where indigenous people are more likely to experience poverty and disadvantage. Poverty rates are considerably higher than for the balance of the population, educational levels are lower, income is lower, housing is inferior and opportunities for advancement are worse. Almost by definition social exclusion is much higher, largely because indigenous people have a different status than other citizens. Social exclusion is also reinforced by government policy, which in most of these OECD countries has isolated the indigenous population on reservations and provides a separate set of social services to them.

Current approaches to improving the conditions of indigenous people in OECD countries are moving more toward a process where responsibility is more fully devolved to communities along with resources to begin a bottom-up development process. Most important, there is increasing recognition by governments and by indigenous people that economic improvement requires stronger economic integration. The challenge is finding a way to provide for continued cultural identity and values in an integrated market economy. While this has not yet happened, in many cases there are sufficient success stories to suggest it is a better approach.

Poverty generates mistrust: In several provinces rural people have started opposing new developments

Extreme poverty negatively affects the relationship between citizens and institutions, causing low levels of trust. As a result, in resource-rich rural provinces people have started opposing new mining developments. Based on their experiences, rural communities consider that mining companies limit their access to land and water, in particular. Mining generates negative externalities for industries such as agriculture, which are not necessarily offset by other employment opportunities for the people who are affected by these impacts. Other forms of compensation, such as royalty payments, do exist but are not associated with stronger growth performance (see Chapter 4).

Box 3.6. Kaikōura and Miraka in New Zealand

New Zealand has a long-standing formal treaty with the Māori that was signed in 1840. After an extended period where the rights of the Māori were not fully recognised, there has been a strong effort in New Zealand to better respect the terms of this treaty. This has resulted in efforts to compensate the Māori for past injustices by: returning land; restoring rights to natural resource use, particularly fishing and forestry; and providing financial compensation. Māori now comprise about 15% of the New Zealand population.

Like indigenous people in other OECD countries, including Australia, Canada and the United States, the Māori are on average poorer, with lower levels of employment and education, and generally worse performance on all socio-economic indicators. Unlike in these other countries, the Māori have direct representation in the national legislature with specific seats reserved for Māori.

Indigenous people maintain a distinct relationship with other citizens. Their treaty rights provide them with specific rights not available to others, but their distinct existence means that they cannot fully assimilate into the dominant culture without losing their identity. A common consequence of this separation is weak participation in the general labour market, often because of physical isolation resulting from separate communities. This means that improvements in employment levels and earned income require developing opportunities near to Māori settlements and that are consistent with cultural norms. Where Māori-oriented activities can be integrated with the rest of the local economy, it is possible to achieve win-win situations for all.

An example of this is tourism development in the Kaikōura District on the South Island. The district was the site of a significant Māori population that relied on fishing and whaling before the arrival of European settlers. Europeans initially focused on whaling, but excessive harvesting reduced the fishing industry and the economy shifted to agriculture and later to a railway centre. In the 1980s, reorganisation of the New Zealand rail industry eliminated this economic function and unemployment increased in the region.

A high level of natural amenities, especially ocean-oriented elements like beaches and marine life, combined with proximity to Christchurch and a growing number of international tourists led to efforts to establish a strong tourism offer. A key element was the creation of Whale Watch in 1987 by members of the Kati Kuri tribe. It was the first whale-viewing enterprise and became a major anchor of a larger regional tourism sector. This now includes other wildlife viewing activities, beach visits, cafes and restaurants, and local art, including Māori artists.

A second example is Miraka, a majority Māori-owned dairy company based in Taupo on the North Island. A number of Māori investment companies are major shareholders and the firm processes milk from local dairy farms operated by Māori and non-Māori families. The main product is milk powder that is exported to Viet Nam, the People's Republic of China and other countries. The company has been profitable almost from its opening day and has steadily expanded production. The key features of the project are that it involves investments from a variety of Māori trusts from different regions, and it buys milk from local farms of both Māori and non-Māori heritage – in both instances showing a high level of collaboration.

Source: OECD (2014b), *OECD Rural Policy Reviews: Chile 2014*, http://dx.doi.org/10.1787/9789264222892-en.

Cajamarca, a rural department in the north of Peru, offers a good example of how the resource competition between the agricultural and mining sectors has impeded economic growth and compromised the provision of public goods to local communities. The province is home to approximately 1.5 million people, a large share of them belong to indigenous minorities. Agricultural and mining activities constitute the base of its economy. The agricultural sector employs 430 000 people across a myriad of small holdings, making it the department's primary source of employment. The mining sector, on the other hand, employs relatively few people (approximately 14 000).

Box 3.7. Building trust between communities and proponents of major resource developments

Social license to operate (SLO) refers to the level of acceptance or approval by local communities and stakeholders of mining companies and their operations. The concept has evolved fairly recently from the broader and more established notion of "corporate social responsibility" and is based on the idea that mining companies need not only government permission (or permits) but also "social permission" to conduct their business.

Increasingly, having an SLO is an essential part of operating within democratic jurisdictions, as without sufficient popular support it is unlikely that agencies from elected governments will willingly grant operational permits or licences. However, the need for and ultimate success of achieving an SLO relies to a large extent on a functioning government and sound institutions. Many mining companies now consider gaining an SLO as an appropriate business expense that ultimately adds to the bottom line. Research shows that an SLO can be achieved where industry invests in developing genuine, trust-based relationships with community stakeholders.

This has important public policy implications. For example, in Queensland, Australia the state government requires mining proponents to develop a social impact management plan in consultation with government and key stakeholders. This provides a framework for identifying risks associated with major resource developments, engaging the community in managing them and ensuring accountability throughout the project life cycle.

Following a social impact assessment, a thorough and well-researched social impact management plan is prepared by the proponent. The plan should:

- reflect the findings and recommendations of the project's social impact assessment, including consideration of the results of engagement with stakeholders
- present only a concise summary of the findings of the social impact assessment, including an analysis of the existing social and cultural area and potential positive and negative impacts (mitigation measures should be described in detail in the project's social impact assessment)
- provide a summary for all stakeholders regarding the potential positive and negative impacts of the project, proposed mitigation and management strategies and implementation actions
- be developed for the life of the project
- promote an active and ongoing role for communities, local authorities and all levels of government through construction, operation and decommissioning.

The social impact management plan establishes the roles and responsibilities of proponents, government, stakeholders and communities throughout the life of a project, in mitigating and managing social impacts and opportunities during construction, operation and the decommissioning of major resource development projects.

Sources: Fraser Institute (2013), "What is the social license to operate (SLO)?", www.miningfacts.org/Communities/What-is-the-social-licence-to-operate; CSIRO (2013), "Social license to operate", www.csiro.au/en/Research/MRF/Areas/Community-and-environment/Social-licence-to-operate; Queensland Department of Infrastructure and Planning (2010), "Social impact assessment: Guideline to establishing a social impact management plan", www.statedevelopment.qld.gov.au/resources/guideline/simp-guideline.pdf.

The department is, however, endowed with vast reserves of gold and copper and there is tremendous potential for the expansion of the sector. For example, Cajamarca is home to Yanacocha, the fourth-largest gold mine in the world, which produced 0.97 million ounces of gold in 2014 (Basov 2015). Yanacocha is an open pit mine located a few kilometres north from the regional capital, the city of Cajamarca. Newmont Mining Corporation, a US company, runs the mine and is the largest stakeholder together with a Peruvian company.

Conflicts between the agricultural and mining sectors have created a situation where potential for economic growth is left unrealised. Competition for scarce water resources, for example, is intense. Agricultural productivity has suffered from the water-grabbing practices of mining developments and resulted in increased poverty for households dependent upon agricultural activities.

New mining developments are therefore subject to considerable local opposition. For example, in 2010, a USD 4.8 billion mining project in the Conga area of Cajamarca was subject to vehement opposition by the local population. The project was anticipated to yield 200 tonnes of gold and 180 000 tonnes of copper per year. The central government approved the project. Local communities, however, elected to strike with the support of the department's governor. In 2011, the strikes escalated into rioting that caused several deaths and was declared a national political emergency. The project has since been blocked.

Box 3.8. **Conflicts over land use due to low institutional capacity: The case of San Martín**

Poor trust in the government and weak institutions (in the sense of both rules and government entities) also affect the potential of San Martín, a relatively wealthy province at the edge of the Amazon basin. Despite the different economic performances of the two provinces, as in Cajamarca, San Martín there is a suboptimal utilisation of regional assets in San Martín, with a disconnect between business opportunities and rural dwellers.

For instance, two factions of indigenous people compete for land use. On the one hand, there are the Quechua communities that migrated from the Andes to cut the forest and farm land in the hills of San Martín; on the other, there are the indigenous communities endemic to the area that make a living out of the forest resource and depend on the traditional landscape.

In this case, the government has not mediated between the two positions. As the land is poor, it cannot be used for long. So each farmer has to cut new pieces of the forest every two years. The result is a dramatic change of landscape. The "use value" of the forest, i.e. the capacity to extract value from the forest instead of simply cutting the trees to access poor quality agricultural land, is poorly understood.

Foreign businesses have taken advantage of the situation and have patented molecules discovered in the plants populating the rainforest. This is not necessarily a bad thing, only it shows that national stakeholders in the region are not considering the right business opportunities due to the lack of information and low institutional capacity.

In recent times, Peru has put in place policy and administrative reforms to improve the management of mining projects. This includes the establishment of the National Environmental Certification Service (SENACE) which was established in 2012. SENACE is chaired by the Ministry of the Environment and includes other key ministries involved in the development and approval of mining projects. SENACE is currently developing improved tools for social impact assessment, and an important aspect for Peru will be ensuring these impacts are effectively monitored and reported on.

Institutional framework for rural development in Peru

Addressing poverty has been a policy focus of successive national governments in Peru. The Ministry of Development and Social Inclusion, and the Ministry of Agriculture and Irrigation play major roles in rural development policy. There are also a number of other national ministries – such as Transport and Communications, and Health – which have developed rural-specific policies. A large number of different social programmes have evolved which provide transfers to poorer households, and invest in public services and basic infrastructure. There are comparatively less resources dedicated to economic development programmes. Subsidies to agriculture were removed in the 1980s, with support shifting to initiatives such as extension services and the development and diffusion of irrigation technologies. Since the 1990s there has also been significant investment in the road network (largely funded by the proceeds of the *canon*), which has benefited rural producers and helped to reduce rural poverty (Webb, 2013).

Subnational governments also play important roles in delivering initiatives that address poverty and economic development issues in rural areas. Regional governments set priorities for development through instruments such as concerted regional development plans. They also have a role in the implementation regional infrastructure and economic development initiatives. Provincial and district municipalities have roles related to the development and land-use plans, improving housing, and investing in infrastructure at a local level. In addition, the *canon* and other fiscal transfers provide district municipalities with significant resources compared to other policy actors. This has enabled, amongst other things, significant improvements to the local road network in rural areas since the early 1990s.

The Ministry of Development and Social Inclusion

The Ministry of Development and Social Inclusion (MIDIS) is very active in rural areas, although its programmes are not specifically conceived for rural areas. MIDIS was created in 2012 to integrate several government agencies and policy packages. It is responsible for, among other things, the co-ordination and delivery of the national policy referred to as "Include for Growth". This national policy prioritises the following five axes, using a life-long approach:

1. childhood nutrition
2. early childhood development
3. development of children and teenagers
4. economic inclusion
5. senior population.

"Include for Growth" is composed of a series of programmes that can be categorised into two groups: those focusing on poverty alleviation and those that try to create income-generation opportunities for people suffering from exclusion and poverty. "Include for Growth" takes a life cycle approach and programmes tend to be organised by age cohorts. These include:

- *Cuna* and *Juntos* that address infant nutrition (0-3 years of age)
- *Qali Warma* and *Juntos* that address early childhood development (3-5 years old)
- *Qali Warma* and *Juntos* that address childhood and adolescence (6-17 years old)
- *Mi Chacra Emprendedora* (also known as *Haky Winay*) and other programmes delivered by a deconcentrated body of the Ministry of Development and Social Inclusion referred to as Foncodes that address economic inclusion (18-64 years old)
- *Pensión 65* that addresses senior protection (65 years and older).

Among these programmes, some focus on social issues while others try to promote job opportunities and better framework conditions (well-being) for rural residents.

Concerning programmes with a focus on social issues, the most important is certainly the conditional monetary transfer programme (CCT) Programa Nacional de Apoyo Directo a los más Pobres (*Juntos*). As of 2014, the programme was active in 1 150 districts spread across 15 departments. Approximately 800 000 households received transfers in 2014. *Juntos'* budget in 2015 was increased to USD 340 million. This makes it the largest programme, in terms of budget allocation, implemented in rural areas, albeit – it should be noted – that technically *Juntos* does not differentiate between urban and rural areas (it could not do so due to the poor regional classification used in Peru), but it is mostly delivered to rural people as they tend to be more exposed to extreme poverty.

Launched in 2005, *Juntos* mirrors the experience of other Latin American countries with CCTs. The overarching objective of these programmes is to break the vicious cycle of poverty via the provision of education and healthcare to children in impoverished communities. The governance of CCT programmes varies across countries. In Peru, for instance, *Juntos* is managed from the centre (MIDIS) and implemented by a network of deconcentrated agencies. The programme puts a lot of pressure on subnational entities, including local and regional governments, as they have to deliver the public services – schools and hospitals – poor people need to use to respect the conditions that give them access to the cash transfer.

These programmes have become very effective at identifying households in need that are eligible for the cash transfer; this is to improve efficiency and reduce free riding. For instance, the *Juntos* programme selects eligible territories according to five criteria: 1) the presence of "Shining Path" (a Peruvian terrorist organisation); 2) level of poverty as measured by the number of households with basic unsatisfied needs; 3) poverty rates; 4) number of children exposed to chronic malnutrition; and 5) prevalence of extreme poverty. Only households with children, teenagers or expectant mothers are eligible for the programme. Households must also be validated by the community prior to enrolment in the programme.

The programme allocates an average of USD 60 to households every month conditional on the fulfilment of three obligations: 1) pregnant mothers must go to health centres for pre-natal testing; 2) children aged 36 months and under must be taken to health centres for development and growth controls; and 3) children must attend school. Households remain enrolled in the programme until their children have either completed secondary school or have turned 19. All households receive USD 60 regardless of the number of children they have.

Juntos provides beneficiary households with approximately 15% of their income, which is lower than in many other Latin American countries, including Colombia (30%) and Mexico (30%). The programme has experienced some notable success. For instance, it has: improved schooling in households participating in the programme; improved access to healthcare for pregnant women and infants; increased the use of banking and financial services (i.e. debit cards); increased the percentage of the population with national identity documents and health insurance; contributed to women's empowerment; increased the income of beneficiary households by 43%; increased food expenditure and non-food consumption in beneficiary households by 15% and 54%, respectively (World Bank, 2009); decreased poverty and extreme poverty rates in beneficiary districts by 14% and 19% respectively (between 2005 and 2009). Furthermore, households receiving benefits from the programme for a year or more have higher chances, with more important impacts in terms of poverty reduction and increase in consumption. Children in beneficiary households are 11% less likely to get sick.

Figure 3.14. **Districts and household enrolment in *Juntos***

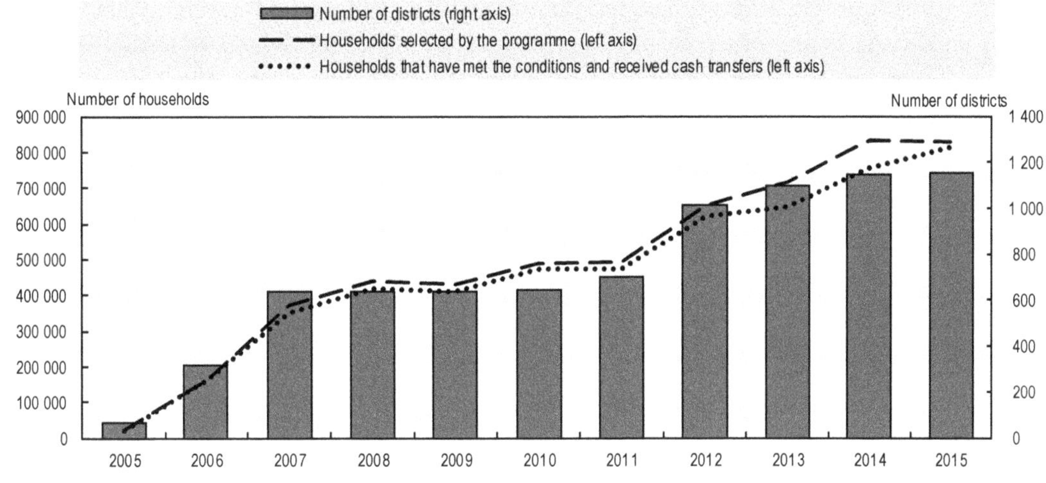

Source: Data from INEI (2015).

Another programme dealing with social aspects is *Qali Warma*, which means "Strong Child" in Quechua. This is a large-scale programme whose aim is to address childhood food insecurity and malnutrition. It has, thus far, equipped close to 50 000 establishments (i.e. primary schools) with a kitchen and, in doing so, has provided fresh food to more than 3 million children. The programme also includes education initiatives to teach children about healthy eating.

Qali Warma was launched in 2012 and is now, in terms of budget allocation, the Ministry of Development and Social Inclusion's largest programme. The programme is delivered via an inclusive governance system that assigns important and active roles to local stakeholders. Each school, for example, must establish a purchasing committee composed of public officials and parents that is tasked with buying foodstuffs and a school feeding committee that consists of teachers and parents that is responsible for monitoring the quality of the food and delivering the food to students. Interviews with national stakeholders have indicated that the programme has successfully addressed health issues and improved children's learning capacities. The programme is due to be extended across all of Peru over the coming years.[4]

The Ministry for Development and Social Inclusion is also responsible for a number of economic development programmes targeted to rural communities.

- *Mi Chacra Emprendedora-Haku Wiñay*[5] (meaning "my enterprising little farm" and "we are going to grow") are just two names of the same programme, which is concerned with increasing the productivity of small holdings, and currently serves 90 000 households. The programme is delivered by Foncodes. Foncodes was founded in the early 1990s with the mandate to develop Peru's primary and secondary road networks. In 2012, however, it was brought under the control of the Ministry of Development and Social Inclusion and has since focused on issues of food security and nutrition.

- The *Mi Chacra Emprendedora* programme promotes agricultural innovation, and in turn improved productivity, via the maintenance of networks of local leaders and systems of peer-to-peer learning. The programme has found particular success in the Andean region. In the department of Cajamarca, for example, local leaders provided assistance and knowledge to small-scale farmers to help them cultivate new profitable and exportable crops including quinoa and *aguaymanto*. These small-scale farmers have realised benefits from the *Mi Chacra Emprendedora* programme in the form of increased incomes and enhanced food security and nutrition. The *Mi Chacra Emprendedora* programme is, however, very much in its infancy. In Cajamarca, for example, the programme has only been implemented in 5 of the department's 12 districts. The said, plans to scale-up the programme and expand its coverage have been made.
- The Economic Inclusion Fund in Rural Areas (FONIE)[6] provides funding for local infrastructure projects identified by subnational governments. The scope of action is the 670 poorest districts, it considers the two poorest quintiles nationally. FONIE finances, preferably simultaneously, the implementation of infrastructure for water and sanitation, electricity, telecommunications, and roads.

The Ministry of Agriculture and Irrigation

The Ministry of Agriculture and Irrigation, also called MINAGRI, is an important player for rural development in the country. It has developed the National Rural Development Strategy which establishes an economic, social and environmental framework to develop agriculture in collaboration with local communities. The policy framework is currently being updated in collaboration with the Ministry of Development and Social Inclusion.

Table 3.13. **National Rural Development Strategy: Policy themes and strategic objectives**

Policy themes	Strategic objectives
Economic, social and environmental sustainability	– Development of competitive productive agricultural and non-agricultural (e.g. tourism, agro-industrial transformation) options in rural zones – Access to active production for rural groups – Rural services to improve the quality of life of the rural population
Sustainable management of natural resources and risk management	– Execution of strategies for the sustainable use of natural resources – Rural economic exploitation that responds to the potential and sustainability of the natural resources – Protection of environmental and cultural heritage based on the knowledge of local populations – Implementation of a system of prevention and mitigation of production weaknesses and rural infrastructure linked to the risks of natural disasters
Promotion of the capacities of rural inhabitants and social inclusion	– Development and provision of an education system in rural zones that would offer services of quality – Strengthening of the organisational and managerial capacity of rural populations – Integration of excluded social groups
Institutional changes that create appropriate conditions for rural development	– Capacity building and focus on decentralised public management and regulations – Strengthening of local governments' and social organisations' management capacity – Participation of the lower levels of governments and civil society in the elaboration of norms and policies

Source: Ministry of Agriculture and Irrigation (n.d.), www.minagri.gob.pe.

In 2015, the Ministry of Agriculture and Irrigation released a National Agrarian Policy which identifies the core challenges for agriculture as the fragmentation of land, low human capital and limited use of technologies, poor access to services, and vulnerability to climate change. The policy sets an objective to enable sustained increases in agricultural income by:

- achieving efficient and sustainable management of water, land and forest resources
- ensuring security and legal stability in access to agricultural resources by communities and farmers
- increasing infrastructure and irrigation technology
- expanding supplementary credit markets, insurance and agricultural services
- strengthening and expanding the capacity of agricultural research and innovation
- improving the productive and entrepreneurial capacities of farmers and women farmers
- achieving full articulation to markets and value chains of domestic farmers.

Table 3.14. **National Agricultural Policy: Policy hub and objectives**

Policy hub	Objectives
1. Sustainable water and land management	– Improve water management for agricultural use – Retrieve, preserve and extend the quality and amount of soil for agricultural use
2. Development of forestry and wildlife	– Improve conditions to develop activities for management, use, renovation and trade in the forestry sector, and the harnessing of wildlife and biodiversity with a special focus on profitability, and socio-environmental and territorial sustainability
3. Legal security over land	– Increase the legal security for land within the agricultural sector
4. Infrastructure and irrigation technology	– Enhance efficiency and operating for infrastructure and new irrigation technologies to facilitate investment nationwide, giving priority to small and medium-scale agriculture
5. Financing and agricultural insurance	– Strengthen and expand market access by agrarian credit and insurance for small and medium farmers
6. Innovation and agricultural modernisation	– Increase innovation by adapting new technologies, looking for agricultural productivity and profitability
7. Management of risk disaster in agriculture	– Implement a framework for risk management disasters in the agricultural sector to ensure the continuity and productivity of small farmers, regarding the issue of climate change
8. Capacity building	– Increase capacity building and agribusiness productivity for small farmers, with a specific approach for women and youth
9. Productive restructuring and diversification	– Promote crop diversification and new technologies procedures, for favorable impacts on social, economic and environmental issues
10. Market access	– Strengthen and expand local, regional, national and international markets for small and medium farmers to be involved in the food supply chain
11. Agricultural health and agrifood safety	– Protect, strengthen and expand the sanitary and phytosanitary heritage as well as food safety
12. Institutional development	– Strengthen governance in the national agricultural sector

Source: Ministry of Agriculture and Irrigation (n.d.), www.minagri.gob.pe.

Likewise, in 2015 MINAGRI developed the National Strategy for Family Farming 2015-2021, which aims mainly at a comprehensive state of intervention for achieving favorable results for farmers and family farmers taking into account a commitment for socio-economic inclusion of rural population. The strategy is composed of three approaches, which aim to guide and organise the basis of sustainable use of natural resources.

Table 3.15. **Family Farming Strategy: Development approaches**

Development approaches	Strategic options
1. Territorial development	– Involves integrating the economic and institutional, dimensions (productive-cultural, environmental and political partners) and provide a comprehensive view of the territory, to promote co-ordination of rural areas with urban ones, through proposals for development of regional and municipal governments. – In this context, the commitment to the exercise of citizenship is key as it allows the recognition and respect of the rights and duties of individuals and overcomes forms of inequity and exclusion by strengthening self-esteem and equality of opportunity between men and women, putting an emphasis on youth empowerment.
2. Sustainable development	– Refers to the process of natural, economic, social, cultural and institutional transformations aimed at a cumulative and durable increase to improve equitable safety and quality of human life, without damaging the natural environment or compromising the foundations of development for future generations (harmony between economic, environmental and social dimensions). – In this context, risk management also arises because Peru is highly vulnerable to the risks caused by natural phenomena or effects of climate change such as flooding, freezing, landslides, droughts, cold fronts, among others.
3. Human development	– This approach emphasises that the purpose of human development is to create conditions and opportunities for enriching human life and not only to increase the rate of economic growth since, according to the approach, the wealth of the economy is, ultimately, only one dimension of the lives of people and not their ultimate goal. – Consequently, National Stategy for Familiar Agriculture (Estrategia Naciona de Agricultura Familiar-ENAF) proposes a model centered on people and their potential. In this context, the strategic commitment to multiculturalism is key.

Source: Ministry of Agriculture and Irrigation (n.d.), www.minagri.gob.pe.

The characteristics of agriculture are uneven across the country. Due, in part, to agrarian reforms during the 1990s, farms are generally small in Peru, and 85% of the population owns less than one hectare of land (EU, 2013). Larger farms, which are also export orientated, are mainly located in the coastal region. Smaller farms are a bigger feature of agricultural production in the highlands and rainforest regions. Importantly, Peru does not provide farmers with subsidies or other forms of public support. The advantage of such a situation is that Peruvian agriculture constantly reacts to signals provided by the international market, and in particular demand and price.

However, in the context of Peru, not having a policy supporting small farmers may expose ethnic minorities living in the mountains to extreme poverty. These farmers have to deal with many sorts of shocks, including El Niño, low international commodity prices and problems accessing local markets. Reflecting this situation, and as in the case of MIDIS, the Ministry of Agriculture and Irrigation implements two kinds of programmes: those to increase agricultural incomes in rural areas and those to improve the economic performance of rural territories. Concerning the first group, MINAGRI participates in inter-ministerial commissions dealing with poverty and food security and is a member of the Multi-Sectoral Commission for Food Security and Nutrition.

The ministry has developed the National Plan for Agriculture that co-ordinates several programmes and provides guidance to subnational governments. It is active in programmes like *Mi Riego* that promote access to water for irrigation. Access to water is inevitably tied to issues of food security and nutrition. *Mi Riego* employs a holistic approach to water management to tackle challenges related to water availability, a lack of relevant infrastructure and water usage. The involvement of the Ministry of Agriculture and Irrigation in programmes like *Mi Riego* facilitates their integration into the National Plan for Agriculture, thereby increasing their sustainability and the political support they receive.

In addition, to supporting agriculture in mountainous areas, MINAGRI co-ordinates the programme *Sierra Exportadora* (exporting mountains). This programme, created in 2006, promotes a range of rural sectors in the mountains, with emphasis on agriculture, livestock, aquaculture, handicrafts, textiles, jewellery, reforestation, agroforestry and tourism, as well as activities of transformation and industrialisation connected with these sectors. *Sierra Exportadora* focuses on the creation of supply chains and clusters of firms, which are considered as any agglomerations of firms in a given mountain territory. The programme is based on the following actions:

- Promotion of investment by elaborating plans for competitive entrepreneurship. These plans are connected with national territorial programmes.
- Implementation of public-private partnerships.
- Access to public funding.
- Technical assistance and capacity building to promote the creation of local value chains.
- Access to national development banks and funds (PROCOMPITE and AGROBANCO, for instance).

Sierra Exportadora also connects with other programmes, such as Agrorural. This co-ordinates a series of projects, including *Sierra y Selva Alta* (forest highlands) and *Aliados* (allies) designed to develop the skills and incomes of agricultural producers in rural areas. *Sierra y Selva Alta* parallels *Mi Chacra Emprendedora* assessed above. It has similar objectives and is delivered by providing information and capacity building to selected members of the local communities (*Yachachiq*) to favour peer-to-peer learning.

Small agricultural producers tend to have limited access to financial markets and insurances. MINAGRI also has several initiatives to develop productive credit programmes, guarantee schemes and insurance systems via AGROBANCO, a state-owned bank focused on agricultural production with 80 offices nationwide.

Box 3.9. *Sierra y Selva Alta* in the province of San Martín

In the province of San Martín, *Sierra y Selva Alta* provides local communities with information and also with some funds to engage them in new activities such as tourism, fish farming and flower production, among others. The programme favours a sustainable use of local environmental assets. This includes:

- Initiatives promoting birdwatching to attract international tourism. The programme pays an ornithologist to work with the community and work with people to identify ways to capitalise on the fact that their territory displays record high biodiversity.
- Likewise for fish farming, projects try to capitalise on the fact that rivers are abundant in the region and there are several species with a good commercial value that can be easily farmed in the rich Amazon's waters.
- Flowers are another abundant resource of the Amazon. Some small-scale pilot projects have started supporting communities to sustainably collect orchids from trees, including from trees cut by farming.

These projects are also assessing the current barriers (regulation) that need to be modified to give the rural people involved with this activity the possibility of benefiting from the immense resources of the forest without necessarily replacing the forest with low-quality agricultural land.

Other national ministries with significant rural programmes

There are a number of other ministries that also have significant rural programmes, and/or national programmes which have a significant impact on poverty and economic development outcomes for rural communities:

- In terms of economic development, the Ministry of Transport and Communications plays a key role in rural development through programmes related to rural roads and departmental roads.
- The Ministry of Transport and Communications delivers the "Pro Región" and "PATS – Support Program for Sub-national Transport" programmes, which are meant to promote the development of transport at the subnational level, with a logistical and competitiveness approach that meets the needs of the productive sector by developing the potential and opportunities in each locality.
- The Ministry of Transport and Communications also delivers the Program of Subsidized Flights (*Programa de Vuelos Subsidiados*) that provides air transport services to isolated areas where there is no private offering (Loreto, Ucayali, Amazonas and San Martín). This represents significant time savings, decreasing one-day travel to 30-40 minutes. It also represents savings rates between 30% and 53% for users.
- The Ministry of Labour and the Promotion of Employment has a focus on linking business and skills development initiatives with poverty reduction. The Responsible Peru programme includes initiatives to provide formal employment opportunities for targeted groups such as women and young people, skills matching, and to promote entrepreneurship.
- The National Water Authority (ANA) implements some policies related to the provision of rural social services, which are related to water resources, such as: drinking water, sewerage and electricity from hydropower.
- From a social policy point of view, the Ministry of Health also has a rural development strategy that develops at least seven major lines of intervention involving rural areas of the country.
- The Ministry of the Environment also plays a key role in terms of environmental and land-use regulation. Spatial planning and land-use regulation is important in terms of helping to identify key natural resources and implementing land-use regulations to help ensure their sustainable use. The ministry is currently working with the region of San Martín to implement zoning rules related to economic development and ecological resources. This will allow the department and municipalities to better identify ecological resources, areas for the location of human settlements, and appropriate sites for forestry and agricultural developments.

There are lots of good projects but they are fragmented and not connected to an agreed national strategy for rural growth and development

The governance of rural policy in Peru is complex and there are multiple actors that deliver programmes affecting rural communities. Granularity of programmes may facilitate the matching between needs and policy responses. However, it is also likely this is leading to duplication and lack of critical mass. As these initiatives are not connected to a regional strategic framework or governance arrangement, it means that complementarities between policies are not realised. This problem is apparent in a disconnect between economic development and social programmes, which will need to be addressed in order to make further progress in reducing rural poverty and growing rural economies.

Box 3.10. Advances in land management in the region of San Martín

Important efforts are currently underway in the process of land-use planning of the San Martín region. Land-use planning is regulated by the Ministry of Environment and uses the ecological and economic zoning as input for the formulation of plans and strategies to intervene in the region. San Martín is a department that has suffered high rates of population migration due mostly to the exploitation of rubber and the opening the marginal road of the forest, which has led to the establishment of human settlements in unsuitable areas, expanding the agricultural frontier and thus generating deforestation.

Economic ecological zoning allowed the authorities to identify the potential and limitations presented by the territory, identifying the areas for the location of human settlements, and the need to preserve and restore ecosystems, optimise the appropriate use of the territory considering its agricultural, forestry vocation and other activities, considering both the urban and rural problems of the territory.

The San Martín region currently has programmes and projects for the implementation of the Regional Forest Plan approved by Regional Ordinance No. 008-2008-GRSM/CR, the same as that produced from the economic ecological zoning, in order to solve deforestation problems faced by the region, thus allowing the recovery and expansion of these forests.

Source: Ministry of Environment (2016).

Box 3.11. Policy complementarity: What is it and how does it work?

The concept of policy complementarity refers to the mutually reinforcing impact of different actions on a given policy outcome. Policies can be complementary because they support the achievement of a given target from different angles. For example, production development policy, innovation policy and trade policy all support the competitiveness of national industry. Alternatively, a policy in one domain can reinforce the impact of another policy.

Sequencing is also important in policy complementarity. Some policies are best put in place simultaneously. For example, innovation, industrial and trade policies must be synchronised to address the issue of industrial competitiveness from all angles. Other policies realise their synergies in a sequential way. For example, investments in broadband infrastructure need to be followed up with specific policies on access and diffusing those services to the population.

Complementarities between policies can be "latent", but can be triggered by specific governance arrangements, for example mechanisms that facilitate co-ordination across levels of government (vertical co-ordination) can help attain complementarity across policies from various levels. Alternatively, they can be induced, by combining different policies through conditionality schemes, or when the complementarities are the result of strategic planning. Employment generation opportunities, for example, can be attached to direct cash transfers to support the inclusion of poor people in production so that they can avoid dependency on income transfers.

Policy complementarities can also be spontaneous when they appear as positive side effects of independent actions of ministries or bodies.

Source: OECD (2014d), *OECD Territorial Reviews: Netherlands 2014*, http://dx.doi.org/10.1787/9789264209527-en.

Peru does not have a full-fledged rural policy, but a large number of programmes. For instance, the government has invested to improve regional accessibility in remote areas since the 1990s. Improved road connections (unintendedly) delivered rural development (Webb, 2013). Likewise, the national conditional cash transfers programme, *Juntos*, has contributed to reducing poverty in the country, reaching out 1 million households, most of which are rural, in 2014. Finally, some smaller programmes promote business and aim to generate rural jobs. This is the case of *Mi Chacra Emprendedora* (also called *Haku Wiñay* – which means "growing together", in Quechua), implemented by MIDIS and its twin programme *Sierra y Selva Alta*, which is implemented by MINAGRI. Having different programmes managed from the centre by different ministries is inefficient. It generates duplications and needless complexity.

The key problem facing rural areas is that rural assets make a significant contribution to national wealth but the income levels and well-being of rural people are low. Sustained economic growth and the implementation of numerous large-scale social programmes – conditional cash transfer programmes among them – have lifted more than 20% of the country's population out of poverty; however, some 50% of rural people remain below the poverty line. Up to 17% of rural children aged 5 and under are malnourished and many of them suffer from stunted growth. It has proven difficult to implement effective policies in programmes in rural areas for a number of reasons. Among them are a lack of information to inform strategic planning processes, capacity constraints at the local level, and generally weak regional governments that are often unable to scale up policies and provide public goods.

Box 3.12. *Mi Chacra Emprendedora* programme

The *Mi Chacra Emprendedora* programme (or its version at the Ministry of Agriculture and Irrigation: *Sierra and Selva Alta*) is an example of a programme that should be scaled up and implemented in food insecure rural regions. The peer-to-peer learning systems impel agricultural innovation and diversification into new, more profitable crops.

The programme also contributes to the establishment of a relationship between the central government and rural communities. This permits communities to articulate their needs and priorities to decision makers at the national level and could also conceivably lead to the more efficient delivery of public services in underserved communities. Enhanced public services provision could, in turn, stem the outflow of rural citizens to urban areas.

Peru's various programmes promoting rural development are insufficiently co-ordinated. The Ministry of Development and Social Inclusion is responsible for a large number of programmes, and it should be responsible for co-ordination of the other ministries. However, it does not have the capacity or the power to co-ordinate a broad rural development agenda. Most programmes have therefore focused solely on the immediate relief of poverty rather than embarking on a more comprehensive policy that deals with the factors generating poverty. For instance, *Juntos* successfully reaches people in need (1 million households in 2014). But it is not able to provide these people with income-generation opportunities: with a pool of skills or capital to sustainably improve their living conditions. Conversely, transferring cash – albeit very efficiently – can generate dependence and lower the incentives to leave the system.

The Ministry of Agriculture and Irrigation is confronted by similar challenges. Its programmes are providing rural citizens with tailored interventions, but most of them are on a small scale and do not co-ordinate with similar initiatives implemented by other branches of the government, including MIDIS (Table 3.16).

Table 3.16. **Programmes provided by the Ministry of Agriculture and Irrigation (select details)**

Programme	Budget 2015 USD	Number of households involved	District or province
High Sierra Project	8.9M	18 533	Lima, Amazonas, San Martín and Cajamarca (total of 85 districts)
North Sierra Project	2.4M	839	Lambayeque, Cajamarca, Amazonas and La Libertad (total of 115 districts)
Sierra Development Project II*	0.8M	0	Arequipa, Puno, Moquegua, Tacna, Apurímac and Cusco (total of 60 districts)
Support for Rural Productive Partnerships in the Sierra (ALIADOS) II	12.9M	16 611	Apurímac, Ayacucho, Huancavelica, Hunauco, Junín and Pasco (total of 480 districts)
My Irrigation	54.4M	4 534	Amazonas, Áncash, Apurímac, Arequipa Ayacucho, Cajamarca, Cusco, Huancavelica, Huánuco, Junín, La Libertad, Lima, Moquegua, Pasco, Piura, Puno and Tacna (total of 64 districts)
Small and medium-sized infrastructure in the highlands of Peru – PIPMIRS	10.6M	Implementation has not begun	Amazonas, Áncash, Ayacucho, Cajamarca, Huancavelica, Huánuco, Junín, La Libertad and Piura (total of 39 districts)

Notes: Number of beneficiary families based on a statement provided in 2015. * The project has been closed.

Source: Ministry of Agriculture and Irrigation (n.d.), www.minagri.gob.pe.

Peru's social programmes are largely detached from the country's competitive agenda, focusing on the creation of employment and income-generating opportunities. The Ministry of Production does not, for example, actively participate in efforts to address poverty and promote local economic development in rural areas. The same disconnect is evident at the subnational level and in non-governmental organisations and citizens' organisations; the engagement of the business community is minimal. For instance, *Juntos* (and the large pool of information the programme collects about households and communities) may operate in co-ordination with a pro-growth programme, or better a policy, that empowers people and creates the conditions to enable them to leave the conditional cash transfer system, after some rounds.

Yet these programmes are establishing an important legacy: they contribute to the creation of stronger rural stakeholders who may be able to influence the national approach to rural development in the near future. Emerging rural constituencies may become important to interface rural communities with investment, including in mining activities, in the coming years. This might facilitate developments and allow the country to increase the volume of its exports in a moment of low international commodity prices.

There is now a general need for strong leadership, a clear vision and greater co-ordination among policies and programmes. Rural development should be based on a whole-of-government approach in which programmes are co-ordinated and scaled up. There is a need for a multidimensional policy that delivers regional accessibility, valorises cultural and natural amenities, and gives communities the power and resources to directly govern some key issues, such land use and local taxes for instance, in their territories. This would provide the country with a full-fledged rural development policy, like the ones that can be found in OECD countries.

Box 3.13. Place-based approach to addressing poverty: Findings from Brazil

Territorial inequality among Brazil's states is very high by the standards of OECD TL2 regions. Inequality in Brazil has been declining steadily since 2004. From 1980 to 1986, inequality in gross domestic product (GDP) per capita among the states experienced a large decline, but then increased again until 1989. During the decade that followed, territorial inequality fluctuated but has been trending downwards since 1998. The trend in territorial inequality strongly resembles the trend in interpersonal inequality, suggesting that the performance and development of different locations are highly linked to overall trends.

Like Peru, Brazil has successfully implemented a large number of social policies intended to benefit disadvantaged citizens, many of them located in disadvantaged areas. However, these programmes are not integrated and economic development and dynamism has not yet taken hold in areas with high levels of poverty. Moreover, these policies are not cost-free. Dependency relationships between citizens and regions receiving the transfers can potentially develop, especially if they depend on external rather than endogenous resources for development and growth in the medium and long term.

Targeted social policies, usually characterised by transfers to households and investment in basic infrastructure and services, have brought many disadvantaged citizens out of poverty. However, it was found that these policies could be enhanced by place-based polices focused on addressing local bottlenecks for development. Brazil's lagging regions have significant gaps in human capital and infrastructure. Targeting these key areas for development through an integrated approach can help put them on the way to a sustainable growth path. This requires national sectoral policies to be targeted in space, so they interact and complement each other in positive ways and avoid unintended consequences.

Source: OECD (2013b), *OECD Territorial Reviews: Brazil 2013*, http://dx.doi.org/10.1787/9789264123229-en.

To realise this outcome, governance arrangements for rural policy will need to be improved. Mirroring the situation in cities, rural regions would benefit from the creation of stronger regional governments that can co-ordinate investment and the delivery of public services. These include rural-urban partnerships that help adjacent communities interact and that facilitate the delivery services and public goods at the right territorial scale. In fact, the lack of an intermediate government level that co-ordinates different streams of national policies is a key challenge in Peru that particularly affects the capacity of the public sector to promote the sustainable development of the country. An effective co-ordination body will also be needed at a national level, coupled with a clear vision and political leadership. For this reason, and given the importance of rural development in the country, the PCM and MEF should play a more proactive role in the rural development agenda to deliver a genuinely whole-of-government approach.

There are a number of experiences from OECD countries that Peru can learn from to address issues related to developing a pro-growth rural development agenda, and improving the alignment and co-ordination of policies. Over the past two decades, the OECD has developed a rural policy agenda which, in part, is designed to address these issues. The following section outlines this and highlights good practices for rural policy makers in Peru.

Lessons from OECD countries for improving rural development policy

The New Rural Paradigm (NRP)

The New Rural Paradigm (NRP) is a framework adopted by OECD member countries to promote development in rural regions. Globalisation, the dramatic reduction in farm employment and the emergence of important non-farm niche markets have generated a common understanding that rural policy falls short of being conceived only as agricultural policy. On the contrary, across OECD countries rural areas are increasingly looked upon as a heterogeneous array of regions where one-size-fits-all policies are no longer suitable to capture the diversity of rural needs and opportunities (OECD, 2006a). In this context, innovative governance structures have been created in many OECD countries to strengthen co-ordination across sectors and levels of government and between public and private actors; and innovative policy instruments aimed to identify and exploit the varied development potential of rural areas. The OECD has labelled this policy shift as the "new rural paradigm" whose two main characteristics are: 1) a focus on places instead of sectors; and 2) a focus on investments instead of subsidies (Table 3.17). The key features of the NRP are:

1. an investment-oriented approach
2. a holistic focus on the entire rural economy and not just a few sectors
3. a bottom-up development strategy that reflects local priorities and an inclusive style that encourages the participation of all potential stakeholders, not just a small elite group.

Table 3.17. **The New Rural Paradigm**

	Old approach	New approach
Objectives	Equalisation, farm income, farm competitiveness	Competitiveness of rural areas, valorisation of local assets, exploitation of unused resources
Key target sector	Agriculture	Various sectors of rural economies (for example rural tourism, manufacturing, ICT industry, etc.)
Main tools	Subsidies	Investments
Key actors	National governments, farmers	All levels of government (supra-national, national, regional and local), various local stakeholders (public, private, non-governmental organisations)

Source: OECD (2006a), *Competitive Cities in the Global Economy*, http://dx.doi.org/10.1787/9789264027091-en.

The aim of the NRP is a better alignment of policies aimed at incentivising rural regions to mobilise their assets and resources. This approach to rural development creates the potential for rural regions to move from lagging status to making a stronger contribution to national development. The strategy does not envision that in this process rural regions will inevitably grow to become large urbanised regions. In the regional hierarchy there are specific roles for both large urban and smaller rural regions and these roles are complementary. Instead, what is contemplated is a process where rural regions develop in the sense of accumulating the types of capital that are appropriate for their particular role in the national and global economies.

The NRP is a framework for thinking about rural policy. It is up to each country to determine how to implement the approach. A necessary first step is the identification of a national rural development strategy, followed by the introduction of policies and programmes, and finally the implementation and evaluation of these interventions on a regional basis. The idea is to integrate and better co-ordinate all national programmes that concern the rural domain and at the same time add flexibility to national policy to ensure that it adapts to the different needs of various rural regions.

The NRP promotes a place-based approach involving top-down and bottom-up development processes. Because the NRP is an investment approach, it implicitly adopts economic development as wealth or a capital expansion approach. In rural regions, the current and optimal mix of capital are likely to differ, and will also differ from those of urban regions. This suggests that there can be important benefits from introducing both urban and rural development approaches. Further, because rural regions are more reliant on natural capital, and natural capital endowments vary considerably across rural regions, it is important to follow a bottom-up approach where each region identifies its particular assets and opportunities, and identifies a specific strategy to make investments that augment its unique capital stock.

The NRP recognises the large variability in the needs and assets of rural regions requiring adaptability and flexibility. This large variability makes it impossible for a central authority to manage the development process. While national governments have the important role of setting out broad goals and acceptable behaviour, it is important to provide a flexible approach at the regional level to finding ways to achieve these goals. National financial support can help or limit this process depending on how it is provided. Where it is provided with some flexibility in how the funds can be used, it can greatly facilitate the development process. However, when funds are tightly restricted to specific uses, the result is typically activity in rural areas that leads to limited development. The region takes the money that is offered and implements the project, but the project provides few long-term benefits, so in effect the money is wasted.

The final part of the NRP is a recognition that an integrated rural policy requires significant co-ordination among various national government ministries, regional and local governments, and private firms. This point is further expanded in Chapter 4. Effective development requires contributions from all actors, but these contributions need a degree of co-ordination. The aim of multi-level governance is to provide at least a forum where each party knows what the other parties intend to do. In some cases this may lead to a co-ordinating agency, but this is neither always necessary nor desirable.

The New Rural Policy 3.0

The current rural framework, however, has evolved since 2006. The OECD Rural Policy Programme has engaged in 12 national rural policy reviews covering a wide spectrum of national conditions and rural regions. Given that each review was conducted with the new rural paradigm as a metric, they contain valuable information on the adoption of this paradigm by member countries.

In addition, the elaboration of a number of rural thematic reviews has also provided a fresh perspective on the changing nature of rural economies and the opportunities and constraints facing rural development. Thematic reviews are also tools to facilitate international policy dialogue and mutual learning. The most recent thematic rural reviews focus on the interactions between urban and rural regions (OECD, 2013d); identification of key factors and bottlenecks for economic growth (OECD, 2008; 2012b); and the links between renewable energy deployment rural development (OECD, 2012a).

Furthermore, recent advancements of the OECD on regional and urban policy have shed light on important dimensions of rural policy. In particular, the elaboration of functional urban areas (FUAs) has important implications for rural policy as FUAs bring about a new framework with which to address rural-urban interactions. This framework also considers medium-sized towns and cities and the elaboration of multidimensional indicators to measure well-being at the regional and local levels. This provides a broader perspective with which to examine differences and similarities in the quality of life across different types of regions.

The OECD's approach is now evolving – from the New Rural Paradigm to the New Rural Policy.[7] Where the New Rural Paradigm provided a conceptual framework, the New Rural Policy focuses on mechanisms for the implementation of effective practices. The various elements of the policy are not distinct – they overlap and mutually support one another.

Table 3.18. **The New Rural Policy 3.0**

	Old paradigm	New Rural Paradigm (2006)	Rural Policy 3.0: Implementing the new rural paradigm
Objectives	Equalisation	Competiveness	Well-being considering multiple dimensions of: 1) the economy; 2) society; 3) the environment
Policy focus	Support for a single dominant resource sector	Support for multiple sectors based on their competitiveness	Low-density economies differentiated by type of rural
Tools	Subsidies for firms	Investments in qualified firms and communities	Integrated rural development approach – spectrum of support to public sector, firms and third sector
Key actors and stakeholders	Farm organisations and national governments	All levels of government and all relevant departments plus local stakeholders	Involvement of: 1) public sector – multi-level governance; 2) private sector – for-profit firms and social enterprise; 3) third sector – non-governmental organisations and civil society
Policy approach	Uniformly applied top-down policy	Bottom-up policy, local strategies	Integrated approach with multiple policy domains
Rural definition	Not urban	Rural as a variety of distinct types of place	Three types of rural: 1) embedded in metropolitan region; 2) adjacent to metropolitan region; 3) far from metropolitan regions

Source: OECD (2016), *OECD Regional Outlook 2016*, forthcoming.

Rural-urban linkages peri-urban, intermediate and remote rural

The New Rural Policy, by combining bottom-up and top-down approaches, can better adapt policy to the needs of different types of rural regions. This flexibility is important given the differences in the types of rural regions, each with its particular urban and rural interactions. Chapter 1 of this review displayed the importance of the choice of a rural definition in determining how much of a country is characterised for policy purposes as urban or rural. In all three general types of rural regions, whenever administrative boundaries are drawn, unless they are tightly drawn around population centres, there will be some incorporation of rural territory into what is defined as urban areas.

The needs and characteristics of remote rural regions, rural regions close to cities and rural regions integrated into functional city regions are very different, despite the existence of strong urban and rural interactions in the three cases.

- There is rural territory that is strongly integrated into an urban context as part of a metropolitan region. In this territory, the development process of the rural territory cannot be decoupled from the larger urban development process.
- There is rural territory that is adjacent to a metropolitan centre but not strongly attached to it. This territory may be incorporated into an administrative region that is considered to be urban, but the territory and its population are in reality still rural. In these regions, while there are some important connections between urban and rural territory, mainly through the flow of goods and services, the two types of territory follow different development paths.
- The third type of rural territory has very weak urban links and is distant from any major urban concentrations. While there are urban places in these remote rural regions, they are small and exert only limited influence on the rural population and landscape.

Functional urban areas, or metropolitan regions, contain a strong degree of symbiosis between the urban and rural parts. This is especially true when urban regions are defined as metropolitan areas that include an urban core and a related hinterland (OECD, 2013d and Box 3.14). These functional regions are based on commuting patterns that attach a rural zone that extends beyond the formal boundary of a city to create a hybrid rural and urban territory. Within this territory the urban function is dominant, but there is a strong degree of symbiosis between the urban and rural parts (OECD, 2013c). These urban and rural territories are linked through flows of people, economic exchanges, shared infrastructure, environmental services and government interaction.

In the case of the Nuremburg Metropolitan Region, there was a conscious effort to extend public transport out into the rural territory to create easy opportunities for rural residents to take advantage of retail opportunities and more advanced services in the core, but also to encourage urban residents to take short trips to the countryside to experience nature. Conversely, because the city of Prague and the adjacent rural territory had uncooperative relations, there were constraints on Prague's growth and uncoordinated housing and transport development.

An important share of rural areas (and population) is contained in FUAs. Particularly when larger administrative regions are used in defining functional areas, as in the case of the United States, the share of rural territory that is embedded within the functional areas is quite large. Indeed, the share of rural population found in metropolitan statistical areas (MSAs) in the United States is larger than the share of rural population in non-MSAs.

In intermediate regions there is typically more balance between urban and rural populations. This balance carries over into the economy where there are often very strong synergies between urban and rural specialisations. In the Lexington, Kentucky MSA (United States), the main city, Lexington, hosts the major financial, retail, health and education functions, but manufacturing tends to be found in adjacent counties, as does a large share of moderate income housing. Similarly, the Geelong region of Australia consists of a city and a large rural area that is divided into several autonomous local governments. The traditional economic manufacturing base of the city is declining, but the high amenity and agricultural production value in the surrounding rural territory is being used to help restructure the regional economy around advanced services. With a high quality of life, largely based on high-quality rural amenities, it is easier to attract the high-skilled professionals that Geelong needs to transform its economy.

Box 3.14. Proximity to cities and economic growth

Large metropolitan areas are important drivers of economic activity within countries and typically have the highest per capita gross domestic product (GDP) of all regions within a country. However, the economic effects of large metropolitan areas are not confined to their borders. They also play important roles for economic activity in surrounding regions. Their size and economic strength implies that they are key markets for many firms in rural areas. Even firms that do not directly sell to metropolitan areas rely on them due to their function as hubs for long-distance travel or because providers of highly specialised business-to-business services can predominantly be found within them. Therefore, large metropolitan areas form the geographical focal point of economic activity even for regions that are a considerable distance away.

Ahrend and Schumann (forthcoming) estimate the relation between distance to metropolitan areas and economic growth. It turns out that the actual travel time required to reach a metropolitan area is a better predictor of economic growth than aerial distance. Travel time indicates the time required to travel by car from the centre of a region to the centre of the closest large metropolitan area and is obtained from Google Maps. In contrast to aerial distance, travel time also accounts for factors such as the state of transport infrastructure and geographical characteristics that affect car traffic.

Between 1995 and 2010, longer travel time to metropolitan areas has been associated with significantly lower growth of per capita GDP at the regional level. The effect is most pronounced when it comes to distance to very large metropolitan areas with more than 2 million inhabitants. However, it is also visible for distance to smaller metropolitan areas. The marginal effect of an additional minute in travel time is greatest at short distances to metropolitan areas. It becomes continuously weaker for longer travel times. Beyond 300 minutes the correlation between travel time and per capita GDP growth disappears.

Figure 3.15 shows the results of a regression of yearly growth rates on a set of dummy variables for the respective travel time brackets (including initial per capita GDP levels and a set of country fixed effects as control variables). The data cover TL3 regions from 18 OECD countries over the 1995-2010 period. The graph shows average yearly growth rates for each group of regions conditional on the control variables. It illustrates that regions within 45 minutes of a metropolitan area with more than 2 million inhabitants grew on average by 1.8% per year. The growth rate is almost half a percentage point higher than the growth rate of regions within 45 to 90 minutes of metropolitan areas of the same size. See Ahrend and Schumann (forthcoming) for further details.

Figure 3.15. **Annual growth rates for regions (time taken to travel by car to metropolitan area)**

Yearly growth rates in %

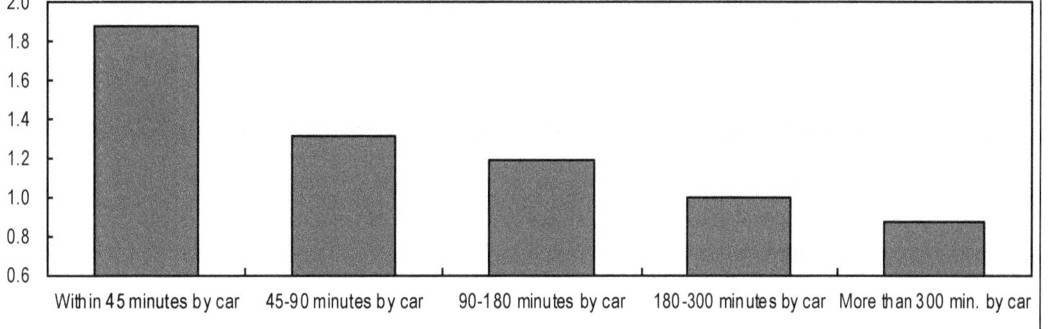

Source: Ahrend, R. and A. Schumann (forthcoming), "Does regional growth depend on closeness to urban centres? The role of economic and geographic distance".

Figure 3.16. **The official definitions of "rural" concept in the United States**

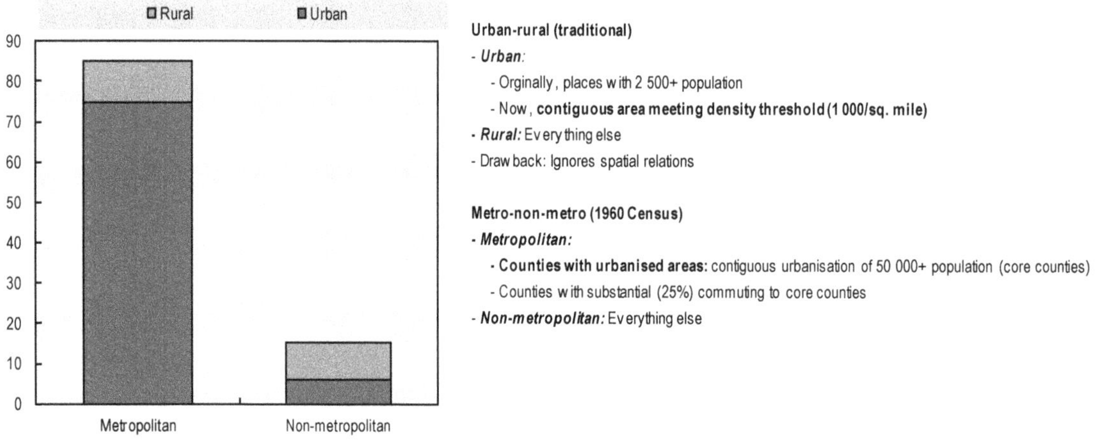

Remote rural regions also display strong urban and rural interactions. In many OECD countries, the majority of the rural territory, but not the majority of the rural population, is found in territory that is only weakly connected to a large urban place. Nevertheless, within these predominantly rural territories there are urban places and some of them can be large towns. Importantly though, the urban places in these regions almost always derive their economic function from the surrounding rural territory. In these more remote rural regions, urban places follow a more traditional urban rile of being market points for the export of rural production and the import of inputs needed for rural production.

In small remote regions such as central Finland, there are considerable problems in providing high-quality public services at a reasonable cost. Individual communities are too small to provide them individually and often can be too far apart to have a single central site for a region. In this case, not only are shared services required among small communities, but attention has to be paid to finding innovative ways to deliver them. Central Poland represents another highly rural region with only small urban settlements. Here, too, the challenge is to organise dispersed local governments to deliver better public services. In the case of Poland, there is not a strong tradition of local co-operation and historically local governments were very weak and took few independent decisions. This has complicated efforts to form effective partnerships among urban and rural areas despite the highly interconnected local economy.

A flexible approach works best for modern rural policies balancing broad and narrow rural policy

Given that rural policy involves a wide number of ministries, the policy framework should on the one hand bring coherence to a complex policy setting and on the other hand adaptability and flexibility to address the specific needs of rural areas. Due to the large number of ministries and agencies with responsibility for some aspect of rural policy, there is a danger for rural policy to be watered down within the internal multiple priorities of these sectoral ministries. In order for rural policy to exist in a way that is "fit for purpose", an institutional framework has to be put in place that provides a proper context. OECD member countries have followed one of two approaches by adopting either a broad or narrow rural policy.

1. broad rural policy refers to the efforts to influence all actions with impacts on rural areas within and by the different administrative sectors as part of the development of the rural society
2. narrow rural policy includes the measures and instruments targeted specifically at rural development.

Broad and narrow rural policy can address the needs of rural policy in different ways. Broad rural development policies are those that adopt a grand overarching design – a cross-sectoral policy in practice, one that attempts to integrate all policies. Included in this frame are those policies and programmes that were designed with other objectives in mind (perhaps without a rural focus or considerations) but which have intended or unintended impacts on rural dwellers and places. In contrast, the more "niche" or "narrow policy" approach is policy designed specifically to address the needs of rural communities (Figure 3.17). Often with the grander scheme, the effort to "address all areas of a rather broad policy framework" such as agricultural policy, transportation policy and energy policy outdistances capacity. As such, the push to co-ordinate all actions and bridge all gaps tends to yield more inertia and inaction than concrete results (OECD, 2006b). The too narrow rural policy delivers results, but also policies that risk being too disconnected from other regional, sector or national polices.

Figure 3.17. **OECD matrix for rural policy analysis**

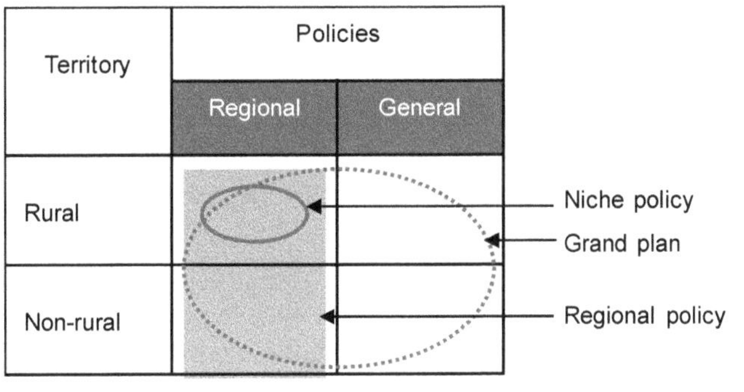

Source: OECD (2006b), *The New Rural Paradigm: Policies and Governance*, http://dx.doi.org/10.1787/9789264023918-en.

A broad rural policy tends to see rural regions as being quite similar to urban regions in terms of their opportunities and constraints, and more importantly in terms of the types of policy instruments that can be provided to them. It largely assumes that there is little need for a territorially specific policy because a single national policy operated by each ministry can adequately meet the needs of people wherever they are located. By contrast, narrow rural policy is inherently territorial in nature. It supposes that there are such fundamental differences between urban and rural regions that a single policy will be ineffective in at least one type of territory. Instead of a single uniform policy, ministries may need specifically targeted policies that are designed to be effective under rural conditions.

Different OECD member countries apply different combinations of broad and narrow rural policy addressing their own needs:

- The government of Spain adopted the Law on Sustainable Development of Rural Areas. This law extends the responsibility of rural policy from a sole actor, the Ministry of Agriculture and Irrigation, to the government at large (OECD,

2009b). By creating the *politica rural de estado*, or a "rural policy of state", it has enabled a way to better co-ordinate the efforts of the regional administration and better link them with the national government. The national body tasked with overseeing this effort is comprised of representatives of different ministries and one representative from each region, the *consejero* in charge of rural development in each region. Mainstreaming rural policy at the national level was key because Spain has a highly decentralised governance structure with extremely autonomous regions. Each region has extensive experience with rural development policy garnered through the LEADER programmes and local action groups. But the approach to a rural governance policy framework was often disconnected at the regional and the national level and yielded suboptimal results (OECD, 2009b). The law essentially formalised much of what already existed in Spain as well as creating a state rural policy with oversight at the national level.

- England has tried to achieve flexibility by adopting a broad rural policy that relies on the general programmes of line ministries to deliver essentially the same forms of support to urban and rural places. But because the EU overlays a narrow approach to rural policy through its Rural Development Funds, there is ultimately a mixed approach to rural development that combines broad (mainstreaming) and narrow (the Rural Development Programme for England, RDPE) approaches. Undoubtedly, mainstreaming equates rural with urban and moves rural beyond the negative of rural "special pleading" to focus on the positive contributions of rural areas to the overall health of the regional and national economy. Since "basing policies just on rural needs" could shadow this view and cause "policy makers to see delivery to rural communities as a marginal activity" and possibly "raise unrealistic expectations", the preference in England is to limit rural-specific interventions to the RDPE (Atterton, 2008). Ironically, mainstreaming rural in the context of England is almost too broad and too narrow, placing it in a space that needs further clarification and support. Thus in England, where the vast majority of the rural population is found within urban metropolitan regions so they have ready access to urban services, the inability to provide any targeted support to rural areas causes problems. For example, while school choice is relatively easy to accommodate in an urban context where there are several schools relatively near any house, it is a difficult situation in a rural location where there is only one school that is accessible.

- Finland has also adopted a mixed approach. The National Rural Policy Programme (*Maaseutupoliittinen kokonaisohjelma*) is drawn up by the Rural Policy Committee and is one of the four special programmes derived from the Regional Development Act (602/2002). It is the main instrument of broad rural policy and as such aims at providing coherence to the different sectoral policies oriented towards rural areas. Revised every four years, the programme contains both a strategic perspective and concrete proposals carried forward by the Rural Policy Committe. The Rural Policy Programme includes a special Rural Policy Programme. The narrow rural policy refers not only to EU programmes but also to other activities of the national rural policy and the main instrument of the narrow rural policy is the Rural Development Programme for the Mainland Finland 2007-13. Thus, Finland has successfully integrated EU programmes at the core of its "narrow rural policy" and is considered a "model" in many respects for other EU countries, especially its LEADER method and its approach to mainstreaming national funds and other EU funds in order to cover the entire countryside.

Whether a broad or narrow perspective is appropriate will largely depend upon the mix of rural territory, as described in the preceding section. It will also largely depend on the types of rural regions in a given country:

- Where a significant share of the rural population lives far from an urban centre and has a quite different quality of life and level of well-being, a narrow rural policy is needed. Differences in conditions and geographic separation make it unlikely that rural residents can rely on urban-oriented policies.
- Conversely, if the majority of the rural population lives in close proximity to urban territory so they can easily take advantage of urban providers of goods and services and are well integrated into the urban economy, then a broad rural policy may be appropriate.

For the case of Peru, a flexible approach combining broad and narrow perspectives might be needed. A broad approach would be needed to better integrate the economic and social development initiatives currently targeting rural areas. This would need to be complemented by a narrow approach which recognises the territorial diversity of the country, and the varying institutional capacities within different regions.

There are a number of different dimensions to this diversity which would need to be taken into account in designing policies:

- Geographic diversity between the coastal, highlands and rainforest areas. This physical geography results in very different climatic conditions and access to markets.
- Proximity to Lima and larger cities. The economies of the coastal regions, in particular, are shaped by urban dynamics.
- Degree of rurality. Rural areas tend to have a higher level of poverty and informality. Indigenous populations experience poorer socio-economic outcomes, particularly in the Amazonia.
- Presence of the mining industry. The mining industry generates particular socio-economic and environmental dynamics which need to be taken account of.

While it would be an exaggeration to say that every region needs a unique rural policy, it is clear that each region requires the flexibility to align national rural priorities with regional needs. Because the rural situation varies considerably, rural policy has to incorporate this diversity if it is to be effective. This kind of flexibility is dependent upon effective multi-level governance and fiscal arrangements, which is the subject of Chapter 4.

Recommendations

Peru has laid the foundations for a contemporary approach to national urban and rural policies. There is a growing interest at the national level in urban policies reflected in the NUDP (2006-15). Investment has been committed to improving the quality and coverage of planning instruments at a subnational level. Rural policies are currently mainly orientated toward the alleviation of poverty, which is understandable given the socio-economic conditions in many rural places. Economic development programmes seek to support rural communities in improving agricultural productivity and natural resource use. These programmes have created local networks and constituencies which provide a platform for a place-based approach to rural development.

There are similar challenges related to co-ordination and alignment across both policy areas. Multiple ministries and agencies at a national level have an interest in urban and rural policies, yet there is a lack of effective whole-of-government co-ordination. Policy and planning frameworks which have been developed are not connected to resource allocation decisions in a co-ordinated way, and their implementation is not consistently monitored and evaluated. There is significant variation in how policies are implemented at a subnational level, and a lack of alignment between different levels of government. In some cases, national ministries take a direct role in the delivery of services at a regional and local level, and in other cases responsibility is given to subnational governments without adequate resourcing. Regions are largely bypassed, which reduces incentives for collaboration between provincial and district municipalities.

These institutional issues mean that the challenges facing Peru's cities and regions cannot be effectively addressed without policy reform. There are a number of challenges which provide a compelling case for change.

- overcrowding of public infrastructure and services, and spatial inequalities within the metropolitan area of Lima
- relative underperformance of Peru's secondary or intermediate cities
- uneven distribution of poverty, which is now concentrating in fewer rural places
- low benefits which tend to be generated for local communities by extractive industries.

Develop a more strategic approach to national urban policy

The Peruvian government should develop a comprehensive approach to urban policy which builds upon the lessons of the National Urban Development Plan (NUDP) 2006-2015, and encompasses the following elements:

- clear policy objectives and indicators, which are outcomes-based, and monitored and evaluated
- leadership of the Presidency of the Council of Ministers and the Ministry of Economy and Finance to ensure co-ordination in urban policies across national ministries (in particular Housing, Construction and Sanitation; Transport and Communications; Environment; and Production)
- incentives and technical assistance for provincial and district municipalities to implement planning instruments and systems for land management (land-use zoning, development approvals and cadastre)
- enforcement of laws to protect public land and property rights, which is currently lacking
- the incorporation of strategic spatial planning into the fiscal framework (for example funding proposals for infrastructure should be required to demonstrate alignment with strategic spatial plans)
- incentives to encourage the matching and co-ordination of policies at the scale of functional urban areas

- an articulation of how cities can contribute to national strategies to lift productivity and promote economic diversification, and an identification of the economic roles and functions of cities within Peru's urban system.

In parallel with this work the government should also work with key stakeholders to identify options for improving the governance of land use and infrastructure for functional urban areas. This includes ensuring each city has an endorsed strategic spatial plan and urban plans, and that there is a co-ordinated process for linking this with investment decisions about infrastructure at a subnational and national level. The government should prioritise reforms for the metropolitan region of Lima, which will then provide lessons for improving planning and governance arrangements in intermediate cities.

Implement a pro-growth rural agenda by:

- ensuring that the vision, objectives and priorities for rural development have a strong focus on productivity and diversification and are included in relevant policies across government (the centre of government – Presidency of the Council of Ministers and the Ministry of Economy and Finance – should work in partnership to ensure buy-in and commitment from different national ministries to this policy agenda)
- prioritise the development of initiatives which are designed to enhance productivity and diversification opportunities for rural communities (e.g. mining, agriculture, fisheries and tourism)
- adapt existing social programmes such as *Juntos* and better link clients with opportunities for skills development, employment and entrepreneurship (this will provide a platform to make further inroads into poverty reduction, and reduce reliance on transfers over time)
- strengthen the role of regions in the planning and co-ordination of rural development initiatives by ensuring concerted regional development plans include a strong focus on rural economic development.

Notes

1. Ordinance No. 1862, December 2014, issued by the Metropolitan Municipality of Lima, related to territorial and urban development planning of the metropolitan area of Lima, is not in line with the national regulation (DS No. 004-2011-VIVIENDA) issued by the Ministry for Housing, Construction and Sanitation (Ministerio de Vivienda, Construcción y Saneamineto - MVCS).

2. Peru eliminated any kind of support to agriculture in the 1980s, when the country was facing a severe economic and budgetary crisis. Since then, its agriculture has become more productive, flexible and able to compete at the international level. However, small farmers are exposed to all kinds of shocks, including those caused by mining activities competing for water and land.

3. Non-traditional exports summed up to USD 11.6 billion in 2014, representing a 5.8% increase from the same period in 2013. Agricultural products – in particular quinoa, cocoa, fresh avocados and grapes – compose the most important sector among non-traditional exported goods, since those represented 36% of the total shipments with added value. The Central Reserve Bank of Peru (BCR) reported that in 2014, agricultural exports amounted to USD 4.2 billion alone (Ojeda, 2015).

4. http://idbdocs.iadb.org/wsdocs/getdocument.aspx?docnum=39557612.

5. The programme is called "*Mi Chacra Emprendedora*" in the Spanish-speaking communities and "*Haku Wiñay*" in those where Quechua is the dominant language.

6. FONIE was created by Article 23 of Law No. 29951 – Public Sector Budget for Fiscal Year 2013. Its purpose was to finance pre-investment studies and/or the execution of public investment projects by the regional or local governments, as well as the sector or private legal entities.

7. The New Rural Policy was endorsed by delegates of the 10th OECD Rural Conference, "National Prosperity through Modern Rural Policy", held in Memphis, Tennessee on 19-21 May 2015.

Bibliography

Ahrend, R. and A. Schumann (forthcoming), "Does regional growth depend on closeness to urban centres? The role of economic and geographic distance", *OECD Regional Development Working Papers*, OECD Publishing, Paris.

Ahrend, R. et al. (2014), "What makes cities more productive? Evidence on the role of urban governance from five OECD countries", *OECD Regional Development Working Papers*, No. 2014/05, OECD Publishing, Paris, http://dx.doi.org/10.1787/5jz432cf2d8p-en.

Atterton (2008), "Demographics of the ageing rural population", *Working with Older People*, Vol 12:3, pp.19-22.

Bartolini, D. (forthcoming), "Fiscal decentralisation and regional disparities: The role of fiscal vertical imbalances", *OECD Economics Department Working Papers*, OECD Publishing, Paris.

Basov, V. (2015), "The world's top 10 gold mines", http://www.mining.com/the-worlds-top-10-gold-mines/

CEPLAN (2015), "Background report for the national territorial review of Peru", unpublished.

CSIRO (2013), "Social license to operate", webpage, www.csiro.au/en/Research/MRF/Areas/Community-and-environment/Social-licence-to-operate.

DCC and MEF (2014), "Diagnostico de la implementación de las políticas de planificación y gestión territorial y urbanística en el Perú", Desarrollo Ciudades Comprometidas and Ministerio de Economía y Finanzas, Lima.

Ernst & Young (2014), "Peru's business and investment guide 2014/2015", Ernst & Young, www.ey.com/Publication/vwLUAssets/Peru-Business-and-Investment-guide-2014-15/$FILE/Peru%C2%B4s%20Business%20and%20investment%20guide%202014-2015-2.pdf.

Feenstra, R.C., R. Inklaar and M.P. Timmer (2015), "The next generation of the Penn World table", *American Economic Review*, Vol. 105/10, pp. 3 150-3 182, www.aeaweb.org/articles?id=10.1257/aer.20130954.

Fraser Institute (2013), "What is the social license to operate (SLO)?", webpage, www.miningfacts.org/Communities/What-is-the-social-licence-to-operate.

Haussmann, R. and B. Klinger (2008), "Growth diagnostic: Peru", Working Paper CSI-111, PE-P1074, Inter-American Development Bank, http://idbdocs.iadb.org/wsdocs/getdocument.aspx?docnum=1640617.

Henderson, J.V. (2010), "Cities and development", *Journal of Regional Science*, Vol. 50/1, pp. 515-540, http://dx.doi.org/10.1111/j.1467-9787.2009.00636.x.

INEI (n.d.), http://www.inei.gob.pe.

INEI (n.d.), Encuesta Nacional de Hogares http://webinei.inei.gob.pe/anda_inei/index.php/catalog/195.Kamal-Chaoui, L. and M. Plouin (2012), "Cities and green growth: Case study of the Paris/Ile-de-France region", *OECD Regional Development Working Papers*, No. 2012/02, OECD Publishing, Paris, http://dx.doi.org/10.1787/5k9fd0fg78bs-en.

Kamal-Chaoui, L. and A. Robert (2009), "Competitive cities and climate change", *OECD Regional Development Working Papers*, No. 2009/02, OECD Publishing, Paris, http://dx.do.org/10.1787/218830433146.

Le Galés, P. (2007), "Governing globalising cities, reshaping urban policies", in: OECD, *What Policies for Globalising Cities? Rethinking the Urban Policy Agenda*, OECD, Paris, http://www1.oecd.org/gov/regional-policy/49680222.pdf.

Merk, O. et al. (2012), "Financing green urban infrastructure", *OECD Regional Development Working Papers*, No. 2012/10, OECD Publishing, Paris, http://dx.doi.org/10.1787/5k92p0c6j6r0-en.

Ministry of Agriculture and Irrigation (n.d.), www.minagri.gob.pe.

Ministry of Environment (2016), National System of Environmental Information (Ministerio del Ambiente- Sistema Nacional de Información Ambiental) INAM-SINIA, http://sinia.minam.gob.pe. Ministry of Housing, Construction and Sanitation (2006), "Plan Nacional de Desarrollo Urbano: Lineamientos de Política de Desarrollo Urbano 2006-2015" [National Urban Development Plan], Lima, www.urbanistasperu.org/inicio/normas%20legales/PLAN%20NACIONAL%20DE%20DESARROLLO%20URBANO.pdf.

Municipalidad Metropolitana de Lima (n.d.), http://www.munlima.gob.pe. Municipalidad Metropolitana de Lima (2016), Ordenanza No. 1 659, www.ceplan.gob.pe/sites/default/files/Documentos/pdf/plan/PDRC/PDRC_LIMA_METROPOLITANA.pdf (accessed 11 February 2016).

OECD (2016), *OECD Regional Outlook 2016*, OECD Publishing, Paris, forthcoming.

OECD (2015), *OECD Territorial Reviews: Valle de México, Mexico*, OECD Publishing, Paris, http://dx.doi.org/10.1787/9789264245174-en.

OECD (2014a), *OECD Regional Outlook 2014: Regions and Cities, Where Policies and People Meet*, OECD Publishing, Paris, http://dx.doi.org/10.1787/9789264201415-en.

OECD (2014b), *OECD Rural Policy Reviews: Chile 2014*, OECD Publishing, Paris, http://dx.doi.org/10.1787/9789264222892-en.

OECD (2014c), *OECD Territorial Reviews: Colombia 2014*, OECD Publishing, Paris, http://dx.doi.org/10.1787/9789264224551-en.

OECD (2014d), *OECD Territorial Reviews: Netherlands 2014*, OECD Publishing, Paris, http://dx.doi.org/10.1787/9789264209527-en.

OECD (2013a), *Green Growth in Cities*, OECD Green Growth Studies, OECD Publishing, Paris, http://dx.doi.org/10.1787/9789264195325-en.

OECD (2013b), *OECD Territorial Reviews: Brazil 2013*, OECD Publishing, Paris, http://dx.doi.org/10.1787/9789264123229-en.

OECD (2013c), *OECD Urban Policy Reviews: Chile 2013*, OECD Publishing, Paris, http://dx.doi.org/10.1787/9789264191808-en.

OECD (2013d), *Rural-Urban Partnerships: An Integrated Approach to Economic Development*, OECD Publishing, Paris, http://dx.doi.org/10.1787/9789264204812-en.

OECD (2012a), *Linking Renewable Energy to Rural Development*, OECD Publishing, Paris, http://dx.doi.org/10.1787/9789264180444-en.

OECD (2012b), *Promoting Growth in all Regions*, OECD Publishing, Paris, http://dx.doi.org/10.1787/9789264174634-en.

OECD (2009a), *How Regions Grow: Trends and Analysis*, OECD Publishing, Paris, http://dx.doi.org/10.1787/9789264039469-en.

OECD (2009b), *OECD Rural Policy Reviews: Spain 2009*, OECD Publishing, Paris, http://dx.doi.org/10.1787/9789264060074-en.

OECD (2006a), *Competitive Cities in the Global Economy*, OECD Publishing, Paris, http://dx.doi.org/10.1787/9789264027091-en.

OECD (2006b), *The New Rural Paradigm: Policies and Governance*, OECD Publishing, Paris, http://dx.doi.org/10.1787/9789264023918-en.

Ojeda, H. (2015), "Peru: Non-traditional exports totalled more than US$11.6 billion in 2014", Living in Peru, 16 February, www.peruthisweek.com/news-peru-non-traditional-exports-totaled-more-than-us-116-billion-in-2014-105288.

Queensland Department of Infrastructure and Planning (2010), "Social impact assessment: Guideline to establishing a social impact management plan", Department of Infrastructure and Planning, Brisbane, Queensland, Australia, www.statedevelopment.qld.gov.au/resources/guideline/simp-guideline.pdf.

Spink, P., P. Ward and R. Wilson (eds.) (2012), *Metropolitan Governance in the Federalist Americas: Strategies for Equitable and Integrated Development*, University of Notre Dame Press, South Bend.

Steffensen, J. (2010), *Performance-based Grant Systems: Concept and International Experience*, United Nations Capital Development Fund, New York, www.uncdf.org/en/node/2304.

Tiebout, C.M. (1956), "A pure theory of local expenditures", *Journal of Political Economy*, Vol. 64/5, pp. 416-434, www.jstor.org/stable/1826343.

United Nations, Department of Economic and Social Affairs, Population Division (2014), *World Urbanization Prospects: The 2014 Revision*, CD-ROM Edition, https://esa.un.org/unpd/wup/CD-ROM.

Valladares, L. and M. Prates Coelho (2016), "Trends in the urbanisation process", *Urban Research in Latin America*, UNESCO, www.unesco.org/most/valleng.htm#trends.

Webb, R. (2013), "Conexión y despegue rural", Instituto del Perú, Universidad de San Martín de Porres, www.lampadia.com/assets/uploads_librosdigitales/2f207-cdr.pdf.

World Bank (2016a), Improved water source, urban and rural (% population with access), http://databank.worldbank.org/data/reports.aspx?source=2&series=SH.H2O.SAFE.UR.ZS&country=.

World Bank (2016b), Rural poverty headcount at national poverty lines (% of rural/urban populations) http://databank.worldbank.org/data/reports.aspx?source=2&Topic=11.

World Bank (2015), "International tourism, number of arrivals", http://data.worldbank.org/indicator/ST.INT.ARVL?page=4.

World Bank (2009), World Development Report, http://web.worldbank.org/WBSITE/EXTERNAL/EXTDEC/EXTRESEARCH/EXTWDRS/0,,contentMDK:23062295~pagePK:478093~piPK:477627~theSitePK:477624,00.html.

World Economic Forum (2013), *The Peru Travel & Tourism Competitiveness Report 2013*, World Economic Forum, Geneva, www3.weforum.org/docs/WEF_TT_Peru_CompetitivenessReport_2013.pdf.

Chapter 4.

Enabling a regional approach: Governance and financial reforms

This chapter provides a diagnosis of the main multi-level governance mechanisms of Peru, as well as an analysis of subnational governments' finance. The chapter has five sections. The first presents an overview of the decentralisation process and its governance. The second section focuses on the distribution of competences across levels of government and mechanisms for co-ordination. The third section analyses subnational revenues and borrowing. The fourth section discusses expenditures at a subnational level, including the fragmentation of investment at a local level. The final section provides the key findings and recommendations.

The statistical data for Israel are supplied by and under the responsibility of the relevant Israeli authorities. The use of such data by the OECD is without prejudice to the status of the Golan Heights, East Jerusalem and Israeli settlements in the West Bank under the terms of international law.

Key findings and recommendations

Key findings

- Peru has come a long way in certain aspects of its decentralisation process. The levels of competencies and expenditure responsibilities of subnational governments are in many aspects similar to those of OECD countries.
- Despite this progress, certain features of the decentralisation have limited its possibility to unleash its full potential. Competences and responsibilities are not clearly defined between the levels of government. Within the decentralisation framework, there are several overlaps in competencies as well as limited definition of the particular responsibilities assigned to each level of government.
- There is a misalignment between responsibilities allocated to subnational governments and the resources and capabilities available to them, which generates a systemic problem in relation to lack of accountability for outcomes. The decentralisation process was too quick in transferring responsibilities to subnational governments that did not necessarily have the human and institutional capacity to take on those responsibilities.
- There is a lack of effective mechanisms and incentives to co-ordinate policies and investments at a subnational level. These co-ordination failures appear at all levels of government, both horizontally and vertically. Policies are delivered on a sectoral basis with actions that may contradict one another at the local level. Co-ordination, rather than fragmentation, is a more binding constraint in relation to the delivery of better public policy outcomes.
- Subnational governments strongly depend upon transfers as a source of income. Transfers are mostly earmarked or consist of deconcentrated expenditures, limiting the autonomy of subnational governments, and particularly regional governments, to adapt policies to local needs and circumstances.
- There are limited incentives and capacity to develop tax revenues at a subnational level. Revenues of subnational governments strongly fluctuate and the central government has a certain degree of discretion in the allocation of resources. Subnational tax revenues are important in decentralised countries to improve policy outcomes, improve expenditure efficiency and accountability.
- The distributional system of the fiscal income from extractive industries (or the *canon* in Spanish) is designed to primarily compensate producing regions for the depletion of natural capital. The absence of stabilisation and equalisation funds has generated significant vertical and horizontal fiscal imbalances and inequalities between regions.
- The lack of effective integration between planning and resource allocation, and programme-based budgeting instruments coupled with a misalignment of incentives (political and administrative) has led to the production of suboptimal and fragmented investments. This is exacerbated by the prominent role of municipalities in allocating funds from mining royalties (the *canon*).
- The delivery and administration of policies, planning and regulatory instruments, and investments are not consistently monitored and evaluated at a subnational level. Public policies are not consistently implemented and there is a wide variety of performance between different subnational governments. The skills and capabilities of the public sector at a subnational level are generally low, and there is a lack of coherent strategy to address this issue.

Recommendations

9. Develop more effective partnerships between levels of government to deliver better policy outcomes by:

   – strengthening the role of the Inter-governmental Coordination Council including by refocusing its role on policy co-ordination between the national and regional governments, and streamlining its agenda on a small number of mutually agreed policy issues

Key findings and recommendations (*continued*)

- strengthening governance arrangements that facilitate policy and investment co-ordination between levels of government at the scale of functional urban areas, and macro-regional scale
- developing a coherent strategy to build the skills and capabilities of subnational governments, which is linked to an accreditation system for increasing responsibilities (including applying the national Law on Civil Service Reform to the local and regional levels)
- putting in place an asymmetric approach to decentralisation, particularly for metropolitan areas, which would allow for the flexibility to better match responsibilities with resources and capabilities
- clarifying the criteria for the creation/amalgamation of new municipalities (including consideration of factors such as fiscal sustainability, efficiency and effectiveness of services, service catchments), and establishing a more transparent and consultative process which includes a public statement providing the evidence and rationale for these decisions
- creating a task force with a mix of technical skills and capabilities (strategic planning, public finance, procurement, project management and evaluation), which can be applied in a flexible way to address critical gaps in skills and capabilities at a subnational level.

10. Develop a coherent package of actions to enable better public investment outcomes at a subnational level by:

- strengthening support for subnational governments to apply results-based budgeting, which is integrated with local and regional concerted development plans
- incorporating multi-year (three- to five-year) capital investment and service delivery plans into the fiscal framework at a regional level and making national transfers conditional upon them (the Presidency of the Council of Ministers/Ministry of Economy and Finance should also ensure co-ordinated input from across national ministries to these plans)
- developing a system of public reporting of service delivery performance at a subnational level, which is transparent, user friendly and enables comparisons between jurisdictions.

11. Designing and implementing an integrated reform to subnational finances which includes the following features:

- increasing the proportion of investment funds (such as the *canon*) which are allocated to the departmental level, and reducing the proportion allocated to the provincial and district levels in order to increase the overall effectiveness of public investment at a subnational level by generating increased economies of scale and the scope for policy complementarities
- creating a stability fund would help balance the cyclical nature of the royalties system (the *canon*)
- strengthening equalisation mechanisms to help compensate for inequalities between subnational governments that are exacerbated by the *canon*
- improving tax administration at a subnational level by pooling administrative capacity at a departmental level, enabling them to collect taxes on behalf of municipalities
- providing subnational governments with the capacity to mobilise their own revenues (e.g. property tax at a municipal level), which would help stabilise public finances while providing clearer accountability for outcomes.

Introduction

Since 2002, Peru has undergone a political and administrative decentralisation process driven both by democratic and economic and regional development objectives. The process sought to bring democracy closer to the people, enhance accountability while at the same time improve the provision of public goods and reduce regional disparities. Peru has made strong advances in terms of political decentralisation with the election of regional governments and transfer of significant responsibilities to the subnational level. However, this has not been adequately integrated with changes to tax and transfer arrangements. This phenomenon, coupled with the initial transfer of responsibilities to subnational governments that did not have the capacities to assume them and which also have limited levels of horizontal and vertical co-ordination, has resulted in the inability of the country to achieve the objectives of the decentralisation process.

Policy inconsistencies and setbacks such as these can be very costly for a middle-income country such as Peru. Decentralisation is associated with higher levels of development, and Peru has been following this path as its economy has developed. Advancing the decentralisation agenda will require, amongst other reforms, better alignment between responsibilities and resources, and a partnership-based approach to delivering policies between central and subnational governments. A more effective approach to multi-level government will enable the country to deliver on the policy reforms set out in the previous chapters of this report.

Decentralisation and governance in Peru

Overview of the decentralisation process

The decentralisation process in Peru is rather recent and has gone through several stop and go phases since the late 1970s. The current process started in 2002, when Congress, driven by democratic and economic objectives, constitutionally declared Peru a "decentralised state".[1] The target was to increase accountability, empower local populations, and improve governance and democratic quality by bringing decision makers closer to citizens. Economic arguments were also put forward; decentralisation would improve the quality and access to public services and reduce regional inequalities. By devolving responsibilities and resources, the objective was to create a model of territorial development based on the principle of subsidiarity.

The current decentralisation process had an accelerated timeline, with 11 major laws that would set the framework for the entire process. This legislation created the framework law for decentralisation, organic laws for regional and local governments respectively, and a fiscal decentralisation law. The key components of the reform were the administrative and political autonomy of elected subnational governments, the principle of fiscal neutrality and tight fiscal rules that would guarantee sustainable debt positions of subnational governments.

In 2002, the existing *departamentos* were set as regional governments with elected representatives with a view that two or more contiguous departments would merge to create regions. This would be encouraged with fiscal incentives and have to be approved by regional referendum. Despite the efforts from the central government, none of the departments accepted to merge into the regions proposed to the referendum held in 2005. After this failed referendum, both the programmed 2009 and 2013 referenda were postponed indefinitely. Despite the fiscal incentives, the elected officials at a departmental level had a lot to lose from potential amalgamation. In the current configuration, departments play the role of the regions proposed in the referendum on the expenditure side, but not in terms of revenues. Furthermore, the failed referendum showed not only that there was overall very little support amongst the population for the creation of larger regions, but also that this lack of support was much stronger in regions where the gross domestic product (GDP) per capita was higher, showing a reluctance to share resources.

The plan initially crafted was to be gradual. It consisted first of a political transfer, with elections at the department level by the end of 2002 and the creation of larger regions by 2005. This was an initial transfer of political legitimacy. The following stage was the transfer of competencies based on an accreditation mechanism. The third step would have been, once the regional governments were created, to transfer the rest of competencies as well as to introduce a sustainable revenue stream (proposed to be half of the tax revenue collected by the national government in the region, aside from the taxes on profits of companies).

A general audit of capacities and a plan to address gaps in skills and capacities was launched in 2004. Regions were transferred competencies depending initially on their capacities. Nonetheless, by 2006 little improvement had been made and the plan for capacity building had been ill implemented. By that year, the new government in place launched the "decentralisation shock". It meant a quicker and deeper transfer of expenditure responsibilities despite the absence of accredited capacities. Subnational governments would pledge to improve their capacities; this modality of accreditation was called: "competences to be developed" (*por potenciar*) (World Bank, 2010; Martinez-Vázquez, 2013). By 2009, 39% of the transfers had been done so under that modality (Defensoria del Pueblo, 2009).

Also, the lack of competences at the subnational level both in terms of planning and implementation of public policies has been identified as one of the key challenges of the decentralisation process. This issue, although widespread, is particularly prevalent amongst those located in rural areas (Muñoz, 2010). The transfer of competencies initially planned under a system of accreditation showed to be a failure both because of the competence gap and because of the lack of implementation of the capacity-building programme.

While there is no ideal degree of decentralisation, there is a broad consensus that the fiscal decentralisation process in Peru is incomplete (World Bank, 2010, 2015; Cheasty and Pichihua, 2015; Martinez-Vazquez, 2013). An unfinished decentralisation has had important aftermaths, such as the lack of accountability and co-responsibility at the subnational level, as well as a negative impact on the effective territorial development; to some extent, the absence of a system of cities (and thus the concentration in Lima), is also symptom of deficiencies in the design of fiscal and institutional decentralisation in Peru (World Bank, 2015).

Governance and administrative system of Peru

Peru is a unitary state structured in the form of a presidential system comprising three independent branches (legislative, executive and judicial), with a two-tier subnational system composed of regions and district/provincial municipalities.

The executive branch, chaired by the President of the Republic, is elected for five years and exercises the functions of the state related to government and administration. The President of the Council of Ministers, named by the President, co-ordinates the national policies with the different ministries, the civil society and the private sector. The rest of the Cabinet is currently comprised of 18 ministries.

The legislative power is unicameral. It is comprised of 130 congressman also elected for five years under a system of closed but not blocked lists in their electoral districts. Congress is in charge of the legislative action and plays a role in supervising and controlling the executive power. It also names the General Comptroller of the Republic, the members of the Constitutional Court, the board of the central bank and the Head of the Supervising Authority for Banks and Insurances. Within the Presidency of the Council of Ministers, the Decentralisation Secretariat (Secretaría de Descentralización) is the structure in charge of subnational government monitoring and co-ordination. The National Strategic Planning Centre (CEPLAN) also plays a co-ordinating role on the planning aspect.

With the decentralisation reform, politically and administratively autonomous regional governments are elected for a period of four years. Local governments have been elected since 1963. There is a one-term limit for elected heads of local executives.

Subnational governments have their own competencies and budget. The regional level currently consists of 25 departments (including the Constitutional Province of Callao, which has the status of a department). The local level has two independent sub-levels: provincial municipalities and district municipalities. Provincial municipalities have a co-ordination role across district municipalities within the province. Currently, the distribution of the administrative sub-divisions is as follows:

- Regional governments: 25 *departamentos* but with 26 regional governments (the department of Lima has two regional governments, one for Metropolitan Lima and the other one for the rest of the provinces of the department) with a median population of 954 000 inhabitants and a median area of 35 900 km^2.
- Provincial municipalities: 196 *provincias* with a median population of around 71 000 inhabitants and a median area of 3 200 km^2; (the *municipalidades provincials*, or capital district of the province, have on average 22 000 inhabitants).
- District/municipalities: 1 671 *municipalidades distritales* with a median population of around 3 300 inhabitants and a median area of 235 km^2; but the median of local governments (*municipalidades provinciales and distritales*) have a median population of 4 500 inhabitants.

There are strong disparities in the sizes and populations of departments, provinces and districts. Indeed, as far as the regions are concerned, population varies from 141 000 to 9 million and land area from 4 700 km^2 to 369 000 km^2. Population in provinces ranges from 4 500 to 9 million inhabitants and land area from 264 km^2 to 120 000 km^2. Population in the provincial municipalities ranges from 1 000 to 407 000. In the districts, population ranges from 177 inhabitants to 1.1 million inhabitants and areas from 2 km^2 to 35 000 km^2 (INEI, 2007). In spite of these disparities, Peru displays levels of municipal size both in terms of area and population above the OECD average due to the size of the territory (see Chapter 1).

Box 4.1. Subnational government structure in OECD countries

The multi-level governance structure of countries varies considerably in the OECD which counts 9 federal states and 25 unitary states. Among OECD member countries, only eight have a structure with three subnational government tiers: the regional/federated level, the intermediary level and the municipal level. Eighteen countries have the same structure as Peru, with two subnational tiers: regions and municipalities. Eight countries have only one subnational tier. The Peruvian two-level municipal system is quite uncommon compared to OECD countries.

Table 4.1. Type and numbers of subnational governments in the OECD: Country by country, 2014-15

Country	Municipal level	Intermediary level	Regional or state level
Federations and quasi-federations			
Australia	565 (local government areas)		8 (states and territories)
Austria	2 102 (municipalities)		9 (*Bundesländer*)
Belgium	589 (municipalities)	10 (provinces)	6 (regions and communities)
Canada	5 253 (census subdivisions)		13 (provinces and territories)
Germany	11 116 (municipalities)	402 (districts)	16 (*länder*)
Mexico	2 445 (municipalities)		32 (states and the federal district)
Spain	8 117 (municipalities)	50 (provinces)	17 (autonomous communities)
Switzerland	2 324 (municipalities)		26 (cantons)
United States	35 879 (local governments)	3 031 (counties)	50 (states)
Unitary countries			
Chile	345 (municipalities)		15 (regions)
Czech Republic	6 253 (municipalities)		14 (regions)
Denmark	98 (municipalities)		5 (regions)
Estonia	213 (local municipalities)		
Finland	317 (municipalities)		1 (autonomous region)
France	36 681 (municipalities)	101 (departments)	27 (regions)
Greece	325 (municipalities)		13 (regions)
Hungary	3 177 (municipalities)		19 counties
Iceland	74 (municipalities)		
Ireland	31 (local councils)		
Israel	252 (local governments)		
Italy	8 047 (municipalities)	110 (provinces and metropolitan cities)	20 (regions)
Japan	1 718 (municipalities)		47 (prefectures)
Korea	227 (local governments)		17 (regional-level entities)
Luxembourg	105 (municipalities)		
Netherlands	393 (municipalities)		12 (provinces)
New Zealand	67 (territorial authorities)		11 (regional councils)
Norway	428 (municipalities)		18 (counties)
Poland	2 478 (municipalities)	380 (counties)	16 (regions)
Portugal	308 (municipalities)		2 (autonomous regions)
Slovak Republic	2 927 (municipalities)		8 (higher territorial units)
Slovenia	212 (municipalities)		
Sweden	290 (municipalities)		21 (county councils)
Turkey	1 394 (municipalities)		81 (provinces and metropolitan municipalities)
United Kingdom	389 (local councils)	27 (counties)	3 (devolved administrations)
Peru	***1 646 (municipalities)***	***196 (provinces)***	***25 (regions)***
OECD34	133 900	4 111	527

Source: Own elaboration based on data from OECD (2015b), "Subnational governments in the OECD: Key data", http://stats.oecd.org/Index.aspx?DataSetCode=SNGF.

Figure 4.1. **Size of districts per number of inhabitants and area**

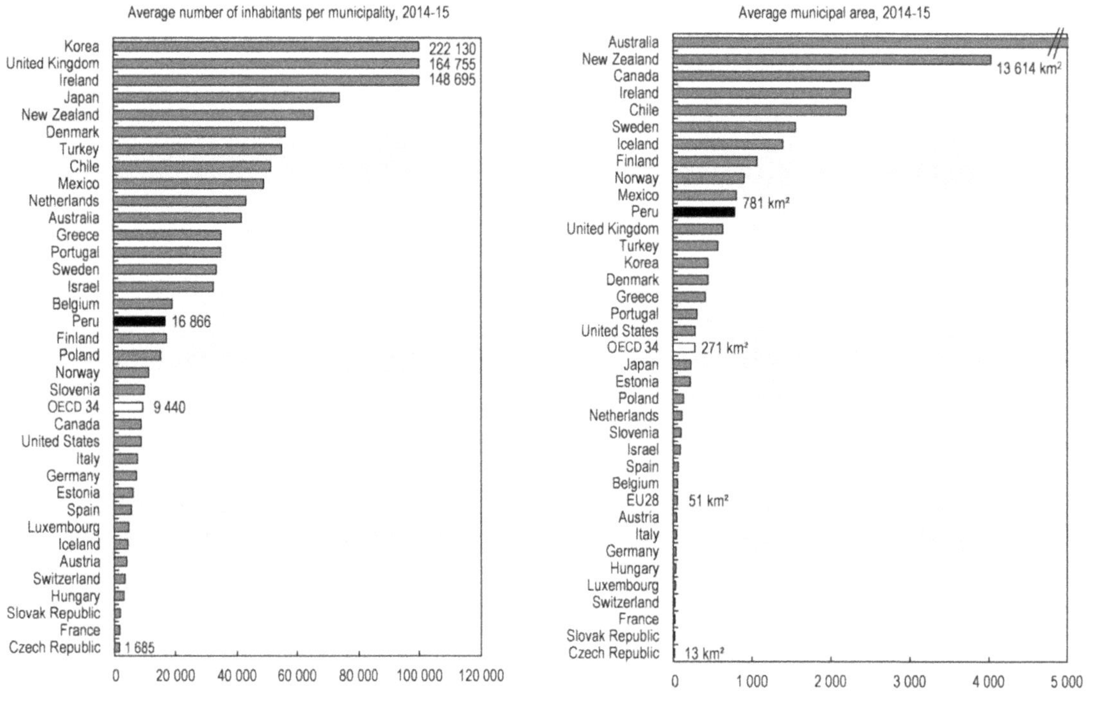

Sources: Own elaboration based on OECD (2015b), "Subnational governments in OECD countries: Key data", http://stats.oecd.org/Index.aspx?DataSetCode=SNGF.

Nonetheless, the territorial division of the country is not fully settled. Indeed, demarcation of the subnational territories is still one of the most pressing issues to be addressed. According to the National Directorate of Territorial Demarcation, 92% of provincial boundaries and 80% of district boundaries are either ill-defined or not permanently demarcated. This particular phenomenon has generated conflicts between subnational governments, particularly given the regulation defining the transfers of resources from extractive industries. Contrary to trends across the OECD, Peru is also creating new municipalities. In the past two years, 29 new municipalities have been created in Peru, and 45 draft laws have been presented in 2016 with the aim of establishing new districts. Currently, the creation of new municipalities unlocks additional transfers from the national government, which creates a perverse incentive. There is a risk that the ongoing creation of new municipalities will contribute to a problem of administrative fragmentation and inefficiency in the country.

Subnational governments play an important economic role

Subnational governments are key economic actors across the OECD, as is the case in Peru. Figure 4.2 shows that subnational governments are responsible for slightly above 40% of overall public expenditure in Peru. Their relative expenditure is higher than could have been predicted by the total level of public expenditure as a share of the GDP because government plays a smaller role in the economy compared to most OECD countries. Subnational governments in Peru play, on average, a more important role in relation to public investment compared to OECD countries.

Figure 4.2. **Weight of subnational expenditure in public intervention**

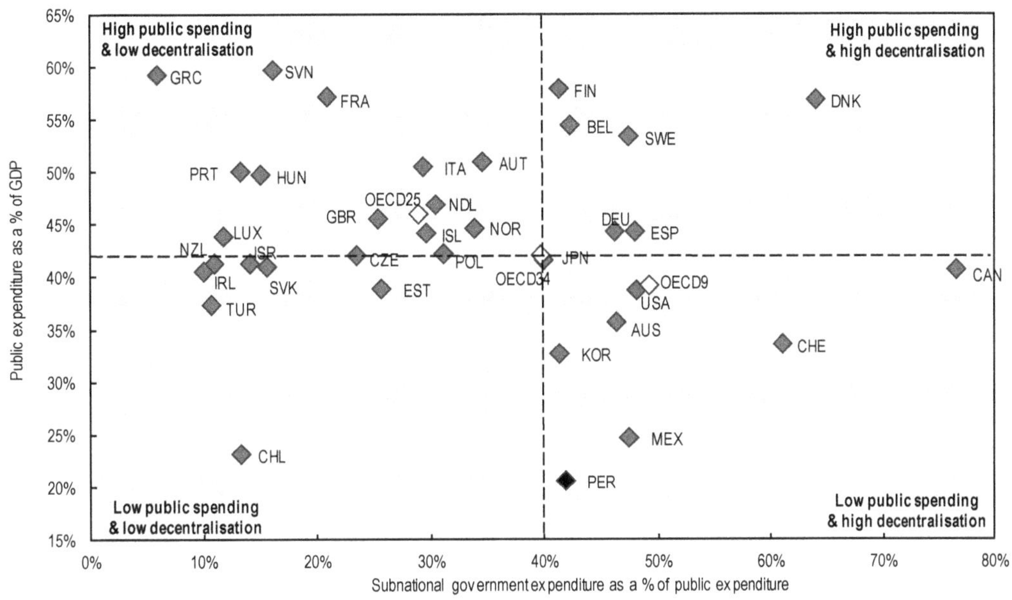

Sources: Own elaboration based on OECD (2015b), "Subnational governments in OECD countries: Key data", http://stats.oecd.org/Index.aspx?DataSetCode=SNGF; and Peruvian Cuenta General de la República 2013 – Ministerio de Economía y Finanzas.

Figure 4.3. **Subnational governments are key economic actors in the OECD and in Peru**

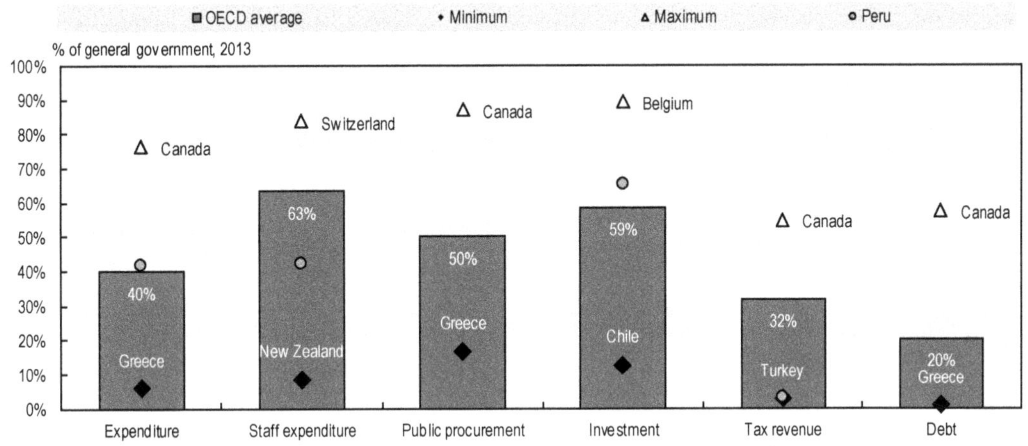

Sources: Own elaboration based on OECD (2015b), "Subnational governments in OECD countries: Key data", http://stats.oecd.org/Index.aspx?DataSetCode=SNGF; and Peruvian Cuenta General de la República 2013 – Ministerio de Economía y Finanzas.

Roles and responsibilities between levels of government are not clear

The decentralisation law of 2002 established the need for a clear division of responsibilities based on the principle of subsidiarity. At the same time, it established a division between three types of competences: exclusive, shared and delegated. As mentioned above, it also stated that the decentralisation was to be done in a gradual, financially neutral and fully funded way. However, responsibilities were transferred simultaneously to all regions independently of their capacities. The organic laws of the executive, regional and local governments respectively provide more detail on the organisation and competences of the latter. These laws show that there is very strong overlap between the missions and competencies across all levels of government. Co-ordination challenges across levels of government need to be carefully managed.

Box 4.2. The OECD approach to multi-level governance challenges

The relationship among levels of government resulting from decentralisation is characterised by mutual dependence, since it is impossible to have a complete separation of policy responsibilities and outcomes among levels of government. It is a complex relationship, simultaneously vertical, across different levels of government; horizontal, among the same level of government; and networked. Governments must therefore bridge a series of challenges or "gaps" between levels, both vertically and horizontally.

These gaps include notably the fiscal capacity of governments to meet obligations, information asymmetries between levels of government, gaps in administrative responsibility, with administrative borders not corresponding to functional economic and social areas at the subnational level, gaps in policy design, when line ministries take purely vertical approaches to cross-sectoral regulation that can require co-design of implementation at the local level and often a lack of human or infrastructure resources to deliver services and design strategies. Countries may experience these gaps to a greater or lesser degree, but given the mutual dependence that arises from decentralisation and the network-like dynamics of multi-level governance, countries are likely to face them simultaneously.

Table 4.2. **Mutual dependence across levels of government: Multi-level governance challenges/gaps in OECD member countries**

Types of challenges/gaps	Co-ordination challenges/gaps
Funding	Unstable or insufficient revenues undermining effective implementation of responsibilities at the subnational level or for shared competences => **Need for shared financing mechanisms.**
Administrative	Occurs when the administrative scale for investment does not correspond with functional relevance, as in the case of municipal fragmentation => **Need for instruments for reaching "effective size" (co-ordination tools among subnational units; mergers).**
Policy	Results when line ministries take purely vertical approaches to cross-sectoral policies to be territorially implemented => **Need for mechanisms to create multi-dimensional/systemic approaches and to exercise political leadership and commitment.**
Information	Asymmetries of information (quantity, quality, type) between different stakeholders, either voluntary or not => **Need for instruments for revealing and sharing information.**
Capacity	Arises when there is a lack of human, knowledge or infrastructural resources available to carry out tasks and to design relevant strategies for local development => **Need for instruments to build local capacity**.
Objective	Exists when different rationales among national and subnational policy makers create obstacles for adopting convergent targets. Can lead to policy coherence problems and contradictory objectives across investment strategies => **Need for instruments to align objectives**.
Accountability	Reflects difficulties in ensuring the transparency of practices across different constituencies and levels of government. Also concerns possible integrity challenges for policy makers involved in the management of investment => **Need for institutional quality instruments => Need for instruments to strengthen the integrity framework at the local level (focus on public procurement) => Need for instruments to enhance citizens' involvement.**

OECD member and non-member countries are increasingly developing and using a wide variety of mechanisms to help bridge these gaps and improve the coherence of multi-level policy making. These mechanisms may be "binding", such as legal mechanisms, or "soft", such as platforms for discussion, and they must be sufficiently flexible to allow for territorially specific policies. Involvement of subnational governments in policy making takes time, but medium- to long-term benefits should outweigh the costs of co-ordination.

Sources: Charbit, C. and M. Michalun (2009), "Mind the gaps: Managing mutual dependence in relations among levels of government", http://dx.doi.org/10.1787/221253707200; Charbit, C. (2011), "Governance of public policies in decentralised contexts: The multi-level approach", http://dx.doi.org/10.1787/5kg883pkxkhc-en.

National government

The national government has a number of exclusive competences (listed in Table 4.3) and shares all other roles and responsibilities with subnational governments, aside from those that are exclusive competencies of subnational governments.

Table 4.3. **Exclusive competencies of the national government**

Planning	– Design of national and sectorial policies
Defence and security	– Defence, national security and army – Internal order, police, border control and crime prevention
Foreign affairs	– Foreign affairs
Justice	– Justice administration
Economic	– Currency management; banking and insurance – Tax system and public national debt – Commercial regime and tariff barriers
Regulatory powers	– Regulation and management of merchant marine and commercial aviation – Regulation of public services under its responsibility – Regulation and management of public services under its responsibility – Regulation and management of national public infrastructure

Regions

Regional governments have the mission to promote the regional economy and development at their level; to encourage investments, and develop activities and public services at their level of competence; in harmony with national policies and national and local development plans. Regions have a Regional Council (normative and audit body-which could be somehow assimilated to a legislative branch) and the presidency (executive body) have a Council for Regional Co-ordination (consultative body) integrated by the president of the region, provincial mayors of the region (60% of the council) and representatives of the civil society (40% of the council). These councils are not operating effectively, and regional governments also lack strategic policy and co-ordinating capacity. The regional level has both exclusive and shared competencies (Table 4.4).

Provinces and districts

Provinces and districts have the mission to promote the local economy and development. They also provide public services under their competencies in harmony with national and regional policies and national and regional development plans. The local level has both exclusive and shared competencies. Provincial municipalities have the same expenditure responsibilities as district municipalities as well as other service responsibilities that extend to the district municipalities within the provincial boundaries. Nevertheless, district municipalities do not depend hierarchically on the provincial municipalities (as mandated by the Organic Law of Municipalities (Ley Orgánica de Municipalidades). All regional and local governments approve their own budgets. The dual coexistence at the same local level of provincial and district municipalities is a peculiarity of Peru's governance arrangements. The specific attributions of provincial governments compared to the district ones are as follows.

- Planning of local development and spatial planning at the provincial level. District governments contribute by presenting their priorities.
- Promoting the strategic co-ordination of the district development plans. District plans concerning the organisation of spatial and land use must respect the provincial plans and norms.

- Promoting, supporting and executing investment and public service projects which have economies of scale at the provincial level. For that, the pertinent agreements are signed with the respective district municipalities.
- Providing general technical norms in the realms of spatial and land use and the protection of the environment.

Table 4.4. **Regional government competencies**

	Exclusive	Shared
Planning and budget	– Plan regional development and execute the corresponding socio-economic programmes – Formulate and approve the concerted regional development plan with the municipalities and the civil society of their region – Approve its internal organisation and budget	
Public investments and public works	– Promote and execute regional public investments in the realms of road infrastructure, energy, communications and regional basic services. This has to be done within a framework of sustainability, competitiveness development, promotion of private investments and stimulation of markets	
Economic policies	– Design and execute regional programmes of basins, economic corridors and intermediary cities – Promote the creation of firms and regional economic units concerting productive and service provision systems – Facilitate processes oriented towards international markets for agriculture, agroindustry, craftsmanship, forestry and other productive sectors depending on potentialities – Develop touristic circuits that could become development axes – Promote the modernisation of small and medium-sized enterprises in the region, particularly articulating education, labour and technological policies	– Promotion, management and regulation of economic and productive activities in the sectors of agriculture, fishery, industry, trade, tourism, energy, oil and gas, mining, transport, communications and environment – Promote regional competitiveness and employment by co-ordinating the use of public and private resources
Urban planning, land property management and housing	– Develop touristic circuits that could become development axes	– Land-use planning
Environment	– Promote sustainable use of forestry resources and biodiversity	– Sustainable management of natural resources and improvement of environmental quality – Preservation and management of natural reserves and protected natural areas
Culture		– Increase accessibility and diffusion of culture and reinforce regional artistic and cultural institutions
Education		– Management of pre-school, primary, secondary and non-university tertiary educational services, taking into consideration the inter-cultural component of the region
Health		– Participation in the management of public health
Citizen participation		– Enhance and strengthen citizen participation by concerting public and private interests
Others	– Develop alliances and agreements with other regions that could foster economic, social and environmental development – Organise and approve technical cases of territorial demarcation within the region – Dictate norms on matters of their competence – Other competencies transferred by law	– Other competencies transferred by law

Table 4.5. **Local government competencies**

	Exclusive	Shared
Planning and budget	– Planning and promotion of urban and rural development and execution of relative plans – Approve of its internal organisation and budget – Formulate and approve the local development plan in dialogue with the community	
Public investments and public works	– Execute and supervise local public works	
Security and public safety		– Public safety
Economic policies		
Urban planning, land property management and housing	– Regulate zoning matters, urban development, territorial conditioning and human settlements – Housing and urban renovation	
Transportation		– Collective transportation, traffic and urban transit management
Environment		– Preservation and management of local natural reserves and protected natural areas – Defence and protection of the environment
Culture		– Culture, tourism, recreation and sports (no details provided by the law) – Conservation of archeologic and historic monuments
Education		– Participation in the management of education
Health		– Participation in the management of public health
Social programmes		– Management of social programmes
Waste		– Waste management
Others	– Manage and regulate local public services destined to satisfy local collective needs – Dictate norms on matters of their competence – Other competencies transferred by law	– Other competencies transferred by law

Functions overlap across levels of government

The division of competences between and across levels of governments stands as one of the main challenges in regards to advancing Peru's decentralisation agenda. The lack of clarity and overlap in the assignment of responsibilities is a key feature of the current system. This undermines democratic accountability and the core objective of the decentralisation process to bring citizens closer to decision making (Muñoz, 2005).

Subnational governments have limited capacity to plan and design sectoral policies. The central government has exclusive competences in the design of national and sectorial policies, taking into account the regional dimension. Furthermore, national ministries are in charge of formulating, planning, directing, co-ordinating, implementing, supervising and evaluating national and sectoral policies under their direction. Some of the planning, designing and formulating of competencies is also assigned to subnational governments. However, in practice national ministries set the framework for the design and execution of key sectoral policies.

The wording of the organic law of regional and municipal governments is very similar and provides numerous functions with little clarity in their definition. Many functions also overlap between the central government and the subnational level (see Annex A for further details). For instance, in the realm of education:

- regional governments have the function to: "formulate, approve, execute, evaluate and administer the education, culture, science and technology, sports and recreation regional policies for the region" and to "design, execute and evaluate the regional educational project, the culture development programs, science and technology, and the sports and recreation development program"
- while local governments have the function to: "design, execute and evaluate the educational project of their jurisdiction, in co-ordination with the Regional Education Office (REO) and the Local Education Management Unit (LEMU) and contribute to the national and regional educational policy with an intersectoral action focus".

Furthermore, some ministries, particularly the new ones created after the decentralisation process, do not take into account the roles and competences assigned to subnational governments. Others have developed and implemented programmes at the national level that do not take into account these competences. This shows a certain resistance from the central government to decentralise. There are a number of key examples of this issue.

- the newly created Ministry for Development and Social Inclusion directly administers the main social programmes of the country, which in principle is a competence of local governments
- the Ministry of Tourism and Foreign Trade still designs and executes regional tourism programmes
- the Ministry of Education still controls the curricular design and there is little or no margin for its adaption at the local level contrary to what the organic law stipulates
- while the management of social conflicts is a subnational competence, the Dialogue Office of the Presidency of the Council of Ministers has taken over most of these initiatives.

It is important to note that the Decentralisation Secretariat and the Public Management Secretariat at the Presidency of the Council of Ministers (see OECD, 2016 for a further description of its competencies) is currently producing a matrix to clarify the competences and responsibilities of the different levels of government. Such a document would be highly valuable for improving clarity in the division of tasks between levels of government.

The governance of the decentralisation is further weakened by the absence of a dispute settlement body that would solve issues of competences and expenditure disputes. The only competent body to deal with such disputes is the Constitutional Court. An administrative body would provide a more transparent way of addressing disputes and reduce the risk of dispute resolution through the budget process. In the absence of an independent administrative body that would settle budget disputes at a lower level than the Constitutional Court, the National Budget Office often acts as a broker to settle expenditures disputes (World Bank, 2010; Martinez-Vázquez, 2013). Those on competencies are often settled by the Presidency of the Council of Ministers (PCM). More serious and politically sensitive issues are informally settled on a case-by-case basis by the President of the Republic and the regional presidents. These kinds of informal arrangements leave a lot of space for the use of discretionary power and generate unpredictable outcomes.

Is fragmentation really the issue?

Compared to OECD countries, the number of regions and municipalities in Peru is not particularly high (see Chapter 1). For example, countries such as France have 36 700 municipalities, Germany 11 327, Spain 8 116 and Italy 8 092. Many OECD countries face higher levels of dispersion in their territorial structure and still manage to properly manage to deliver public services. Although high fragmentation levels is deemed to be negative for the quality of public service provision because of co-ordination costs and missed exploitation of economies of scale, bigger administrative units have also shown to be potentially linked to higher transaction costs (Carr, 2004; Dollery and Robotti, 2008,). This is particularly relevant in the case of Peru with many areas that have low population densities and strong socio-geographic differences.

Box 4.3. **Explaining the failure of the municipal amalgamation law**

Much like in the case of the referendum to amalgamate departments, the central government passed the Law of Municipal Amalgamation in 2007, creating a fiscal incentive for the consolidation of two districts reaching a population of 8 000 inhabitants or of three reaching 12 000 inhabitants. The incentive was a 50% premium over the FONCUMUN transfer received by non-amalgamated districts over 15 years. The premium was to be earmarked for investments.

Despite the fiscal incentives provided by the amalgamation law, no districts made use of it. Two main drivers have been at play to counterbalance these fiscal incentives. The first one, like in the case of the departmental referenda, was the opposition from elected municipal authorities who would have seen their positions disappear. The other one has to do with the significant increase of transfers coming from the *canon* with the raw material so-called "super-cycle". Departments receiving important transfers from the *canon* funds were reluctant to share their resources with have-not departments.

Later that year, and realising the lack of success of its initiative, the government introduced a law allowing the association of local governments (*mancomunidades*) for the provision of public services at a higher level, thus allowing to take advantage of the potential economies of scale in the service delivery and investment projects. Despite what seemed to be an initial success – with the creation of 184 *mancomunidades* – only very few have managed to pool resources.

Addressing fragmentation can help achieve better economies of scale in public administration and service delivery, and this has been a general trend across OECD countries. Analysis shows this is particularly beneficial within urban areas as there is a penalty associated with fragmentation, whereas this finding does not hold for rural areas (see Chapter 3). However, Peru, contrary to the general trend in the OECD, has been creating more local governments in recent times. Since 2013, 29 new districts have been created, and there are currently 45 district creation proposals in Congress as of 2016. The average size of these new districts remains above the OECD average, with 11 607 inhabitants. Nonetheless, this average hides the fact that only 22% of the districts created were above the OECD average size, and that the median size of these districts was of 4 300 inhabitants. Two of the created districts were significantly bigger than the others with 61 000 and 150 000 inhabitants. The latter were both located in urban areas, increasing urban fragmentation.

The costs and benefits of addressing fragmentation in urban and rural contexts will have to be carefully considered. Other issues such as lack of effective co-ordination, the overlapping of competencies, and the lack of skills and capabilities in the regional governments are also pressing issues to be addressed for decentralisation to work. The government should also adopt an asymmetric approach to decentralisation and strengthen incentives for co-operation between municipalities. These incentives are important in achieving better economies of scale in public administration and service delivery.

Peru needs to be very careful when considering the creation of new districts to avoid fragmentation, particularly in urban areas. If new districts were to be created, a deep and transparent analysis of the fundaments would have to be considered. Current incentives that drive this demand for the creation of new districts should be addressed. Some of the criterion of that process would have to at least consider and balance the following elements:

- The fiscal sustainability of the newly created district.
- The capacity of the district to efficiently and effectively deliver public services and fulfil its responsibilities.
- The correspondence between the administrative division and the socio-economic functionality of the area in which it would be created. This is particularly important to avoid further fragmentation in urban areas.
- Socio-political factors mainly related to political representation and accountability.

Improving horizontal and vertical co-ordination

Peru lags behind benchmark countries in the co-ordination of public policies (OECD, 2015a). The issue starts with the weakness of the centre of government in the co-ordination of public policies due to the lack of collaboration within and between national ministries. Peru's poor performance can be explained by a number of factors, such as weakness in the prioritisation and implementation phases for policies involving several ministries and the lack of leadership from the centre of government (see OECD, 2016).

The centre of government is characterised by a lack of systemic co-ordination between national development planning and budget decisions. CEPLAN, which produces the National Strategic Development Plan (PEDN), has very limited leverage to enforce the application of the long-term strategies of the government. Aside from the PEDN, prepared at CEPLAN, several line ministries (such as Production or Trade) have their own national plans which are not strongly aligned (OECD, 2015a). Furthermore, these plans are not linked with the two policy frameworks set by the Ministry of Economy and Finances (MEF) to increase coherence in the delivery of public policy, which are the Multi-Annual Investment Plan and the *Presupuesto por Resultados* (result-based budgeting), nor are they place based. Strengthening the centre of government by better integrating the PCM and MEF will be central to better co-ordination of policies at a subnational level.

To improve co-ordination between levels of government, Peru passed a law in 2007 to establish inter-governmental commissions. These commissions include line representatives of national ministries and subnational governments and manage the decentralisation process across different sectorial policies (e.g. work and employment promotion, energy and mines, and women and vulnerable populations). These commissions are also in charge of developing the matrices of competencies, which was outlined earlier in this chapter. By the end of 2015, only three of these commissions were considered to be active by the Decentralisation Bureau: health, labour and education. The lack of implementation is partly due to lack of agreement about the mechanisms to elect representatives of local governments on these bodies.

Figure 4.4. **Perceptions of co-ordination among public institutions, 2012**

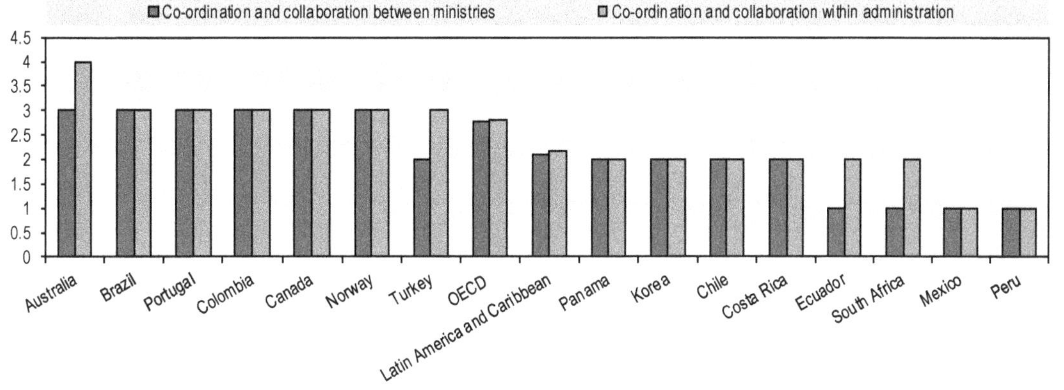

Notes: 0 represents very little co-ordination and 4 strong co-ordination. The *Institutional Profiles Database* provides an original measure of countries' institutional characteristics through composite indicators built from perception data. The perception data were gathered through a survey completed by country/regional economic services (*services économiques*) of the French Ministry for the Economy and Finance and the Agence Francaise de Developpement's offices

Sources: IPD (2012), "2012 governance data", *Institutional Profiles Database*, www.cepii.fr/institutions/EN/ipd.asp; OECD (2015a), *Multi-dimensional Review of Peru: Volume 1. Initial Assessment*, http://dx.doi.org/10.1787/9789264243279-en.

Despite the existence of some formal mechanisms, in practice, co-ordination between national and subnational government is inconsistent and *ad hoc*. The main co-ordination and dialogue channel between the central and regional governments is done via direct informal dialogue of mayors and regional presidents with the central government authorities. Neither the association of mayors nor that of regions have institutionalised channels of communication with the central government. Other interactions occur on a case-by-case basis via the deconcentrated administrative bodies of the central government. Furthermore, there are mismatches in the organisational structures, which sometimes leave some regional offices with no counterparts to interact and others with too many national offices and agencies to interact with.

To address problems associated with a lack of co-ordination between levels of government, the MEF has put in place an instrument to enhance the territorial articulation of its budgeting process (Work Plan for Territorial Articulation, or Plan de Trabajo de Articulación Territorial). This process begins by identifying the roles and responsibilities of subnational actors in the implementation of a determined budget programme. The process of articulation also seeks to create a typology of projects which should then help subnational governments in the planning and implementation of investment projects. The typology of projects is done at the central level and validated with a sample of at least five regional governments and ten local governments. The line ministry in charge of the budget line is then tasked with the diffusion of the project typology, as well as of the proposal of indicators and objectives of the budget line at each level of government in consultation with subnational governments.

Box 4.4. Main mechanisms for vertical and horizontal co-ordination in OECD countries

Vertical co-ordination mechanisms

Legal mechanisms (binding laws and legislation) are the strongest method for organising multi-level governance relations. This mechanism is often used with respect to fiscal resources and to allocate competencies.

Standard setting. Many OECD countries establish universal standard setting to ensure a similar level and quality of service provision across the country. In Sweden, for example, municipalities enjoy a high degree of autonomy in the provision of public services, but need to meet nationally set standards and regulations.

Contracts or agreements between national and subnational governments concerning their mutual obligations, i.e. assignment of powers of decision, distribution of contributions (including financial commitments) and contract enforcement mechanisms. These arrangements offer several advantages: they allow for customised management of interdependencies; they are useful tools for dialogue that can be used for clarifying responsibilities and making mutual commitments explicit; they open possibilities for judicial enforcement; and they can be used as learning mechanisms. In federal and decentralised countries, "contracts" are a particularly important tool for promoting co-operation, coherence and synergies among levels of government. Examples include "arrangements" in Canada, "joint tasks" in Germany, *accordi* in Italy and *convenios* in Spain. Challenges with contracts that have been observed across OECD member countries include high transaction costs, a power bias towards higher education compliance by all parties.

Strategic co-ordinating committees and partnership groups. The interests and inputs of key actors from different levels are co-ordinated through joint representation on administrative bodies or working groups. These committees can serve as forums for improved communication and dialogue on subjects of common interest. They can also help align interests and timing, and set the basis for signing contracts and agreements among levels of government. Finally, they can help disseminate good practices between different levels of government, or horizontally across regions. In some countries, co-ordination bodies are leading actors in fiscal capacity building by representing the interests of the local or regional level to national level decision makers. In Norway, for example, the Association of Local and Regional Authorities provides a forum to discuss the framework for distributing revenues in relation to the tasks carried out by local governments, the financial situation of local government and efficiency measures. In the Czech Republic, the Union of Municipalities and the Association of Regions have representatives on the national government's Board of Deputy Ministers for Regulatory Reform and Effective Public Administration, and represent the regions' interests in the Czech parliament, the Cabinet and in European institutions. In Spain, examples include the sectoral conferences and the Conference of the Presidents of Autonomous Communities.

Horizontal co-ordinating mechanisms

The governments of the German *Länder* co-operate through the Council of Prime Ministers and 19 subject-specific standing conferences of ministers. The council/standing conferences are not part of the German government and cannot pass legislation. Nevertheless, they play an important role in the federal system. Councils have two primary functions. In policy fields where legislative powers reside with the *Länder*, they are the main forum for policy co-ordination across the *Länder*. In policy fields where the Länder have limited powers, council/conference resolutions articulate common interests of the *Länder* to other actors, such as the federal government or the European Commission. Co-operation in the council/conferences is consensus based and most decisions are made unanimously. Formally, the Council of Prime Ministers and most other permanent conferences require the approval of 13 of the 16 German *Länder* to pass a resolution. Although resolutions are not legally binding, they have a strong symbolic power, and are almost always enacted by *Länder* governments.

Box 4.4. **Main mechanisms for vertical and horizontal co-ordination in OECD countries** *(continued)*

Some permanent conferences also draft model laws and regulations to support state administrations and to further harmonise laws across states. The Council of Prime Ministers convenes four times a year. After the council meetings, prime ministers meet with the German Chancellor. Subject-specific permanent conferences have their own meeting scheduled and tend to meet between one and four times a year. The federal minister in charge of the respective portfolio typically attends the meeting in an observing role. Several permanent conferences have established additional committees to discuss particular topics in more detail. The administrative structure of permanent conferences varies depending on their responsibilities. Some permanent conferences have their own permanent secretariats with sizable staff numbers while others use the administration of the state that holds the rotating presidency of the permanent conference.

The Association of Regions of the Czech Republic (AK CR) was founded in 2001 to represent the collective voice of the Czech regions. It associates the Czech Republic's 13 regions and the capital Prague. The supreme body of the AK CR is the council composed of the president of each region and the Mayor of the capital, Prague. The association offers services ranging from representing regional interests in parliament, the Cabinet and European institutions, to drawing up various reports, standpoints and initiatives. The council elects a chairman and three vice-chairmen, and decides on setting up commissions. Commissions serve as advisors to the council. Actual commissions include the Commission for Regional Development, the Commission for Public Administration, the Commission for Regional Financing, the Commission for Education, the Commission for Health Services, the Commission for the Environment and Agriculture, and the Commission for Transportation. Commission sessions serve for monitoring and issuing standpoints on major national and European issues in their area of competence. The council meets once every six to eight weeks on a rotating basis in one of the regions. External guests, from the central government administration, members of parliament, public organisations or international companies, may also be invited to the meetings. The association has a small secretariat and is financed through membership fees.

Source: OECD (2014g), *Spain: From Administrative Reform to Continuous Improvement*, http://dx.doi.org/10.1787/9789264210592-en.

This process, which started three years ago, is a significant step forward to improve co-ordination between levels of government, linking budgets with results and to avoid the duplication of action between levels of governments. The mechanism, using a functional and practical approach to budgeting, could be an important tool to help define the roles and responsibilities of the different levels of governments. Despite these positive signs, the programme of territorial articulation of the budget has yet to reach a more extensive number of budget lines while insuring that application of the instrument maintains its place-based and bottom-up rationale. Co-ordination failures require a broader and more strategic and multi-annual approach, issues on which there is still room for improvement.

The horizontal and vertical co-ordination at the subnational levels has also proven to be deficient despite the incentives set out by the MEF and the existence of formal institutions. With regard to horizontal co-ordination, some attempts have been observed in recent years, such as the *mancomunidades* grouping municipalities. However, as mentioned above, of all the constituted *mancomunidades*, only a few have pooled resources. Other formal mechanisms such as the regional and local co-ordination councils and the inter-regional co-ordination boards have shown to have significant weaknesses and do not seem to fulfil their missions.

There are not effective mechanisms or incentives to facilitate vertical co-ordination between the regional and municipal level, which is almost non-existent. Additionally, at the municipal level, there are no co-ordination tools between provinces and districts. Regional and local co-ordination councils often do not meet despite the legal obligation to do so and the concerted regional development plans have not been implemented across the majority of regions.

Lack of continuity in political and administrative leadership at a subnational level is another barrier to effective co-ordination. At a subnational level, there are one-term limits for political representatives who generally appoint senior members of the administration. This turnover reduces the capacity to develop the informal relationships which are important to facilitating vertical and horizontal co-ordination. It also means that key public sector skills and capabilities are not developed adequately at a subnational level. These arrangements and practices impede the capacity of the system to deal with transitions, while at the same time increasing the number of transitions. The result can be measured, for instance, in terms of investment projects, where there is a sharp decrease in investment during the first year of every administration.

In sum, Peru is not an overall particularly fragmented country but rather a country that suffers from a lack of effective co-ordination. In that sense, efforts in strengthening regional and provincial governments, implementing an asymmetric approach to decentralisation, and incentivising local governments to co-ordinate in delivering public resources could yield much greater benefits. Fragmentation in OECD countries has not been found to be a binding constraint for growth and public service delivery in rural and intermediary areas, although it does have a negative effect in urban areas (see Chapter 3). Reducing fragmentation in Peru's urban areas by incentivising policy and investment co-ordination at the scale of functional areas should be a priority. This reform should be carried out alongside reducing incentives for the creation of new districts. This would allow better outcomes from decentralisation while limiting the costs and disruption associated with forced mergers.

Subnational revenues and borrowing

Fiscal systems are essential to making decentralisation work (OECD, 2014b). Fiscal arrangements, to a large extent, shape the capabilities and performance of subnational governments. A review of subnational policies should start with an analysis of the fiscal framework: own revenues, transfers and debt. The fiscal capacity of lower levels of government and the control exercised by local governments over their own revenues and expenditures are especially important in decentralised countries.

There is limited fiscal autonomy in relation to revenues at the subnational level

Peru has a lower degree of decentralisation in revenues than in expenditures. The failure to create macro-regions and a lack of clarity in the transfers of competences have prevented subnational governments from having a significant share of tax resources to finance their responsibilities. As a result, subnational governments have little capacity to generate their own revenues and therefore rely heavily on transfers.

Box 4.5. The Compartir Project: Streamlining training and recruitment processes in the public sector

In late April 2012 the Spanish National Institute of Public Administration (Instituto Nacional de Administración Pública, INAP) conducted a study on the possibility of sharing and collaborating between the various public administrations – the general administration and the regional governments and town councils – to streamline the programmes of the various training and recruitment centres. This started the "Compartir" ("Sharing") project. However, the "Compartir" project has gradually given rise to an Administration 2.0 culture which has made it possible for the work carried out by the central government to be agreed with the other government bodies so that everyone can benefit from their results. Among others, the project has obtained the following outputs:

Education and training: INAP has developed a project to create a repository of online courses, under which the various government bodies make their own resources available to the other government bodies. The repository contains over 270 courses, reducing the cost of having to prepare them independently. Over 70 loans have been formalised, avoiding the need to enter into contracts for a similar number of actions. In addition, a single central self-teaching platform will be developed using the MOOC (Massive Open Online Course) concept for all state primary and secondary schools, which will allow any government employee or citizen wishing to do so to take part in freely available courses. The concept is: "public money at the service of society as a whole".

Recruitment: A roadmap has been developed for the validation of recruitment processes in the public administrations through an INAP/regional government task force led by the Basque Institute of Public Administration (Instituto Vasco de Administración Pública).

Knowledge management: A social and knowledge ecosystem has been created, with a bank of learning resources and a non-exclusive social network that can benefit all the public administrations without the need to create their own banks and networks.

Management by responsibility: INAP has produced a dictionary of responsibilities of the senior posts in the general administration, to create, from 2014, a task force that includes the autonomous regions that have made the most progress in this area in order to create an integrated dictionary of responsibilities.

In addition, the Ministry of Finances has created an online training platform for autonomous communities' public officials. The platform has been providing fiscal courses since 2006. In 2013, 34 courses were carried out focusing on 18 different subjects relevant to the general administration and the autonomous communities. These online courses are a parallel effort to the Institute for Fiscal Studies' (Instituto de Estudios Fiscales) I continuous training and knowledge-building activities on international subjects provided to public managers and new upcoming and current public officials.

Public training follows a horizontal and vertical co-operative approach as observed in subjects related to public finance and training provided to officials from town and provincial councils, extending capacity-building efforts to other levels of the territorial state administration.

Source: OECD (2014g), *Spain: From Administrative Reform to Continuous Improvement*, http://dx.doi.org/10.1787/9789264210592-en.

Tax revenue is still highly concentrated on the central government, leaving only a residual role to subnational governments. The number of taxes assigned to subnational governments, particularly to departments, is limited, and the latter do not have any room to determine their rates. The vast majority of taxes are raised by the central government: close to 87% of total tax revenues in 2012. Peru has seen little evolution on that matter; in 1995 the central government collected 88% of all taxes. These phenomena can also be observed in most OECD countries, although the ratio in the case of Peru is much higher than the OECD average for unitary countries (68% of public tax revenues and 80% in unitary states).[2] Subnational governments receive the following types of transfers to finance their responsibilities:

- natural resource and customs revenue (the *canon* and custom funds), which should be spent on capital investment
- transfers from the national government (essentially deconcentrated expenditures with some level of discretion in the transfers)
- compensatory funds for regional governments (FONCOR) and municipal governments (FONCOMUN).

Table 4.6. **Revenue sources at the subnational level: Breakdown by sources**

% of total

	2002	2008	2014
Regional revenues			
Transfers from the national government (grants)	87.2%	62.5%	78.2%
Canon and customs revenues	6.2%	16.5%	10.1%
Donations	0.2%	9.3%	3.8%
Compensatory transfers (FONCOR)	0.0%	8.7%	2.9%
Charges and tariffs	6.5%	3.0%	2.6%
Borrowed resources	0.0%	0.0%	2.5%
Local revenues			
Canon and royalties	7.8%	38.9%	37.3%
Compensatory transfers (FONCOMUN)	32.5%	23.7%	21.7%
Transfers from the national government (grants)	7.5%	6.2%	15.3%
Charges and tariffs	30.7%	14.3%	11.5%
Local taxes	12.1%	9.4%	10.9%
Donations	9.3%	7.4%	3.3%
Borrowed resources	0.0%	0.0%	0.0%

Source: Own elaboration based on data provided by the Ministry of Economy and Finance.

In addition, subnational governments can borrow but are subject to very restrictive conditions, as analysed in the following section. Figure 4.5 shows the sources of revenues for the subnational governments. The breakdown of local revenues has changed significantly since the beginning of the decentralisation process. While in 2002 charges and tariffs were the main source of revenues, currently the main source of revenues is the transfer of *canon* and royalties. By contrast, at the regional level, the sources of revenues have, despite some significant fluctuations, experienced less dramatic change; and transfers from the national government had consistently accounted for more than 60% of their income – with peaks in some years of almost 90%.

There are significant differences between regional and local governments in terms of sources of revenue. As will be further developed, regional governments are particularly dependent on discretionary transfers from the central government, while local governments depend more on formula-driven transfers (*canon* and FONCOMUN). In the latter case, the *canon* is the biggest source of revenue of local governments, and despite being formula driven, its distribution is highly uneven across the country.

Figure 4.5. **Breakdown of subnational government revenues, 2014**

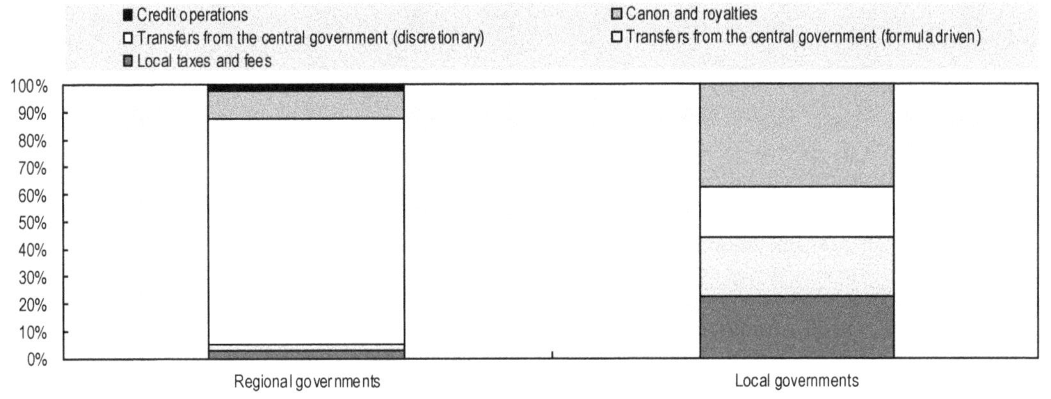

Source: Own elaboration based on data provided by the Ministry of Economy and Finance.

Peru's subnational governments are much more dependent on central government transfers than OECD countries. Indeed, the weight of grants is 30 percentage points above the OECD average in terms of a share of overall subnational revenues.

Figure 4.6. **Sources of revenue of subnational governments in OECD countries and Peru**

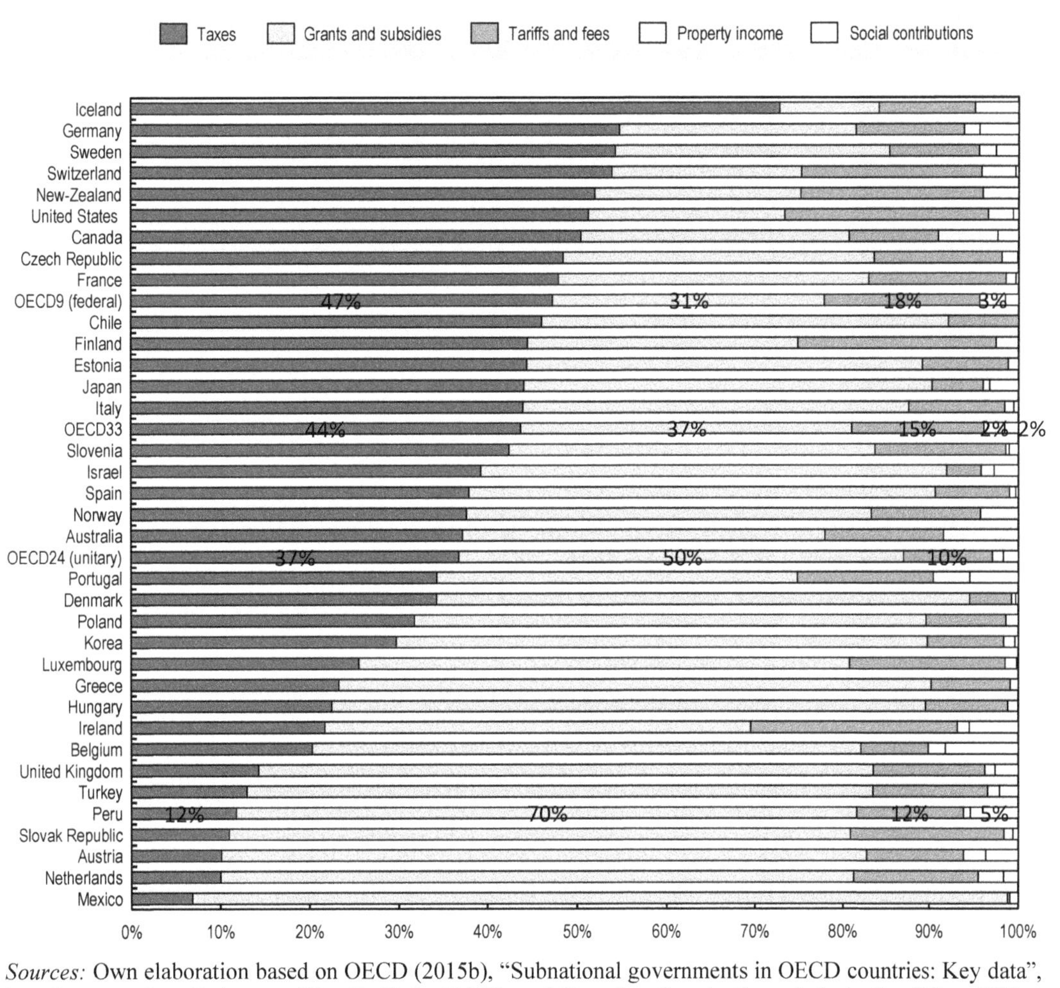

Sources: Own elaboration based on OECD (2015b), "Subnational governments in OECD countries: Key data", http://stats.oecd.org/Index.aspx?DataSetCode=SNGF; and Peruvian Cuenta General de la República 2013 – Ministerio de Economía y Finanzas.

At the local level, own resources represent only around 22% of the total local revenue: approximately 11% local taxes and the rest are charges and tariffs. As a result, subnational governments exhibit a high dependence on transfers from the central government, which generates a problem of vertical fiscal imbalance. This imbalance is even more striking in the case of regions. Since the decentralisation process started, departments have assumed important expenditure responsibilities with a tax base that makes them completely reliant on central government transfers and earmarked resources.

Figure 4.7. **Fiscal imbalances in OECD countries and in Peru at the subnational level**

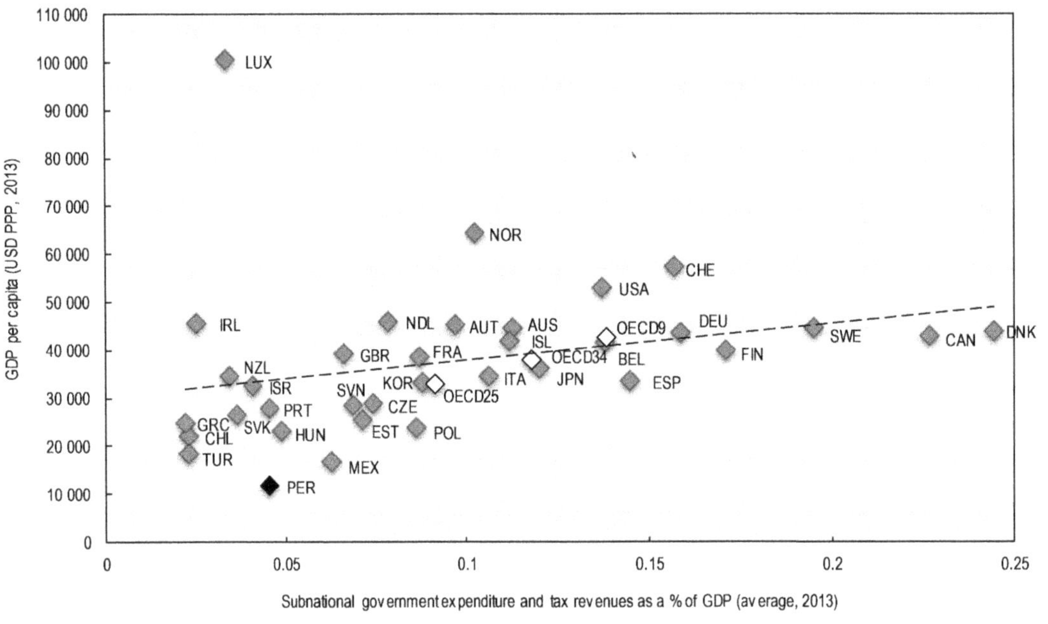

Sources: Own elaboration based on OECD (2015b), "Subnational governments in OECD countries: Key data", http://stats.oecd.org/Index.aspx?DataSetCode=SNGF; and Peruvian Cuenta General de la República 2013 – Ministerio de Economía y Finanzas.

Municipalities do not have the power to decide on the rate and basis of their local taxes. They can only create charges and tariffs which have less tax-collection potential and have to be directly tied to the provision of a particular service and be proportional to its cost. Additionally, the tax base at the local level is very narrow and is constituted mainly by only three taxes: the property tax on land and buildings (*impuesto predial*), the tax on the property of vehicles (*impuesto al patrimonio vehicular*), and the tax on property transfers (*impuesto de alcabala*).

In addition, strong regional socio-economic disparities and the spatial concentration of economic activity in Lima leads to a poor tax capacity to collect taxes outside the capital. Lima is responsible for over 80% of total tax revenues collected by municipal governments, and the per capita collection of revenue in Lima is approximately two times higher than the potential collection of intermediate cities (World Bank, 2015).

Weak tax administrative capacity also has a negative impact on tax collection. To foster the tax administrative capacity of subnational governments, tax administration agencies (SATs) were created for the larger municipalities. These agencies enjoy a high degree of financial and administrative autonomy as they are financed by a share of collected taxes and fines. The main remaining challenge is setting up a tax administration for medium and smaller municipalities, where tax collection is poor. Implementing SATs in every district is not as cost-efficient, as it would require significant investments in staff and implied high current expenditure.

Figure 4.8. **Breakdown of taxes at the local level, 2014**

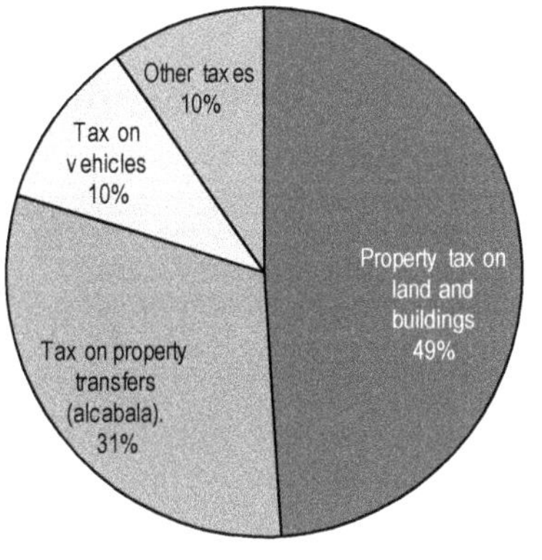

Source: Own elaboration based on data provided by the Ministry of Economy and Finance.

Property tax (on land and buildings) is, by far, the mainstay of the local taxation in Peru, as it is in almost all OECD countries. Peru's distinctive feature is that only the largest municipalities (mainly Lima-Callao) actually collect this tax. Small municipalities and the poorest areas mostly do not collect property taxes. As a result, the collection of the property tax in Peru barely reaches 0.21% of GDP (0.34% of GDP when considering the tax on property transfers), well below the Latin America and Caribbean (0.8% of GDP) and the OECD averages (1.8% of GDP).[3] There are three factors which explain this poor tax collection at the subnational level:

1. Many local governments do not have cadastres, and where they do exist, they are mostly outdated. Cadastres are a necessary condition for an effective, transparent and accurate management of the property tax. The poorest and/or smaller districts cannot afford to update or develop their cadastres, which diminishes their capacity to raise revenue. As of today, property taxes are determined by tariffs set by the Ministry of Housing, Construction and Sanitation.

2. Many subnational governments, and particularly in the poorest regions, have very weak tax administrations.

3. There are strong levels of political inertia limiting the level of incentives to improve tax collection. The current system with strong spending responsibilities but no co-responsibility in the tax collection does not create incentives for improved collection. In addition, the lack of clarity in the distribution of competencies across levels of government further develops political inertia and reduces accountability. The distribution of the royalties system may also diminish the incentives for tax collection efforts from *canon*-receiving subnational governments, although empirical evidence does not suggest it has been the case yet in Peru.

These three factors not only have an direct impact on tax collection, but they are also a development policy per se. Cadastres are an important tool contributing to better evidence-based policy making by providing better knowledge of the local dimension.

Cadastres are also an essential input for land-use management and planning. It is also an important tool for service delivery, not only because it is a source of revenue but also because it allows better sizing and developing public service delivery provision. Finally, following the logic developed by Hernando de Soto (1989), it can be used as a development tool to increase access to finance of the population by allowing them to leverage their assets.

Figure 4.9. **Property tax collection in selected Latin American and Caribbean countries, 2013**

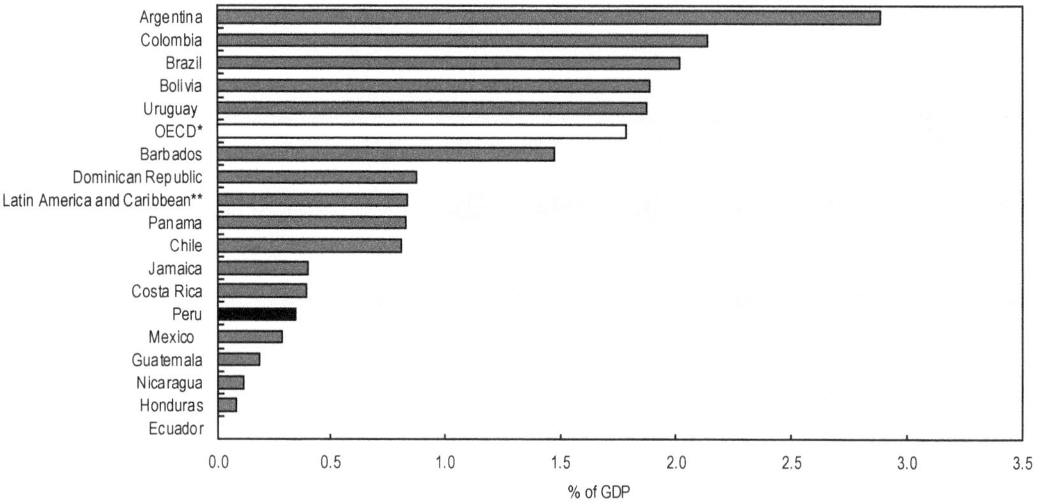

Notes: * Represents the unweighted average for OECD member countries ** Represents a group of 20 Latin American and Caribbean countries. Chile and Mexico are also part of the OECD 34 group. Estimated figures for Bolivia and Uruguay. Data for 2013 in Mexico and OECD average.

Source: OECD et al. (2015), *Revenue Statistics in Latin America and the Caribbean 2015*, http://dx.doi.org/10.1787/rev_lat-2015-en-fr.

In order to strengthen municipal capacity to raise its own funds, in 2010 the Incentive Program to Improve Municipal Management included among its goals increases in property tax collection. This incentive plan consists of providing further transfers to performing municipal governments. Some municipalities, such as Alto Selva Alegre in Arequipa – the best-performing municipality according to the ranking –, have received more money from this incentive programme than from *canon* transfers. The plan contributed to increase property tax collection by 13% in the year following the creation of this incentive (World Bank, 2015). Nonetheless, it does not yet include (but should in the future) incentives for increases in property tax collection for smaller cities and remote areas. No improvements have been seen on that matter in those types of municipalities. On a wider spectrum, as shown in Figure 4.9, there is wide room for improvement in terms of local tax collection since Peru lags behind LAC and OECD averages.

The low degree of revenue autonomy, or the corollary high degree of dependence of subnational governments on intergovernmental transfers, exposes the system to serious weaknesses that can be summarised as follows (Martinez-Vazquez, 2013):

- the dependency on revenues from transfers limits the efficiency and accountability of subnational governments
- it also reduces the overall level of fiscal responsibility of subnational governments because it is unlikely that subnational authorities will perceive the correct

marginal cost of public funds when their cost is simply to ask for more funds from the central government

- a transfer-dependent system poorly complements the emphasis on a hard budget constraint and borrowing discipline introduced in other elements of Peru's decentralisation design.

Box 4.6. Principles for the design of growth-friendly local tax systems

In general, the criteria for a growth-friendly national tax also apply at lower levels, but there are some additional constraints (Johansson et al., 2008):

- as a basic principle, local authorities should rely on taxes that provide, for households or firms, a link between taxes paid and public services received (Oates and Schwab, 1988)
- because firms and households are mobile, such taxes should be relatively non-redistributive and applied to less mobile tax bases (to avoid base erosion); inter-personal redistribution is probably better addressed at a higher level
- local tax bases should not be highly sensitive to business cycles, since local governments lack the capacity to run counter-cyclical policies
- they should not encourage localities to try to "export" the tax burden to other jurisdictions, as this distorts markets and breaks the basic link between taxation and benefits
- the tax base should be evenly distributed across jurisdictions (to avoid strong disparities and/or the need for huge fiscal equalisation systems).

These criteria point to the attractiveness of the property tax as a revenue source for local governments. Over-reliance on personal or corporate income taxes risks distorting the location decisions of households and firms and/or encouraging undesirable forms of tax competition, particularly if local authorities have discretion to adjust rates or offer tax breaks and other incentives. Corporate tax revenues are in any case mobile, highly cyclical, geographically concentrated and prone to shift the tax burden onto non-residents. Too much reliance on consumption taxes, especially sales taxes, would tend to divert revenues and distort markets.

Source: Blöchliger, H. and O. Petzold (2009), "Finding the dividing line between tax sharing and grants: A statistical investigation", http://dx.doi.org/10.1787/5k97b10vvbnw-en; Johansson, Å. et al. (2008), "Tax and economic growth", http://dx.doi.org/10.1787/241216205486; Oates and Schwab (1988), "Economic competition among jurisdictions: Efficiency enhancing or distortion inducing?", http://econweb.umd.edu/~oates/research/economic%20competition%20among%20jurisdictions.pdf.

Reforms in the realm of tax collection by subnational governments are important to solve the issues above, but may show little utility if they are not coupled with an overarching reform of the transfer system and expenditure responsibilities. Currently subnational governments have no incentives to collect their own taxes, which coupled with a lack of clarity in responsibility for expenditures is not conducive to delivering good public policy outcomes.

Intergovernmental transfers are leading to suboptimal investment

Transfers remain the main source of funding for subnational governments

Reliance on transfers from higher levels of government often limits subnational medium- to long-term planning and renders them vulnerable in times of economic difficulty (OECD, 2014b). This can make it difficult for cities and regions to budget and plan effectively, to ensure public service delivery and maintenance, and to invest in more strategic long-term priorities. In Antofagasta (Chile), for example, local projects are often designed with little certainty as to whether or not funding will be available, making it difficult to manage funding flows and ultimately discouraging potential investors (OECD, 2013c). Over-reliance on transfers may also undermine incentives for efficiency and accountability in local spending (OECD, 2012; 2013a).

In any case, subnational governments across the world tend to be highly dependent on transfers from higher levels of government, a tendency exacerbated in Peru as shown above. Own revenues are virtually never sufficient to cover their expenditure obligations, which are often determined by the delegation of responsibilities from above. The full range of different types of grants and transfers used by central governments goes beyond this discussion, but OECD work points to a number of basic guidelines for central governments to keep in mind.

Box 4.7. Efficiency of intergovernmental grants

Table 4.7 summarises the efficient use of various types of grants. The concrete aims are classified in terms of the general purposes of subsidisation, equalisation and financing. These, in turn, can be distinguished according to whether: 1) the central government takes the initiative to impose or influence subnational service provision or investment (e.g. delegation of functions); or 2) the subnational government itself takes the initiative. The instrument column indicates the various types of grant instruments available, as well as some regulatory instruments that may achieve more efficiently the aims for which grants are often used. Discretionary grants are mentioned as a possible instrument for co-funding purposes. Co-funding arrangements are used in some countries to finance projects with objectives that are hard to achieve using matching grants and where both central and subnational governments have to be committed. The table should not be seen as a prescriptive blueprint, since much depends on institutional architecture and country context. Nonetheless, it provides a framework that can serve as a starting point for thinking about the way grants are designed and used.

Table 4.7. **Lessons for efficient use of grant instruments**

Purposes and types of grant or regulatory instrument	Central government initiative			Subnational government initiative	
	Imposed programmes or standards	Compensation of spillovers	Temporary projects and programmes	Basic services	Fringe services
Financing					
Extension of subnational tax base	X			X	X
Non-earmarked general purpose grants	X			X	
Non-earmarked block grants	X				
Earmarked discretionary grants			X (co-funding)		
Earmarked matching and non-matching grants	(X)		X (risk sharing)		
Subsidisation					
Earmarked matching grants		X (national spillovers)	X (experiments)		
Imposition of co-operation		X (regional spillovers)			
Equalisation					
Imposition of horizontal grants	X			X	
Non-earmarked general purpose grants	X			X	

Source: Bergvall, D. et al. (2006), "Intergovernmental transfers and decentralised public spending", http://dx.doi.org/10.1787/budget-v5-art24-en.

These guidelines represent only a starting point, however, as much depends on the specific rules applied to grant use – such as, for example, the ease or difficulty with which municipalities or other local authorities can combine grants from different sources and/or pool grants across administrative boundaries in order to pursue service provision or investment at a larger territorial scale. One advantage of general purpose grants is that the conditions attached to earmarked grants often make it harder to adopt solutions that cut across policy sectors or administrative jurisdictions. This is an area where the United States, for example, has been making a particular effort: its Partnership for Sustainable Communities is largely designed to facilitate better co-ordination at the local and regional levels of federal funds emanating from different sources (OECD, 2013b).

The transfer of spending responsibilities by the national government coupled with the limited tax autonomy and poor tax collection of subnational governments, makes the latter strongly dependent on intergovernmental transfers. The central government has created seven types of resource transfers to subnational governments. The most important ones are FONCOMUN (formula based – for the local level), FONCOR (formula based – for the regions), ordinary transfers (discretionary – for both) and the *canon* – (formula based – for both). The dependence of the regional level on the transfers from the central government is particularly high, since they only have direct control over 5% of their income. Local governments face a similar issue, although slightly more limited. Still, 78% of their resources are transfers from the national government, of which 37% are from the *canon*. Nonetheless, before the explosion of *canon*, local governments were strongly dependent on non-*canon* central government transfers (Figure 4.10).

Figure 4.10. **Evolution of the origin of local government resources**

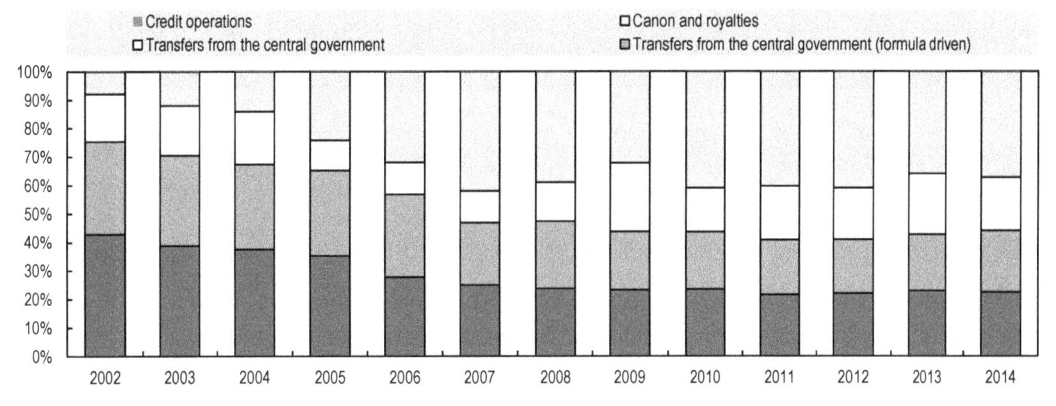

Source: Own elaboration based on data provided by the Ministry of Economy and Finance.

The main source of income for regional governments and a still relatively important source of income for local governments are the so-called "ordinary resources". They account for around 80% of the regional governments' resources. These ordinary transfers are divided into two kinds of transfers: 1) those set at the beginning of the year in the Institutional Opening Budget; and 2) those transferred throughout the year on a project basis. Transfers assigned in the Institutional Opening Budget are the result of a bargaining process during the design of the National Budget Law. After consideration of budget ceilings, the MEF assigns financial resources to the subnational governments.

Ordinary resources transferred at the beginning of the year are mostly earmarked and destined to cover primary expenditures made on behalf of the central government for the payment of wages and pensions in the sectors of education and health. This leaves subnational governments with comparatively limited scope for re-prioritising funding allocations transferred to them by the national government, and adapting them to the needs and circumstances of their territory. Therefore, this arrangement can be characterised as largely deconcentrated rather than decentralised. Ordinary resources transferred throughout the year on that basis are estimated to reach up to two-thirds of the regional government level (World Bank, 2010; Martinez- Vasquez, 2013). This incremental approach to resource allocation decreases the incentives for linking strategic planning with budgeting allocations. Improving the planning system (as presented in chapter 2) at the sub-national level by building their capacity along with introducing stronger performance based incentives would give subnational governments gradually more scope for prioritisation of expenditures –while maintaining coherence with national priorities. This would also increase their level of accountability for increasing efficiency and delivering better outcomes

Figure 4.11. **Evolution of the origin of regional government resources**

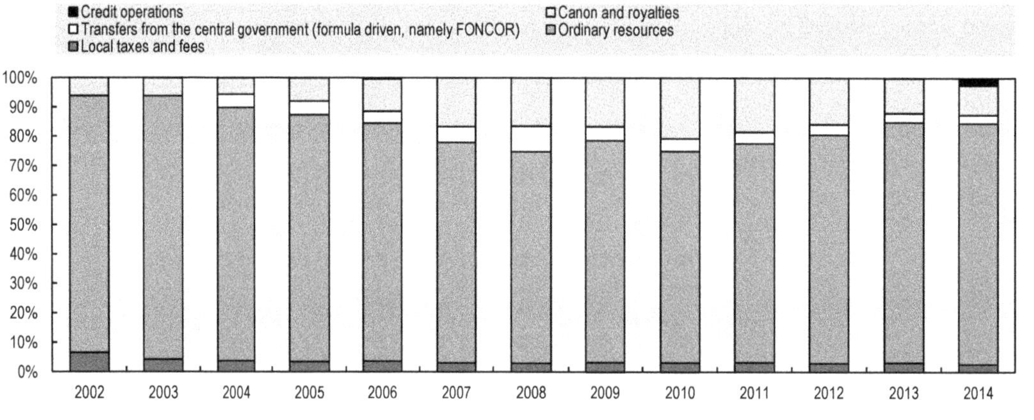

Source: Own elaboration based on data provided by the Ministry of Economy and Finance.

The increasing role of the canon *in subnational finances*

Commodity-based transfers (*canon* in Spanish) have become an important source of income for subnational governments due to the substantial increase of the revenues of extractive activities over the last decade. Mining firms in Peru paid USD 3.3 billion in taxes in 2013, or about 1.6% of GDP, 9.7% of the total tax revenue and 7.3% of total government revenue.[4] In 2013 the mining sector represented 12% of Peru's GDP. Between 2002 and 2014, the level of transfers to subnational governments increased by 4 245%, from PEN 164 million to PEN 7.1 billion.

Figure 4.12. **Evolution of *canon* transfers to subnational governments**

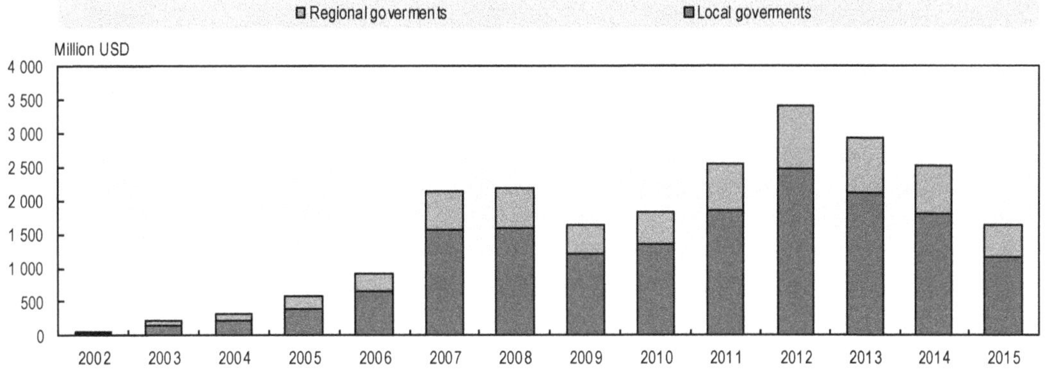

Source: Own elaboration based on data provided by the Ministry of Economy and Finance.

The Constitution specifies that the *canon* is allocated proportionally to regions from which natural resources are extracted. Although the *canon* is the largest source of revenue for subnational governments, only a small number of municipalities receive it. The distributional system of the *canon* mostly focuses on local governments, which receive 70% of the overall transfers. Regional governments only receive 15% of the *canon* and 5% is allocated to investments in science and technology. The *canon* funds, as determined by law, can only be used to finance capital investment.

Box 4.8. **The distributional system of the *canon***

The current system of revenue distribution – the *canon* – was created in 2001. The objective was to share the resources extracted from the subsoil with the regions and local governments; compensating producing regions for the exploitation of non-renewable resources. The *canon* transfers are not related, nor tied to the transfer of extra responsibilities aside from the ones already transferred during the decentralisation process. It is simply an additional transfer, above the transfer system established in the decentralisation process.

This revenue is distributed between the central government, regional governments and local governments under a formula-based system. Only producing subnational governments receive *canon*. There are different types of *canon* for the different types of non-renewable natural resources. They are all based on a similar model whereby half of the revenues are kept by the central government while the other half is transferred to the subnational level (this latter part is called the *canon*). In the case of the mining *canon*, the central government collects the taxes from the mining firms and then distributes it as follows:

- 25% to the regional government of the producing region (5% of which is invested in public universities in producing regions)
- 40% to municipal governments in the producing region based on population and UBN
- 25% to municipalities within the producing province based on population and UBN
- 10% to the district municipality of the producing district (of which 30% has to be invested in the community where the mining is located).

The *canon* resources can only be spent on capital investment, under the rationale that revenues from non-renewable resources should be spent on promoting long-term growth and not on current expenditure. A recent change in the regulation has allowed slightly looser assignation of the resources, and has allowed 20% of the overall sum to be assigned to maintenance and planning of the different public investment projects.

This distribution criterion for the *canon* was established before the fiscal decentralisation started at a time when the price of raw materials was relatively low. The original system did not take into account the potentially distortive effect that an increase in prices might produce. The current distribution of the *canon* contributes to fiscal imbalances in two ways.

First, it creates a horizontal imbalance. All the transfers go to producing regions, and more specifically to producing provinces. Six regions of the country account for more than 70% of the overall transfers, while 14 regions receive less than 3% of that sum. At the provincial level, those differences are even more telling since 4 out of the 1 853 municipalities receive more than the 50% of the *canon* funds attributed to the local governments (World Bank, 2015).

Figure 4.13. **Distribution of *canon* and royalties, Peru**

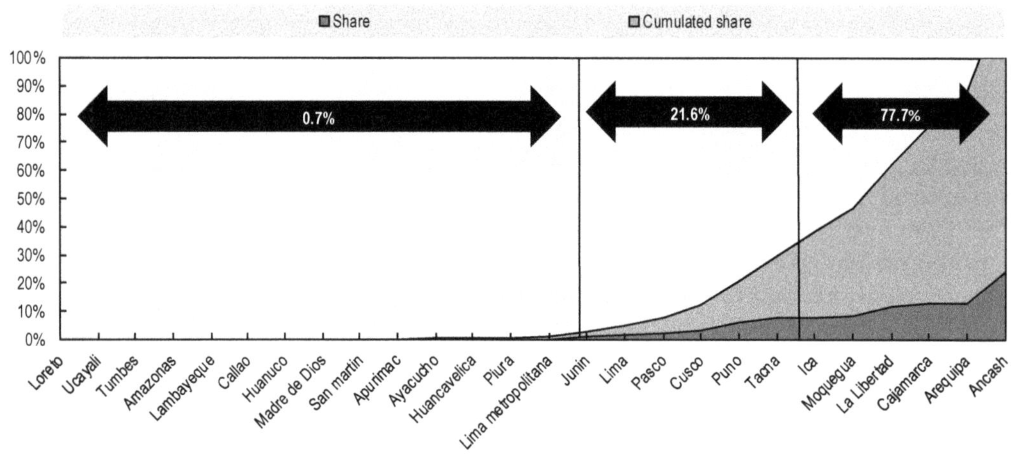

Source: Contraloría General de la República (2014), "Estudio del proceso de decentralización en el Perú".

The second imbalance is a vertical one. Local governments in the producing regions receive 80% of the overall transfer while the regional governments only receive 15%. This creates a strong disparity in resources between levels of government. This system provides local governments with a lot of leverage and reduced incentives to co-ordinate with regional governments given the level of resources they receive.

Colombia, which had a similarly distortive system prior to the 2011 reform of its transfer system made to address these issues could provide some lessons for Peru. Nonetheless, Peru demands a solution adapted to its context. In 2007, a tentative to reform the system had to be aborted because of strong mobilisation in producing regions. Colombia has a political context – particularly related to the FARC conflict – which allows higher levels of consensus for pacification and reconstruction. Also, the Colombian system is based on the presence of strong regional governments, which is not the case in Peru where decentralisation has not been completed since the failure to create regions. Strengthening the regional level will be key to sustaining the reform. Finally, the prices of raw materials, and particularly mining products, have decreased in the past years, reducing the window of opportunity to create consensus.

Canon *funds exacerbate socio-economic disparities and increase volatility in local revenues*

The allocation of the *canon* does not consider socio-economic needs of subnational governments because it is based on the principle of compensating producing regions for the depletion of their natural capital. Some studies find that it is likely that the uneven *canon* funds distribution is increasing spatial disparities in the country (World Bank, 2010; OECD, 2015a). Regions such as Moquegua or Tacna receive most of the *canon* transfers while they have a very small share of their population with UBNs. On the other hand, regions such as Loreto or San Martín receive very little *canon* while they display high shares of their population with UBNs.

Box 4.9. Transfer system in Colombia

Before the 2011 reform, 80% of royalties were distributed to the regions where minerals and hydrocarbons were extracted; only 20% were distributed according to other criteria. Starting in 2012, distribution to regions rich in extractive resources was substantially reduced and criteria were revised in order to distribute the revenue in a more targeted and geographically diverse fashion. Prior to 2012, 80% of the royalties were distributed to regions that represented 17% of the Colombian population; in 2012, the same share, 80% of royalties collected, reached regions representing 70% of the population.

Despite the substantial contribution of revenue from royalties to regional and local governments in minerals and energy-producing regions, the receiving governments are among the least developed regions in Colombia such as la Guajira. Indeed, poverty levels were higher than the national average in six of the eight regions that received the largest share of royalties by 2005.

The 2012 reform aimed at improving the effectiveness of investment and infrastructure spending funded by royalties and to conditions to extract more resources. Indeed, 3% of the transfers went to administration and oversight of projects and 2% to research and mapping of the resources. The remaining expenditure envelope is distributed between a territorial pension fund (10%); investments in science, technology and innovation (10%); a stabilisation fund (30%); the remaining half went to investment-related projects in the producing regions (10%), investment projects in the poorest regions (23%) and to a project-based fund for all the other regions (15%).

Figure 4.14. **Distribution of royalties in Colombia, post-2012 reform**

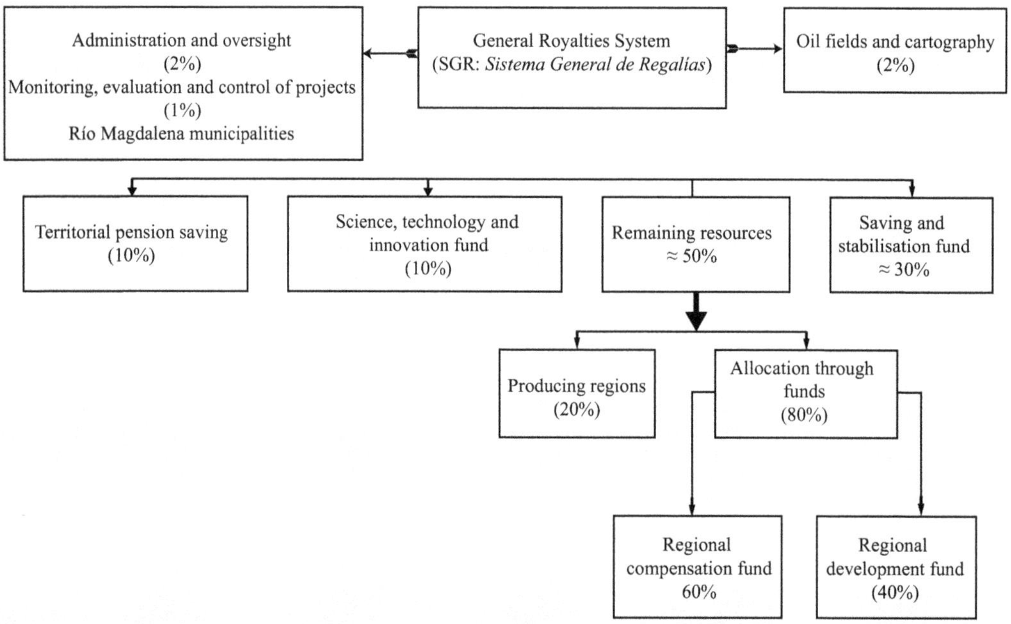

Source: OECD based on Acto Legislativo 05 (2011), Decree 0750 (2012) and Decree 4923 (2011).

The share going to producing regions has gradually decreased from 50% in 2012 to 20% from 2015 onward. In the medium term, therefore, the producing regions will obtain about 10% of the total revenue from royalties in direct expenditure, compared to 80% before the reform.

Source: OECD (2014d).

Figure 4.15. **Regional transfers per capita and unsatisfied basic needs per region, 2014**

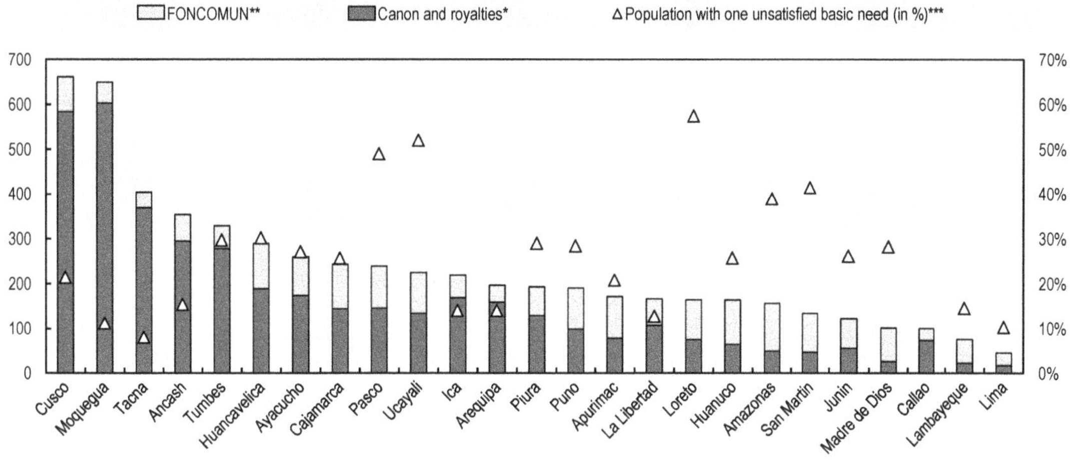

Notes: Average year nominal exchange rate. *All *canon* and royalties are included in this calculation including the gas, forestry or customs. ** FONCOMUN is the municipal compensation fund. This fund seeks to promote investment at the municipal level with a redistributive objective. Priorities are set to the poorest municipalities and particularly in rural areas and marginal urban areas. *** The components of unsatisfied basic needs are: quality of the house, non-overcrowding of the house, access to sanitary services, school attendance and economic dependency. No data for Callao.

Source: OECD calculations based on INEI for population (2014 data) and unsatisfied basic needs (2013 data) and Ministry of Economy and Finance for FONCOMUN and *canon* and royalties data.

In addition to contributing to regional disparities, the *canon* funds increase the volatility of subnational revenues, as this stream is directly affected by the fluctuation of the international prices for commodities. This is a common challenge faced by most countries with abundant natural resources, but in the case of Peru it is particularly important since the *canon* represent a large share of local government revenues. Their fiscal structure gives them less capacity to offset a decline in these funds, and results in higher revenue fluctuations at a local level.

Revenue uncertainty has a negative impact on the planning, programming and management of investment spending. In the context of current declines in commodities prices, the high degree of uncertainty in the *canon* funds complicates the management of large investment projects. During the first half of 2015, some municipalities were forced to cut the budget three times due to the decline of the *canon* funds.

Peru should improve public spending predictability by mitigating the *canon* fund's volatility through a stabilisation fund. International experience suggests that stabilisation funds can help stabilise growth and maintain competitiveness. Counter-cyclical expenditure and stabilisation tools can prevent price volatility from resulting in macroeconomic instability that also harms non-extractive sectors. There are different models internationally that Peru could learn from in this respect. In particular, Colombia, which links its stabilisation fund to subnational investment.

Box 4.10. Stabilisation funds: International experiences

Colombia

The General Royalties System in Colombia is connected to a Savings and Stabilisation Fund (FAE) to share the proceeds from Colombia's natural resources across generations. The FAE is managed by the Central Bank of Colombia, which is a signal of its independence. Moreover, the FAE was introduced with a new fiscal "golden rule" (June 2011), which will further protect Colombia's economy from the boom and bust of commodity prices. Once fully implemented, the FAE will absorb up to 30% of the total royalty revenues. In particular, the FAE will also accumulate revenue windfalls (i.e. extra revenues from the growth of counter-cyclical fiscal policies during economic downturns). In 2012, 25% of the total revenue generated by the General Royalties System was allocated to the FAE. In the future, this percentage will grow proportionally with the expected increase in royalty revenues.

Up to 10% of the budget allocated to the FAE in the previous year can be used to set up counter-cyclical investment programmes. These investment programmes will be shared among territorial entities in the same proportions as the Regional Compensation Fund and the Regional Development Fund.

Chile

Chile's fiscal finances are heavily dependent on the volatile price of copper, its leading export. In the past, the volatility of the price of copper had an extremely negative impact, and in 1987, the Copper Stabilisation Fund was set up, partly to insulate fiscal revenues from cyclical fluctuations in the price of copper. When the price rises above a certain target, the extra revenue is deposited in the fund and is not available for the budget. Similarly, when it falls below a certain target, the revenue shortfall in the budget is compensated for through withdrawals from the fund. In September 2006, the Chilean Congress approved a new Fiscal Responsibility Law (FRL), an important step in strengthening its fiscal framework. This created a legal framework for the structural balance rule; created a Pension Reserve Fund to address pension-related contingencies; transformed the Copper Stabilisation Fund into a broader sovereign wealth fund called the Economic and Social Stabilisation Fund; and introduced explicit, formal mechanisms for capitalising the central bank. The Ministry of Finance regulates the investment of revenue collected through taxes with advice from a Financial Committee, and the Central Bank of Chile is designated as asset manager. Detailed reporting on the investments undertaken, return on investments and the positions of the funds is conducted monthly by the Ministry of Finance.

Sound macroeconomic management has allowed the Chilean government to run counter-cyclical fiscal policies. In 2001, it adopted a structural fiscal rule stipulating that the government maintain a structural surplus equivalent to 1% of GDP, a percentage that was relaxed in 2008 to 0.5% of GDP, and was further reduced to 0% to allow for a fiscal stimulus during the crisis. The rule was suspended *de facto* in February 2010 due to the earthquake.. This structural balance rule involves estimating the fiscal income that would be obtained net of the impact of the economic cycle, and in particular of commodity price cycles, and spending only the amount that would be compatible with that level of income. It is calculated using projected government revenue when the prices of copper and molybdenum, a by-product of the production of copper, are at a sustainable level over the long term, defined as ten years, and GDP growth is at a sustainable medium-term rate. These rates are determined by an independent panel of 20 members of the private sector and academia, as well as (in the case of the price of copper) representatives of COCHILCO, the copper advisory agency, and CODELCO. Every year, at least three members of this committee are replaced to ensure an orderly turnover. Chile's economic outlook shifted drastically during the world economic crisis in the last quarter of 2008. Nevertheless, the structural surplus and the stabilisation funds accumulated during the profitable years were used to launch a fiscal stimulus package in January 2009, which boosted public investment programmes and transfers. This stimulus included investments in infrastructure, small enterprise development and subsidies to low-income households. The Chilean stabilisation fund represented 5.5% of GDP in 2011, down from 13% in 2008.

Box 4.10. **Stabilisation funds: International experiences** (*continued*)

Norway

In Norway, the government Petroleum Fund was established in 1990 to build up financial reserves to preserve an equitable share of petroleum revenues for future generations and to prevent short-term fluctuations in the oil price from influencing spending in the current and following years' budget. The fund is fully integrated into the state budget, and net allocations reflect the total budget surplus (including petroleum revenues). It remained empty until 1996 as a result of the recession of the early 1990s, but has seen a rapid build-up in assets in recent years. The government decided in 2005 to establish the Government Pension Fund, which includes the former Petroleum Fund (renamed the Government Pension Fund – Global, or GPFG) and the National Insurance Scheme Fund (renamed the Government Pension Fund – Norway). Its real return is to provide a partial prefunding of future pension liabilities. This fund mainly transforms depleting oil and gas resources into financial assets.

The rationale is that since this wealth belongs to present and future generations of Norwegians, the capital should be preserved, and only the returns consumed, to allow future generations to choose how to allocate these earnings. The so-called 4% rule stipulates that the central government deficit excluding petroleum revenues and adjusted for the cyclical position of the mainland economy should, over time, equal 4% of the value of the GPFG at the end of the year prior to the budget year. A non-petroleum structural deficit equal to 4% of the GPFG is not a binding target for any particular year. The government is free to deviate from it under various circumstances, notably when discretionary fiscal action seems necessary to stabilise the economy, or when the value of the GPFG changes erratically. The Ministry of Finance projects the value of the GPFG to increase from about 160% of mainland GDP at the end of 2011 to about 185% by 2025.

Source: OECD (2014d), *OECD Territorial Reviews: Colombia 2014*, http://dx.doi.org/10.1787/9789264224551-en.

Other intergovernmental transfers do little to compensate for the inequalities generated by the canon

Increases in the *canon* transfers have led to major investment unbalances across regions. Indeed, there are three instruments which should act as equalisation mechanisms, but which have very limited impact. The first two are investment funds – the Regional Equalisation Fund (FONCOR) and the Fund for the Promotion of Regional and Local Public Investment (FONIPREL), which is a competitive fund – transferred to subnational governments. Compared to *canon* transfers, though, their weight and hence equalising effect is fairly limited. FONCOR has a further weakness in the medium and long run related to fact that it does not have a direct source of funding attached to the fund. The third fund, FONCOMUN, is a transfer to local governments which can freely dispose of it (see Box 4.11 for further details). FONCOR and FONCOMUN are allocated according to demographic, geographic and socio-economic criteria. Nonetheless, all local governments of the country receive transfers from FONCOMUN given that a minimum amount has been set, thus reducing its potential equalisation effect. Compensatory transfers seek to transfer financial resources to subnational governments to enable them to provide their citizens with a similar level of public services despite differences in economic wealth.

The third mechanism is direct investments from the central government in regions. The latter has more potential compensating power but does not seem to be particularly targeted towards reducing regional UBNs. For instance, per capita central government investment is particularly high in regions such as Madre de Dios which received ten times more central government investments than Loreto while it has less than half its share population with UBNs (Figure 4.16). As a result, public investment in regions is highly unequal and has no correlation with the level of UBNs of the population.

Canon-receiving regions have high levels of per capita investments compared to non-receiving regions. For example, Moquegua has levels of public investments per capita close to PEN 3 500 while in Lambayeque they are barely above PEN 500.

Box 4.11. Focus on FONCOR and FONCOMUN

The Regional Equalisation Fund (FONCOR), (the third main source of funding for regional governments after ordinary funds and the *canon*) underwent an interesting reform in 2009 which could inspire future equalising and *canon*-related unbalances.

Allocation of the fund is formula driven; regional investment needs are calculated on the basis of population, poverty, unsatisfied basic needs, location near borders and effectiveness in the execution of investment projects. That sum is then deducted from the amounts transferred to the regional governments for the *canon*. The transfers are distributed proportionally amongst regions with a positive balance in terms of investment needs. This distribution system leads to regions with higher *canon* transfers than investment needs to receive no transfers for the concept of FONCOR.

Despite these advances, the fund has little equalising power because of its size compared to the *canon*. In 2004, when FONCOR was established, the overall value of the fund matched that of *canon* transfers but since then, with the explosion of the value of *canon* transfers, it now represents only 3% of the transfers to regions against 10% for the *canon*. Its potential equalising effect is thus limited.

At the local level, the municipal compensation fund (FONCOMUN) initially allocated resources to the provincial and district municipalities to promote investment, taking into account the unsatisfied basic needs. It is now a fund that is freely used by local governments (for capital or current expenditures). Provincial municipalities retain 20% of resources and distribute the remaining 80% between the districts of each province according to population criteria, management capacity and area. However, FONCOMUN is not a true compensatory fund as the distribution does not take into account the fiscal potential of districts or their tax collection nor the *canon* funds received by the municipalities. In other words, all municipalities, even the richest, receive this fund. In addition, it cannot be considered an effective equalisation fund as it depends on sales taxes collected in a given area (it is a VAT-based fund). Attempts have been made to reform the allocation criteria of the FONCOMUN, to prevent municipalities with higher revenues from receiving this fund. However, this proposal did not succeed.

Source: OECD analysis based on information provided by the Ministry of Economy and Finance.

Overall government spending (current expenditures and investments) shows higher per capita equalisation on spending but correlation with UBNs is limited. This phenomenon is mainly due to the fact that both the Municipal Compensation Fund[5] (FONCOMUN), ordinary resource and public spending as a whole are driven more by population factors than by the needs of the population. Figure 4.17 shows that most disparities in overall public spending come from subnational spending, and particularly local governments, where the *canon* disparities are most important. Central government expenditure acts as per capita equaliser particularly in regions such as Lima or Callao, but do not target specifically UBNs.

In addition to *canon* funds and the formula-based transfers, subnational governments receive ordinary transfers, which are assigned following budgetary priorities defined by the national government. This allocation is used to finance payroll expenses, goods and services, and public investment. Most of these allocations are earmarked by the central government and cover primary expenditures. There is a part of these transfers which is more discretionary, the one based on specific resource requests and project-based transfers. As a result, subnational authorities, especially governors, spend a lot of time and energy negotiating their grants with the MEF. Increasing the integration of these discretionary transfers with strategic planning processes and consistently evaluating outcomes will increase the likelihood of better policy outcomes.

Figure 4.16. **Public investment per capita in regions and population with unsatisfied basic needs, 2014**

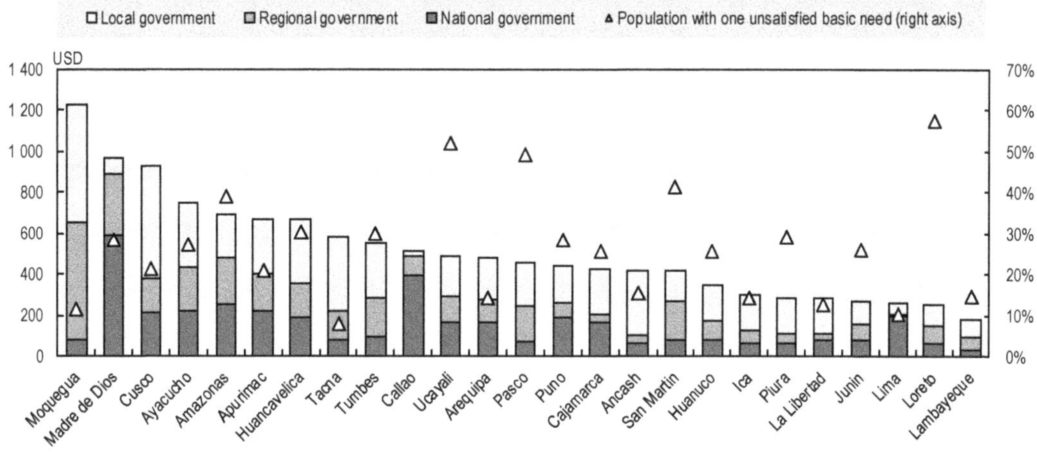

Note: Average year nominal exchange rate.

Source: Own elaboration based on data provided by the Ministry of Economy and Finance and INEI.

Figure 4.17. **Government spending per capita and unsatisfied basic needs, 2014**

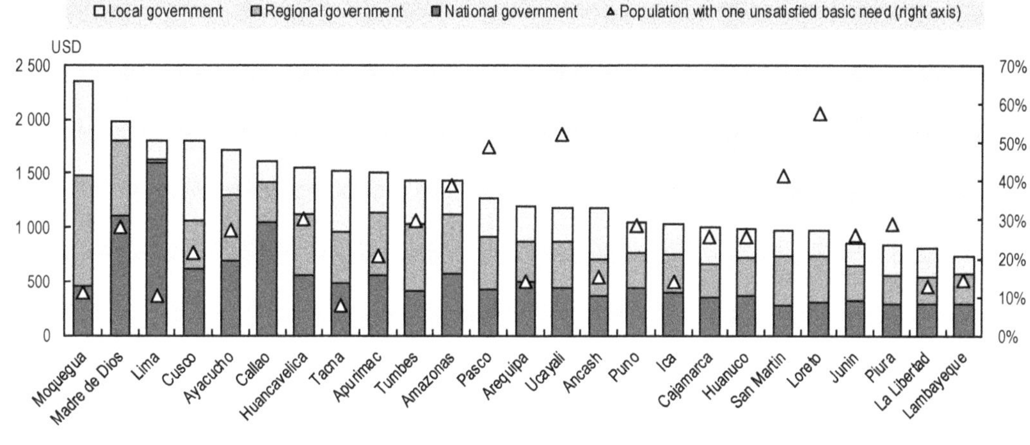

Note: Average year nominal exchange rate.

Source: Own elaboration based on data provided by the Ministry of Economy and Finance and INEI.

Many OECD countries use fiscal equalisation measures to ensure citizens can be provided with similar levels of public services at similar levels of taxation despite differences such as higher levels of socio-economic disadvantage and low population densities. In some countries (such as Australia and Germany) this significantly reduces or eliminates differences in revenue-raising capacity. Currently, equalisation measures in Peru do not bridge this gap.

Box 4.12. Snapshot of fiscal equalisation in OECD countries

Equalisation mechanisms are extensively used in OECD countries, introducing either vertical transfers (from the central government to financially weak subnational governments) or horizontal transfers (from wealthy jurisdictions to the poor ones). Not only federal countries but also unitary countries have put in place equalisation procedures as a key pillar of their fiscal policy. Across the OECD, fiscal equalisation transfers average around 2.5% of gross domestic product (GDP), 5% of general government spending and 50% of intergovernmental grants.

The differences in GDP per capita across jurisdictions provoke unequal tax-raising capacities and, thus, differences in public service provision. In addition, the cost of public services is another factor that leads to unequal public service provision: special groups such as children, the elderly, the disabled, etc. will raise the cost of public services and the geographical factors will also impact on the cost per service unit.

Equalisation arrangements can hence be broken down into revenue versus cost equalisation. While the former equalisation aims mainly to reduce differences in tax-raising capacity, the latter reduces the cost of providing public services. Most OECD countries apply various equalisation arrangements, although the combination of vertical and cost equalisation tends to be prevalent.

Across OECD countries, equalisation has a strong redistributive effect: on average it reduces pre-equalisation disparities by more than two-thirds and, in some countries – such as Australia, Germany and Sweden – revenue-raising disparities are virtually eliminated. Equalisation mechanisms should be tailor-made for each country. Fiscal equalisation depends on a set of institutional factors such as size and number of sub-central governments, their geographical distribution, spending assignments and fiscal resources allocated to each jurisdiction, among others. However, based on OECD countries' experiences it is possible to state a few general rules on the reform of equalisation:

- Equalisation should rely on only a few core indicators that reflect inter-jurisdictional differences in tax-raising capacity and/or spending needs. These indicators should be immune to any manipulation by subnational governments in order to pre-empt any unfair allocations to jurisdictions or spending excesses by either sub-central governments or central government. Equalisation should cover the main subnational taxes and public service responsibilities in order to prevent jurisdictions from setting taxes strategically or core services from remaining structurally underfunded.
- The institutional set-up should help underpin the efficiency of equalisation while keeping equity objectives intact. Horizontal equalisation tends to be more efficient than vertical equalisation in terms of redistribution achieved per monetary unit spent. In all countries, disparities in revenue-raising capacity across jurisdictions are much greater than those in service cost. They should therefore be the first priority of equalisation. The size of a jurisdiction should not enter into the equalisation formula, the possible exception being large agglomerations where living costs are high.
- In order to improve transparency, equalisation should be clearly separated from tax sharing and other intergovernmental grants whose purpose is not redistribution. Equalisation should, ideally, be a single transfer that offsets differences in tax-raising capacity and/or one or more transfers that meet differences in spending needs in the main policy areas devolved to subnational governments – education, healthcare and infrastructure. Donors and recipients should be clearly visible.
- The impact of equalisation should be regularly monitored. Periodical reviews of the system should assess to what extent equalisation helps reduce inter-jurisdictional inequality and how it affects the efficiency of the public sector, development incentives, overall spending and tax levels. Equalisation should, in particular, come under scrutiny to ascertain whether it provides insurance against asymmetric shocks. If it does not, equalisation and stabilisation should be addressed by two separate transfer systems.

Source: OECD (2013a), *Fiscal Federalism 2014: Making Decentralisation Work*, http://dx.doi.org/10.1787/9789264204577-en.

Borrowing at the subnational level in Peru

Fiscal discipline has also been a key pillar in the Peruvian decentralisation process. Since the fiscal decentralisation process started in Peru, there has been particular emphasis on avoiding runaway subnational borrowing and bailouts leading to macroeconomic instability as have occurred in other LAC countries (Martinez-Vazquez, 2013). In this sense, levels of debt are not a pressing issue for subnational governments in Peru. Nonetheless, borrowing could be used more effectively to address infrastructure gaps.

Fiscal rules proliferated during the first decade of the fiscal decentralisation. The Peruvian fiscal framework was characterised as having a high number of fiscal rules (eight) and poor compliance due to the amount of rules, the lack of capacity to apply them and the lack of enforcement capacity. In an effort to reduce the number of parameters to comply with, Peru recently adopted a reform of the fiscal framework reducing the number of subnational fiscal rules to two:

1. restraining total (non-financial) public expenditure to the rolling average of the last four years' revenues
2. capping the debt by limiting the ratio of total debt on the average of the past four years' current revenue to 100%.

Sanctions for non-compliance were also reformulated in this new fiscal framework. Non-compliant subnational governments are not allowed to contract or issue debt of any kind. In addition, a restriction on fiscal transfers from the Fund for the Promotion of Regional and Local Public Investment (FONIPREL) is foreseen in the new fiscal rules.

Enforcement mechanisms are a key pillar for making fiscal rules work. In 2014, the first year in which the new fiscal rules were in force, only 50% of the regional governments and 59% of local governments met both fiscal rules (spending and debt limits). Peru should consider including incentives for compliance, as well as giving technical support for subnational government compliance and reporting. The achievement of the spending, deficit and debt targets will not only have a direct impact on Peruvian national macroeconomic outcomes, but also on the quality of services delivered.

A new spending rule has recently been approved for current and capital spending, with the objective of achieving greater consistency between the increase in the stock of public capital and the amount spent on equipment and maintenance of that stock (Cheasty and Pichihua, 2015). This should help maintain the quality of infrastructure over time.

In addition, in the recent fiscal reform, subnational governments were required to submit a multi-year report on fiscal management, which is a helpful tool for improving medium-term financial planning and transparency at the subnational level. This new obligation will gradually come into force between the years 2015-20 on all subnational governments. Although the objective of these reports is to ensure sound fiscal management, it would be desirable that they also help strengthen medium-term planning of public policies at the subnational level.

Peruvian subnational public finances are in good shape

Despite the limited success in compliance with the fiscal rules, at aggregate level, Peru presents a very sound subnational fiscal position and in comparison with OECD countries (Figure 4.18). Currently, subnational public debt represents only around 2% of GDP. Recently adopted regulation for the computation of subnational debt, now including obligations with the pension funds, has lifted debt levels to 4% of GDP, very sound levels by OECD standards. This is directly linked to the robust growth of government revenue during the upswing and sound fiscal management. In this sense, Peru should maintain the fiscal discipline at the subnational level, especially in a context of slowing revenue growth due to the economic slowdown. Without abandoning fiscal responsibility, improving the cohesion across territories should also be a core objective of the fiscal policy.

Figure 4.18. **Contribution of subnational government debt and debt levels as a share of GDP in OECD countries**

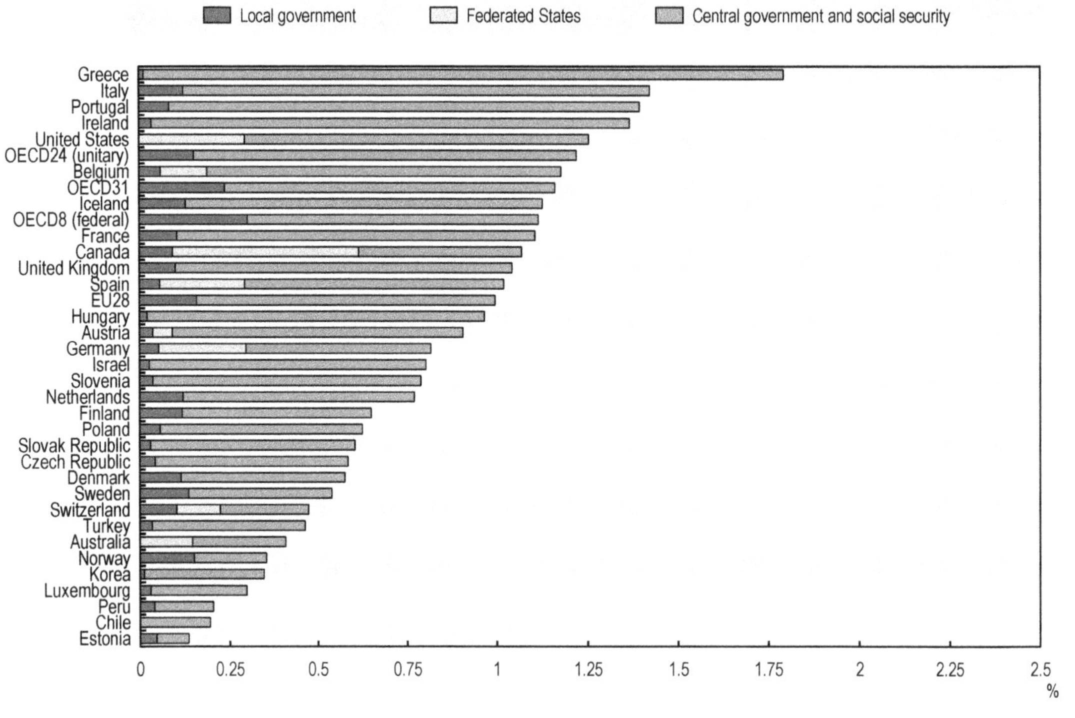

Sources: Own elaboration based on OECD (2015b), "Subnational governments in OECD countries: Key data", http://stats.oecd.org/Index.aspx?DataSetCode=SNGF; and Peruvian Cuenta General de la República 2013 – Ministerio de Economía y Finanzas.

Debt levels in Peru are not only low but also very concentrated in regions or cities with higher financial capacities such as Lima. Lima is the only subnational government with access to financial and foreign markets. Other regions have fairly limited levels of debt, confirming the sustainability of subnational debt once debt levels are desegregated.

Indebted subnational governments have a stable perspective on their debts since they are mostly *vis-a-vis* the central government; bond issuing is *de facto* forbidden for most subnational governments, leading to low levels of financial debt in loans and bonds. This, coupled with the fact that subnational governments are very controlled in the borrowing market by the central government, provides further stability against financial market volatility.

One lesson learnt from OECD countries is that a sound design of fiscal rules has to be tailored to the specific economic and institutional characteristics of each country. In the case of Peru, revenue flows to subnational governments are directly affected by the volatility of international prices for commodities. A key challenge therefore is to include in the fiscal rule a stabilisation mechanism to better manage these resources and to avoid fluctuations that negatively affect the planning of public policies at the subnational level.

Peru still exhibits a significant infrastructure gap, so the fiscal framework may include elements to favour public infrastructure investment. In addition, in a new context with lower commodity prices, the funding of investment projects will be reduced. Creating new fiscal spaces may be of interest for Peru. Priority should be given to generating more fiscal space in the long run, beyond immediate cyclical considerations, rather than simply allowing for more discretionary fiscal space during economic slowdowns (Carranza, Daude and Melguizo, 2011).

Many OECD countries include a "golden rule" in their fiscal discipline to protect public investment. The rationale is that higher public investment translates into higher growth, and thus more revenues to sustain debt levels. The most common solution is to set a balanced budget while authorising borrowing only to finance public investments. Spain's experience linking public investment with fiscal discipline at the local level is of interest here. Spain's recent reform allows municipalities with fiscal surpluses and low thresholds of public debt to invest a share of their surplus in public investments that guarantee the financial sustainability of the projects. The remaining surplus must reduce public debt.

While the fiscal position of Peruvian subnational governments is good, one major cause of resistance to granting more autonomy to subnational actors may be a fear of jeopardising macroeconomic stability. This is common in many OECD countries. In Chile, for instance, one of the main barriers for the decentralisation reform proposed in 2009 was the fear of jeopardising the macroeconomic stability achieved in recent decades. The experience of OECD countries suggests that every initiative to extend the decentralisation process requires a special effort to communicate to the public the potential medium- and long-term efficiency gains the reform can bring, and the potential productivity and competitiveness both of the different regions and the country as a whole. In particular, it is important to demonstrate that the benefits of reform outweigh its costs, and that decentralisation does not increase overall public expenditure and debt.

Subnational expenditures

On the spending side, subnational governments have assumed important responsibilities, especially in public investments and in the delivery of essential public services, such as health and education, which are the main competences assigned to subnational governments. One distinguishing feature in Peru is the high share of public investments at the subnational level: 64% of the total, above the average of OECD countries. This was initially driven by the boom in commodity revenue during the last decade, which finances investment in the production areas. Stimulus measures from the central governments have helped maintain the level of subnational investments despite a decrease in *canon* transfers. The level of overall public investments in the country is also high compared to OECD standards, partly due to a catch-up effect and to the mechanics of the *canon*, whose funds must be directed towards public investments.

Subnational governments have a key role in the economic and social development of the country

Subnational expenditure has risen, from 33% in 2004 to around 40% in 2014, as a share of total public expenditure (Table 4.8). The entire increase observed in subnational expenditure over that decade is mainly a consequence of the boom in commodities revenues, not to new powers assigned to subnational governments (World Bank, 2010). Over this period the share of public expenditure remained fairly constant at a regional level whereas local expenditures increased considerably, due to the increases in the *canon* funds. Since 2012, the decrease in *canon* transfers has been compensated by increased transfers from the central government earmarked for investment.

Table 4.8. **Public expenditure by level of government**

As a % of the total

	2004	2014
National government	67.0%	61.2%
Regional government	19.6%	19.3%
Local government	13.4%	19.8%

Source: Own elaboration based on data provided by the Ministry of Economy and Finance.

Figure 4.19. **Subnational expenditure breakdown by level of government**

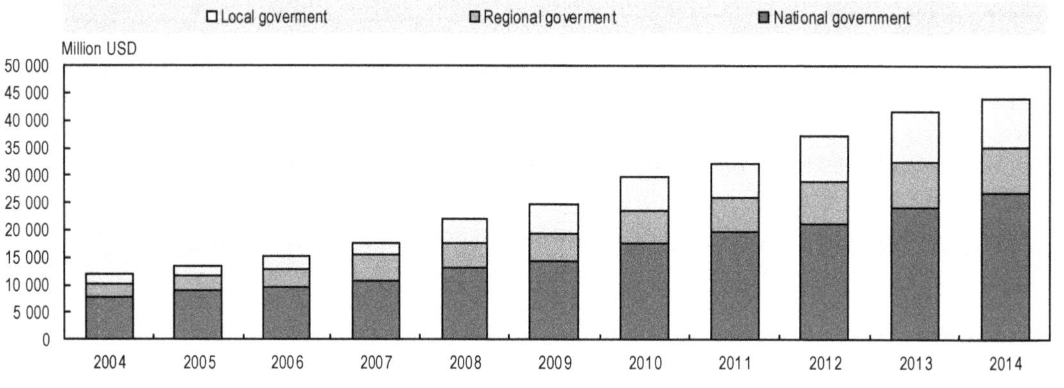

Note: Average year nominal exchange rate.

Source: Own elaboration based on data provided by the Ministry of Economy and Finance.

The vast majority of the expenditure responsibilities of regional and local governments are shared with the national government. The exclusive competencies of the national government are mainly the legislative function, national defence and security, foreign affairs, judicial services, and the management of public debt. In these areas, the national government accounts for almost 100% of total expenditure. Peru is close to the OECD average in terms of the composition of expenditure of subnational governments, aside from their role in economic affairs (Figure 4.20).

Figure 4.20. **Structure of expenditure by level of government, 2014**

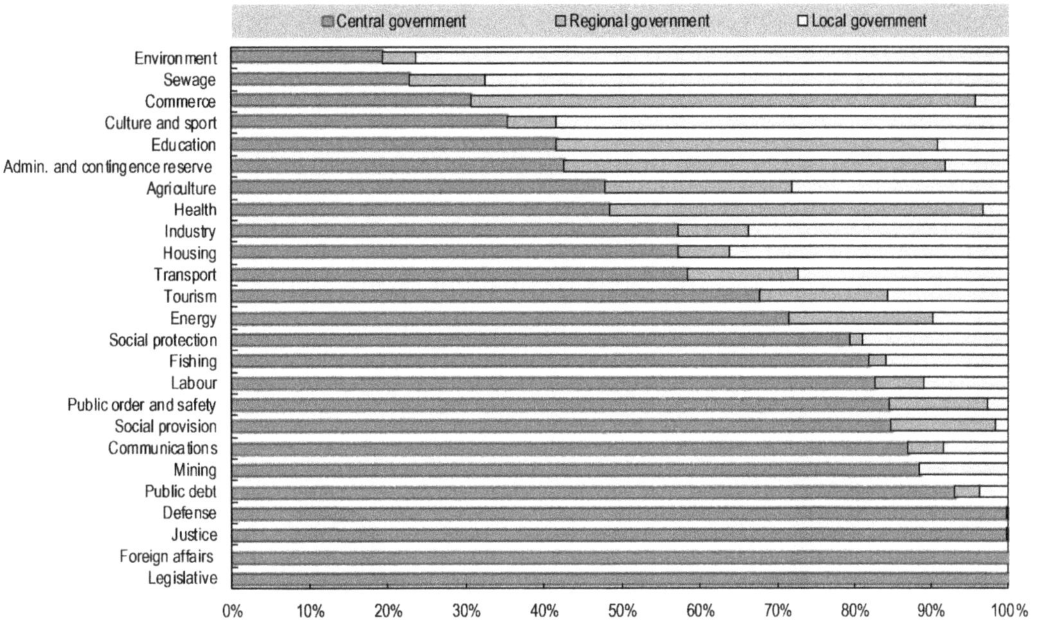

Source: Own elaboration based on data provided by the Ministry of Economy and Finances.

Figure 4.21. **Subnational government expenditure by function, OECD and Peru**

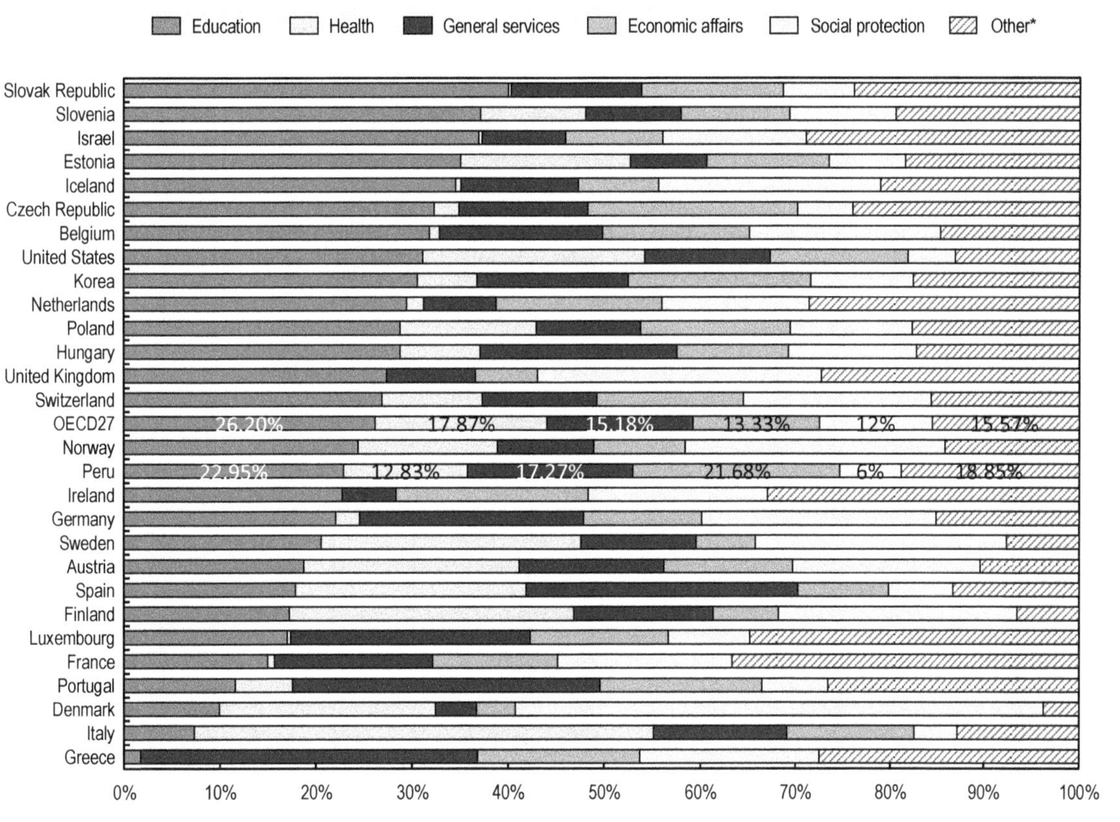

Sources: Own elaboration based on OECD (2015b), "Subnational governments in OECD countries: Key data", http://stats.oecd.org/Index.aspx?DataSetCode=SNGF; and Peruvian Cuenta General de la República 2013 – Ministerio de Economía y Finanzas.

The functional composition of expenditures by level of governments, shows that subnational governments are responsible for the bulk of social sector expenditure, although there are significant differences between the composition of regional and local budgets:

- At a regional level, education constitutes one-third of expenditure, followed by health services (30%), planning and management (27%), transport (7%), and public order and security (6%).
- At a local level, the largest share of expenditure is allocated to transport (23%), followed by sewage (17%) and environment (11%). Education is the main social expenditure at the regional level, accounting for a 10%.

Figure 4.22. **Breakdown of regional (left) and local (right) expenditure in Peru, 2014**

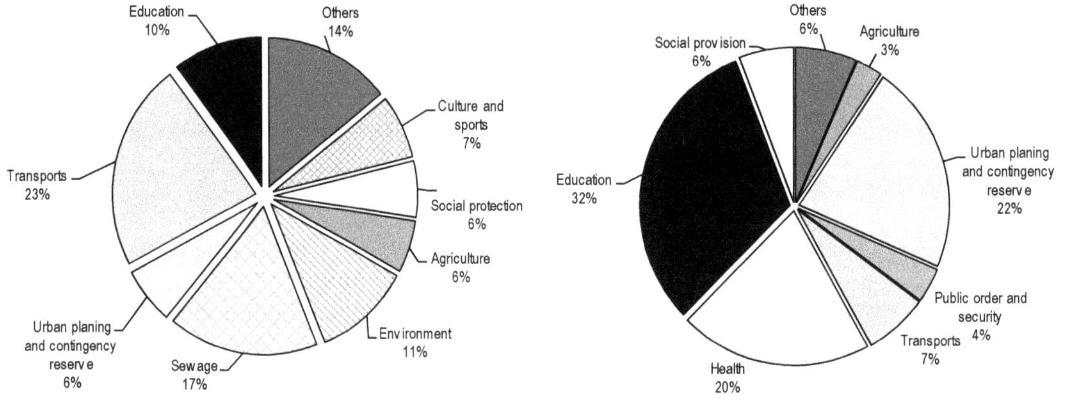

Source: Own elaboration based on data provided by the Ministry of Economy and Finance.

Capital expenditures by subnational governments have been progressively growing over the past decade to a level comparable to the OECD average of 56%. Currently local governments account for 38% of total public investment, while the central government accounts for 44% and regional government only 18%.

Figure 4.23. **Government spending per type, 2014**

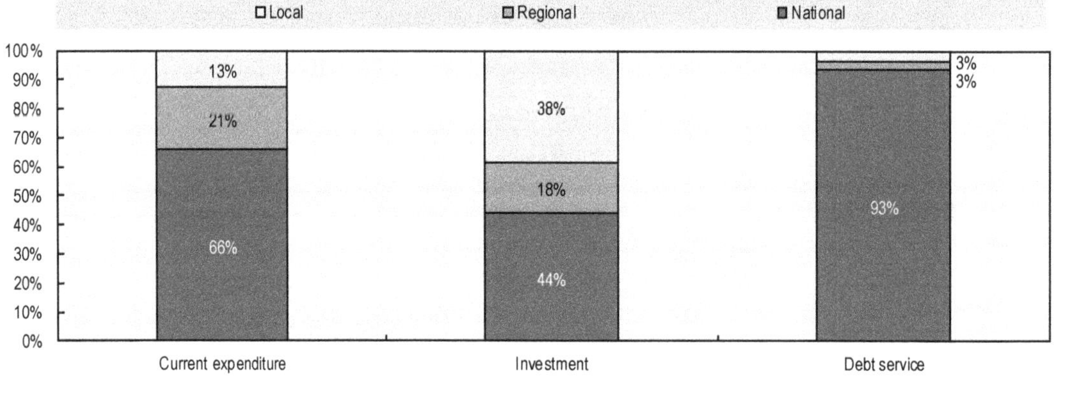

Source: Own elaboration based on data provided by the Ministry of Economy and Finance.

Figure 4.24. **Current and capital expenditure at the subnational level**

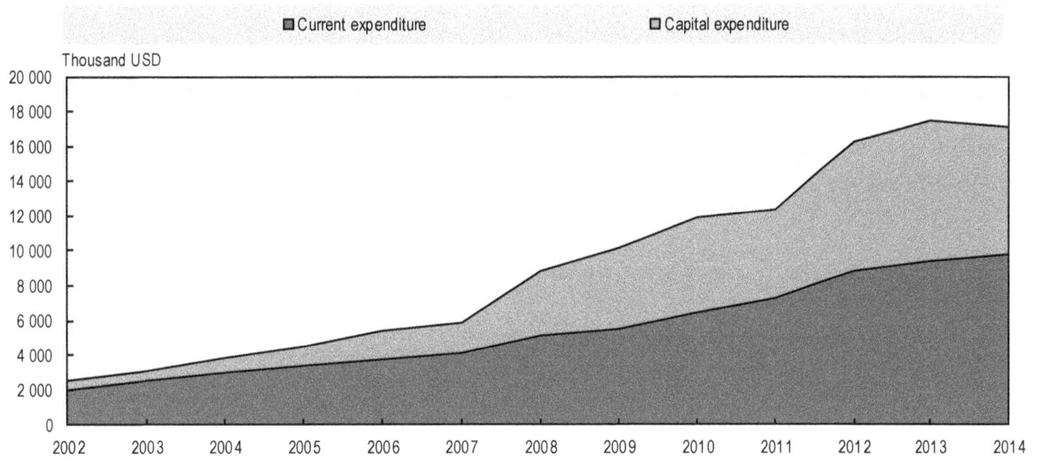

Note: Average year nominal exchange rate.

Source: Own elaboration based on data provided by the Ministry of Economy and Finance.

In comparison with OECD countries, Peru has very high levels of public investment as a share of GDP. Subnational governments are slightly above-average investors compared to OECD countries. The combination of both makes subnational governments in Peru not only key investors in the economy but also very important national economic actors.

Figure 4.25. **Share of total public investment in GDP and share of subnational governments in public investment, OECD and Peru**

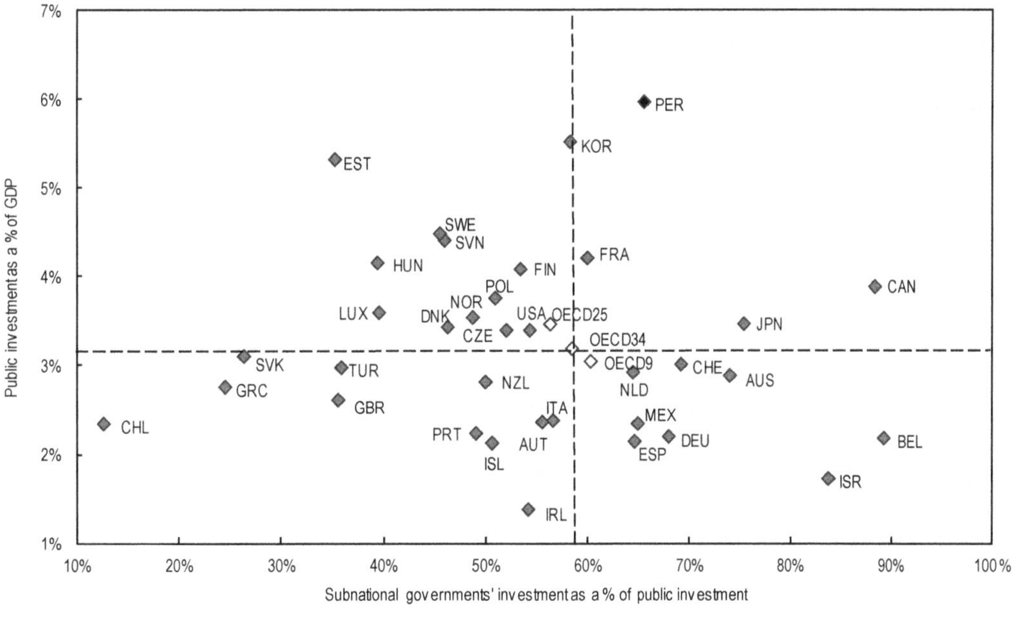

Sources: Own elaboration based on OECD (2015b), "Subnational governments in OECD countries: Key data", http://stats.oecd.org/Index.aspx?DataSetCode=SNGF; and Peruvian Cuenta General de la República 2013 – Ministerio de Economía y Finanzas.

Despite this overall increase, investment figures also show volatility, particularly at a local level. Due to lower commodity prices, investment at the local level in 2011 fell by 15% from the previous year. Since 2012, the decrease in the *canon* transfers has been compensated by an increase of funds earmarked for investment from the central government. Between 2012 and 2015, *canon* transfers decreased by PEN 4 billion while transfers increased by PEN 6 billion. Despite sustaining the level of subnational investment, this trend has led to a decrease in the autonomy of subnational governments in determining investment decisions.

Table 4.9. **Public investments in Peru**

Million USD

	Central government	Regional government	Local government	Total
2004	911	234	480	1 625
2005	1 075	323	657	2 055
2006	1 000	456	918	2 374
2007	1 280	686	1 067	3 033
2008	1 636	948	2 398	4 982
2009	2 159	1 318	3 054	6 531
2010	3 198	1 754	3 540	8 493
2011	3 522	1 710	3 092	8 324
2012	3 206	2 522	4 637	10 365
2013	3 563	2 644	5 226	11 433
2014	4 125	2 293	5 037	11 455

Source: Own elaboration based on data provided by the Ministry of Economy and Finance.

Local governments allocated the vast majority of their investments to meet UBNs. The largest expenditure items were transport infrastructure (25%-30%), sanitation (around 20%) and education (around 10%). Regional governments mostly invest in transport (around 30%), health (around 20%), and education and agriculture (around 15% respectively).

Higher overall investment levels have often resulted in suboptimal outcomes at a subnational level

The World Bank (2010) has shown that regions with more investment capacities (e.g. *canon*-receiving regions) have more and better quality public services, but they have much lower levels of public expenditure efficiency. The lack of efficiency in the marginal levels of investment coupled with the strong levels of disparity in the distribution of the *canon* calls for a reform in the management system of extractive activity royalties, much as in the case of Colombia (OECD, 2014d). Regions with higher needs receive lower shares of the *canon* and are deemed to have higher marginal returns on public investments in terms of public service provision. Reallocating part of the revenues to the latter could have significant equalising effects while providing improvements in public service delivery across the board.

Canon transfers have not been associated with higher growth rates. Indeed, regions with higher levels of per capita *canon* transfers have had a tendency to have lower growth rates than those receiving fewer *canon* transfers. For instance, Moquegua, Tacna and Áncash, three of the regions with the biggest per capita *canon* transfers, have had growth rates significantly lower than the national average. In contrast, Cusco, the second-largest receiver of *canon*, has had the highest national growth rate over time. Regions such as

Ayacucho or Ica have amongst the highest growth rates in the country while being average *canon* receivers. Behind this data there is probably a catch-up phenomenon at play, but the other question that Figure 4.26 raises is the efficient utilisation of the resources from the *canon*.

Table 4.10. **Destination of subnational investments**

	2011		2014	
	Regional	Local	Regional	Local
Planning, management and contingencies	4.5%	10.2%	4.4%	7.2%
Defense and security	0.0%	0.0%	0.0%	0.0%
Public order and security	1.8%	1.7%	2.5%	3.7%
Justice	0.0%	0.0%	0.1%	0.0%
Labour	0.0%	0.0%	0.1%	0.2%
Trade	0.1%	1.0%	0.1%	1.9%
Tourism	0.6%	0.4%	0.7%	0.3%
Agriculture	14.6%	7.9%	13.5%	6.1%
Fishery	0.2%	0.1%	0.2%	0.0%
Energy	3.7%	1.8%	1.7%	1.6%
Mining	0.1%	0.0%	0.1%	0.0%
Industry	0.0%	0.1%	0.0%	0.1%
Transport	26.4%	27.7%	28.5%	24.7%
Communications	0.0%	0.3%	0.1%	0.2%
Environment	1.3%	4.2%	1.3%	3.2%
Sanitation	19.1%	22.4%	6.5%	21.8%
Housing and urban planning	0.3%	2.8%	1.9%	4.9%
Health	9.9%	2.3%	19.3%	2.3%
Culture and sports	1.6%	5.4%	2.0%	7.3%
Education	15.3%	9.7%	16.5%	12.9%
Social security	0.4%	2.0%	0.4%	1.5%
Social programmes	0.0%	0.0%	0.0%	0.0%
Public debt	0.0%	0.0%	0.0%	0.0%

Source: Own elaboration based on data provided by the Ministry of Economy and Finance.

Figure 4.26. ***Canon*** **per capita and regional growth rate**

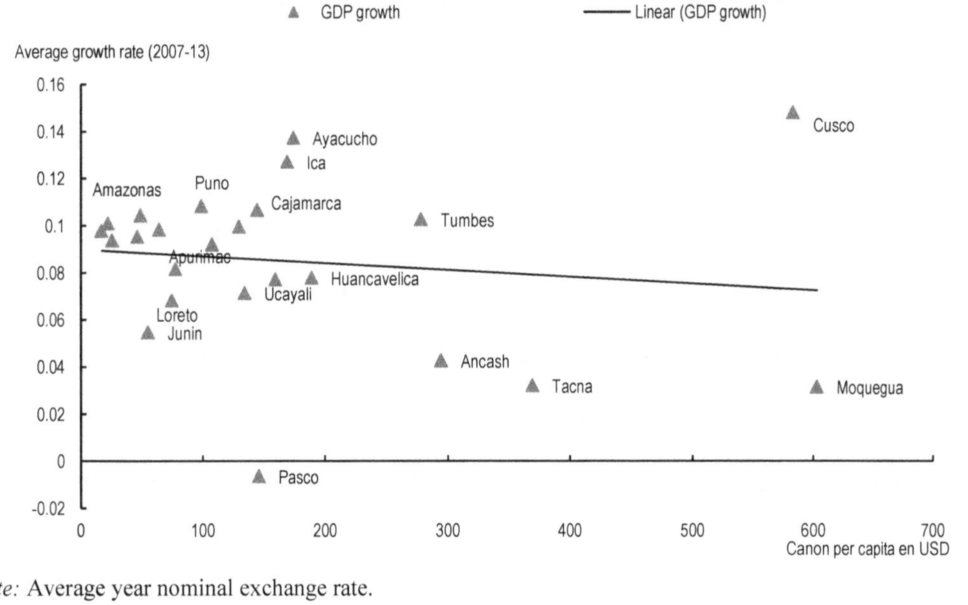

Note: Average year nominal exchange rate.

Source: Own elaboration based on data provided by the Ministry of Economy and Finance and INEI.

Easy access to significant levels of revenue has the potential to distort incentives for the efficient allocation of resources, which is not the case in Peru (Sanguineti 2010; and Natural Resource Governance Institute, 2015)). Nonetheless, World Bank (2010) has shown that despite better public policy and quality service delivery in the region receiving *canon*, those regions have much lower levels of public expenditure efficiency. Furthermore, there has been no strong correlation between regional growth levels and *canon* resource availability (World Bank, 2010; Cheasty and Pichihua, 2015; OECD, 2015a). The lack of efficiency in the marginal levels of investment coupled with the strong levels of disparity in the distribution of the *canon* call for a reform in the management system of extractive activity royalties, much like it has been the case in Colombia (OECD, 2014d).

A strong obstacle for the efficiency of public spending is the small size of investment projects. In 2012, the average size of investments by the national government was USD 2 million, USD 2.4 million for regional governments and USD 0.5 million for local governments (Table 4.11). This phenomenon is mainly induced by the transfer system and its governance, the lack of horizontal and vertical co-ordination capacity to allow the pooling of resources for bigger projects, and the lack of administrative capacity to deal with bigger projects (see Chapter 2 for the OECD Principles on Effective Public Investment across Levels of Government). This transfer system, as shown before, has turned local governments into the main investors of the country. By nature, subnational governments tend to have smaller investment projects than regional and subnational governments.

Regional governments seem to be a better level for subnational investment. Table 4.11 shows that the regions have managed to increase the size of their investments with the raw material super-cycle despite the relatively small share of the *canon* resources that they are assigned. Investments at the regional level have shown over time to have scalability potential to reach levels of size per investment higher than those of the central government. This level of investment seems to be pertinent to carry out place-based investments while at the same time guaranteeing lower levels of fragmentation and benefiting from economies of scale and network. This argument, coupled with higher capacities at the regional level than those at the local level, would be a solid basis for reforming the *canon* distribution system by strengthening the regions *vis-à-vis* local governments.

Table 4.11. **Average size of public investment projects**

Million USD

	Average												
	2001	2002	2003	2004	2005	2006	2007	2008	2009	2010	2011	2012	Total
National government	0.718	10.774	3.34	1.713	1.191	1.295	1.852	2.213	2.612	2.685	3.686	5.215	3.108
Regional government	0	0.258	0.506	0.763	0.753	0.773	1.025	2.389	3.201	3.716	3.433	6.435	1.938
Local government	0	0	0.333	0.373	0.315	0.366	0.587	0.721	0.909	0.835	1.035	1.372	0.571
Total	0.239	3.677	1.393	0.95	0.753	0.811	1.155	1.774	2.241	2.412	2.712	4.341	

Note: Average year nominal exchange rate.

Source: Contraloría General de la República (2014), "Estudio del proceso de decentralización en el Perú".

Current governance and fiscal arrangements encourage fragmented investments at a subnational level

Most subnational expenditures can be deemed as being deconcentrated rather than decentralised. These funds are usually delivered by individual ministries with low flexibility in terms of regional discretion. This strong control makes it hard for subnational governments to: adapt investments to local needs and circumstances, integrate policies and investments across different programmes and ministries, and balance capital and recurrent expenditures. This phenomenon has been further deepened by the decrease in the *canon* transfers.

Capital investments made from the *canon* have to go through the National System of Public Investment (SNIP) (Box 4.13), which is a system that controls the quality of investment and its social returns. Projects have to justify their social utility and sources of financing over time have to be guaranteed. In practical terms, it means that the investing government has to prove that it either has the funds to utilise the investment or that it has signed an agreement with another institution which will provide directly or indirectly the investment with the current expenditures associated to its functioning. For instance, if the money is used to build a school, the local government must have previously signed an agreement with the Ministry of Education which guarantees the presence of teachers for that school as well as guaranteeing the availability of funds to cover current expenditures to run the school.

Guaranteeing current expenditures and co-ordination may be difficult. This type of governance system thus creates incentives for investments in projects with small levels of primary expenditure and low co-ordination requirements despite potentially higher social returns from other projects.

Box 4.13. The National System of Public Investment

The National System for Public Investment (SNIP) was created in 2000 to improve the quality of public investment. The system seeks to guarantee that projects are efficient, sustainable and cost-effective. All investment projects from the central, regional and local governments are concerned and analysed.

The control is divided into three phases:

- Pre-investment phase: where initial studies are carried out to prove the viability and the social and economic returns of the project. It is a key phase since it is necessary to obtain the approval for the following phases.
- Investment phase: where definitive studies are made and the investment is executed.
- Post-investment phase: consists in the operation and maintaining of the investment and *ex post* evaluation of the project.

All projects need to be declared viable before going to the investment phase. In order to be approved, projects need to be socially profitable, sustainable and in accordance with the policy objectives. The diagnosis considers the problem that the project seeks to solve, its causes and the effect of the project. The analysis also considers issues of sizing and costs to determine an overall cost-benefit analysis and ultimately its profitability. Small projects (below PEN 10 million, which was modified in 2015 to reach PEN 20 million) benefit from a simplified procedure, and for those below PEN 1.2 million the procedure is further simplified.

Despite a certain number decentralised organs in the SNIP, the Ministry of Economy and Finance, via the General Direction for Public Investment (DGIP) is the highest technical-normative authority of the system and has a lot of weight in the process. It is in charge drafting the necessary norms for the functioning of the SNIP, regulating processes and procedures, dictating the technical norms that projects have to meet, declaring the viability of projects that require debt or guarantees from the state, guaranteeing that the approved projects match both the technical and legal requirements, guaranteeing that during the investment phase projects are consistent with the conditions and approved parameters and realise sample evaluation on the quality of viability approvals granted by the competent organs of the SNIP.

Box 4.13. The National System of Public Investment (*continued*)

Some relevant elements about the SNIP:

- The SNIP does not have a system of prioritisation, it is blind (noting that the Ministry of Economy and Finance has recently developed a tool to prioritise public expenditure based on a number of factors, including socio-economic disadvantage).
- The central government lacks knowledge about local realities.
- There is a lack of capacity to connect investment projects with the different governmental plans (also partially due to the weakness of these plans signalled in this Chapter). Nonetheless, the Municipal Incentives Plan (Plan de Incentivos Municipales) does, independently from the SNIP, incentivise investments in line with the provision of key basic needs (which does not guarantee that they are aligned with the Plan de Desarrollo Concertado).
- Now, within the investment projects, up to 20% of the value of the project can be assigned to maintenance. The remainder of the costs have to be covered by current income or by engagement from other governmental bodies – for example engagement from the Ministry of Education to pay the teachers. In order to have a project approved, subnational governments have to show how they are going to finance the long-term sustainability of their investment.
- The SNIP sometimes invalidates projects which are not of the competence of the subnational government that presents it until they sign an agreement with the competent authority to carry out the projects, thus avoiding the presence of white elephants. In education projects, for example, the Ministry of Education has to approve of the new school to guarantee the presence of teachers in the new school.
- The central government can sometimes bypass the SNIP when the project is considered a national priority (i.e. the Transoceanica).
- Since 2013, productive and competitiveness programmes can also be considered as investments.
- The national government greatly supports regional governments to go through the SNIP.

Source: Ministry of Economy and Finance and Contraloría General de la República (2014), "Estudio del proceso de decentralización en el Perú".

In order to speed up investments at the subnational level, "Works for Taxes" (*Obras por Impuestos*, OpI), a new mechanism to finance investment projects, was created in 2008. It allows the different levels of government to delegate the provision of public infrastructure to private firms in exchange for tax credits. Through December 2015, the mechanism had been used 188 times for a total value of investments of PEN1.9 billion. For this pipeline, the amount of projects financed rocketed from 2 in 2009 to 86 in 2014. This mechanism appears to have benefited regional and local governments by increasing the execution of infrastructure projects, accelerating local infrastructure, using the know-how of private companies to increase the quality of their investments, and enhancing the reputation and image of local governments by helping them to reach their goals and objectives (OECD, 2015a).

Local governments have mainly used the OpI to invest in transport, sanitation and education whereas regional governments have mainly used it to invest in transport, health and sanitation. Subnational governments submit a list of priority projects to the SNIP. The list of projects can come directly from the governmental body or from private firms, that present projects to the governmental body which in turn validates the project and acts as a vehicle by presenting it to the SNIP. This has helped produce more infrastructure at a faster pace.

Table 4.12. **Investments and projects**

	Number of investments	Amount invested (million USD)	Average investment per project (million USD)
2009	2	2.0	1.0
2010	5	3.5	0.7
2011	7	99.1	14.2
2012	19	68.6	3.6
2013	35	178.4	5.1
2014	86	229.3	2.7
2015	43	94.2	2.2
Total	197	96.5	0.5

Note: Average year nominal exchange rate.

Source: Own elaboration based on data provided by the Ministry of Economy and Finance.

Despite its fast growth, this mechanism presents a number of risks, and further analysis is required concerning its outcomes.

- Private firms assume responsibilities in the provision of public infrastructure and services without a proper policy framework and which can be used to benefit individual firms. Given the system of governance of the mechanism, and despite providing room for projects bigger than the national average, investments are still fragmented into administrative divisions and little or no co-ordination takes place. "Works for Taxes" promotes small investment, hampering the upscaling in investment projects and so reinforcing the existing fragmentation. The framework was improved in 2015, its effect on outcomes remains to be analysed. Since 2014, the central government can also use this mechanism. It can also use it jointly with subnational governments. This new piece of regulation should help increase the size of projects.
- Projects do not go through the traditional public investment control mechanisms. The procedure is not as stringent and can be done in-house by the firm or by another firm selected by the financing firm. This could lead to conflicts of interest and clientelism, despite the fact that projects have to be approved by the council of subnational governments and go through the SNIP. The new regulation enhances the possibility of oversight from the General Comptroller. Nonetheless, the latter remains relatively weak and understaffed (OECD, 2015a).
- Financing firms are not necessarily in the best position to draft investment projects.
- Oversight and execution remain weak and incentives may be misaligned. Firms do the hiring themselves, with the approval of the government the executing and oversight firm.
- There is lack of clarity between corporate social responsibility and public investment related to the use of this mechanism. Firms tend communicate around the use of this mechanism as if it were corporate social responsibility, although it is not.

Despite these limitations, Peru has adopted a number of key reforms for improving governance in recent years, such as fiscal framework projections and performance budgeting, with the objective of increasing the effectiveness of public expenditure. The performance-based budgeting system is a relatively new process in Peru (introduced in 2008), which is been gradually implemented in all entities of public administration and at all levels of government. Performance-based budgeting constitutes a new approach to budgeting, using output and outcome measures to allocate resources. In light of the experience of OECD countries, performance budgeting can be seen as an effective tool to link budget and strategic planning (see Chapter 2). Peru has also started developing the above-mentioned plan for territorial articulation of its budget. Despite certain downfalls, it is a positive step toward increasing the degree of inclusion of subnational governments in the budgeting process.

Figure 4.27. **Number of investment projects financed by "Works for Taxes"**

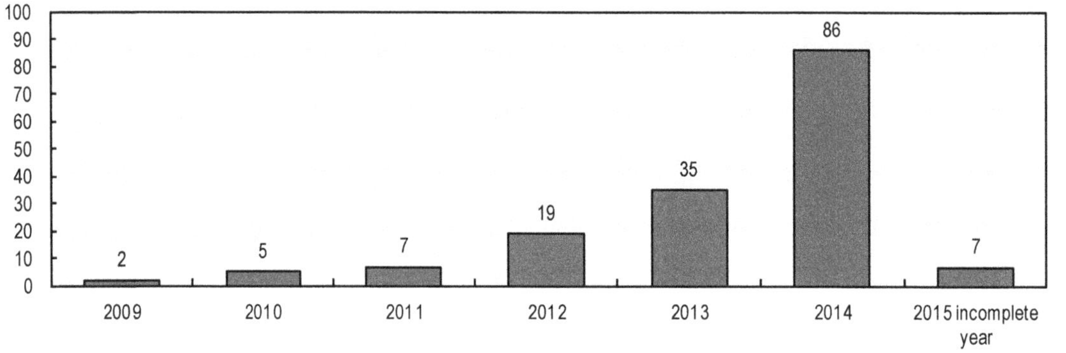

Source: Own elaboration based on data provided by the Ministry of Economy and Finance.

The experience at the subnational level is still relatively recent in Peru, but improvements have been made, such as the establishment of a common set a basic performance indicators frequently used by subnational governments. This provides subnational authorities with common basic management objectives which are focused on the most vulnerable segments of the population.

Currently performance budgeting is still mainly concentrated at the national level and has a sectoral approach as each line ministry is in charge of using performance budgeting in its budgetary programmes. There is still room from improvement in reducing the space blindness of the budget and vertical integration. The challenge for Peru in using performance-based budgeting is twofold.

1. Increase the degree of implementation of performance budgeting at the subnational level, as it is important that subnational governments integrate performance information into the budgetary decision making in the areas where they have discretion to allocate budgetary resources.
2. Performance budgeting should move towards a more horizontal approach, in which the product inputs of several line ministries are involved.

Key findings and recommendations

The quality of public goods and services delivered at the subnational level is a key issue to lifting productivity and achieving inclusive growth for Peru. Improving the quality of public investment and services in developing countries is always a question of resources, but it is also a question of governance. Governance determines, for instance, how efficiently costs are shared throughout the metropolitan area and how service delivery is co-ordinated across local government layers. Better spending will lead to better service delivery and, thus, better social outcomes. With respect to the previous analysis, Peru should consider implementing the following recommendations to mainstream the use of public resources with greater spending at the subnational level.

Developing a more effective partnership between levels of government to deliver better policy outcomes

Better horizontal interactions between different ministries and agencies of the central government and vertical ones across departments, provinces and districts, are a necessary condition for efficient and effective planning, programming and budgeting at the subnational level. Peru should consider promoting co-ordination mechanisms across subnational governments. The experience of OECD countries in establishing horizontal and vertical co-ordination tools could be of interest to Peru.

In the case of Peru, regions can play an effective role in the co-ordination of the provincial municipalities and district municipalities. For example, regions could also play an essential co-ordination role within the proposed regional development agencies (see Chapter 2). Since the establishment of macro-regions has become unlikely, efforts in the coming years could be focused on consolidating the existing regional governments by clearly defining responsibilities for spending and attributing a co-ordination role to the regions. In addition, as mentioned above, attributing a sufficient tax base to regions is also recommended and would foster greater accountability.

The government should also consider returning to a more asymmetric place-based decentralisation. Currently, small municipalities have the same requirements as bigger ones, although they do not have the same capabilities nor necessarily the same types of issues. Avenues could be explored for example in metropolitan areas.

The provision of public services typically requires the intervention of different levels of government. Even with a regulatory framework that better defines the competences of each level of government, it is impossible to have a complete separation of policy responsibilities. This implies that vertical co-ordination arrangements are crucial for policy coherence. In this regard, OECD member countries, especially federal or decentralised countries like Spain, are increasingly developing and using a wide variety of multi-level co-ordination mechanisms. These governance arrangements are supposed to promote collaboration among different levels of government, to improve the coherence and complementarities in their interventions, to exchange information and knowledge, to reduce administrative overlaps and duplications, and in general, to increase the quality and efficiency of public service delivery. These mechanisms may be "binding", such as contracts, or "soft", such as platforms for discussion (Box 4.2).

In addition to fostering vertical co-ordination mechanisms, Peru should consider strengthening the role of subnational government associations or networks to foster horizontal co-operation. Local government associations are an important supporting structure for municipal management and can play a very important role in the design and discussion of national policies and regulations on decentralisation. At the regional level, associations can play a similar role with intermediary governments and also provide technical support. Horizontal inter-regional co-operation can make it easier to find common positions in negotiations with the central government, and thus facilitate vertical co-ordination. It can also help as a forum for interchanging knowledge and best practices among regions, or for conducting shared projects or initiatives.

Fostering public sector skills and capacities at the subnational level

Peru should apply the new civil service law to subnational governments to promote a professional subnational government civil service, introducing merit and capacity criteria, especially in those posts which are highly technical. This reform is particularly important at the subnational level, where key management functions such as planning and budget management, investment programming or financial administration, are renewed with a change in government.

It is very important for the success of the decentralisation process that local government capacities are effectively strengthened, helping them to better exercise their powers and responsibilities and to provide a good level of service. In Spain's decentralisation process, three important measures were taken to guarantee that subnational governments have the proper capacities to develop their new tasks.

1. The Constitution envisaged different speeds in the decentralisation process. Autonomous communities could decide on taking up different packages of competences, taking into account their capacities. This may be useful for Peru as it may be desirable to introduce temporarily asymmetric competencies while significant differences in administrative capacity at the subnational level persist.
2. In terms of the allocation of tasks and responsibilities, mentioned above, regions could be strengthened, as they have greater potential to attract qualified personnel and to benefit from economies of scale. Transferring some competences to the regional level – at least momentarily – in terms of planning and finance, which local governments cannot manage, could be a way to escape the trap of the misstepped asymmetric decentralisation that was initially envisioned.
3. When regions assumed core competences such as health and education, public employees were also transferred to these administrations. Since then, regions have been responsible for the management of this staff, taking important decisions such as fixing wages or the recruitment process. Regions are also responsible for training their staff. However, the process has not worked efficiently.

Finally, as the process of forming a true civil service is relatively long, the central government could envision the creation of a task force which could operate in the regions for planning and financing. This task force would provide the necessary human capital to lagging regions to properly accomplish their mission while providing knowledge transfer spillovers. This task force could provide critical support in tasks such as planning, delivery of complex projects, evaluation of policies and projects, and providing framework regulations; typical areas where subnational governments lag behind (see Chapter 2).

Developing a coherent package of actions to enable better public investment outcomes at a subnational level

In the current context of economic slowdown, pressures to increase the level of investment will continue as a means of implementing an effective countercyclical policy in the country. Peru has an opportunity to make reforms in the existing regulation by focusing on the quality of the investments. The main challenges for Peru in regards to this are:

- multi-year planning and prioritisation of public investment
- increasing the quality and scale of investments
- monitoring and evaluation.

The OECD developed 12 Principles for Effective Public Investment across Levels of Government (OECD, 2014a) to set priorities, overcome difficulties in these areas and improve multi-level governance in public investment (see Chapter 2). These principles can provide useful guidelines for Peru by identifying good practices related to the multi-level governance of public investment.

Regarding co-ordination across levels of governments, the OECD Principles for Effective Public Investment across Levels of Government highlight the key role of the central government, setting the general legal framework to enable sound relations, vertically among the different levels of government and horizontally among the different national sectorial policies and among the different regions or municipalities. This legal framework should target inter-regional disparities and regulate fair and effective fiscal relations among the different levels of government. Central governments may help local governments carry out their new mandates by offering technical support, co-ordinating the creation of economies of scale in the production of some local public goods and services, and perhaps most importantly, in monitoring and evaluating the performance of subnational governments. Colombia's experience of co-ordinating investments through the governance tool *contratos plan* provides some lessons to help Peru further develop some of the mechanisms it has created recently (see Chapter 2).

In addition to establishing co-ordination mechanisms, Peru should consider establishing the right incentives to scale-up investment projects. In this sense, subnational governments with a four-year mandate have no incentives to run large-scale projects; rather, they will only consider those projects that can be completed during their term. Additionally, as technicians also change, the stability of investment projects is compromised as well. These elements would have to be coupled with improvements in both monitoring and evaluation which are currently very low (OECD, 2016c) and multi-year planning and prioritisation.

The current boom of investment expenditure initially driven by the *canon* will lead to an increase of the current expenditure in the medium to long term. Most capital investments (building roads, schools, hospitals, etc.) require recurrent expenditures for their maintenance. This cannot be fully financed by the *canon* funds given some of the restrictions in the use of these funds, so subnational governments should have to use other transfers since subnational tax receipts are small. To face this problem, any project funded through royalties should be required to be financially sustainable and giving the necessary budget to subnational governments to finance these operating costs.

Furthermore, Peru should minimise other instruments that are currently causing investment fragmentation ("Work for Taxes") and rather focus on means to reduce the incentives for fragmentation in the mechanisms in place while enhancing those that foster larger scale investments. Some districts apply participatory budgeting, that is, the allocation of a percentage of their budget is decided by citizens, which in practice leads to small-scale projects. Currently, the amount of resources decided by participatory budgeting is small, but there are voices that are demanding an expansion of this practice. It is important that citizens also have the opportunity to participate in regional planning, and this is integrated with the budgeting process to ensure effective investment outcomes.

Finally, Peru needs to be very careful when considering the creation of new districts to avoid fragmentation, particularly in urban areas. If new districts are to be created, a deep and transparent analysis of the fundaments would have to be considered. Current incentives that drive this demand for the creation of new districts should be addressed.

Some of the criterion of that process would have to at least consider and balance the following elements:

- The fiscal sustainability of the newly created district.
- The capacity of the district to efficiently and effectively deliver public services and fulfil its responsibilities.
- The correspondence between the administrative division and the socio-economic functionality of the area in which it would be created. This is particularly important to avoid further fragmentation in urban areas.
- Socio-political factors mainly related to political representation and accountability.

Mobilise revenues at a subnational level

Peru has significant space to strengthen tax collection and, thus, increase permanent revenues. Despite the huge economic growth achieved during the last decade, Peru continues to have one of Latin America's lowest tax revenues: in 2013, tax revenue in Peru amounted to 16.4% of GDP, 4.6 percentage points below the average registered in Latin America and well below the OECD average of 34%.[6] Improving the low tax collection rate is key to close the existing socio-economic gaps in Peru, to enhance opportunities at the local level and to effectively address the shift in the economic environment, with the collapse of commodities prices.

All levels of government should be engaged in achieving an effective tax revenue mobilisation and, particularly, subnational governments can play a very effective role mobilising revenues mainly by widening the tax base by reducing informality. Among other reasons, the low fiscal collection rates in Peru is related to the large informal economy; there is a need for putting in place the right set of incentives both on the part of business as well as the public sector to address this issue.

In a decentralised fiscal system, subnational governments will play a key role by strengthening tax regulation enforcement, as they will have more incentives to control informal activities in order to increase their fiscal revenues. This has to be coupled with further reforms on the revenue and expenditure side. They may improve regulation and provide economic actors with better framework conditions. In addition, subnational governments may be able to produce better public services, and hence increase the cost of informality if it is related to the absence of access to these services.

Subnational governments in Peru have wide room to improve tax collection by following these recommendations:

- Improving tax administration at the subnational level. This is almost non-existent, especially in small municipalities given the costs that tax administration implies. In this sense, economies of scale could be achieved by the central government or regions as a middle level of government, assuming the function of collecting subnational taxes on behalf of the municipalities. This is highly relevant given that some of Peru's districts are small (nearly 60% of districts have less than 5 000 citizens), and do not necessarily have the managerial capacity to collect taxes appropriately. In some OECD countries, for instance France, the collection of subnational taxes remains centralised and then the resources are transferred to the municipalities. Additionally, improving human resources capacities at the subnational level and promoting tax awareness are also necessary conditions to develop a professional tax administration at the subnational level. This part of the reform is essential for any improvement in tax collection.

- Progressively develop a tax system at the regional level. A pending issue of the fiscal decentralisation in Peru is providing regions with their own tax resources to finance their public services. This would require a review of the taxes assigned to each level of the administration in order to find a proper mix of regional taxes by assuming taxes that are currently assigned to the national or local level. In addition, regions could help create new fiscal spaces by creating new taxes and which would be destined to them with the agreement of the national government. This could prove to be particularly important in low-revenue countries like Peru.
- Progressively increase tax autonomy at the subnational level. Peru should consider increasing tax autonomy by offering some leeway, within a determined framework (such as a band), to subnational authorities to take decisions regarding tax rates and tax bases. Allowing subnational authorities to decide on the allocation of their own taxation could be an incentive to raise more taxes and, thus, promoting fiscal co-responsibility and accountability. Additionally, the list of taxes assigned to the subnational level could be enlarged. Properties of desirable local level taxes are that they are: buoyant, with revenues roughly changing in proportion to the economic base; horizontally equitable, providing equal treatment to taxpayers in similar circumstances; relatively efficient, causing low distortion in economic activity; relatively low in administrative costs; and politically acceptable. Such a reform must be conceived as a package, and come hand in hand with the previous and following points:
  - Increasing fiscal space at the local level by raising the collection of the property tax. This tax has a steady revenue flow capacity and provides stability to municipal finances without creating distortions for economic growth. To this aim, Peru should consider the following:
    - Developing a unified cadastre. Peru has three different land registries with different purposes and without any co-ordination amongst them. The potential benefits of having a well-managed cadastre go beyond the mobilisation of revenues, as it is an effective tool to achieve non-fiscal objectives such as spatial planning and better protection of property rights.
    - Updating the database on land and properties to widen the property tax base. Taking into account the good results achieved thanks to the revenue-raising incentives, Peru should expand these incentives to the poorest municipalities, where there are limited resources to update their land registries. Alternatively, Peru could follow the example of Chile, where municipalities do not manage the cadastre nor the collection of the property tax, which are functions assumed by the central government. It could also be linked to the regional taxation agencies.
    - Giving powers to subnational governments to fix the rate of the property tax. In Spain, for example, the national government fixes the minimum and the maximum tax rate and subnational governments fix the tax within these limits.
- Fostering fiscal transparency. Increasing taxes is not easy in any country but a close articulation of the use of collected taxes will help to give more visibility of the positive effects of having a sound tax collection. Particularly critical at the

local level is to invoke the social contract – to ensure that those citizens who will pay more to their local government under revenue reforms feel that they are getting some benefit from doing so and are being treated fairly in the process. All levels of government need to make efforts to report tax collection comprehensively and to improve accountability. Additionally, fighting against corruption would increase the trust citizens have in their institutions and would facilitate the context for any tax reform (OECD, 2016c for further details).

Reform the transfer system

A period of price decreases could raise challenges in terms of political economy of reform to implement changes. However, improving the design of the *canon* and other transfers will be fundamental to successfully advancing the decentralisation agenda and delivering better regional development outcomes. Some of the issues that these proposals seek to solve are:

- the level of volatility in subnational governments' finance
- the lack of efficiency in public spending
- the absence of an equalisation fund
- the lack of a pro-growth strategy for *canon*-receiving regions.

In terms of the first issue, Peru should look into the creation of a stabilisation fund with a threshold system in order to balance the need for investment today while limiting the pro-cyclical effect of the excess in incomes. Such a mechanism would contribute to strengthening subnational finances. The logic would be that above a certain threshold of transfer value – which could be computed as an average of, for instance, the previous five – a share of the sum would go to this fund. In the lower part of the cycle, say if the revenues are a certain percentage below the average of that same time period, the fund would help compensate the decrease in income. Such a reform, coupled with higher levels of own resources in subnational revenues, would definitely help increase both the predictability and strength of subnational finances.

In relation to the efficiency of public spending, several avenues can be explored. Some of them have already been mentioned above, such as the required balance between current and capital investment, the need to strengthen human capital, the necessary reform of the system that controls public investments with the adoption of the OECD Principles for Effective Public Investment across Levels of Government. Peru should also consider a more strategic multi-year approach to investment that is conditional upon regional planning (see Chapter 2).

A first step forward would be to transfer resources only to determined validated projects, which would have to be aligned with the regional development plans. In that sense, *canon* transfers would not be transferred without any counterpart, but there would be an obligation for results, or at least of alignment with the regional objectives. Financial incentives could be created to further strengthen co-ordination and investments in UBNs and the regional development needs. This would entail a reform of the SNIP, which would also have to be modified to create further incentives for scaling up investments. Currently smaller projects demand less quality and lead to less controls from the central government, thus creating clear incentives to produce smaller investments.

Another step forward would be reversing the transfer system, to transfer a higher proportion of resources to the regional governments to increase the scale and quality of investments. The current system of *canon* transfers creates vertical inequalities. Indeed, it provides more funds to local governments than to regional governments. As it has been shown, this leads to small average sizes in investments and issues in terms of investment co-ordination. A way forward would be to invert the system of distribution and attribute a bigger investment role to regions by transferring a larger share of the *canon* to the regions rather than to local governments. Regions have both better management capacities and could realise economies of scale in investment projects, while at the same time exploiting the potential of network investments.

As outlined in Chapter 2, Peru lags behind in R&D investments both at the private and public level. The *canon* currently obliges to invest 5% in the universities of the region. Nonetheless, results from this system do not seem to be compelling; hence, Peru could diversify part of those investments. This part of the grant could be used not only for research, but also for more applied research and innovation, and technological transfers. Opening investments in the CITEs could be an option. Schemes including the private sector could also be envisioned. Introducing fair and open competition in the distribution of grants could also help improve their impact.

Finally, the *canon* system contributed to the provision of strong regional inequalities. Evidence also suggests that there are strong diminishing returns to the *canon* transfers. There is a strong rationale for a transfer system with more of an equalisation component. Peru could explore the creation of a regional compensation fund which would transfer funds above a certain threshold to non-producing regions on a formula basis (take advantage of lower prices of mining products to set this threshold as low as possible for political economy of reform feasibility). One option might be using these resources to increase FONCOR and FONCOMUN, while giving more strength to FONCOMUN as an equalisation mechanism.

In addition to *canon* funds and compensatory transfers, subnational governments receive other transfers – grants – which are assigned following budgetary priorities defined by the national government. Thus, the current system of grants in Peru lacks clear structure and the allocation is made on a discretionary basis, to finance payroll expenses, goods and services, and public investment in line with local needs. In addition, the national government also contemplates historic budgets to assign grants, as well as specific resources requests made by subnational governments. This means that subnational authorities, especially governors, spend a lot of time and energy negotiating their grants with the Ministry of Economy and Finances.

Still, grants constitute the major source of financing of regional governments (almost 80% of the total regional resources). While at the local level the importance of this category of resources is less (15% of the total municipal resources), grants play a very substantial role by financing investments in those municipalities that do not receive *canon* funds. Since 2008 Peru has been gradually implementing a performance-based budgeting approach to allocate these grants, thereby reducing the degree of discretion and improving the quality of public finances. Currently, 58% of the government budget, excluding pensions and debt service, is allocated under the principles of performance-based budgeting (Cheasty and Pichihua, 2015). As shown in OECD countries, performance-based budgeting could significantly increase the efficiency of public resources, which is particularly important in a low-revenue country like Peru. Peru should make efforts to progressively expand performance budgeting in partnership with subnational governments in the coming years and, in parallel, reduce the degree of discretion of grants (see Chapter 2).

Notes

1. Article 43 of the Constitution declares that Peru have "An unitary, representative and decentralised government".
2. See OECD (2015a; 2015b).
3. Source: OECD (2014f).
4. Information on GDP and total government revenue from the Banco Central de Reserva del Perú (BCRP). Information on taxes from SUNAT.
5. Historically, FONCOMUN – financed by 2% of the VAT collected in the country – was the main source of income of local governments. It is a formula-driven transfer created in 1994 initially destined for investment, and ensures the functioning of all municipalities based on equity and compensation criteria. Transfers are allocated based on population and the share of the population with unsatisfied basic needs. The population criterion is the most important one and weighs for 85% in the calculation of the transfer. FONCOMUN has had a hard time playing a compensatory role, since resources are limited and they are also channelled to *canon*-receiving local governments. The highest transfer from FONCOMUN was 17 times lower than the highest *canon* transfer. Furthermore, the coefficient correlation between *canon* transfers and FONCOMUN transfers was zero for provincial municipalities and close to zero for district municipalities
6. Source: OECD (2014f).

Bibliography

Aguilar, G. and R. Morales (2005), "Las transferencias intergubernamentales, el esfuerzo fiscal y el nivel de actividad", *Documento de Trabajo*, No. 144, Instituto de Estudios Peruanos, Lima, http://bibliotk.iep.org.pe/bib_img/24480-8-1.pdf.

Ahmad, E. and M. García-Escribano (2011), "Constraints to effective fiscal decentralization in Peru", in: Martinez-Vazquez, J. and F. Vaillancourt (eds.), *Decentralization in Developing Countries: Global Perspectives on the Obstacles to Fiscal Devolution*, Edward Elgar, Cheltenham, United Kingdom.

Ahmad, E. and M. García-Escribano (2006), "Fiscal decentralization and public subnational financial management in Peru", *IMF Working Papers*, WP/06/120, International Monetary Fund, Washington, DC, www.imf.org/external/pubs/ft/wp/2006/wp06120.pdf.

Alfaro, J. and M. Rühling (2007), "La incidencia de los gobiernos locales en el impuesto predial en el Perú", Instituto de Investigación y Capacitación Municipal, Lima, www.mef.gob.pe/contenidos/pol_econ/documentos/Incidencia_GL_Imp_predial_Peru.pdf.

Arreaza, A. and A. Reuter (2012), "Can a mining windfall improve welfare? Evidence from Peru with municipal level data", *CAF Working Papers*, No. 2012/04, Development Bank of Latin America, Caracas, www.caf.com/media/4239/mining-windfall-welfare-peru-municipal-data.pdf.

Astudillo, M. and N. Zúñiga (2012), "Algunas consideraciones sobre el impuesto predial. Una referencia al caso de México", *INCEPTUM: Revista de Investigación en Ciencias de la Administración*, Vol. VII/12, pp. 271-294, http://inceptum.umich.mx/index.php/inceptum/issue/view/14/showToc.

BCRP (2008), "Potencial y limitantes de las exportaciones no tradicionales", *Notas de Estudio del BCRP*, No. 15, 7 March, Lima, www.bcrp.gob.pe/docs/Publicaciones/Notas-Estudios/2008/Nota-Estudios-15-2008.pdf.

BCRP (2007), "Determinantes y evolución de la competitividad en el Perú", *Notas de Estudio del BCRP*, No. 15, 16 March, Lima, www.bcrp.gob.pe/docs/Publicaciones/Notas-Estudios/2007/Nota-Estudios-15-2007.pdf.

Berganza, J. (2012), "Fiscal rules in Latin America: A survey", *Documentos Ocasionales*, No. 1 208, Banco de España, Madrid, www.bde.es/f/webbde/SES/Secciones/Publicaciones/PublicacionesSeriadas/DocumentosOcasionales/12/Fich/do1208e.pdf.

Bergvall, D. et al. (2006), "Intergovernmental transfers and decentralised public spending", *OECD Journal on Budgeting*, Vol. 5/4, OECD Publishing, Paris, http://dx.doi.org/10.1787/budget-v5-art24-en.

Bitran, E., S. Nieto-Parra and J.S. Robledo (2013), "Opening the black box of contract renegotiations: An analysis of road concessions in Chile, Colombia and Peru", *OECD Development Centre Working Papers*, No. 317, OECD Publishing, Paris, http://dx.doi.org/10.1787/5k46n3wwxxq3-en.

Blöchliger, H. and O. Petzold (2009), "Finding the dividing line between tax sharing and grants: A statistical investigation", *OECD Working Papers on Fiscal Federalism*, No. 10, OECD Publishing, Paris, http://dx.doi.org/10.1787/5k97b10vvbnw-en.

Canavire-Bacarreza, G., J. Martinez-Vásquaz, and C. Sulveda (2012), "Sub-national revenue mobilization in Peru", International Center for Public Policy, Working Paper No. 12-09, Andrew Young School of Policy Studies, Georgia State University, Atlanta, Georgia, http://icepp.gsu.edu/files/2015/03/ispwp1209.pdf.

Carr, J.B. (2004), "Perspectives on city-county consolidation and its alternatives", in: Carr, J.B. and R.C. Feiock (eds.), *Armonk City-County Consolidation and its Alternatives: Reshaping the Local Government Landscape*, M.E. Sharpe, New York, pp. 3-25.

Carr, J.B., K. LeRoux and M. Shrestha (2008), "Institutional ties, transaction costs, and external service production", *Urban Affairs Review*, Vol. 44/3, pp. 403-427, http://dx.doi.org/10.1177/1078087408323939.

Carranza, L., C. Daude and Á. Melguizo (2011), "Public infrastructure investment and fiscal sustainability in Latin America: Incompatible goals?", *OECD Development Centre Working Papers*, No. 301, OECD Publishing, Paris, http://dx.doi.org/10.1787/5kg9xf1ncvzw-en.

Charbit, C. (2011), "Governance of public policies in decentralised contexts: The multi-level approach", *OECD Regional Development Working Papers*, No. 2011/04, OECD Publishing, Paris, http://dx.doi.org/10.1787/5kg883pkxkhc-en.

Charbit, C. and M. Michalun (2009), "Mind the gaps: Managing mutual dependence in relations among levels of government", *OECD Working Papers on Public Governance*, No. 14, OECD Publishing, Paris, http://dx.doi.org/10.1787/221253707200.

Cheasty, A. and J. Pichihua (2015), "Fiscal dentralization: Progress and challenges for the future", Chapter 10 in: Santos, A. and A. Werner (eds.), *Peru: Staying the Course of Economic Success*, International Monetary Fund, Washington, DC.

Contraloría General de la República (2014), "Estudio del proceso de decentralización en el Perú", Lima.

Contreras, C. (2004), "Centralismo y descentralización en la historia del Perú independiente", in: Contreras, C. (ed.), *El Aprendizaje del Capitalismo: Estudios de Historia Económica y Social del Perú Republicano*, Instituto de Estudios Peruanos, Lima, pp. 273-305.

Corporación Andina de Fomento and Georgia State University (2010), "Abriendo espacios fiscales: La descentralización de fuentes de ingresos y el desarrollo de la capacidad recaudatoria de los gobiernos regionales y municipales en Perú", prepared for the Ministry of Economy and Finance, Government of Peru.

Dargent, E. and P. Muñoz (2012), "Peru 2011: Continuities and changes in politics without parties", *Revista de Ciencia Política*, Vol. 32/1, pp. 245-268.

Dayton-Johnson J., J. Londoño and S. Nieto-Parra (2011), "The process of reform in Latin America: A review essay", *OECD Development Centre Working Papers*, No. 304, OECD Publishing, Paris, http://dx.doi.org/10.1787/5kg3mkvfcjxv-en.

De Cesare, C. (2012), "Improving the performance of the property tax in Latin America", Policy Focus Report, Lincoln Institute of Land Policy, Cambridge, Massachusetts, www.lincolninst.edu/pubs/2071_Improving-the-Performance-of-the-Property-Tax-in-Latin-America.

De Ferranti, D. et al. (2002), *From Natural Resources to the Knowledge Economy: Trade and Job Quality*, The World Bank, Washington, DC, http://dx.doi.org/10.1596/0-8213-5009-9.

De Mello, L. (2010), "Fiscal decentralisation and public investment: The experience of Latin America", *OECD Economics Department Working Papers*, No. 824, OECD Publishing, Paris, http://dx.doi.org/10.1787/5km347r2hhbp-en.

De Soto, H. (1989), *The Other Path: The Invisible Revolution in the Third World*, I.B. Tauris, London.

Defensoría del Pueblo (2015), "Reporte de conflictos sociales", No. 134, www.defensoria.gob.pe/modules/Downloads/conflictos/2015/Reporte-Mensual-de-Conflictos-Sociales-N-134-Abril-2015.pdf.

Defensoria del Pueblo (2009), "Hacia una descentralización al servicio de las personas: Recomendaciones en torno al proceso de transferencia de competencias a los gobiernos regionales", *Serie Informes Defensoriales*, Informe No. 141, Lima, www2.congreso.gob.pe/sicr/cendocbib/con_uibd.nsf/D1A17E3C8BE15D5005257591 0082F22C/$FILE/DefensoriaInforme141.pdf.

Defensoria del Pueblo (2008), "¿Uso o abuso de la autonomía municipal? El desafío del desarrollo local", *Serie Informes Defensoriales*, Informe No. 133, Lima, www2.congreso.gob.pe/sicr/cendocbib/con4_uibd.nsf/4A8106894089547505257DD3005FA5D3/$FILE/1_pdfsam_informe_133.pdf.

Del Valle, M. (2013), "Ingresos fiscales por explotación de recursos mineros e hidrocarburos en Perú", *Resumen de Políticas*, IDB-PB-197, Inter-American Development Bank, http://publications.iadb.org/bitstream/handle/11319/1512/RRNN_Peru.pdf.

Del Valle, M. et al. (2010), *Descentralización y Sostenibilidad Fiscal: Los Casos de Colombia y Perú*, Inter-American Development Bank, Washington, DC, https://publications.iadb.org/handle/11319/2704?locale-attribute=en.

Dollery, B. and L. Robotti (2008), *The Theory and Practice of Local Government Reform*, Edward Elgar Publishing, Cheltenham, United Kingdom.

Gallup Organisation (2015), *Gallup World Monitor* (database), http://www.gallup.com/services/170945/world-poll.aspx.

Gonzalez, O. et al. (2012), *Peru: Public Expenditure Review for Peru: Spending for Results*, Public Expenditure Review, The World Bank, Washington, DC, http://documents.worldbank.org/curated/en/2012/06/17204328/peru-public-expenditure-review-peru-spending-results.

Guasch, J.L. (2004), *Granting and Renegotiating Infrastructure Concessions: Doing it Right*, The World Bank, Washington, DC, http://elibrary.worldbank.org/doi/abs/10.1596/0-8213-5792-1.

Hanushek, E. and L. Wöbmann (2007), "Calidad de la educación y crecimiento económico", Document No. 39, PREAL, www.oei.es/pdfs/documento_preal39.pdf.

Hernando de Soto (1989), The Other Path: the invisible revolution in the Third World, Harper and Row, New York.

Herrera Catalan, P. and P. Francke Ballve (2007), "Análisis de la eficiencia del gasto municipal y de sus determinantes", CIES, Pontificia Universidad Católica del Perú, edición Julio 2007, Lima.

IMF (2015a), *Peru: Staying the Course of Economic Success*, IMF Publications, Washington, DC, www.elibrary.imf.org/staticfiles/misc/pdf/peru_extract_en.pdf.

IMF (2015b), "2015 Article IV Consultation with Peru", *IMF Country Report*, No. 15/133, International Monetary Fund, Washington, DC, www.imf.org/external/pubs/cat/longres.aspx?sk=42956.0.

INEI (2007), National Census, National Institute of Statistics and Informatics, Lima.

IPD (2012), "2012 governance data", *Institutional Profiles Database*, www.cepii.fr/institutions/EN/ipd.asp.

Johansson, Å. et al. (2008), "Tax and economic growth", *OECD Economics Department Working Papers*, No. 620, OECD Publishing, Paris, http://dx.doi.org/10.1787/241216205486.

KIPF/OECD (2015), *Institutions of Intergovernmental Fiscal Relations: Challenges Ahead,* OECD Fiscal Federalism Studies, OECD Publishing, Paris, http://dx.doi.org/10.1787/9789264246966-en.

Korinek, J. (2015), "Managing the minerals sector: Implications for trade from Peru and Colombia", *OECD Trade Policy Working Papers*, No. 186, OECD Publishing, Paris, http://dx.doi.org/10.1787/5jrp6wrc2r7l-en.

Loayza, N. (2008), "El crecimiento económico en el Perú", The World Bank, Washington, DC.

Loayza, N., L. Serven and N. Swgawara (2009), "Informality in Latin America and the Caribbean", *Policy Research Working Paper*, No. 4 888, The World Bank, Washington, DC, http://web.worldbank.org/archive/website01241/WEB/IMAGES/WPS4888.PDF.

Lora, E. (2001), "Las reformas estructurales en América Latina: Que se ha reformado y como medirlo", *Documento de trabajo des BID*, IDB-WP-346, Inter-American Development Bank, Washington, DC, www19.iadb.org/intal/intalcdi/PE/2012/10450.pdf.

Maldonado, S. (2015), "The political effects of resource booms: Political outcomes, clientelism and public goods provision in Peru", mimeo, University of California, Berkeley, http://dx.doi.org/10.2139/ssrn.2510376.

Marcel, M., J.P. Martinez and M. Sanginés (2012), "El presupuesto basado en el desempeño: Una vía para mejorar el gasto público", Chapter 2, in: *Las Instituciones Fiscales del Mañana*, Inter-American Development Bank, Washington, DC, www19.iadb.org/intal/intalcdi/PE/2012/11274.pdf.

Martinez-Vázquez, J. (2013), *Fiscal Decentralisation in Peru: A Perspective on Recent Developments and Future Challenges*, International Center for Public Policy, Andrew Young School of Policy Studies, Georgia State University, Atlanta, Georgia, http://scholarworks.gsu.edu/icepp/45.

Morris, S. and C. Blake (2009), "Political and analytical challenges of corruption in Latin America", in: Morris, S. and C. Blake (eds.), *Corruption and Democracy in Latin America*, University of Pittsburgh Press, Pittsburg, Pennsylvania.

Muñoz, P. (2010), "¿La política importa? Los determinantes políticos de la eficiencia del gasto municipal", CIES, Lima, www.cies.org.pe/sites/default/files/investigaciones/informe_final_paula_munoz.pdf.

Muñoz, P. (2008), *La Incertidumbre de la Política Regional. Estudio sobre la Articulación entre el Gobierno Regional y los Gobiernos Locales de Puno (2003-2007)*, Asociación Servicios Educativos Rurales/Oxfam, Lima, www.ser.org.pe/files/la_incertidumbre_de_la_politica_regional_-_final_0.pdf.

Muñoz, P. (2005), *El Diseño Institucional Municipal 1980-2004 y sus Implicancias para las Zonas Rurales*, Servicios Educativos Rurales, Lima.

Natural Resource Governance Institute (2015), "Local level resource curse: The 'cholo disease' in Peru", Revenue Watch Institute, www.resourcegovernance.org/sites/default/files/SubnationalresourcecurseresearchDRAFT.pdf.

Oates, W. and R.M. Schwab (1988), "Economic competition among jurisdictions: Efficiency enhancing or distortion inducing?", *Journal of Public Economics*, Vol. 35/3, pp. 333-354, http://econweb.umd.edu/~oates/research/economic%20competition%20among%20jurisdictions.pdf.

OECD (2016a), *Financing Democracy: Funding of Political Parties and Election Campaigns and the Risk of Policy Capture*, OECD Publishing, Paris, http://dx.doi.org/10.1787/9789264249455-en.

OECD (2016b), *OECD Public Governance Reviews: Peru 2016*, OECD Publishing, Paris, forthcoming.

OECD (2016c), *Public Sector Integrity Review of Peru*, OECD Publishing, Paris, forthcoming.

OECD (2015a), *Multi-dimensional Review of Peru: Volume 1. Initial Assessment*, OECD Development Pathways, OECD Publishing, Paris, http://dx.doi.org/10.1787/9789264243279-en.

OECD (2015b), "Subnational governments in the OECD: Key data", http://stats.oecd.org/Index.aspx?DataSetCode=SNGF.

OECD (2015c), *The State of Public Finances 2015: Strategies for Budgetary Consolidation and Reform in OECD Countries*, OECD Publishing, Paris, http://dx.doi.org/10.1787/9789264244290-en.

OECD (2014a), OECD Effective Public Investment across Levels of Government Toolkit, OECD, Paris, www.oecd.org/effective-public-investment-toolkit.

OECD (2014b), *OECD Regional Outlook 2014: Regions and Cities: Where Policies and People Meet*, OECD Publishing, Paris, http://dx.doi.org/10.1787/9789264201415-en.

OECD (2014c), *OECD Rural Policy Reviews: Chile 2014*, OECD Publishing, Paris, http://dx.doi.org/10.1787/9789264222892-en.

OECD (2014d), *OECD Territorial Reviews: Colombia 2014*, OECD Publishing, Paris, http://dx.doi.org/10.1787/9789264224551-en.

OECD (2014e), *OECD Territorial Reviews: Netherlands 2014*, OECD Publishing, Paris, http://dx.doi.org/10.1787/9789264209527-en.

OECD (2014f), *Revenue Statistics in Latin America 1990-2012*, OECD Publishing, Paris, http://dx.doi.org/10.1787/9789264207943-en-fr.

OECD (2014g), *Spain: From Administrative Reform to Continuous Improvement*, OECD Public Governance Reviews, OECD Publishing, Paris, http://dx.doi.org/10.1787/9789264210592-en.

OECD (2013a), *Fiscal Federalism 2014: Making Decentralisation Work*, OECD Publishing, Paris, http://dx.doi.org/10.1787/9789264204577-en.

OECD (2013b), *OECD Territorial Reviews: Brazil 2013*, OECD Publishing, Paris, http://dx.doi.org/10.1787/9789264123229-en.

OECD (2013c), *OECD Territorial Reviews: Antofagasta 2013*, OECD Publishing, Paris, http://www.oecd.org/greengrowth/oecd-territorial-reviews-antofagasta-chile-2013-9789264203914-en.htm.

OECD (2012), *Promoting Growth in all Regions*, OECD Publishing, Paris, http://dx.doi.org/10.1787/9789264174634-en.

OECD (2009a), *Governing Regional Development Policy: The Use of Performance Indicators*, OECD Publishing, Paris, http://dx.doi.org/10.1787/9789264056299-en.

OECD (2009b), *Regions Matter: Economic Recovery, Innovation and Sustainable Growth*, OECD Publishing, Paris, http://dx.doi.org/10.1787/9789264076525-en.

OECD (2008), "La política fiscal como herramienta de desarrollo en América Latina", *OECD Observer*, OECD Publishing Paris, www.oecd.org/dev/41578326.pdf.

OECD (2007), *Linking Regions and Central Governments: Contracts for Regional Development*, OECD Publishing, Paris, http://dx.doi.org/10.1787/9789264008755-en.

OECD (2005), *Building Competitive Regions: Strategies and Governance*, OECD Publishing, Paris, http://dx.doi.org/10.1787/9789264009479-en.

OECD/ECLAC (2012), *Latin American Economic Outlook 2012: Transforming the State for Development,* OECD Publishing, Paris, http://dx.doi.org/10.1787/leo-2012-en.

OECD/IDB (2014), *Government at a Glance: Latin America and the Caribbean 2014: Towards Innovative Public Financial Management*, OECD Publishing, Paris, http://dx.doi.org/10.1787/9789264209480-en.

OECD/ITF (2015), *ITF Transport Outlook 2015*, OECD Publishing, Paris, http://dx.doi.org/10.1787/9789282107782-en.

OECD et al. (2015), *Revenue Statistics in Latin America and the Caribbean 2015*, OECD Publishing, Paris, http://dx.doi.org/10.1787/rev_lat-2015-en-fr.

Pedagrio. S. (2014), "Corrupción y economía ilegal. El estado: Un protector más que un botín", Argumentos – *Revista de Análisis y Critica*, Vol. 8/3, http://revistaargumentos.iep.org.pe/articulos/corrupcion-y-economia-ilegal-el-estadoun-protector-mas-que-un-botin.

Peruvian Cuenta General de la República 2013 - Ministerio de Economía y Finanzas, http://www.mef.gob.pe.

Plataforma Interinstitucional de Gobiernos Descentralizados (ANGR, AMPE, REMURPE) (2014), "Avanzar en la descentralización fiscal", Peru.

Proética (2013), *VIII Encuesta Nacional Sobre Percepciones de la Corrupción en el Perú 2013*, Proética.

Salazar, R. and J. Pablo Ramos (2007), "Increased transparency helps curb corruption in Costa Rica", in: *Global Corruption Report 2007: Corruption in Judicial Systems*, Transparency International/Cambridge University Press, pp. 190-194.

Sánchez Urribarrí, R.A. (2008), "Characteristics of the judiciary vs. corruption perception", *Sistemas Judiciales*, pp. 88-99, http://sistemasjudiciales.org/content/jud/archivos/notaarchivo/361.pdf.

Sanguinetti, P. (2010), "Canon minero y decisiones fiscales subnacionales en el Perú", *CAF Working Papers*, No. 2010/01, Development Bank of Latin America, Caracas, www.caf.com/media/3180/201001SanguinettiFebrero2010.pdf.

The Economist Intelligence Unit (2016), "Country report: Peru", The Economist, London.

Tirole, J. (1996), "A theory of collective reputations (with applications to the persistence of corruption and to firm quality)", *Review of Economic Studies*, Vol. 63/1, pp. 1-22, http://dx.doi.org/10.2307/2298112.

UNHABITAT (2014), "Urban development financing: The challenges of local governments in developing countries", Expert Group Meeting on Urban Development Financing, Barcelona.

United Cities and Local Governments (2010), "Local government finance: The challenges of the 21st century", Second Global Report on Decentralization and Local Democracy, Gold 2010, United Cities and Local Governments, Barcelona, Spain, www.cities-localgovernments.org/gold/Upload/gold_report_2/2010%20EXECUTIVE%20SUMMARY%20baixa.pdf.

USAID (2015), "Informe anual sobre el estado del proceso de descentralización 2014", Lima.

World Bank (2015), "Perú – Hacia un sistema integrado de ciudades: Una nueva visión para crecer", The World Bank, Lima, www-wds.worldbank.org/external/default/WDSContentServer/WDSP/IB/2015/12/01/090224b083851ac3/2_0/Rendered/PDF/Per0000Hacia0u0a0visi0n0para0crecer.pdf.

World Bank (2012), *Country Partnership Strategy for the Republic of Peru for the Period FY2012-FY2016*, The World Bank, Washington, DC.

World Bank (2010), "The decentralization process and its links with public expenditure efficiency in Peru", Public Expenditure Review, The World Bank, Washington, DC, http://documents.worldbank.org/curated/en/2010/06/17204303/peru-decentralization-process-links-public-expenditure-efficiency-peru-el-proceso-de-descentralizacion-y-su-relacion-con-la-eficiencia-del-gasto-publico.

Yamada, G. and R. Montero (2011), "Corrupción e inequidad en los servicios públicos en el Perú", *Working Paper*, No. 87, CIES, Lima, http://old.cies.org.pe/files/documents/DyP/DyP-50.pdf.

Annex A. Functions assigned to subnational governments

Table A.1. **Functions assigned to subnational governments**

Regional governments	Local governments
1. Formulate, approve, execute, evaluate and administer the education, culture, science and technology, sports and recreation regional policies for the region.	1. Promote sustainable human development at the local level, favouring the development of educational communities.
2. Design, execute and evaluate the regional educational project, the culture development programmes, science and technology, and the sports and recreation development programme.	2. Design, execute and evaluate the educational project of their jurisdiction, in co-ordination with the Regional Education Office (REO) and the Local Education Management Unit (LEMU) and contributing to the national and regional educational policy with an intersectorial action focus.
3. Diversify the national curriculums, incorporating significant contents of their socio-cultural, economic, productive and ecological reality.	3. Promote curriculum diversification adding significant content to their socio-cultural, economic, productive and ecological reality.
4. Promote a culture of rights, peace and equality of opportunities for everyone.	4. Supervise the pedagogic and administrative management of the educational institutions under their jurisdiction, in co-ordination with the REO and the LEMU and strengthening their institutional autonomy.
5. Promote, regulate, incentivise and supervise services related to elementary, primary, secondary and non-university higher education; in co-ordination with the local government and in accordance with the policies and regulation of the sector.	5. Construct, equip and maintain the infrastructure of the educational establishments in their jurisdiction in accordance with the agreed Regional Development Plan and the assigned budget.
6. Modernise the decentralised educational management systems and favour the formation of educational networks, in co-ordination with the Ministry of Education.	6. Support the creation of educational networks as an expression of participation and co-operation between the centres and the educational programmes of their jurisdiction.
7. Execute and evaluate, jointly with the local government, the literacy programmes.	7. Promote and organise the Local Education Participative Council in order to generate agreements and to foster the citizens' surveillance and control.
8. Integrate the different educational regional programmes in an integral policy oriented to the improvement of the region's productivity; the equality of opportunities, integration and inclusion at the regional level; the strengthening of the citizen participation; and to the development of a culture of respect and recognition for diversity.	8. Support the incorporation and development of new technologies for the improvement of the educational system. This process enhances relationships with other sectors.
9. Permanently promote intercultural education.	9. Promote, co-ordinate, execute and evaluate with the regional government the literacy programmes within the frame of national policies and programmes.
10. Promote and incentivise investigation and extension in the universities and other higher educational institutions.	10. Strengthen the supportive spirit and the collective work oriented to the development of social, harmonious and productive coexistence; the prevention of natural disasters and the security of the citizens.
11. Promote and disseminate cultural expressions and foster artistic and cultural institutions of the region, in co-ordination with the local government.	11. Organise and support cultural centres, libraries, theatres and art workshops in provinces, districts and populated centres.
12. Protect and preserve, in co-ordination with the local government, the national cultural heritage of the region, as well as the non-official cultural property of the region.	12. Foster the protection and promotion of the cultural heritage of their jurisdiction and the defence and preservation of the archaeological, historical and artistic monuments, contributing with the relevant national and regional organisations.
13. Design and implement infrastructure and equipment policies with the local government.	13. Promote the culture of prevention through education for the preservation of the environment.
14. Identify, implement and promote the use of effective and efficient new technologies in order to improve the quality of different levels of education.	14. Promote and administrate, directly or through agreement or concession, zoos, botanic gardens and natural forests.

Table A.1. **Functions assigned to subnational governments** (*continued*)

Regional governments	Local governments
15. Develop and implement information systems and make them available to the population.	15. Promote sustainable tourism and regulate the services related to that purpose in co-ordination with the relevant entities.
16. Periodically and systematically evaluate the achievements of the region in educational matters and support the evaluation and measurement of the Ministry of Education, as well as contribute to the development of an accreditation and certification policy for educational quality.	16. Foster a civic culture of respect for public goods and maintenance, cleanliness, conservation and improvement of the local property.
17. Encourage and participate in the design, execution and evaluation of research projects and educational experimentation and innovation that will contribute to regional development and the improvement in the quality of the education service.	17. Promote participative, educational and recreational spaces aimed at local elder adults.
18. Develop the professionalisation, capacity-building and actualisation processes for teachers and administrative personnel, in accordance with the continuous formation national plan.	18. Regulate, co-ordinate and promote sports and child recreation through the construction of sport and recreational centres or the temporary use of appropriate urban zones for this purpose.
19. Strengthen, in accordance with the local government, educational institutions by promoting their autonomy, innovation capacity and democratic functioning, as well as the intersectorial articulation with the participation of the society.	19. Promote diverse cultural activities.
20. Articulate, advice and supervise local management unities in the administrative and pedagogical fields.	20. Promote the consolidation of a democratic culture and strengthen the cultural identity of the rural, native and afro-Peruvian population.
21. Promote and articulate the participation of universities, enterprises and civil society institutions in the execution of regional development plans.	

Source: Art. 47 of the Organic Law of Regional Governments and the Organic Law of Municipal Governments and World Bank (2010).

ORGANISATION FOR ECONOMIC CO-OPERATION AND DEVELOPMENT

The OECD is a unique forum where governments work together to address the economic, social and environmental challenges of globalisation. The OECD is also at the forefront of efforts to understand and to help governments respond to new developments and concerns, such as corporate governance, the information economy and the challenges of an ageing population. The Organisation provides a setting where governments can compare policy experiences, seek answers to common problems, identify good practice and work to co-ordinate domestic and international policies.

The OECD member countries are: Australia, Austria, Belgium, Canada, Chile, the Czech Republic, Denmark, Estonia, Finland, France, Germany, Greece, Hungary, Iceland, Ireland, Israel, Italy, Japan, Korea, Latvia, Luxembourg, Mexico, the Netherlands, New Zealand, Norway, Poland, Portugal, the Slovak Republic, Slovenia, Spain, Sweden, Switzerland, Turkey, the United Kingdom and the United States. The European Union takes part in the work of the OECD.

OECD Publishing disseminates widely the results of the Organisation's statistics gathering and research on economic, social and environmental issues, as well as the conventions, guidelines and standards agreed by its members.

OECD PUBLISHING, 2, rue André-Pascal, 75775 PARIS CEDEX 16
(04 2016 13 1 P) ISBN 978-92-64-26284-3 – 2016

www.ingramcontent.com/pod-product-compliance
Ingram Content Group UK Ltd.
Pitfield, Milton Keynes, MK11 3LW, UK
UKHW051458290926
15471UKWH00008B/1271

9 789264 262843